THE NI

ELECTORAL SYSTEM

NO *POLITICAL* PARTIES

Copyright © 2020 by Michael Anguelo

All rights reserved. No part of this book may be reproduced or transmitted in any form or by any means, electronic or mechanical, including photocopying, recording, or by any information storage and retrieval system, without permission in writing from the copyright owner, ask for it please.

"The alternate domination of one faction over another, sharpened by the spirit of revenge natural to party dissension ... is itself a frightful despotism."

G Washington

MY PETITE BIOGRAPHY

Born in Cuba, in 1929. I served the Cuban Air Forces for three years as Aircraft Mechanic during the conflict with the Communist insurgency attack the Cuartel Moncada, where the Castro's brothers were apprehended after the massacre they carried out of several civilians and military hospitalized in the Military Hospital, they were apprehended and trial for their crime, After the trial and incarcerated for life for the crime they perpetuated, the President Batista gives Amnesty to the Communist insurgents criminals Castro and his brother Raul, shameful and fatal decision.

In 1955, Diaz-Balart gave a speech before the Cuban House of Representatives in opposition to the Amnesty granted to his former brotherin-law, Fidel Castro, for his involvement in the 1953, the attack was descried as a col-blooded massacre on the Moncada Barracks.

Diaz-Balart was elected Senator in 1958, but was unable to take office due to Fidel Castro's rise to power on January 1, 1959, he eventually emigrated to U.S with his sons Lincoln, Mario and Jose whom become later Senator and Reprehensive of the United State.

Resigned from my military rank and emigrated to U.S. of America. Enrolled and served U.S. Air Forces for five years at Marruecos North Africa as jet Engine Mechanic, in 1961 I got out the service with an Honorable Discharge and became an entrepreneur.

I open and administrated two FAA repair Stations, starting from 2 employees, I bought the company, from zero to a $ 2 million in sales, and 63 employees, unfortunately I pretended to do a family company and that ended up in a family feud where my brothers took my company away from me in a legal battle accusing me of embezzling the company funds, "sometimes your worth enemy is your own family".

Nevertheless, after that, I open the second company, with my sons and it did not work out well either. In the new company I had the same success with 53 employees, with the same sales amount. My success was based in creativity, good management, problem solver, and hard work, but again I have other misfortune, this time was the raid to my new company by DOT, FBI, FAA and local Police, due an allegation by one of my competitors, Sermatec International. They filed a complaint of a Suspect Unapproved Illegal Repairs against my company and the DOT raid my Company without an investigation, I lost everything in a court battle.

Say to myself "The good Lord do not want me to be an entrepreneur", so at 81 years old, l I enrolled in MDC. college and four years later I graduated college as an Associate in Arts. Presently I am self-studding to get my diploma in Political Science. Nevertheless, my misfortune, I start authoring this book.

Today I am focused writing this book pretending to enlighten the voters and officials elected, the necessity of make a reform within the complete elimination of all political parties, factions' system that is affecting our Democracy-Republic, which is a Fusion of the two ancient government systems not of political parties. In the Fusion Electoral System there is no need for politics parties war between the factions, instead the voters united will elect our officials' servants without the intervention of any party-political tendencies that is causing distressful dangerous political wars, and they are the one choosing their presentative to elect the President. Founding fathers George Washington dislike the idea of political divisions. Dedicate this political History in his memory.

CUBA

DEDICATION

I dedicate this book to my Sons, Grandsons, Voters, Legislators, Government Officials and peoples of the world in general, trying to enlightening the necessity of the abolishing all existing political parties System, and instead replaced by my Fusion Electoral Tribunal System. in our Democracy-Republic systems that melting together form what I call it "The New Fusion Electoral System" No partisan elections to concluding the political competitiveness between parties, and have a more harmonious and transparent elections for the benefit of peoples in this imperfect crumbling world and in memory of George Washington.

Michael Anguelo

THE NEW FUSION ELECTORAL SYSTEM

FOR ALL

The New Fusion Electoral System

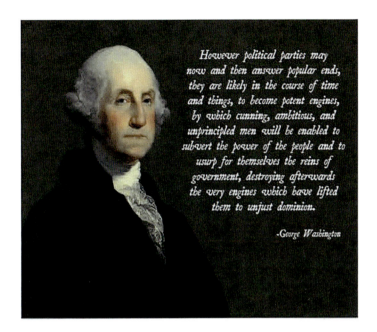

GENERAL GEORGE WASHINGTON

OUR CAPITAL HILL

GEORGE WASHINGTON
FARE-WELL

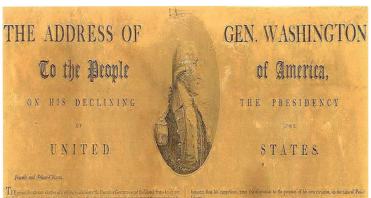

TABLE OF CONTENTS

CHAPTER 1 1

CHAPTER 2 25

CHAPTER 3 51

CHAPTER 4 60

CHAPTER 5 78

CHAPTER 6 99

CHAPTER 7 117

CHAPTER 8 143

CHAPTER 9 154

CHAPTER 10 167

CHAPTER 11 169

CHAPTER 12 188

CHAPTER 13 197

CHAPTER 14 204

CHAPTER 15 225

CHAPTER 16 243

CHAPTER 17 263

CHAPTER 18 271

CHAPTER 19	285
CHAPTER 20	293
CHAPTER 22	333
CHAPTER 23	354
CHAPTER 24	374
CHAPTER 25	395
CHAPTER 26	415
CHAPTER 27	434
CHAPTER 28	453
CHAPTER 29	469
CHAPTER 30	482
CHAPTER 31	490
CHAPTER 32	510
CHAPTER 33	519

THE NEW FUSION ELECTORAL SYSTEM

Analyzing the American electoral process, every election and the political parties' participation, for the past 40 years, I become more convinced that our political system is terrible defective and must be changing.

This procedure outrage, shameful action of war between political Factions, because the way our elections are more conflictive, as a results the nation is divided in two or three, opponents political parties, up to the point that we, the people, are forced to spend millions of dollars, of our nation treasure funds of our tax contribution, a waste of the nation reserves for this nonsense hostilities between two political parties that do not benefited in any way our Democratic-Republican System, but only to the media, and politician that taking the election of our government's officials, as a business for profit, and a competition game, for their own benefit, when the only parties that should exist, are those that are in favor, and those that are opposed, we do not need name, no flag, no color, simple the voter's decision.

I sincerely try to express my ideas to the world, in benefit of the human kind, an uncomplicated idea that may cause substantial changes in the election system of today's political structure in the Capitalist Democracy-Republic system of the World.

Everything commence with a simple idea, like the day when a person sought that implanting Democracy and Republic System, to organize, respect others opinions, given freedom and to control the behaves of the humanity in the political aspect, of that era, was necessary a change for better government, and public benefit. With the same principles I am launching my idea to the World, not for my own benefit, but for all peoples of the world. Political Parties Divide the nation instead of united the people to elect its candidate peacefully.

Michael Anguelo

The purpose of my book is to enlightening legislators and public in general the importance of modifies the Electoral System in America and nations of Democratic self-governing System around of the world, to facilitate a smooth selection of the Public Servants and the President of the Nation, without the necessity of political parties that it means what it is, a divider of the citizens choice in a political conflict within two or more political tendencies that do not benefit the Democracy neither the Republic are just political-divisions of the nation, what in reality we have a blend. It is of what our system is composed, a fusion of the two Systems Democracy and Republic. With the need of an electoral System that aids the people, in selecting our Public Servants without any political parties that cause, according "President George Washington opinioned, "The political parties harm the nation"

Michael Anguelo

MICHAEL ANGUELO SYSTEM

The purpose of this book is not to make money is to enlightening and advising legislators and public in general the importance of modifies the Electoral System in America and nations of Capitalist-Democratic System around of the World, to facilitate a pacific selection of the Public-Officials and the President of the Nation, without the necessity of any political parties, a divider of the citizens in a political hostility within two or more political tendencies that do not benefit the Democracy neither the Republic, are just political-partitions of the selections voters, what in reality we must have a blend. It is of what our system is, a Fusion of the two Systems Democracy and Republic, not of political factions.

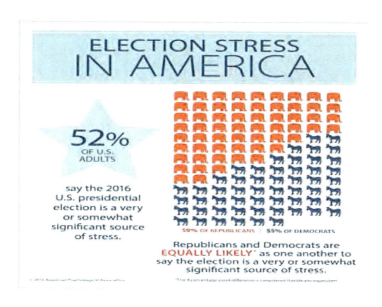

THE OLD FUSION SYSTEM
OLD FUSION STRATEGIES

History of Democracy-Republic Elections System

The old Fusion System was a multiple party nomination founded, Fusion Party in South Dakota. The party had formed in 1896 from an alliance of Democrats, Republicans, and Populists who opposed to the platform of the state Republican Party.

Old-Fusion works as follows: For primary election, ballots were-tallied separately for each party and the candidate with the most votes within each party wins that party's nomination. A single candidate who appears on two parties' ballots can thus win the nomination of both parties, or one party but not the other, or neither.

For general elections, the candidate's votes on each party's ballot they were-added together to determine the winner. This allows a minor party the opportunity to supply the margin of victory, on its own ballot line, in a close race between the two major party nominees. This has happened many times in U.S. history.

Under the United States' winner-take-all election system, office-seekers were-typically elected by a simple plurality of votes cast in single member election districts. Since minor parties are unable to win elections on their own, they suffer from a wasted-vote syndrome. That is, many who support the minor party's ideology and program decline to demonstrate that support at the polls, since they are reluctant to "waste" votes on candidates with no serious chance of winning.

Old-Fusion mitigates this syndrome by allowing minor parties to join electoral coalitions with other parties, minor and/or major, behind candidates with a realistic chance of success. It gives minor party supporters an opportunity to express their support without "wasting" their votes, and thus gives minor parties the opportunity to contribute their votes, and thus gives minor parties the opportunity to contribute to, and share legitimate credit for, a candidate's victory. In this way, Old-Fusion enables minor parties to attract the participation of those who support their policies, expand their base of voter support, and thereby enter the mainstream of electoral politics. It is a powerful tool for minor parties that wish to engage in serious electoral competition.

Old-Fusion, although now banned in an overwhelming majority of the states, was a characteristic feature of U.S politics throughout much of the 19th century. It was particularly important in the Midwest and West, where it occurred in some degree in every election in the late 19th century. Historian Peter C. Argersinger described its importance to third party competition in an article on anti-fusion laws in the American Historical Review.

Old-Fusion helped keep a significant third-party tradition by guaranteeing that dissenters' votes could be more than symbolic protest, that their leaders could gain office, and that their demands might become heard. Most of the election victories normally attributed to the Granger, Independents, or Green-backers in the 1870s and 1880s were a result of Fusion between those third-party groups and Democrat

By "Fusion" with one of the (highly competitive major parties, third parties were able to influence election results, and thus public policy.) They were also better able to keep their popular base. A vote for a major party candidate endorsed by a third party ballot line allowed the third party voter to retain his or her political identity by casting a vote as a member of a third party with commitments different from the major parties, without sacrificing political effectiveness, that is, without being required to "waste" their votes on an independent candidate with no chance of winning. State law bans on Old-Fusion date from the 1890s, and were part of an extensive recasting of American electoral politics associated with that period, which included the "Jim Crow" system in the South, and accelerated after the realigning election of 1896 in which the Republican Party took control of state legislatures throughout the country.

The Party took control of state legislatures throughout the country. The first bans were-enacted shortly after the election of 1892, which was marked by the national appearance of the Populist "People's Party" and extensive Old-fusion between democrats and Populists in the campaign eventually won by Democrat Grover Cleveland. In response to the Populists' strong showing and the threat of a resurgent Democratic Party, Republican dominated state legislatures went ahead to enact bans on Old-Fusion. By

1907, the practice had become banned in Oregon, Washington, Michigan, Ohio, Illinois, Indiana, Iowa, North Dakota, Pennsylvania, Wisconsin, Wyoming, California, Nebraska, Kansas, Minnesota, South Dakota, Idaho, and Montana. As this report shows, some forty states plus the District of Columbia presently ban Old Fusion. Bearing clear political motivation, the bans had exactly the intended effect of keeping control of the elections.

After their passage, Republican dominance of American national politics was-assured for another forty years, only interrupted by the plurality victory of Woodrow Wilson in 1912, due to the Roosevelt/Taft split, and a razor-thin re-election victory in 1916. Twelve more years of GOP domination followed, until the Great Depression swept in the New Deal Democrats in 1932.

The Populist movement was-effectively silenced as an electoral force. Third parties, while they continued to form, were more Candidate-Centre and much less durable and effective as ongoing organizations. They never again achieved the influence they once had in state politics.

Old-Fusion survives today in only ten states. The most prominent is New York, which supplies a sort of laboratory experiment for its effects for minor parties. Throughout the 20thcentury, a rich tradition of vital third parties have exerted clear influence on New York state politics. Among them have been the Conservative, Liberal, Right-to-Life, and American Labor parties. Political scientist Daniel Mazmanian describes some of the virtues of the New York Old-Fusion system in Third Parties in Presidential Elections: The essential attribute of New York's modified two-party Fusion system is the options it provides to both individual voters and political parties. For the issue-oriented voter the presence of durable third parties afford a greater variety of choices among party platforms and candidates than does a two-party contest. Alternative arenas are available for potential activists who find the major-party organizations either preoccupied with winning office or dominated by an older generation of politicians. Furthermore, the system does not force voters to choose between 'throwing their vote away' or voting for one of the two major parties. The modified system allows third parties to keep them specialized constituencies while contributing to election outcomes through coalitions with the major parties. Finally, the ability of third parties to survive over time makes them vehicles for contemporary issues and innovative programs that otherwise would have to await acceptance. By much broader audience before the major parties would address them.

The New Fusion Electoral System

Thus, durable third parties, even more than the short-lived third parties that emerge in the present national two-party system, hold the potential for stimulating political discussion and compelling politicians in power to stay abreast of current public trends. Changing the election laws of other states to replicate those of New York would not, of course, automatically generate third parties or placate those groups demanding new forms of political participation. But it would entirely tend to ease change. New York Times Magazine, who recommends that: A genuine third party must attract regular Democrats and Republicans by nominating some of them to run as candidates with the third-party nomination as well as that of the Liberal-Conservative Party in New York democratic primary, as a candidate of its own party as well. Though LaFollette was willing to accept the second nomination, the Wisconsin Board of Elections followed the mandate of Wisconsin's Old-Fusion ban and refused to place his name on the Labor Farm ballot because he was already a candidate in the Democratic primary.

Labor Farm was not successful in Swamp v. Kennedy trial. The trial judge dismissed the complaint, the Court of Appeals affirmed, and the Supreme Court refused to grant review. But three highly respected conservative judges on the Seventh Circuit Court of Appeals, Judges Ripple, Posner, and Easterbrook, dissented from their fellow judges' refusal to rehear the case, writing that: The Supreme Court has recognized that the right of a party to nominate a candidate of its choice is a vital aspect of the party's role in our political structure. Same person as another party is an important aspect of that right. It allows a party to form significant political alliances. When a minor party nominates a candidate also nominated by a major party, it does not necessarily "leech onto" the larger party for support. It may, and often does offer the voters a very real and important choice and sends an important message to the candidate. On the view that a "split among the circuits" is likely to persuade the Supreme Court to take review in another case, the CND is working with third parties outside of Wisconsin on new lawsuits in other judicial circuit. It became addressed exclusively to multiple party nomination, whereby two parties nominate the same candidate on their respective ballots, and does not focus on laws, common throughout the states, which prohibit candidates from running as both independents and party nominees.

It does, however, take notice of "sore loser" rules or rules that forbid candidates who lose primaries in their "own" parties from running in the general election as candidates of other parties, but which do not, in themselves, forbid candidates who are successful in their own I primaries from also running on other tickets. As the report shows, only ten states in the United States permit Old-Fusion generally, four by explicitly authorizing it (Connecticut, New York, Utah, and Vermont), the other six by silence on the subject (Arkansas, Delaware, Idaho, Mississippi, South Carolina, and South Dakota).

In addition, at least five states permit "write-in Old-Fusion" (where one or more of the multiple party nominations is-won by means of write-in votes), although these states ban Old-Fusion on the ballot (California, Maine, Massachusetts, Nebraska, and New Hampshire). Two other states allow Old-Fusion for certain judicial races but ban it for all others (Maryland and Pennsylvania). Seven ban multiple party nominations on the general election ballot, even if fusion occurs during the primary or convention nominating process, by specifically requiring the candidate to choose one party before the general election (Arizona, Indiana, Iowa, Kansas, Michigan, Montana, and North Dakota), and two other states have a similar statute (Kentucky and Washington). Louisiana has no party nominations per se, and is, therefore, a special case: Candidates were selected for the general election in a nonpartisan primary, making Old-Fusion irrelevant.

The purpose of this New Fusion Elections System' book is to advise legislators and public in general the importance of modifies the Electoral System in America and nations of Democratic System around of the world, to facilitate a smooth selection of the Public Servants and the President of the Nation, without the necessity of political parties that it is what it is, a partition of the citizens in a political hostility within two or more political tendencies. When this report is sponsored by CND as an aid in the effort to restore Old-fusion its once prominent place in this country's politics. Its goal is to map out the status of Old-Fusion throughout the United States. It is based on the statutes themselves court decisions, attorneys' general opinions, correspondence with officials (attorneys general, secretaries of states, etc.) of the various states, and separate studies conducted by ACORN and the Connecticut State Legislature

THE NEW FUSION ELECTIONS SYSTEM AND HOW IT WORKS

- Voters elect their Representatives, as Senators, Governors, City Mayors and all the government officials elected by the peoples vote, who will be the people voice in the presidential election. It is a simple solution to dismissing the political party's discrepancy and have a more transparent and an efficient election.

- To become a candidate, the aspirant must fill an application with the Electoral Tribunal System, composed by 13 members of qualified citizens or professionals with a university degree, to perform an investigation of the Candidates, for any unclear past. Its purposes are function as a filter, to keep away the corrupt aspirants out the race, and to have transparency in the elections.

- There will be only seven (7) candidates to the presidency, with a University degree in Economy, Business Administration, Engineering, Architect, and others administrative professions.

- A degree in law, military, police of any king will not be allowed to be taking part in the Fusion Election System. Never-the-less they may run for any other public servant candidatures, or get a University degree in the professions mentioned above to become accepted as Presidential Candidate, the reasons are because we need administrators no Litigators, Prosecutors, Policeman, or Warriors.

- The others public officials will participate as Candidates in the elections in groups of five(5) per positions per states this number may be increased in none-numbers only up to five exp. (5) senator per state, (5) governors per state and therefore, all in a group of (5) the candidate with more vote is the winner the rest are advisors.

- In the Presidential election, the candidate with more votes is the elected President.

- The second with more votes, will be the Vice-President.

- The rest become advisor, and they can take part in further elections.
- There will be no losers, all are winners, and can take part in the upcoming Fusion Elections System again as many times they want, without the participation of any political parties involved.
- In Fusion Elections they may participate as many times they desire without the participation of any political parties involved and is ban the campaigns with the typical insults, candidate that uses blasphemous insults will be disqualified and through out of the election contest.
- What you have read above is results of a modification to the inappropriate of the existence Political Elections system that is controversial and inefficient, if substitutes by The New Fusion Election System, this controversy quickly will end and as a result we will have a pacific election with no political wars.
- In this new Fusion Electoral System, we eliminated all political parties having only the choice of the one who agreed and the one who does not agree, by this measure there is no need of political parties and the end of political wars between parties, humans naturally divide in two groups.
- As I mentioned there will be only seven presidential candidates, by this reason there will be no an equal finish situation, the candidate with more votes will become the winner, the second will be the vice president, and the rest will become advisor to the presidential administration, there will be no losers all are winners, and have the opportunity to participate in the future elections again.
- The nominations to any candidature are done only by the New Electoral Tribunal by application, not nomination, composed by thirteen members with a University degree, to prevent an equal end situation.
- I am launching my idea to the world, not for my own benefit because I am 90 years old and my goal is to enlightening the Voters and Public Servants, for a more honest election without political fights; for all peoples of this distress World. Political Parties Divide the nation instead of united the people to electing their candidate's honesty and peacefully. The number of thirteen has no link with the superstition

Michael Anguelo

FUSION THE NEW ELECTORAL SYSTEM

History of Democracy-Republic Systems

Thoughts:

The Political Parties' confrontations are destroying our United States of America. George Washington opinion "Political Parties are a menace that will harming our nation, I warn you" he told to Tomas Jefferson and Alexander Hamilton, founders of today Democratic and Republican Parties. What you learn in the medias today is that Democrat Party is intending to impeaching the President for allegations not confirmed of wrong doing, naturally the motive is not patriotic, instead, I believe is political gain by Democrats Vs. Republican, is a shame, without political parties this controversial should not take place.

Michael Anguelo

ELECTIONS HISTORICAL

The Democrat president Barack Obama visit to Cuba
and checking hands with a murder Dictator Communist
is a picture for the Hall of Shame

CHAPTER 1

HISTORY OF DEMOCRACY REPUBLIC SYSTEMS

Problems of the inefficient modern Political Electoral System.

To your information, the Geeks created the Democracy and the Republic was a Roman system. From the creation of Rome in c. 753 BIC. to c. 509 B.C., it was a monarchy, ruled by kings. In 509 the Romans opted for a mix the two system in one well organized system, in a new form of government, with 3 branches, Consuls, Senate, and the Assembly, and simply called Democracy-Republic Systems.

Then almost a millennium later in America, we mixed the Democratic System with the Republic System, and was called the Democrat-Republic System a fusion of the two system, with no divisions, all was doing well until one unfortunately day Mr. Alexander Hamilton and Mr. Thomas Jefferson, commenced a political war and each took a name of the Democrats-Republican, in two separated political coalitions, Hamilton as the Democrats, and Thomas Jefferson as the Republicans.

George Washington remained nonpartisan, throughout the two terms of his presidency. He warned them the danger of political parties to dividing the nation. Nonetheless, Alexander Hamilton formed the first political party during Washington's term, called the Federalists, today the Democrat Party.

Thomas Jefferson had no choice and showed the Anti-Federalist party today Republican Party in 1792, the year after Hamilton formed the Federalist Party, today in the dangerous form, are in continue conflict against each other. Hamilton and Jefferson remain political enemy for the rest of their life, and they die days of each to the another. Coincidence?

Modern parties' directors, as uncooperative and unpredictable in the dangerous form, are in continue conflict against each other. The supporters, it would hardly do something to call them, the fractions, of the Gracchi seem more like mobs than parties. In Aristocracies or states with a limited suffrage the most important political conclaves often had much the character of family gatherings, and the political decisions makers by them took the form of what today would be called gentlemen's agreements. This is true particularly of the ancient Democratic party. The supporters, it would hardly do something to call them, the factions, of the Gracchi seem more like mobs than parties. In Aristocracies or states with a limited suffrage the most important political conclaves often had much the character of family gatherings, and the political decisions makers by them took the form of what today would be called gentlemen's agreements.

To manage the hundreds of thousands and millions of new voters thus created political managers have compelled to devise forms of organization of an ability, extent, and flexibility previously unknown in the world's history. As to the practical efficiency of this modern political machinery there can be no doubt; indeed, this has made the chief point in the formal accusation against present day parties. For with it there has come a certain preponderance of party organization as against party principles and a centralization in the hands of party Leaders and Bosses of controls subject to misappropriation for dishonest benefits and private ends. Not anywhere in the world have these progresses, both moral and malevolent, occurred on a larger scale than in the United States. Undeniably they present the greatest internal party problem which now confronts us.

Summing up the various elements presented in the fore going pages and which, as the most immediate method of securing their acceptance, appoints and supports certain candidates for public office. A definition may now become offered, as follows: A political party is a voluntary organization of individuals or groups of individuals supporting certain principles and policies as greater to all others for the general behavior of government. In place of far as party organization is concerned, an absolute revolt has brought about by the extension of the electoral suffrage which occurred in the United States roughly between 1810 and 1840, and subsequently in Great Britain, France, Belgium, Norway, and other countries with liberal governments.

To handle the hundreds of thousands and millions of new voters therefore formed political bosses had compelled to plan procedures of the organization of a dimensions, extent, and flexibility up till then unknown in the world's history. As to the practical efficiency of this modern political machinery there can be no hesitation; certainly, this has made the chief point in the formal allegation against present day part for this has become a certain preponderance of party organization as against party principles and a centralization in the hands of party leaders and bosses of controls subject to misuse for dishonest interests and private ends. No world has these developments, both good and evil, occurred on a greater scale than in the United States.

Unquestionably they present the greatest internal party problem which now confronts us, the pretending impeachment of the President. Summing up the various elements presented in the fore going pages a definition may now become offered, as follows: A political party is a voluntary organization of individuals or groups of individuals advocating certain principles and policies as superior to all others for the general con duct of government, and which, as the most immediate method of securing their adoption, designates and supports certain of its leaders as candidates for public office.

INEFFICIENCY OF MODERN PARTIES
American Political History

As principles are considered to hold good over extended Permanence periods of time, parties inspired by them are presumed to of parties be able to count upon a somewhat prolonged lease of life with many transmutations and vicissitudes the present Democratic party can be traced back to the beginnings of our national life. Both great English parties can claim a continuous existence of more than two and a half centuries.

There is a scientific said, that every atom of a man's body is replaced by others in seven years. A process of similar character goes on more slowly perhaps in the case of parties which persist through extended periods. However, the time element affords neither a definite nor a convincing test of party character. Certainly, none would deny this character to the late Progressive movement, for example, simply because of its rapid disintegration after the campaign of 19 12.

In that campaign it played a role of major importance and was fully equipped as far as candidates, platform, and organization were concerned, to perform all the functions of a party. Realistic, it failed in its effort to gain control of the government, but success in this is not a necessary qualification for party standing. The prohibitionists supply a situation in opinion.

In fact, a party may remain in a minority throughout the greater part or even the whole of a long existence and yet perform every purpose typical of such an association. Although the immediate aim of a party is to gain control of the government by placing a sufficient number of its own leaders in office, failure in this aim does not prevent the possibility of working out a great and beneficent impact. From the social point of view, therefore, the immediate success or lack of it on the part of individual parties may be a matter of small importance.

What is important is that such organizations shall contribute unhelpfully to the fight for the expansion of nationwide lifespan goal. Taking this bigger point of view, parties which have but a small resulting, or which endure for a brief time only, may nevertheless be of great interest and significances.

At all times it should be impressed upon researchers of parties that politics is life, not simply literature. The voters should be encouraged to attend campaign meetings, conventions, caucuses, conferences of reform and other organizations; to write fact statements followed by comment on the speeches and proceedings at such gatherings; to interview leaders and candidates; and finally to compare and disapprove of such written statements and the accounts published in local newspapers.

On the specific topic discussed in this Chapter. Eras of the derivation of the word party (Latin, partidos) calls good feeling attention to the fact that ordinarily the people of a country are divided into two or more political campgrounds in America, each con tending for the control of the government. Sometimes this is not the case. At the outbreak of the World War, for example, party strife was followed by an armistice and an alliance in several of the destructive nations. In our own country during the called Era of Good Feeling (1816-32) there was only one party in the field, because were not political disputing. The great mass of the people of the country were in general agreement currently as to the broad principles and policies upon which the government was to be con ducted.

To one who looks below the surface, however, the Era of Good Feeling was a period of individual policies. Groups following rival leaders contended vigorously for office. But even currently the prevalence of personal interest was not absolute. While each of these political groups professed allegiance to the principles of Jeffersonian Republicanism, it also looked to make distinctions concerning these principles which it regarded as of fundamental importance class.

Except during such unusual periods, however, a party interests as the origin of the such unusual periods, however, a party interests as the origin of the word itself suggests, a portion of the people, grouped against other similar portions, each con tending for the control government.

From this time, it has been argued that the principles and policies of each party, no matter how strongly they are advocated as an ideal guide for the whole conduct of the state, must in fact be only partial views strongly tinged with the particular interests of the group or groups making up the party. consequently, the factual end of a party, according to one writer, the end of which it is itself aware is, in ordinary times, to promote not the general interest, but the interest of a class, a section or some one of the many groups of citizens which are to be found in every state in which there is political life, an interest which is always rather the other, and generally, however not always, to some degree is less than the nationwide consciousness. It is impossible to deny the general validity of this statement. In some cases, a party honestly admits that it is made up of members of a convinced meeting and that it is working primarily in the interests of that meeting. This is true, for instance, of the Communist party which, wherever it is organized, claims to be the party of the workers which is a fallacious proclamation. It is false, also of several other parties in European countries where party divider is supported to an extreme unknown in the United States. On the other hand, our two principal parties which seek to make converts in all ranks of society naturally deny this allegation.

Whether or not they admit the charge that they are parties focus by class interest large parties and small parties to act alike support that the programs they advance represent interests of the real interest of the state or the people as a whole. Of the state sequence there is a reason for so doing so. Only by making this argument good or at least acceptable to most of the people can a party hope to conquer control and keep itself within. Quite apart from this self-seeking motive, however, the assertion may be fully justified by the facts in certain situation. History records on many occasions when a given party has laid-down principles and implemented policies, which were in the best benefits of the state at the time. In the case of a party containing a considerable majority of the people drawn from all social classes it is easily conceivable that the collective group interests which help to frame its platform may enumerate policies according largely with the best interest of the party Discipline and tolerance of parties the people as a whole.

And indeed, the interests of a small class may possibly agree for a time with those of the state, especially if the class concerned is of superior intelligence or of superior political or economic ability. On the other hand, it is of course true that party is dominated by narrow class awareness have at times uncertain an already dishonest state to pieces. With the possible exception of such cases the preparation of principles and policies by political parties, even when shaded by class benefits, is a public service, likewise, which parties alone render on an adequate scale the question may well be raised, however, as to whether there is not a certain unfairness in comparing actual party platforms with ideal platforms assumed to be in the best interests of the state. As a rule, it is only the actual party platforms which have sufficient power and organization behind them to determine the action of government. Moreover, often historians only discover the so-called ideal courses of policy long after the event.

If they exist simultaneously it is only in the brains of philosophers or of a few intellectuals, whence, indeed, they may appear in time to permeate and bless the communality. Unconstitutionality in actual party platforms before they may hope to be realized. In fact, however, actual party platforms and ideal formulations of policy do not compete. To contrast the two parties to the of disparagement former is, therefore, meaningless.

Like many other associations pursuing political ends either exclusively or as part of their activities, parties are unpaid assistant submissions of the voters. Rules, customs, traditions, discipline of a sort, and distinctions between leaders and supporters they do, indeed, own, but they are occasionally enforced with the conscientiousness and neutrality distinctive of the implementation of law in a well-ordered state. In this genial tolerance lies one of the reasons for the peculiar friendliness in which the typical partisan holds his party.

American political history its problems and the Inefficiency of modern parties.

NATURE OF PARTIES
The Nature and Activities of Parties

It appears so abundant nearer to him, so much more human in its aims and struggles, than the stern, just, powerful, and far more distant state. In an extremely happy passage professor Merriam has given expression to this feeling. The party, he writes, is in a sense a political church which does not require very regular attendance or extremely strict faith, Party plat forms vs. ideal platforms.

But still it provides a home-based and it looks after the disconnected if he pays the minimum of party contributions, involving in the associate with and sporadic support of some one of its wealthy elite, even nonetheless a minor one. Or, changing the sign, the party is an honorable awareness, like a baseball team in which the discrete is powerfully involved from time to time political families other than parties are frequently Appeal of somewhat exclusive as to their relationship. Parties cannot be able to pay for, to take such a position. They can never have too large a following. Naturally they are most interested in enrolling actual voters, but they by no means neglect other classes of residents, or even individuals who have not acquired his naturalization, mostly if the final is soon to be added to the people entitled to vote. Thus, we find parties inspiring the naturalization of foreigners, granting party representation to inhabitants of regions, and establishing clubs of young men soon to become first voters or of women in states which had not yet approved them the suffrage right to vote. Indeed, there is scarcely a class, race, creed, group, or encouragement of any sort to which the prejudiced politician does not make a petition.

Although tolerant in their discipline and cordial in their Party invites to potential supporters, modern political parties are considered by huge and extremely specialized organizations. In this respect they fluctuate abruptly from the parties of earlier centuries. The parties of classic antiquity impress the reader of olden times, and still more the modern party Boss, as awkward and unreliable in the dangerous.

This is true particularly of the ancient Democratic parties. The followers, it would hardly do to call them the followers of the Gracchi, Roman like social reform by the Gracchi brothers, seem more like Mobs than parties. In nobilities or states with a limited suffrage the most important political meetings often had much the character of family meetings, and the political decisions reached by them took the form of what today would be called the oral gentlemen's agreements. So far as party organization is concerned, a veritable revolution was brought about by the extension of the electoral ballots which occurred in the United States roughly between 1810 and 1840, and subsequently in Great Britain, France, Belgium, Norway, and other countries with liberal governments. As to the practical efficiency of this modern political machinery there can be no doubt; indeed, this is made the chief point in the accusation against present day.

Nowhere in the world have these developments, both good and evil, occurred on a greater scale than in the United States party systems. Unquestionably they present the greatest internal party problem which now confronts us with the struggle between Democrats and Republicans of these 21 Century elections of 1920. Definition of party as follows: A political party is a volunteer group of individuals or groups of individuals supporting certain principles and policies as higher to all others for the general behavior of government, and which, as the most direct method of securing their acceptance, designates and supports certain of its leaders as candidates for public office. Although there has been a great increase of interest in the subject of recent years, the number of general works dedicated entirely to American political parties is still quite limited. Of those which rank as systematic dissertations the most valuable is C.E. Merriam, The American Party System (1922), which deals with the function of the political party in the community and examines the composition of parties in terms of political and social forces, rather than of historical evolution or of political apparatus. As in the case of certain religious sects, nicknames maliciously invented by enemies are sometimes assumed defiantly by parties and afterward borne with pride.

Party names small light on the character of the party assuming it. Of course, the task of selecting a name is much easier in the case of parties devoted to a single issue, as, for example, our Green backers and Prohibitionists. But no single title can do justice to parties advocating a wide range of policies. Certainly, there is little of descriptive value in the terms Republican and Democratic as used in our national politics. The Democrats of today are the lineal descendants of those who in Jefferson's time called themselves Republicans. By their Federalist opponents they were labelled Democrats or Democratic-Republicans, in insolence and ridicule.

At the present time so-called Democratic parties also exist in a number of European countries, but they have no connection whatever with the party bearing the same name in the United States and differ from it widely both in configuration and in resolutions. The terms Radical, Liberal, Moderate, Progressive, and Conservative are also much in favor as party names. In their general significance each of these has some value as showing a certain attitude toward political innovation. As party names, however, they are used very loosely. Parties calling themselves Liberal contrast widely from country to country, and the same is true of each of the other terms in the above list. On the other hand, it is true that Socialist parties hunt equitably certain common goals in all countries and have established international connections of a Communist party with the purpose to dominates a population of workers and succumbing them as slavery of the Government. In popular speech several terms are used more or party and less exactly to characterize fanatical system of government. Thus, gathering a distinction is drawn often between a party and a gathering. Originally the two words were 3 synonymous; indeed, they are so used occasionally at the present time. In his famous dictionary Doctor Johnson defines faction as a party in the state and quotes it without qualification of any sort as an equivalent for the word party.

At that time both terms were in hostile position. With the extension of the activities and the purification of the aims of parties that came in the nineteenth century the concluding word gradually lost its violent significance and became first trustworthy and finally even praiseworthy.

Meanwhile all the malevolent and contemptuous meanings fall away upon party, which is currently associated with the ideas of opposition, trickery, unscrupulousness, self-seeking, negligence of the common good, and revolutionary designs upon the Government. With more or less disposition the word is also employed at times to designate the groups into which a party is divided before or after a split by oppositions between its leaders or by crashes of economic, sector, or other interests. Another distinction commonly made is that between the (ins) and the (outs) that is, between the party (outs) equal finish backup the government and those in antagonism. Where these roles are overturned from time to time the distinction may seem to be of slight value.

References: O. Ray, Introduction to Political Parties and Practical Politics (2d ed., 19 17); M. Ostrogorski, Democracy and the Party System in the United States (19 10), being an abridgment of the second volume of his earlier extended work, Democracy and the Organization of Political Parties (2 vols., 1902); J. Macy, Party Organization and Machinery (1904) ; and J. A. Woodburn, Political Parties and Party Problems in the United States (1903), which is still of great value, particularly for its historical chapters (I to VIII, inclusive). C. L. Jones, Readings on Parties and Elections in the United States (1912), is a collection of well-chosen materials in this field.

For general reference purposes the most extensive and helpful work is A. C. McLaughlin and A. B. Hart, Cyclopedias of American Government (1913). The American Party System, p. 402. Cf. also G. Wallas, Human Nature in Politics, p. 83. From this source many party titles of greater or less vogue have been drawn, see our Quid's, Loco-Focus, Know-Nothings, Hunkers and Barnburners, Stalwarts and Half-Breeds, Snappers and Ant Snappers. Ref: A. D. Morse, op. cit., p. 69. Getting back to our New Fusion Electoral System is not a party, is an Electoral System fusion with two government System the Democracy and the Republic, in on single idea, without the intervention of the corrupt system of political parties.

In the past, a Fusion System existed, introduced in New York's fusion voting system as a unique process that gives third parties political power in a system dominated by two major parties. But it was not always this rare. Electoral fusion played a key role in 1800s politics and contributed to the success of many third-party candidates. The Old Electoral Fusion allows one candidate to become nominated by multiple political parties. This allows smaller parties to have an impact on the election and forces lawmakers to pay attention to the platforms of these parties. It also allows voters to support the platform of a party, such as the Working Families Party in New York, without sensitivity like their vote will go to waste if they do not cast it for a Democrat or Republican parties in this New Fusion Electoral System of the 21 Century, we eliminated all political parties having only the choice of those who agreed and those who does not agree, by this opportunity there is no need of political parties and is the end of political confrontations between parties.

TWO PARTIES TWO PROBLEMS

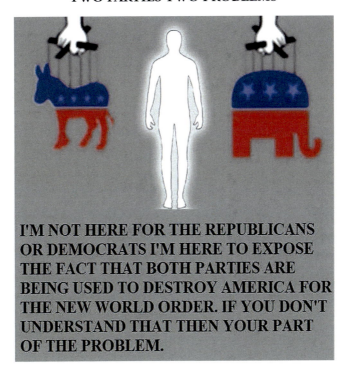

The political parties as we know them did not begin to develop until the late 1600s. The ancient Greeks, who were pioneers in developing Democracy, had no organized political parties in the modern sense. The senate of the ancient Romans had two groups that represented people with different interests the Patricians and the Plebeians. The Patricians represented noble families. The Plebeians stood for the wealthy merchants and the middle class. Although these two groups often mingled, at times they voted as factions, or parties, on issues that were important to the groups they represented.

For many centuries after the fall of Rome (AD 476), the people of Europe had little voice in politics. Thus, there were no true political parties only factions that supported one noble family or another. Political parties developed as representative assemblies gained power. In England, this change began after what was called the Popish Plot of 1678.

The Founding Fathers disliked political parties, calling them "factions" motivated by self-interest. Washington was so upset over the quarrelling between Hamilton (Federalists) and Jefferson (anti-Federalists) that he devoted much of his Farewell Address to the evils of parties. The people who supported Hamilton and Adams were called Federalists (supporters of the Constitution) but they were not an organized political party. The first organized party in America was made up of the followers of Jefferson, who, starting in the 1790s, called themselves Republicans or Jeffersonian Democratic-Republicans. Hamilton and those who opposed Jefferson, kept the name Federalist. Jefferson's Republican Party has no ties to the current Republican Party. In fact, the current Democratic Party considerer Jefferson and Andrew Jackson as the founders of their party.

The leaders of the American Revolution did not like the idea of parties and political battles between parties. Upon his retirement from public life in 1796, George Washington warned Americans against "faction" (parties).

James Madison thought parties were necessary, although he did not entirely approve of them. Alexander Hamilton thought that faction was always a vice to be guarded against.

Thomas Jefferson declared in 1789, "If I could not go to heaven but with a party, I would not go there at all." Nevertheless, the men who held these views founded the first two fatal American political parties.

References: MLA (Modern Language Association) style, "Political Parties." The New Book of Knowledge®. 2007. Grolier Online. 25 July 2007.

Chicago Manual of Style: Flanders, Stephen

UNITED STATES GOVERMENT ORGANIZATION

American Political History

United States Government is a combination of federal, state, and local laws, bodies, and agencies that manages conducting the operations of the United States Administration. The federal government of the United States placed in Washington, D.C. the capital of the nation. The institutions of all governments appear from basic principles. In the United States the one basic principle is representative Democrat-Republic systems, is a Fusion of the two systems, not as political parties, which defines as system in which the people govern themselves by electing their own leaders without the participation of any political parties. The American government functions to secure this principle and to further the common interests of the people.

The New Fusion Electoral System

The New-Fusion of the Democracy and the Republic Systems in America is based on six essential ideals: (1) People must accept the principle of majority rule. (2) The political rights of minorities to become protected. (3) Citizens must agree to a system of rule by law. (4) The free exchange of opinions and ideas must not become restricted. (5) All citizens must be equal before the law. (6) Government exists to serve the people because it derives its power from the people. These principles form the basis of the Democratic and the Republic System in the United States, which looks to create a union of diverse peoples, places, and interests.

To implement its essential Democratic-Republic ideals, the United States has built its government on four elements: (1) Popular sovereignty, meaning that the people are the ultimate source of the government's authority; (2 Representative Government; (3 Checks and Balances; (4 Federalism, an arrangement where powers are shared by different levels of government; and (5 Politicians are not allowing to promote dominant leaders in any form.

Every government has a source of its sovereignty or authority, and most of the political structures of the U.S. government apply the doctrine of popular sovereignty. In previous centuries, the source of sovereignty in some countries was the Monarchy, the divine right of Kings to rule. In United States of Americans places the source of authority in the public who in a Democratic-Republic society governed. In this idea the citizens collectively stand for the nation's authority. They then express that authority individually by voting to elect candidates, no leaders, without the need of political parties, to represent them in a Presidential Election, in order to represent them the voters elect their representatives to represent the voters in electing the President.

"I know no safe repository of the ultimate powers of the society but the people themselves, and if we think them not educated enough to exercise their control with a wholesome discretion, the remedy is not to take it from them, but to inform their decision. This was an experimental idea at the time, but today United States of America take it as accepted". wrote Thomas Jefferson.

The second principle of United States Democracy-Republic Systems is a representative government. In a representative government, the people delegate their powers in the elected officials to be them in the presidential election to elect the most competent President, this is the system I proposes.

In turn these elected officials are the will of the people and ensure that the government is answerable to its citizens. In a New Electoral Fusion System, (Democracy-Republic), the people exercise elections, which allow adult citizens of the United States the chance to have their voices heard and to influence government though their representatives. With their vote, they can remove officials who ignore their intentions or who betray their trust.

Administration' Officers are responsible as representatives of the people; this accountability is an important feature of the United States of America system of representative government, with the New Fusion Electoral System, in order to truly work, however, representative elected officials must represent all the people to elect the new President.

The third principle of American Democrat-Republic are the systems of checks and balances. The three branches of Government, are the Legislative, the Executive, and the Judicial restraint and stabilize one another through their separated functions, but no fighting as the political parties existing do today, instead, cooperation and mutual Team Work are the success. The legislative branch, represented by Congress, must pass bills before they can become law. The executive branch namely, the President can veto bills passed by Congress, thus preventing them from becoming law. In turn, by a two-thirds votes, Congress can override the president's veto. The Supreme Court may invalidate acts of Congress by declaring them contrary to the Constitution of the United States, but Congress can change the Constitution through the amendments process, I greed if political parties has not become included.

The fourth principle of democracy in the United States is federalism. In the American federal system, the states, and the national government divide authority. This division of power helps curb abuses by either the national or the state governments and no one have absolute power.

UNITED STATES GOVERMENT ORGANIZATION

American Political History

The nature and Activities of Parties in General Politic offers many avenues of approach. Groups of voluntary activities is the most obvious of these, but it is by no means a political Parties or the sole one party, as the Communism do. The American citizen who is interested in public affairs meet an extraordinarily substantial number and variety of voluntary organizations each engaged in the work of influencing the conduct of government. Some of these associations limit themselves to a single issue or a single field of activity, as, for example, the Short Ballot Organization, the Anti-Saloon League, the Civil Service Reform League, the American Protective Tariff League, the American Association for Labor Legislation. Others cover in some manner the general activities of the government of a city, a state, or even of the nation. An alert city club keeps up a constant fire of comment and criticism upon the acts both of commission and omission of all the departments of municipal government. Bureaus of research offer constructive and elaborate suggestions to city or state governments. The National Voters' League turns a searchlight on Congress every month and incidentally manages to enlighten various other branches of the federal government. The League of Women Voters discusses every political question, national, state, or local, of interest to its membership. In addition to these purely political associations many organizations primarily concerned with other fields, labor unions, Church federations, Synagogue temples, commercial and professional bodies, and the like, are accustomed to act whenever their interests affected by government.

AMERICAN POLITICAL HISTORY
AND THE SOLUTIONS

They offer opportunities for constructive statecraft which no one interested in politics can afford to ignore. However, they are supplements, rather than substitutes for, political parties. At least it is evident that the latter perform certain essential of political parties as may found scattered throughout the statute books of our states the making of nominations regarded, and rightly so, as the fundamental test of a political party. It has the further merit of easily applied for administrative purpose.

They may even discuss the records of party candidates and advise the public to make selections among them as is the custom of various Voters' leagues, but this is not the same thing as selecting them in the first instance and thus accepting responsibility for them. If any such organization decides to transcend its ordinary limitations and names candidates, it buys at once the characteristic of a political party. The making of nominations is not only the distinctive activity of a political party, it is, moreover, a public service of the greatest importance and significance. Especially in a country like our own with an extremely substantial number of elective offices and often recurring elections the volume of work involved.

At times they accused of nominating men of known incompetence and bad reputation; at other times it is charitable to assume that they have been deceived in the character of their own nominees. However, nominations must be made by an Electoral Tribunal only not by parries nominations, at the appointed intervals if the work of government is to go on. And among our many organizations devoting themselves to political ends parties alone always stand ready to assume this problem. To formulate party principles and party policies may preparation seem a much higher duty than nominating candidates. In of principle this connection, though, it is worth remembering that to a large part of any electorate make only when they dramatized by forceful and sympathetic personalities, fighting in the public arena for power to realize hem, do they provoke a full popular response. Certainly, it is much easier merely to formulate political ideals and loudly call upon all good men for their support, than to undertake the further steps of securing representative and responsible candidates and backing them in their campaign for office.

That is one of the reasons why so many individuals and voluntary political organizations other than parties' content themselves with the first of these activities. However, this may be, the political necessity and social utility of the added functions which parties alone assume must conceded, frankly. In an oft-quoted passage from Edmund Burke party is Burke definition of denned as a body or men united, to promoting by their party joint endeavors the national interest, upon some principle in which they are all agreed. Usually this statement criticized as idealism rather than definition, as an attempted glorification by the brilliant Whig pamphleteer of his own party in contrast with the irresponsible cabal of King's Friends whom George III had collected around him.

PROGRESS OF PARTIES PRIOR CIVIL WAR

American Political Parties History

As it stands the statement does indeed seem to lay stress upon philosophies and the promotion of the national interest to the exclusion of other and perhaps lower ends for which parties have striven not only in Burke's time, but later. However, the words quoted above should be read in find it impossible to conceive that any one believes in his own politics, or thinks them to be of any weightiness, who refuses to adopt the means of having them reduced into practice. It is the business of the speculative philosopher to mark the proper ends of government. It is the business of the politician, who is the philosopher in action, to find out proper means toward those ends, and to employ them with effectiveness.

Therefore, every honorable connection will affirm it is their first purpose, to pursue every just method to put the men who hold their opinions into such a condition as may enable them to carry their common plans into execution, with all the power and authority of the state. As this power attached to certain situations, it is their duty to contend for these situations by The Fusion Electoral Tribunal, Included the making of nominations. The added sentences make it clear that Burke's conception of party, however ideal in other respects, included the very practical function of bringing men forward for office. Finally, it involves the idea that a body of men who hold to certain political principles with sincere conviction and a sense of their importance will, by the fact, of take the further step of selecting and supporting men who, when placed in office, will happenings to realize these principles. In other words, a party needs to this extent a higher voltage of conviction than those political associations which do not make nominations, only though Fusion Electoral Tribunal.

Meaning, While the formulation of party principles and party of platforms prejudgment is not the most distinctive of party functions, it is nevertheless of high importance and great social utility. It is an activity that, as we have noted, is common not only to political parties, but also to other organizations which do not make nominations, and which therefore are not to counted properly as parties. In most cases, however, the programs laid down by such organization or appear to shelter, every governmental question of reputation. Although many boards may be evasions, falsifications, or devout clichés, it is the party theory of itself that the principles it clutches provide all that is needed for higher guidance, while the policies it proposes supply a detailed program quite sufficient for the general conduct of government in case the party is given control. And of course, in each case these principles and policies encouraged, if not as ideal, at least as noticeably and demonstrably superior to those of other parties with which it is competing for sovereignty.

Party professions of conviction, it perceived, include definition of both principles and policies. Logically it is quite possible to make a distinction between the two, although application of the distinction is not always easy. The principles of a party have defined as the durable convictions held in common by its members as to what the state should be and do.

The policy of a party, on the other hand, understands all that the party does to set up I its principles; it includes, therefore, the whole of the party's conduct. Principles showed in the end which made thought; policy in the end which sought after; policy in the means employed for the attainment of the end. Party principles have a greater permanence Relation of and a higher validity than party policies. The latter principles to must square with the former, but in practical politics considerable stretching is sometimes necessary to make them seem to do so.

The senate of the ancient Romans had two groups that represented people with different interests, the Patricians, and the Plebeians. The Patricians represented noble families. The Plebeians in such cases, however, it is always possible to keep convincingly that the changes made are matters of policy only; or that they justified Anson D. Morse. Political parties as we know them did not begin to develop until the late 1600s. The ancient Greeks, who were pioneers in developing Democracy, had no organized the middle class. Although these two groups often mingled, at times they voted as factions, or parties, on issues that were important to the groups they represented.

For centuries after the fall of Rome (AD 476), the people of Europe had little voice in politics. Thus, there were no true political parties only factions that supported one noble family or another. Political parties developed as representative assemblies gained power. In America we were busy creating political methods that we called Political Parties that eventually will contaminates all World with a party revolution that did not helping today much. Hamilton and those who opposed Jefferson, kept the name Federalist. Jefferson's Republican Party has no ties to the current Republican Party.

In fact, the current Democratic Party considerer Jefferson and Andrew Jackson as the founders of their party. The promoters of the American Revolution did not like the idea of parties and political battles between parties.

Upon his retirement from public life in 1796, President George Washington warned Americans against faction (parties). James Madison thought parties were necessary, although he did not entirely approve of them. Alexander Hamilton thought that faction was always a malevolent to safeguarded in contradiction of Government. Thomas Jefferson declared in 1789, "If I could not go to heaven but with a party, I would not go there at all."

There are other forms of political systems, which are prevalent in different countries of the world. Those systems have existed for a long time, like: Monarchy, Oligarchy, Anarchy, Democracy, Socialism, and Republic, etc. Of these forms of government, Democracy-Republic is The New Fusion Electoral System is a no partisan system, are quite often juxtaposed, but there is a fine line amidst the two systems, when is divided in political parties, is converted in two political adversaries, dividing the country, and become an eternal political competition that don't benefit anything, but, politicians, the media Etc. but not to the people.

Reference: Using as References and History Book, by Robert C Brooks, I respond his allegations with a solution to the American Electoral Problems, with my theory of the New Fusion Electoral System, based in the nonpartisan political disagreement, as President George Washington did in his two administrations.

Reference: Flanders, Stephen. "Political Parties." The New Book of Knowledge®. Grolier Online APA (American Psychological Association) Flanders, S (2007). Political Parties. The New Book of Knowledge®. Retrieved July 25, 2007.My book is sort of an American Political History and The New Electoral System that I called The New Fusion Electoral System no partisan elections.

WHAT IS THE DEMOCRACY SYSTEM?

American Political History

Greek Democracy History: Democracy refers to the system of masses, i.e. a political system dominated by citizens of the country. Under this system, the public have a certain degree of power and authority and takes part in the decision-making process of the government choice. Athens was not the only city in Ancient Greece that instituted a Democratic regime.

Aristotle points to other cities that adopted governments in the Democratic style. However, accounts of the rise of Democratic institutions are about Athens, since only this city-state had enough historical records to guess on the rise and nature of Greek Democracy.

Before the first attempt of a Democratic government, Athens ruled by a series of chief magistrates, and the Areopagus, made up of ex-anchors. The members of these institutions were aristocrats who ruled the politics for their own advantage. In 621 BC, Draco codified a set of notoriously harsh laws designed to reinforce aristocratic power over the public.

till, a growing problem of aristocratic families feuding among themselves to obtain as much power as possible led to a point where most Athenians were subject to harsh treatment and enslavement by the rich and powerful. In the 6th century BC, the Athenian laboring class convinced Plato's ancestor Solon, premier anchor at the time, to liberate them and halt the disputing of the nobility. What soon followed was a system of chattel slavery involving foreign slaves. Solon then issued reforms that defined citizenship in a way that gave each free dweller of Attica a political function: Athenian citizens had the right to take part in assembly meetings. By granting the formerly aristocratic role to every free citizen of Athens who owned property, Solon reshaped the social framework of the city state. Under these reforms, a council of 400 members (with 100 citizens from each of Athens's four tribes) called the boule, ran daily affairs, and set the political agenda.

Not long afterwards, the nascent democracy was overthrown by the tyrant Peisistratus, but was reinstated after the expulsion of his son, Hippias, in 510. Cleisthenes issued reforms in 508 and 507 BC that undermined the domination of the aristocratic families and connected every Athenian to the city's rule. Cleisthenes formally named free inhabitants of Attica as citizens of Athens, which gave them power and a role in a sense of civic solidarity. He did this by making the traditional tribes politically irrelevant and instituting ten new tribes, each made up of about three agreements, each consisting of several demonstrators.

Government, Politics & Diplomacy, every male citizen over 18 had to registered in his demonstrators. The third set of reforms was instigated by Ephialtes in 462. While Ephialtes's opponents were away trying to demist aid the Spartans, he persuaded the Assembly to reduce the powers of the Areopagus to a criminal court for cases of homicide and sacrilege. At the same time or soon afterwards, the membership of the Areopagus extended to the lower level of the propertied citizenship. In the wake of Athens's disastrous defeat in the Sicilian campaign in 413 BCE, a group of citizens took steps to limit the radical Democracy they thought was leading the city to destruction. Their efforts, initially conducted through constitutional channels, culminated in the establishment of an oligarchy, the Council of 400, in the Athenian coup of 411 BCE. The oligarchy endured for only four months before it replaced by a more Democratic government.

WHAT IS THE REPUBLIC SYSTEM?

American Political History

THE ROMAN REPUBLIC HISTORY:

The Republic System was founded by the Roman society under the Republic was a cultural mix of Latin, Etruscan, and Greek elements, which is especially visible in the Roman Pantheon. This political organization was strongly influenced by the Greek city states of Magna Graecia, with collective and annual magistracies, overseen by a senate. The top law lords were the two consuls, who had an extensive range of executive, legislative, judicial, military, and religious powers. Whilst there were elections each year, the Republic was not a Democracy, but an oligarchy rule, as a small number of large families called gentes monopolized the main magistracies. Roman institutions underwent considerable changes throughout the Republic to adapt to the difficulties it challenged, such as the creation of pro-magistracies to rule its conquered provinces, or the composition of the senate. Unlike the Pax Romana of the Roman Empire, the Republic was in a state of virtual perpetual war throughout its existence.

Its first enemies were its Latin and Etruscan neighbors as well as the Gaul's, who even sacked the city in 387 BC. The Republic nevertheless proved extreme resilience and always managed to overcome its losses, however catastrophic. After the Gallic Sack, Rome indeed conquered the whole Italian peninsula in a century, which turned the Republic into a major power in the Mediterranean. The Republic's greatest enemy was doubtless Carthage, against which it waged three wars. The Punic general Hannibal famously invaded Italy by crossing the Alps and inflicted on

Rome two devastating defeats at the Lake Trasimene and Cannae, but the Republic once again recovered and won the war thanks to Scipio Africans at the Battle of Zama in 202 BC. With Carthage defeated.

Rome became the dominant power of the ancient Mediterranean world. It then embarked in a long series of difficult conquests, after having notably defeated Philip V and Perseus of Macedon, Antiochus III of the Seleucid Empire, the Lusitanian Viriathis, the Numidian Jugurtha, the great Pontic king Mithridates VI, the Gaul Vercingetorix, and the Egyptian queen Cleopatra.

At home, the Republic similarly experienced a long streak of communal and political crises, which ended in several violent civil wars. At first, the Conflict of the Orders opposed the patricians, the closed oligarchic elite, to the far more many publics, who finally achieved political equality in several steps during the 4th century BC. Later, the vast conquests of the Republic disrupted its society, as the immense influx of slaves they brought enriched the aristocracy but ruined the peasantry and urban workers. In order to solve this issue, several social reformers, known as the Populates, tried to pass agrarian laws, but the Gracchi brothers, Saturninus, or Clodius Pulcher, were all murdered by their opponents: The Optimizes, keepers of the traditional aristocratic order.

Mass slavery also caused three Servile Wars; the last of them was led by Spartacus, a skillful gladiator who ravaged Italy and left Rome powerless until his defeat in 71 BC. In this context, the last decades of the Republic marked by the rise of great generals, who exploited their military conquests and the factional situation popular Rome to gain control of the political system. Marius, between 105-86 BC, then Sulla (between 82-78 BC dominated in turn the Republic; both used extraordinary powers to purge their opponents. These multiple tensions lead to a series of civil wars; the first between the two generals Julius Caesar and Pompey.

Despite his victory and appointment as autocrat for life, Caesar was murdered in 44 BC. Caesar's heir Octavian and lieutenant Mark Antony defeated Caesar's assassins Brutus and Cassius in 42 BC, but then turned against each other. The final defeat of Mark Antony and his ally Cleopatra at the Battle of Actium in 31 BC, and the Senate's grant of extraordinary powers to Octavian as Augustus in 27 BC – which effectively made him the first Roman emperor, therefore ended the Republic.

THE FUSION OF OUR DEMOCRACY-REPUBLIC SYSTEM.

American Political History

The United States is Both a Republic and a Democracy Fusion, together the two systems in one, that I called Fusion. One way to phrase this is the United States of America is a representative Republic and a representative Democracy, Is a fusion of two systems, not two political parties.

In the Fusion System, people Democratically vote for their representatives, who represent them in general elections to elect the President without the use of a political parties. In its science means the process of merger or mixing of two systems, this is the definition of a Fusion System, symbolizes specifically to a form of government in which elected officials represent the citizen body and exercise it power according to the rule of law under a constitution, including separation of powers with an elected head of state the President, referred to as a Constitutional republic in a representative democracy, the Fusion system is a mix of Republic System and a Democratic System, no political Parties involved the Roman Republic (República Romana) was the era of classical Roman civilization beginning with the overthrow of the Roman Kingdom, traditionally dated to 509 BC, and ending in 27 BC with the establishment of the Roman Empire.

It was during this period that Rome's control expanded from the city's immediate surroundings to domination over the entire Mediterranean world, and all Europe world, the entire West World, with this action, Roma' enlightened all known European world. For centuries after the fall of Rome (AD 476), the people of Europe had little voice in politics. Thus, there were no true political parties only factions that supported one noble family or another. Political parties developed as representative assemblies gained power. In England, this change began after it called the Popish Plot of 1678.

The leaders of the American Revolution did not like the idea of parties and political battles between parties. Upon his retirement from public life in 1796, George Washington warned Americans against factions. James Madison thought parties had required, although he did not entirely approve of them. Alexander Hamilton thought that party was always a wickedness to protected conflicting to. Thomas Jefferson declared in 1789, "If I could not go to heaven but with a party, I would not go there at all". Nevertheless, the men who held these views, co-founder the first two fatal American political parties.

Chicago Manual of Style: References: MLA (Modern Language Association) style: Flanders, Stephen. Political Parties. The New Book of Knowledge®. 2007.

Grolier Online. 25 July 2007 Flanders, Stephen. Political Parties. The New Book of Knowledge®. Grolier Online (accessed July 25, 2007). APA (American Psychological Association) style: Flanders, S. (2007). Political Parties. The New Book of Knowledge®. Retrieved July 25, 2007, from Grolier Online,

CHAPTER 2

FIRST U.S.A PRESIDENTIAL ELECTION

American Political Elections History

On this day in 1789, America is first presidential elections held with George Washington nominated to run for the candidature of the Presidency. Voters cast ballots to choose state electors; only white men who owned property could vote, as it did in the elections of 1789. As expected, George Washington gained the election and was sworn into office as President on April 30, 1789.

The United States still uses the old Electoral College system, established by the U.S. Constitution, which today gives all American citizens over the age of 18 the right to vote for the party of his preference to elect the President.

In Fusion system the same voters will in an election of the primaries chosen officials to be them in the presidential election to elect the President. The President and vice president are only elected by federal officials chosen by the voters to be them in the election presidential, instead of the direct popular vote.

WASHINGTON FIRST ELECTION

Like my system, there were no political parties in those days and stay that way until Alexander Hamilton and Thomas Jefferson start the division of the country in two Political Parties. Today political parties usually nominate their schedule of electors at their state conventions or by a vote of the party's central state committee, with party loyalists often picked for the job. In my Electoral System, a Fusion Electoral Tribunal will do nominations previews a request for contending for taking part in the election. In the present election each state voters can choose as many officers as it has, senators and representatives in Congress. To win the presidency, a candidate needs a majority of 270 electoral votes out of a possible 538.

On the first Monday after the second Wednesday in December of a presidential election year, each state's electors meet, usually in their state capitol, and simultaneously cast their ballots nationwide.

This is ceremonial: Because electors always vote with their party, presidential elections decided on Election Day. Although electors not constitutionally mandated to vote for the winner of the popular vote in their state, it demanded by tradition and required by law in 26 states and the District of Columbia (in some states, violating this rule is punishable by $1,000 fine).

Historically, over 99 percent of all electors have cast their ballots in line with the voters. On January 6, as a formality, the electoral votes counted before Congress and on January 20, the commander in chief sworn into office. Critics of the Electoral College argue that the winner takes all system makes it possible for a candidate to elected president even if he gets fewer popular votes than his opponent.

The New Fusion Electoral System

This happened in the elections of 1876, 1888 and 2000-2016. However, supporters contend that if the Electoral College were done away with, heavily populated states such as California and Texas might decide every election and issues important to voters in smaller states would be ignored, it is an unfairness.

NEW FUSION REPUBLIC-DEMOCRACY ELECTIONS WITHOUT PARTIES

American Political History

In our Electoral system, there are two political parties that are hostile each other for many reasons, including personal and political ambition. Like two political territorial armies, the parties fight one another in a party political dispute, to obtain the approval by many of the voters, with the Fusion System this is not the situation, without political parties, without names, without flags, only the peoples vote decisions.

Agree with President George Washington that political parties divided the nation, and the public opinion, which is extremism characterized with names, colors, flags, and emblems. The human nature already divided into two groups or fractions, no names, only those who agree, and those who do not agree. Those are the true political opinions, not parties. In a nonpartisan Fusion System, common people are who trough they representatives elect a President, they elect their representatives, whom, then elect the President.

Because most electors do not have the knowledge of how to elect the best candidate, to become the President, to effetely govern the nation, the majority, induced by the advertising media, because politician pay marketing, and advertised as a product, to divert the real purpose of electing a President.

No party man myself, Washington wrote to Thomas Jefferson, and the first wish of my heart was, if parties did exist, to reconcile them. As our first and only independent president, Washington's independence was a function not only of his original place in American history but also of political principles he developed over his lifetime.

To Washington, moderation was a source of strength. He viewed its essential judiciousness as a guiding principle of good government, rooted in ancient wisdom as well as information period of open-mindedness.

Much could be achieved by prudence, much by conciliation, and much by firmness. A stable, civil society depends on resisting fanatical extravagances. The Constitution did not mention political parties, and during the debate over the confirmation, James Madison and Alexander Hamilton acclaimed the Constitution's spirit of moderation in contrast to the bigoted spirit of those who are ever so much persuaded of their being in the right in any controversy.

Washington was nonpartisan but he was not neutral. He was decisive after consulting differing opinions. He seeks information from all quarters, and judges more independently than any man I ever knew, attested Vice President John Adams. Washington understood the danger of manipulators in a democracy. He was an enthusiastic advocate of moderation as a means of calming partisan passions and creating problem-solving alliances. Adams also believed that without the great political virtues of humility, patience, and moderation, every man in control becomes a voracious creature of prey.

And it was a source of personal pain for Washington to see his Cabinet decadent into overstated uncertainties and malicious defamations during his presidency. Most frustrating was to watch his motives twisted and attacked for partisan gain by dishonorable scribblers in the newspapers. Even in the days after winning independence from Britain, Washington warned of the dangerous interaction between immoderations. There is a natural and necessary progression from the extreme of anarchism to the extreme of tyranny, he wrote in his Circular Letter to the States, and arbitrary power is most easily established on the ruins of liberty abused to licentiousness. As liberty in France turned to anarchy and then tyranny during his administration, it confirmed his deepest instincts.

As a young man, Washington devoured the popular early eighteenth-century essays of Joseph Addison in the Spectator of London.

Addison was the author of his favorite play, Cato, and while reflecting on the sources of England's bloody civil war in the 1640s, he had written an influential essay on the Malice of Parties. It's worth quoting at length: There cannot a greater judgment befall a country than a dreadful spirit of division as rends a government into two distinct people, and makes them greater strangers, and more averse to one another, than if they were actually two different nations.

The effects of such a division are pernicious to the last degree, not only with regard to those advantages which they give the common enemy, but to those private evils which they produce in the heart of almost every particular person. This influence is very fatal both to men's morals and their understandings; it sinks the virtue of a nation, and not only so, but destroys even common sense. A furious party spirit, when it rages in its full violence, exerts itself in civil war and bloodshed; and when it is under its greatest restraints, naturally breaks out in falsehood, detraction, calumny, and a partial administration of justice. In a word, it fills a nation with spleen and rancor, and extinguishes all the seeds of good nature, compassion, and humanity.

Addison was not the only wise voice warning the revolutionary generation against t danger of hyper-partisanship. The English poet Alexander Pope declared that party spirit is but the madness of many for the gain of a few.

The early 18th-century British opposition leader Henry St. John, 1st Viscount of Bolingbroke, described parties as a political evil. Informed by experience in both journalism and politics, Bolingbroke wrote, that a man who has not seen the inside of parties.

I believe that the common people are more skilled to elect public servants, and then the public servants elected by the people, Mayors, Councilors, Representatives, Senators, Governors and other public servants elected by the peoples, will elect the President, they are more capable to elect the president, with-out the intervention of wicked political party's propaganda.

Participant's applicant for a public position will chose by a Supreme Electoral Tribunal, which is similar as the Supreme Court of Justice, this court, and the tribunal, both are composed by 13 citizens with impeccable past and, with a University Education, and clean criminals' records.

Candidates must fill an application to the Electoral Tribunal. The choice application, of each candidate would be asking to declare their political prospectus and approved by the Electoral Supreme Electoral Tribunal.

Present biblically the biography to creates confidence to voters and make a list of ensures and promises, to inform the voters. Candidates will become banned by the Electoral Supreme Court law, not to accuses mutually to prevent insults and personal scandals, and coarse language. The voter can choose freely, without intimidations of any kind, their representatives, the public servants, learn only what the candidate promises are and their principles, and their vote is sacred and secret: In the primary election, voters elect their representatives, e.g.: Senators, Representatives, Governors, Mayors, and other public servants elected by the voters, whom then will elect the President.

The rest of the electoral process is a continuation of the electoral regular process existent, with no political parties involved, with some modifications. The Election Process is a fundamental part of the American system of government, which founded on the principle that the power Elections provide how the American people delegate this power to the elected Representatives, whom will elect the President. By voting for government officials, the public makes choices about the policies, programs, and future directions of government action. At the same time, elections make government officials accountable to their constituents. Elected officials must conduct themselves in a responsible manner and consider popular interests and the responsibilities for those why they elected. Otherwise they will be on the way to be fire-weed out of office impeached.

This system depends primarily on the voters. The electoral process can only work if people take participation on it.

Elections supply how the American people delegate this power to the elected Representatives, who will elect the President. By voting for government officials, the public makes choices about the policies, programs, and future directions of government action. At the same time, elections make government officials

Reference: John Avlon is the Editor-in-Chief of The Daily Beast and the author of Washington's Farewell: The Founding Father's Warning to Future Generations, out today from Simon and Schuster. accountable to their constituents.

Elected officials must conduct themselves in a responsible manner and consider popular interests and the responsibilities for those why they elected. Otherwise they will be on the way to be fire-weed out of office. This system depends primarily on the voters. The electoral process can only work if people take participation on it.

NEW FUSION RESPONSIBILITIES AND THE ELECTIONS

American Political History

In the United States, elections held at regular intervals. National presidential elections take place every four years. Congressional elections occur every two years, together with the State and local elections at the same time. In addition to elections for office, many state and local ballots include referendums and initiatives, which allow the people to directly determine a government policy.

- State and local governments handle organizing elections. State, county, and municipal election boards administer elections. These boards set up and staff polling places and verify the eligibility of individuals who come to vote. State laws specify the qualifications of candidates and how elections are to administer, including registration procedures, the location of polling places, and even the kind of ballots used. Political affiliations not required in open New Fusion primary.

(3) Federal Senators aspirants per States, (3) Governors, (3) Mayor, etc. the reason of "3" is because if a tie occurs one will be the decision vote, if one is elected the rest will become advisors, there are not boundaries for congressional and state. The primaries elections that will exist are allow by the Supreme Electoral Tribunal only.

POLITICAL PARTIES AND ITS PROBLEMS

American Political History

Political parties are not the most representative of the peoples, inclusive organizations in the United States it is a division of the peoples, it must be eliminated because are unconstitutional. They had made up of citizens who may differ in race, religion, age, and economic and social background, but who share certain perspectives on public issues and leaders. In the Fusion Electoral System, you do not have to have a political party, flag, color or name, political parties are a waste of people's time and resources. Parties are the enemy of the American peoples, an engine that divided the nation's elections in two or more disunion of voter's fashions. The party recruit candidates for office, organize primary elections so that the voter's members can select their candidates for the primary election, and support their candidates who represent them in the general election. In the Fusion System where the Electoral Fusion Tribunal and the voters approve the candidates that had educated by schools, Churches, Synagogues, and others non-political institutions.

Originally our nation Founders had opposed to political parties, believing them to be fractions' intent on manipulating the independent will of the voters. But by the early 19th century political parties had become the most polarized political organizations in the United States, converting a responsible citizen opinion in a political war with no sense. They made certain that their members got to the polls. They also organized members of Congress into stable voting blocs based on voter's idea, no partidos.

These coalitions united the legislators and helped the president create an alliance between the executive and legislative branches. Since the mid-1850s, when the Republican and Democrat Party was formed, the two major parties in the United States have been in confrontation in a political war since then. The Democratic Party traces its beginnings to the Jeffersonian Democratic-Republicans. In the 19th century, political parties were powerful enough that they could often motivate voting turnouts of over 80 percent, that is not a good reason to educates the voters their responsibilities to vote, what really increases the turnout of voters is through education in our Schools, Synagogues and Churches across the nation, as a result, appear so similar that many voters lose interest, because the lack of political education of citizen obligations and responsibilities.

ROLE OF THE MEDIA IN THE ELECTORAL PROCESS

American Political History

The media, especially television, have played a role in the increasing cost of campaigns because candidates spend a large amount of money on advertising themselves like a consumer's product. It is like the form of advertising a product, as a car, a house, pair of shoes, Etc., this scums trash filth is unnecessary in the Fusion System, where the peoples vote by analyzing candidates Biographies and their aptitudes and political promises, then choosing the best candidate, to represent then in an electing a President in the General Elections. In a political campaign, individual candidates spend more money on media advertising than ever before.

In 1860 the Republicans spent only $100,000 on Abraham Lincoln's presidential campaign and on those of all Republican House and Senate candidates. In 1988 Republican candidate George Bush spent $70 million, just on the presidential race. During the 1998 elections, a 60-second spot on prime-time television cost as much as $100,000 every time it ran. As a result, campaigns have become more expensive, forcing candidates to concentrate more in fund raising and less on presenting issues to voters, which in the Fusion Electoral System is not necessary to be that way. The media, have also played a role in the diminishing importance of political elections, and permit candidates to present themselves and his ideas and aptitudes, without any aid from their political candidates, only through the Fusion Electoral Tribunal, using their own money or companies sponsors with some limitations.

Candidates running for office use the media to gain popularity, like a product. By appealing to the public through the media, candidates erode the authority of political institution. In the old National party conventions, which officially nominate candidates for president and vice president, used to be exciting meetings where the party leaders decided who would be nominate, in the Fusion System nominations are performed only by the Fusion Electoral Tribunal.

Today presidential elections have become independent political entrepreneurs who go to the voters rather than to party leaders. Although candidates still rely on parties for campaign money to a certain extent, the power of the media has focused attention much more on individual candidates rather than on the parties they stand for. This has made personal campaign organizations more efficient moneymaking tools than the national parties, in the Fusion Electoral System will be no nominations by parties. With this practice the sacred obligations of electors are prostituted by the candidates' campaigns and publicities, also in the Fusion Electoral System there is not be Presidential and Vice President or any other candidate nominations, they are approved only by the Fusion Supreme Electoral Tribunal, the only authorized nominator for the futures elections candidates though an application makes a formal petition of the right to participates in the election. Reference: Flanders, Stephen. "Political Parties." The New Book of Knowledge®. Grolier Online APA (American Psychological Association) Flanders, S. (2007). Political Parties. The New Book of Knowledge®. Retrieved July 25, 2007.

CURRENT TRENDS AND ISSUES

American Political History

Democrats and Republicans face the vanishing of the political show ground in the future because they will be substituted by the New Fusion Electoral System. The traditional of campaigning will disregarded by the New Fusion Electoral System. Politicians spend less time on ordinary campaigning, such as visiting neighborhoods' conscious them self as respectable folks. Instead they are insisting the voter by several elements to enhance their chances of election; some of these elements were unheard of as recently. These include short television advertisements with no defamations and offenses that infuriates the political adversary unreasonably, polls, direct mail, and political consultants who offer advice on how to shape a campaign, and insults to the adversary will prohibited by the Electoral Fusion System.

Furthermore, party leaders will not exist because there will be no parties in the Fusion system, parties will not exist or permitted, neither negative advertising about what an opponent has done wrong, rather than a presentation of what a candidate will do correct for the peoples. Meanwhile proposed policies reduced to slogans, as the shortness of television spots has limited viewers' abilities to make choices based on a positive information's. Because the voters will see a little difference among candidates, voters often fail to cast a ballot for lack of elector's education, and election turnouts have declined because the same, a sense of voting knowledge, what is not that important in the new Fusion Electoral System, voters get the information they need trough the Supreme Electoral Tribunal, public, private and Public Schools, Synagogues and Churches, of any denominations.

Politicians depend on huge campaign contributions from corporations and powerful special interest groups. One answer to this problem is to rely entirely on public financing only. Another is to limit the amount that any candidate can spend on a campaign, rather than control the amount that any individual or group can give. Modern campaigns are expensive propositions, and Americans are increasingly dissatisfied with the way they are financed. Politicians depend on huge campaign contributions from corporations and powerful special interest groups. One answer to this problem is to rely entirely on public financing. Another is to limit the amount that any candidate can spend on a campaign, rather than control the amount that any individual or group can give.

Yet in 1976 in the case of Buckley v. Valeo, the Supreme Court ruled that Congress cannot limit campaign spending because spending money on politics is a form of constitutionally protected free speech. Today there are no limits on how much money a candidate or party can spend, and no limits on how much a wealthy candidate can donate to his or her own campaign. All this could be changed if we take control of these political practices with the New Fusion Political Electoral System and the Supreme Electoral Tribunal. There are not privates' contributions permitted, since candidates advertising are trough the New Electoral Fusion System, however, limits on some kinds of contributions will be permitted if is done through the New Electoral Fusion Tribunal, to finance candidates' promotions, by this restricting corruptions will not happen. For instance, $2,000 is the most any individual can donate to any candidate in a single election.

A limit of $250,000 placed on the amount that can company give to the New Electoral Tribunal, in the name of selected candidates, which then be redistributes the funds in various media promotion in benefit of this candidate. The top amount that can give to the New Electoral Tribunal in in benefit to all candidates in a federal election is $250,000 per contributors by corporations. funds to prevent corruptions.

THE NEW FUSION ELECTORAL SYSTEM

American Political History

Through the process of many elections, I become more, convinced that our political system must be changing. This is a violent, outrage, shameful act of political fighting, the way elections and politician are more, and more, conflictive, the nation is divided in two or more opponent's political parties, no counting the Independent Parties that is a possible stabilization of the election, in some cases, but never had won a presidential election.

Ezra Taft Benson comments: "If you vote for the slighter of two evils parties, you are still voting for the evil… Always vote for the best possible candidate, whether they have a chance of winning or not. Then, even if the worst possible candidate wins, God will bless our nation more because more people were willing to stand up for what is right and not for a party."

Up to this point we, the people, are been asking by the law, to pay millions of our hard-earned money, for our tax contribution, and using it to support elections that is a worsening of the nation treasure, for this nonsense hostilities, between two political parties that do not benefited in anyway our decision of elect the President, only to the media, reporters, and politician that making the selection of our government servants officials, as a war game, when the only parties that should exist, are those that are in favor, and those that are opposed, no name, no flag, no color, simple the voters through their representatives, to elect the President.

Meanwhile, George Washington remained nonpartisan, throughout the two terms of his presidency. President George Washington warned, them, of the danger of the political parties. However, Alexander Hamilton formed the first political party during Washington's term, called the Federalists, today the Democrat Party. Thomas Jefferson have no choice to take another party name, as the Anti-federalist party.

PARTY DESIGNATION AND CLASIFICATION

American Political History

Democrat-Republic is the perfect system, that I consider the best: but everything needs improvements with the time. The political system of plural political parties does more harm than benefit to the peoples of the Democratic-Republic Electoral system, The Fusion System will be the new system of all nations throughout the world. It will benefit, because the New Fusion System gives us, all the rights of freedom, and protections, as freedom of speech, human rights and all the other rights, through the constitution, redacted more than two centuries ago.

The harm of the present system is by the confrontation between political parties, supposedly, designed to become a competition between two ideas, in favor to benefit the citizen of the nation, that was a noble idea, but with the time, it became an aggressive political war, between two or more political parties, not for the benefit of the people, instead for political gain, personally gain or for a party gain, against other than rivals parties, as we can experiences in the present time, with the fight of Democrats and Republican for a borders-wall between Mexico and United States, in order to stop all kind of aliens, good and bad for our country.

The plural politics parties divide the citizens of a nation System, like a civil political war where no body get physical hurt, but only the public's pockets. War game, that benefits only the medias, the networks and some other profiteers that love the controversy between participator of a political administration position, of the existing parties, Republican, Democrats, and Independent.

The idea of dividing psychologically the people's political opinions, do more harm than benefits to the political system, the solution is: Beginning with the presidency, the President, should be elected by the elected officials, public functionaries or officials elected by the people's votes, at the level of Governor, Mayors, Senators, Representatives and others public servants will be elected by voters in a primary election.

Now those elected functionaries, elected by the people-voters to represent them in the Presidential elections, will elect the President of the United States, and as results we would not need political parties to elect them. The political system, need to work as teams, not as adversaries, political parties make war between them, instead of political parties, we definitely have supporter and opponents, let them divide by them self without having a political ideology, name, color or flag.

With the present system, politicians from both or more parties attack each another in the both chambers of legislation, interrupting the bills and laws for the benefit of the people, in an extreme of the time it is not for people's benefits; instead, for political gain, by blocking the adversary party in power. All this will end with a system with no political parties just The New Electoral Fusion System. If the legislator haves no need to debates for political and personal gain, the system will function smooth and efficient for the people's strong existence. The Democracy Republic system or "The New Electoral Fusion System," it will work better as a government team, not as political party's division-ism, and adversaries, concentrating in creating the best legislation for the benefit of the nation only, not for political or personal gain, as how they present political parties system does. The peoples will divide them self in those that agree and those that does not agree. Why we need political parties? We do not.

NEW FUSION THE BEST ELECTORAL SYSTEM

American Political History

I persuasively try to express my ideas to the world, in benefit of the humankind, an uncomplicated idea that may cause substantial changes in the political system of today's world. Everything commence with a simple idea, like the day when a person sought that implanting Democracy and Republic System, to organize, respect others opinions, given freedom and to control the behaves of the human in the political aspect, of that era, was necessary a change for better government, and public benefit, with the same principles I am launching my idea to the world, not for my own benefit; but for all peoples of the world benefits.

Do you think that the political parties' benefits or damage the efficiency of the Democracy-Republic system? They do more harm than benefit, because one, two or more political systems is a division among people's societies, a division of the nation's electors in a nonsense political battle that should not benefit the citizen at entirely. The only one who benefits from this war is principally, the mass media and others profiteers that love this political controversy for their own benefit, the fact is a business is to them, they inflaming and exaggerate the events that occurred to get profit, inducing to a political war, to inflames the animus of the contenders, and confusing the voters. The media is a necessary tool to inform rather than encouraged war between political factions.

The idea came to me after I analyzing the why? well it is clean reality, the whole idea behind this political war, is greed, greed for fame, greed for money, greed for power, not for the people's benefits, but in the majority of this cases, is greed.

We must stop this political nonsense by simply eliminating all political parties, for the good of Democracy-Republic, call it The Fusion Electoral System, and the people, to do reforms when those party foundations will not exist.

Ending the political parties' systems, the Government will regulate the candidates to an official's position, selected by a Supreme Electoral Tribunal, composed by 13 honest citizens, with some University education or similar education level and scrutinized by the Supreme Court of Justice. Each contender should fill an application form, with all the information required, in order to be investigated by the Supreme Electoral Tribunal, and the Supreme Court of Justice, no one with obscure pass, will accepted as a candidate. I n the political race, nobody with obscure or criminal past, is allowed to participate in the contend, only the honest and with good principles, willing to do the best for the people, and the nation, will participate in the selection for a public position, to be a politician is not a business, is a patriotic obligation for a public job.

There are thousands of positions, from a simple City Mayor, up Representatives and Senators of the nation, it is not complicated and easy to select the candidates in the primary election, they will be the peoples voice to elect the president. Each City or States will be responsible and involved in this selection, the rest is letting the peoples know the qualities of each candidate by publishing a complete biography of each of the contenders, and each of their promises to be accomplishing when in service if he or she is elected. With this idea, there not needed for political parties because the Presidency will be elected by elected officials Representatives of the people vote.

Political parties divided the nation, and public opinion, is a fanatical political institution, with names, color, flag, and emblems. When human by nature, divided into two groups with no names no names, only those who agree, and those who do not agree. In a non-political party democratic system common people are not able to elect a president, because most of them do not have the right information of the how to selected the best candidate to govern the nation. Candidates often leads by the advertising media influence of the politicians that pays for the advertising, they advertised them self as angels, diverting the real purpose to get elect, not all but a large portion seeking political or benefices gains.

The common people are more capacitated to choose public servants in a primary election. In this procedure, the public servants elected by the people as their voices and representative vote, to elect the wright President, Councilors, Governors, Representatives, Senators and other public servants elected by peoples votes, they representing the people to elect the President, without the intervention of political parties, as legitimate representation of people's votes.

Politicians applying for a public position will be done by the Supreme Electoral Tribunal, which will be screening the politic with impeccable past, with a college or university education.

In the election, each candidate would allow to declare their political history, as his biography, certified by the Electoral Fusion Tribunal, to build trust to the voters and show it intentions.

In this new Electoral Fusion System, candidates must not accuse mutually, to prevent insults and personal scandals. The voter can choose freely, without cohesion of any kind, their representatives, the public servants learn only what the candidate and their conscience, and their vote is sacred and secret. Candidates are prohibiting accuses mutually, each another to prevent insults and personal scandals as a result will be throughout the race.

FUSION THE NEW ELECTORALSYSTEM

American Political History

Politic offed many avenues of approach in electing a candidate by political parties, which is not the correct way of conducting the choice of our nation administrators. Party activity is the most obvious of this offer but is not the best one. The citizen of United States of North America, who is curios in public affairs, will find many avenues, lager, and variety of voluntary organizations, dedicated in the influence of government conduct which wind out in political disorder, this have contributed at it.

These associations are limit to a single issue, the single field of activity, associations: The Group of Women Voters, Civil service Reform Liege, The American Association for Labor Legislation, The National Voters' Group, and many more others organizations that in a way or other affect the government functions which is a nonconformity of the simple option of electing a correct government, Samples: Women Voters Group discuses every political issue, national, state and local, the interest to its membership, when is concern to women protection and rights, and that is good for their rights and regain, they are the reason of our existence for ended they deserve our respect and consideration.

The National Voters' Liege turn a search on Congress every month, including to managing to illumine many other branches of the federal Government, which is good as long not interferes with the Government process. Adding to those poorly political associations a large number of organizations concerning Labor Unions, Church Federations, Commercial and Professional Organizations, and they like to accustomed to take action whenever their interests are affected by the government, is in some cases revolutionaries' ideas subversion and could be penalized by the law, to prevent chaos and revolutionaries' subversions, that could wind out with a civil war of the nation, to prevent this irregularity we must eliminate all political parties, is where they start.

Adding to those poorly political associations a large number of organizations concerning Labor Unions, Church Federations, Commercial and Professional Organizations, and they like to accustomed to take action whenever their interests are affected by the government, is in some cases revolutionaries' ideas subversion and could be penalized by the law, to prevent chaos and revolutionaries' alterations, that could wind out with a civil war of the nation, to prevent this irregularity we must eliminate all politicos parties.

The value of the contributions of those organizations is consider a benefit, as long it is with the noble purpose of protection of their Civil Rights. This organization offer opportunities for constructive art of conducting state affairs, when no one interested in politics, can afford to ignore. Anyhow, they are supplements, rather than substitutes of Political System, in any way. At least it is clear that the presently they perform certain important political functions not undertaken even such of those other organizations, as are primary political in an unscientific and as symbols only.

The most characteristic qualities to shows these groups as a political gathering, if its leaders became candidates for public office though the regular Fusion Electoral System. In a legal definition of political group's scatters throughout the status books of our states, they can point out a nominee, but not a nomination regarded, as the fundamental test of a political gathering. It has the merit applied for administrative purpose. Voluntary political organizations nonpartisan engages in variety of activities, but they do not take part in the political ground. They may discuss the activity and record of group's candidates and can recommends the public to make choices among them as is the custom of Voters' Association, but not to appoint them.

Organizations or nominate them, political groups allowed to select a candidate of their choice, but not to nominate them, only the Electoral Fusion Tribunal, will be apt to approve its nomination as candidate, prior an application has turn out to be made.

The making of a nomination is the distinguishing activity of the Fusion Electoral Tribunal System, a public service of the importance and significance. Is foregone conclusion that political parties often do this work poorly. At the times the nominees some are accuses of ineffectiveness and low character, in other situation is accused of dishonesty and bad moral character, the war among nominees is detriment to the Electoral System that we have seen in the past primaries elections, the candidates insult and an accuse one to the other candidate, it is a scandalous, regretful, and criminal, it will stop with my New Electoral System and The New Fusion Electoral Tribunal, all this irregularity will be terminated.

However, the nomination conducted at the pointed intermissions if the work of Government is to go on. And among our many organizations devoted themselves to political ends alone always stand ready to assume this burden. To express assemblies' principles and policies may seem a much higher duty than nominating candidates. In this connection, however, it is worth remembering that to a large bare principal and polices makes, but a weak application.

Only when they are documentary by strong and understanding personalities, fighting in the public ground for power to realize them, that it is a nonsense political fighting. Do they provoke a full popular response? Unquestionably, it is much easier, In United States with large numbers of legible electable officers with frequent elections, the volume of work involved in only selecting candidates is immense, nevertheless in the New Electoral Fusion System a Supreme Electoral Tribunal will nominate the candidates in its place. In charged to verify, if the candidate has not an obscure hidden criminal past, there is why a non-patrician system will certify that the candidates will not enter in a political fight.

No doubt this task is imperfect; it should be the function of the Supreme Electoral Tribunal system. They may even discuss the records of candidates and advise the public to make selections among them as is the custom of various Voters' leagues, without the use of any party, but it is different from decide on them in the first instance, and thus accepting a support for them. If any such organizations decide to transcend its ordinary limitations and actually names candidates, but not necessarily they cannot appoint a candidate without go through the Supreme Electoral Tribunal, to screen them, it is moreover, a public service of the greatest importance and significance, should be elected by the people's voters only, without any political dividers. To implant groups' principles policies may be a monumental duty than the nomination of candidates, therefore we should not have any political divider, as parties, they destroyed and damage the system.

It is worth remembering that a large part of electoral, plain principles and polices, make but a wobbly appeal. When they dramatized by forceful and merciful personalities, fighting in the public arena for power, to realize them, is a shame and a disgrace, to do they draw out something hidden a full popular response. It is much simple merely to design political ideas and loudly call upon good men for their support, instead of a political party, then undertaking the further steps of securing representative and responsible candidates, without the need of a political party, and baking them in a campaign for office position, only by the decision of the Supreme Electoral Tribunal, without the intervention of political parties.

It is the reasons why so many individual voluntary political organizations, without the parties' content, with the first of this activity is elect a candidate without a political party. This may be, the political necessity and one of the glitterati of the added responsibilities which only voters must concede.

Therefore, every moral connection will affirm, it is the first resolution, to pursue every just method to put the men who hold their thoughts into such disorder as may allow them to carries their mutual plans into the execution of it, with all the power and authority of the state. As this power committed to certain opinion, it is their duty to contend for this situation. It involves the idea that a man who hold certain political principles with sincere conviction and sense of their importance, will take the future step of selecting and supporting men who is verified and screened by The Supreme Electoral Tribunal, then placed in office e by the peoples vote, without the necessity of a political party, will realize these principles. Them have the need to this extent a higher steam of conviction than those political associations which do not make nominations, but support candidates only are tolerable.

PARTIES NOMINATION

NATURE OF THE PARTIES

American Political History

At times they accused of nominating men of known incompetence and bad reputation; at other times it is charitable to assume that they have been betrayed in the charisma of their own candidates. Nevertheless, The Fusion Supreme Electoral Tribunal System must make the nominations only, at the appointed intervals if the work of government is to go on. To formulate groups principles and groups policies may design and give the idea of considerable and advanced responsibility than nominating candidates, if authorized by the Supreme Electoral Tribunal. In the attitude of this assembly, however, it is worth remembering that to a large part of any electorate naked principles and policies make but then again, a weak appeal.

Only when the dramatized by forceful and sympathetic personalities, fighting in the public ground for control to realize them, then they produce a full popular reply. Certainly, it is much easier merely to formulate political ideals and loudly call upon all good men for their support, than to assume the further steps of securing representative and responsible candidates and backing them up in their campaign for office. That is one of the reasons why so many individuals and voluntary political organizations other than content themselves with the first of these actions.

However, this may be, the political necessity and social utility of the other functions which political groups alone assume of must conceded honestly. Usually this statement criticized as idealization rather than explanation, as an attempted glorification by the brilliant opponent pamphleteer of his own idea in contrast with the irresponsible cabal of ruler's friends, whom George III had gathered about him, and as it viewpoints the announcement does. Reference:1 Thought on the Cause of the Pretend Discontents, References in the published 1770, Works, vol. I, p.530 by Burke. y from Simon and Schuster.

THE EVILS OF POLITICAL PARTIES

American Political History

Definitely, seem to apply weight upon ideologies and the promotion of the national interest to the exclusion of other and perhaps lower ends for which parties have striven not, only in Burke's time, but later. Though, the words quoted above should be read in connection with the following sentences from the same paragraph, for my part, I find it impossible to conceive that anyone believes in his own politics, or thinks them to be of any weight, who refuses to adopt the means of having them reduced into practice. It is the business of the speculative philosopher to mark the proper ends of government. It is the business of the politician, who is the philosopher in action, to find out proper means toward those ends, and to employ them with effect.

Therefore, every honorable connection will avow it is their first purpose, to pursue every just method to put the men who hold their opinions into such a condition as may enable them to carry their common plans into execution, with all the power and authority of the state through a well-regulated Supreme Electoral Fusion Tribunal, only. As this power attached to certain situations, it is their duty to contend for these situations. Included the making of nominations through the Supreme Electoral Fusion Tribunal.

The other sentences make it clear that Philosopher Burke's conception of political groups, however ideal in other respects, included the very practical function of bringing men forward for office, through the New Electoral Fusion System. Finally, it involves the idea that a body of men who hold to certain political principles with sincere conviction and a sense of their importance will, by that very fact, take the further step of selecting and supporting men who, when placed in office, will attempt to realize these principles, through my New Electoral Fusion System. In other words, a candidate requires to this extent a higher energy of conviction than those political associations which do not make nominations.

NATURE OF POLITICAL PARTIES

American Political History Political parties' principles, on the other hand, place forward as having complete qualities; party platforms tend to become longer each year as the result of efforts to cover, or appear to cover, every governmental question of importance. Although many article platforms' may be evasions, misrepresentations, or deep commonplaces, it is the political parties' theory of itself that the principles it holds furnish all that is needed for higher guidance, while the policies it proposes supply a detailed program quite sufficient for the general conduct of government in case the political party is given control. And of course, in each case these principles and policies encouraged, if not as ideal, at least as distinctly and demonstrably superior to those of other groups with which it is contending for supremacy. Political parties are a vocation of persuasion, it will see as, include destruction of peoples' confidence.

Definition of both principles and policies. Logically it is quite possible to make a distinction between the two, although application of the distinction is not always easy. The ideologies of a political parties have been defined as the durable principles held in common by its members as to what the state should be and do is like an indoctrination of the votes mind. The policy of a political parties, on the other hand, understands all that the group does in order to establish its principles; it includes, therefore, the parties' conduct, principles are disclosed in the end which a sought; poring the magical imposes for the attainment of the end, concluding in a political war.

Political parties' principles have a greater permanence relation of and a higher validity than groups policies. The latter principles to must square with the former, but in practical politics considerable stretching is sometimes necessary to make them seem to do so. In such cases, however, it is always possible to keep convincingly that the changes made are matters of policy only; or that they justified. The Electoral Fusion Tribunal will supervise it. Illustrations of the distinction between party principles and party policies in American political history will be found in chaps, iv and v. and now through this version of the book as The New Fusion Electoral System.

References: Anson D. Morse, What Is a Party? Political Science Quarterly, vol. xi, p. 68 (March 1896).

Michael Anguelo

POLITICAL PRINCIPLES THE CANING

ELECTORAL CORRUPTIONS PROBLEMS

American Political History

Adjustment of principles and policies to contemporary needs looking for issues by great emergencies or exceptional conjunctures of affairs never likely to repeat; or that, indeed, they are necessary to the life of the state itself. To finalize the closing argument, it may add that the preservation of the state manages to pay for the only possible means of returning to the original principles of the political parties after normal conditions have re-established. As matter of fact, therefore, groups policies shift rapidly with the current demands of politics, and political meetings principles themselves are subject to new interpretations over longer periods of time. To survive, a political party must adjust itself to new circumstances, and it is the New Fusion Electoral System.

A political party may have plentifully with principles and policies which are too far in advance of prevailing ideas, and for that reason it may suffer calamity. Radical minor groups usually ascribe their small following to this condition. Many of the supporters of the Progressive political party believe that its abandonment after 1912 was in part due to the same reason.

Sceptics are accustomed to say that a political party may survive without values, merely by force of its organization, its traditional following, and the control of support. The most real of practical politicians are, however, fully aware of the danger of such a situation.

Usually they make vigorous efforts to disentangle themselves by looking for problems, as the popular phrase has it. For a political party which appears to be without principles naturally falls a prey to the suspicion that it is nothing but a selfish combination of office hunter's incapable or unwilling to solve the problems of the day. And in our nationwide politics at least a political group which finds itself in this situation is in danger of a serious decline of power or even of a fragmentation.

SITUATIONS OF PARTY LIFE

American Political History

They cannot afford to be unconvinced with the wider electorates of the present day. Popular education, the press, freedom of thought and speech, have all contributed to drive dishonesty in disloyal and make it more problematic. overall, there is reason to believe that the danger from this basis is many extents under the present gathering system than during the eighteenth and preceding centuries. Certainly, it is much less in advanced countries with a well-developed party life than in retrograde Totalitarianism countries where such a development is impossible. There was a sound historical foundation for the eighteenth-century view that parties were violent and destructive in their worse phases, oppressive and dishonest at greatest. Under the Republic and Democratic conditions of the nineteenth century parties must sloughing head off all the life threatening and many of the slight forms of dishonesty existing during earlier and present regimes. They have abandoned violence for peaceful processes, they have substituted constructive for destructive activities, they pursue conciliation instead of oppression. The same century that witnessed an enormous increase in their size, organization, and material power witnessed a striking if not equally great advancement of their determinations methods, and moral standing, nevertheless party system is an invitation of the natural instinct of the man in its all of viciousness, verbal or in some cases physical, prompted by the press, the media, and political ambitions. Today United States seems more like United States of America by the action of the political fight because the two party's existence. Nancy Pelosi as Democrat obstacles the President Trump in placing the wall, to stop unwelcome element intruding illegally our borders, but that does not mean he is not doing what the country need to secure our borders, and make our Nation the best place to live in the World, if they want to come, welcome but legally like I did, to contributing not to destroy.

**PRESIDENT TRUMP'S BORDER WALL
YOU ARE WELCOME, BUT DO NOT ILLIGALY**

CHAPTER 3

NATURE OF POLITICAL PARTY

America Political History

As principles are considered to hold good over extended periods of time, political gatherings inspired by them are presumed to be able to count upon a somewhat prolonged tenancy of life with many transmutations and vicissitudes the present Democratic political party can be traced back to the beginnings of our national life as the Republican party. Both shameful American parties can claim a continuous existence of more than two and a half centuries of fights between them in an eternal war.

It said that a man's body every atom will replaced by others in the course of seven years and when there are many copies, the original becomes diffused and that is how we get old. A process of similar character goes on more slowly perhaps in the case of political parties, with so countless copies they get old fashioned, which persist through extended periods of time.

However, the time element affords neither a definite nor a convincing examination of political parties' attractiveness. Certainly, none would deny this attractiveness to the late progressive movement, for example, simply because of its rapid fragmentation after the campaign of 1912. In that campaign it played a role of major importance and fully equipped as far as candidates, platform, and organization were concerned, to perform all the functions of a political party.

It is true, that it failed in its effort to gain control of the government, but success in this is not a necessary requirement for the grouping stand-up. The Prohibitionists offer a case in an argument. In fact, a political party may remain in a minority through the greater part or even the whole of a long existence and yet perform every role characteristic of such group.

Although the immediate aim of a political party is to gain control of the Government by placing enough of its own leaders in office, humiliation in this aim does not preclude the possibility of exercising a greater and beneficent impact. From the social point of view, therefore, the immediate success or lack of it on the part of individual group may be a matter of small reputation.

What is important is that such organizations shall contribute helpfully in the main to the development of national life and good well been of the nation. Taking this wide-ranging opinion of understanding, it is evident that political parties which have but a small following, or which endure for a short time only, may nevertheless be of great interest and significance.

THE NATION DIVITIONS PROBLEMS
American Political History

Periods of the beginning origin of the word party, Latin, parities or in English language meaning social gathering and engaging in a usually drunkenness celebration, calls the attention to the fact that ordinarily the people of a country are divided, it is not a party, instead is a partition, a faction, a division of the peoples, each competing for the control of the Government. At the outbreak of the World War, for example, party uncared for the disaster will follow by not making a peace armistice and an alliance or at least a negotiation in nearly of the aggressive countries in order to prevent a bloodshed.

In our own country during the so-called Era of Good Feeling (181632) there was only a unity of voters in one party in the arena, which truly was not a party, it was a fusion of the two systems of a Democracy and the Republic system. The great mass of the people of the country were in general agreement, at that time, as to the extensive wide-ranging principles and policies about which the elections of Government was to be conducted.

Remained to one who looks below the surface; however, the Era of Good Feeling was a period of personal politics parties following interesting advantaged competitor fought insensitive persuasively for office advantage.

But even currently the prevalence of personal interest was not absolute. While each of these political groups professed loyalty to the principles of Jeffersonian Republicanism, it also sought to make distinctions concerning these philosophies which it observed as of a significant importance retro, except, during such unusual periods, however, a political party benefits as the origin of the word itself suggests, a part (portion) of the people, arrayed against other similar parts (portion), each contending and competing for the control of the Government administration in an ambition way.

Henceforth it has argued that the principles and policies of each political parties, no matter how strongly they supported as an ideal guide for the whole conduct of the state, must in fact be only partial views powerfully streaked with the interests of the party or parties. Therefore, the true end of a party, according to one writer, the end of which it is itself conscious is, in ordinary times, to encourage not the general interest, but the interest of a class, a party or some one of the many sectors citizen is to be found in every state in which there is political life, an interest which is always something other and generally, though not always, somewhat less than the national and self-interest.

Reference: 1 J. A. Woodburn, Political Parties and Party Problems, p. 31.10.

HOW THIS MESS STARTER

NATURE OF PARTIES

American Political History

It is impossible to deny the general foolishness of this Political party opinion. In some cases, a political party, honestly, confesses that personalizes of class it is made up principally of memberships of a certain class and that it is the working primarily in the benefits of that philosophy. This is true, for instance, of the Socialist party (Communist Bolshevik Party) which, wherever it organized, claims to be the exclusive political party for the benefited of the workers, which proven to be false, instead it benefits a group of the Klan' leaders. It is substantially true also in an amount of other political parties in European countries where division is carried to an extreme, unknown until today, in the United States, up to now in this political time of the 21 Century, where party is really a division of the people.

On the other hand, our two principal political parties, which pursue to make converts in all ranks of society, naturally deny this accusation. Nevertheless, it often urged against them by their fundamental opponents, the free enterprise, I prefer Capitalism without Political parties, the New Fusion style than any other ideologies.

There seems to be no reason, however, to doubt the sincerity of a political party simply because it proclaims that its ideologies and policies designed in the benefits for a few, rather than with freedom, with support and self-determination for all. Each class in a society wears its own eyeglasses and see its usually unconscious of that fact in the explanations it makes of political situations and the necessities of it. Whether or not they admit the responsibility that they are political organization predominated by class interested in large groups and small groups realizes to act alike preserve that the programs they develop characterize benefits of the real attention of the government or the people. In opportunity if you go for. Reference: Cf. A. D. Morse, op. cit., p. 80. II, The New Fusion Electoral System.

ELECTORAL PROBLEMS

American Political History

Should be indeed, the interests of a small class may coincide for a time with those of the state, especially if the class concerned is of superior intelligence or of superior political or economic ability. On the other hand, it is of course true that partisan organizations subjugated by narrow class interest have at times turn an already twisted government to bits, as the case of the Democrat and Republican of todays 21 Century is happening.

Except for such cases the formulation of principles and policies by political parties, even when touched affected by class interests, is a public service, furthermore, which political party alone make on an acceptable scale. The question may well raise, though, as to whether there is not a certain injustice in comparing, actual political party platforms with ideal platforms assumed to be in the best interests of the public. As a rule, it is only the actual political party platforms which have enough control and organization behind them to determine the action of the Government.

Too often historians only discover the called ideal progresses of the process long after the event. If they exist in present-day it is only in the brains of theorists or of few academics, hereafter, absolutely, they may give the impression in period to permeate diffuse and devote to the community.

There is a nonsense of this conflict if we may eradicate eliminate the debate by the political parties, in a system lacking of parties there will be no discrepancies, because the legislature and the policymaking are working systematized composed for the same objective, that is, in the benefited of the peoples, that are their person over you after all.

Unquestionably a great public service thereby made, while in the end the ideas of the thinkers must incorporated in actual party platforms before they may hope to realize. In fact, however, actual political parties' platforms and perfect preparations of procedure do not contend fight. To the divergence discrepancy of the two parties to the ridicule of the earlier is, so therefore, ridiculous irrational.

Mark Twin quote

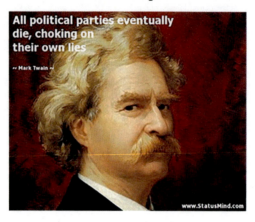

Like many other associations pursuing political ends either exclusively or as part of their activities, political parties are voluntary associations, nonetheless a disunion of the peoples.

Rules, customs, traditions, discipline of a sort, and differences between privileged and supporters they do, certainly have, but they occasionally imposed with the crookedness and detachment disinterestedness distinctive of the implementation of law in a well-ordered government. In this genial fanaticism lies one of the reasons for the irregular weakness in which the typical prejudiced grips his party.

NATURE OF PARTIES

American Political History

It seems so much closer to him, so much more human in its aims and fights, than the strict, just, controlling, and far more unfriendly to the government. In an extremely happy passage Professor Merriam has given expression to this feeling. The party, he writes, is in a sense a dogmatic and ecclesiastical which does not require very regularly being present or very strict creed; but still it provides a home based and it looks after the specific attendance if he pays the minimum of the party payments fees, involving in the acquaintance associate with and occasional support of someone of its member of the landed wealthy elite, even nonetheless a minor one.

Naturally, they are most concerned in sign up actual voters, but they by no means disregard other classes of citizens, or even individuals who do not have citizenship, particularly if the ultimate is soon to added to the electorate.

Thus, we find political organizations encouraging the naturalization of foreigners, granting political party representation to increase the populations of regions or colonies, and forming clubs of young men soon to become first voters or of women, in states which had not yet have approved them the voting rights. Indeed, there is hardly barely a class, race, creed, group, or persuasion of any kind to which the partisan politician does not make a request. In this respect they differ sharply from the parties of earlier centuries. The political organizations of classic antiquity olden days impress the reader of history, and still more the size and efficiency of modern party organizations. With a Fusion System these practices are old-fashioned.

Reference: The American Party System, p. 402. Cf. also G. Wallas, Human Nature in Politics, p. 83.,

ELECTORAL PROBLEMS

American Political History

Description of a political party modern director Bosses are, as inept incompetent and unreliable untrustworthy in the crooked way. This is true particularly of the ancient Democratic parties. The followers of it would hardly do to call them the supporters of the Gracchi seem more like Mobs than parties. Gracchi; In aristocracies or Roman states with a limited suffrage the most important politician was Tiberius Semiprecious .163–133 BC, and his younger brother, Gaius Semiprecious, 153– 121 BC, known as the Gracchi. Roman tribunes and reformers. Tiberius tried to redistribute public land among the poor but was assassinated in the resulting insurrection for political ambitions.

Political parties often had much the character of domestic congregation's worshipers, or participate in usually drunkenness celebration and the political decisions, grabbed by them took the form of what today would be called gentleman-agreements. As far as party organization is concerned, an authentic rebellion was brought about by the extension of the electoral suffrage which occurred in the United States between 1810 and 1840. That was a period when American Politic infested the world with the political-party idea disease sickness, and afterward in Great Britain, France, Belgium, Norway, and other countries with liberal governments, this is an example of how a nonsense idea have change the political idea in Democracy of the World.

To manage the hundreds of thousands and millions of new voters thus created political managers Bosses obliged grateful to express forms of organization of an ability, extent, and flexibility previously unknown in the world's history. As to the practical efficiency of this modern political machinery there can be no doubt; indeed, this made the principal point in the normal allegation against present day political establishments creations. For with it there has come a certain preponderance of the political organization as against groups principles and a centralization in the hands of political parties' Leaders and Bosses of controls subject to misapplication for dishonest interests and impounded ends. Nowhere in the world have these developments, both good and evil, occurred on a greater scale than in the United States.

Unquestionably the parties present-day are the greatest internal organization awkward uncooperative which now annoys aggravates us with the political fights. Summing up the various elements presented in the foregoing pages a definition may now be offered, as follows: A political party is a voluntary organization of individuals or groups of individuals advocating certain principles and policies as superior to all others for the general conduct of government administration, and which, as the most immediate method of securing their adoption, designates and supports certain of its leaders as candidates for public office. Although there has been a great increase of interest in the subject of recent years, the number of general works devoted entirely to American political parties still quite limited. Of those which rank as systematic organized dissertations critiques the most appreciated are Democratic and Republican parties.

In my new Electoral Fusion System, there is not parties at all, is just only the people decisions to elect a candidate, not a political parties' decisions. Reference:1 A. D. Morse, op. cit., p. 69.

Political Groups (2 vols., 1902); J. Macy, Party Organization and Machinery (1904); and J. A. Woodburn, Political Parties and Party Problems in the United States (1903), which is still of great value, particularly for its historical chapters (I to VIII, inclusive). C. L.

Jones, Readings on Parties and Elections in the United States (1912), is a collection of well-chosen materials in this field. For general reference purposes the most extensive and helpful work is A.C. McLaughlin and A. B. Hart, Encyclopedia of American Government (1913).

ONLY IN GOD WE TRUST

CHAPTER 4

ELECTORAL PROBLEMS

Political Organization, Designations and Classification Popular

American Political History

The names chosen by political groups to appoint themselves are choice of seldom occasionally accurately correctly or comprehensively descriptive. Practical politics develops a racy vernacular replete with slang. From this source many groups titles of greater or less vogue have gone under: witness our Quid's, Loco Focus, Know-Nothings, Hunkers and Barn-burners, Stalwarts Half-Breeds, Snappers and Anti-Snappers. This are example of voter's ignorance, as in the case of certain religious sects, nicknames maliciously invented by enemies sometimes assumed defiantly by parties and afterward accepted with pride. Such was the origin of the names of both the Whig and Tory groups in England and Democrats and Republican in America. Small Even when the title chosen is a word formerly have descriptive a serious political meaning, it may nevertheless throw party names small light on the character attractiveness of the party word assuming it.

Of course, the task of selecting a name is much easier in the case of parties devoted to a single issue, as, for example, our Green-backers and Prohibitionists. But no single title can do justice to groups supporting a wide range of procedures. Certainly, there is little of descriptive value in the terms of Republican and Democratic as used in our national politics, because they are no the names of political parties, they are a representation of two ancient-governments systems that have the Democrats of today are the lineal descendants of those who in Jefferson's time called themselves anti-federalists.

THE NEW FUSION ELECTORAL SYSTEM

By their Federalist opponents they called Democrats or Democratic Republicans, in disrespect and mockery of the two great ancient system. At the present time called Democratic parties also exist in number of European countries, but they have no connection whatever with the party bearing the same name in the United States and differ from it widely both in structure and in resolutions.

The terms Radical, Liberal, Moderate, Progressive, and Conservative are also much in favor as party names. In their general meaning each of these has some value as showing a certain insolence on the way to partisan revolution uprising. As party names, however, they used very uncertainly tentatively. Parties calling themselves Liberal contrast extensively from country to country, and the same is factual of each of the other terms in the above list.

On the other hand, it is true that Socialist-Communist parties pursue definite common aims in all countries and have established international connections, but in the reality, a is a false sound remained for the hard work electors or political groups, just the elite is only benefit. In popular speech number of terms used more or party and less exactly to characterize partisan organizations. Thus, get-together a distinction drawn often between a party and a faction.

Recent numbers of the American Political Science Review, Political Science Quarterly, Annals of the American Academy of Political and Social Science.

Reference: C. E.H. Croly, Marcus Alonzo Hanna (1912); Tom L. Johnson, My Story (1913); Brand Whitlock, Forty Years of It (1916); Anna

Howard Shaw, (1915; T. Roosevelt, Autobiography (1913; W. D. Lewis, The Life of Theodore Roosevelt (1919; and W. E. Dodd, Woodrow Wilson and His Work (1921. On, the nature of political parties— references may be found in the systematic treatises on American political parties listed, and also in the following: G. Bradford, The Lesson of Popular Government, Ch. XXI; J. Q. Dealey, The State and Government (1921, Ch. XX; R. G. Gettell, Introduction to Political Science (1910, Ch. XXI; A. N. Holcombe, State Government in the United States (1916, Ch. VII; L. H. Holt, Introduction to the Study of Government (1915; S. Leacock, Elements of Political Science (1913, Ch. VIII; J. Schouler, Ideals of the Republic (1908, Ch. X; J. A. Smith, The Spirit of American Government (1907, Ch. VIII; W. F. Willoughby, Government of Modern States (1919, Ch. XVII; and W. Wilson, Constitutional Government in the United States (1908), Ch. VIII. The most original and thorough discussion of the definition of political parties from the pen of an American writer is to found in an article by A. D. Morse, What Is a Party? in the Political Science Quarterly Vol. XI, p. 68 (March, 1896).

PARTY DESIGNATIONS VS POLITICAL ORGANIZATION.

American Political History

Originally the two words were synonymous; indeed, they used so occasionally at the present time. In his famous dictionary Doctor Johnson defines faction, part of a large group, as a party in the state, meaning social gathering engaging, unusual drunkenness, and quotes it without qualification of any sort as an equivalent for the word party, Instead of political organization or groups.

With the extension of the activities and the purification of the aims of the political groups that came in the nineteenth century the latter word gradually lost its offensive significance and became first trustworthy and finally even worthy. Meanwhile all the evil and opprobrious connotations descended upon faction, which is currently associated with the ideas of disagreement, intrigue, unscrupulousness, self-seeking, recklessness of the common good, and rebellious designs upon the government is the correct interpretation. With more or less animus the word is also employed at times to designate the groups into which a group is divided before or after a split by rivalries between its leaders or by clashes of economic, sectional, or other interests. Another distinction commonly made is that between the ins and the outs, is that, between the organization or parties (outs) supporting the government and those (in) in opposition. Wherever these roles are reversed from time to time the distinction may seem to be of slight value. As a matter of Right, Left and Center, Haves and have nots Constitutional and revolutionary organizations fact, however, it involves considerable differences both of outlook and of activity. The (ins) are inclined to be optimistic in temper and defensive in tactics, while the (outs) are suitable to be pessimistic and aggressive. When political conditions bring about a long retention of power by the government party and the consequent exclusion of the opposition, these psychological and tactical differences become very sharply defined.

In the various countries of continental Europe, the terms Right, Left, and Center, are often employed to appoint conservative, radical, and moderate groups, respectively. floor assigned to the representatives of the Clerical (Catholic) party, and the word Centrum so came to be associated. The usage arose from the practice of assigning parliamentary seats, which arranged semi-circularly in the legislative halls of these countries, so that the conservative representatives placed to the right of the speaker, the radicals to his left, and the moderates in the center. When groups divisions are many such terms as Right Center, Left Center, Extreme Right, and Extreme Left come into use. In the Reichstag of the former German Empire the center with that group behaves. According to another popular saying the struggle between the haves and the have not, is the basis of all political party's disunions.

In scientific phraseology the followers of Karl Marx have elaborated this idea that, so many disgraces have created in the world, is held responsible to this absurd of the Marxist idea, fortunately in The New Fusion Electoral System, we all are equals, no Left No Right no Center, only legislators working together harmoniously to obtain the same goal, the best for the peoples of the nation.

They conceive the Socialist party as representative of the proletarian masses, which destroy the self-worth of the people and as a result a total failure of the total economic disaster and distension all other parties together, regardless of their widely diverging aims, as more or less frankly representative of the anti-capitalism classes. Political Parties are also often classified in the countries of continental Europe as belonging to two groups, first, those which support the existing state, and second, those which want to overthrow it. Thus, under the former German Empire the Social-Democrats, and the Polish, Danish, and Alsace-Lorraine parties belonged to the second and 91all other parties to the first of these groups

PARTIES ELECTORAL PROBLEMS
American Political History

While they accept the constitution, they may favor its amendment in important, always, however, by legal methods. The word opportunist occasionally used in American opportunist can politics, always in a bad sense as implying a party's trimmer or one willing to sacrifice consistency to expediency and principles to policies. It enjoys a better fame in France, for to the efforts on more than one occasion of so-called opportunists they present the Republic saved from rebellion. In fact, a speculator may devote to his principles as a member of any other political organization, added so, indeed, because he is unenthusiastic to endanger them by rapid and across the board action.

As regards policies, however, he considers it wise and prudent to distinguish between those which are suitable for acceptance in their entirety or not subject to cooperation, and, on the other hand, those which may be accomplished gradually, or suspended for the present, or made the basis of negotiation with other parties. In this better sense of the word not only our two major parties, but the Communists as well, may be said to have frightened a speculator policy on many occasions to Perpetuating in power, as in Cuba, Venezuela, Nicaragua, North Korea and many more, not counting China and Vietnam that have adopted a new system called Socialist Democratic Republic, but never the less they are an oppressive Dictatorship. Directly opposed in beliefs and methods to favorable incompatible the opposing or reactionaries of politics. The talented or in latter conceive their program to be of such supreme importance that they reject all compromise and claim upon its immediate acceptance. Naturally, this attitude often made the but then of ridicule of censure. It is impossible, however, to doubt the sincerity of incompatible political organization.

Since membership in them usually requires much greater courage than membership in more tolerant political organizations and offers less prospect of office or reward of any kind. They have occasionally encouraged brutality if it is necessary. Indeed, at times the only course of action open to them has been that of passive resistance. There have been many intransigent political groups in European countries, most of them devoted to what seemed hopelessly lost causes. Yet some of them have gained their ends, especially at times of general unsettled, and contributed to the world's advance thereby.

Following the Great War, the map of Europe was redrawn, and its political systems readjusted along lines formerly advocated by various intransigent parties. In the United States the Prohibitionist group has consistently pursued an opposing policy in the better sense of the term. Macaulay's contrast with the popular distinction's, historians and philosophers have often at political organizations tempted to point out fundamental bases of group divider. Thus, in discussing the origin of the two great English political organizations, he wrote: In one sense, indeed, the distinction which then became obvious had always existed, and always must exist. For it has its origin in diversities of temper, of understanding, and of interest, which are found in all societies, and which will be found till the human mind ceases to be drawn in opposite directions by the charm of habit and the charm of novelty.

Everywhere there is a class of men who hold with friendliness to whatever is ancient, and who, even when convinced by overpowering reasons that innovation would be beneficial, consent to it with many reservations and presentiments. We find also everywhere another class of men confident in hope, bold in assumption, always pressing forward, quick to discriminate the inadequacies of whatsoever exists, disposed to think lightly of the dangers and inopportuneness which appear enhancements. If in her England's establishments, freedom, and order, the and disposed to give every transformation recognition for existence a development. advantages ascending from insurgency, and the advantages arising from that remedy have been combined to an extent in a different place strange, we may attribute this happy individuality to the strenuous conflicts and the alternate victories of two challenging associations of announcement, a confederacy enthusiastic for authority and the distant past, and a confederacy passionate for liberty and progress. Interesting as is this bit of theorizing, it obviously imperfections of does not begin to do justice to the large variety of political inclinations existing among humankind. In countries with nations a two-party system one of the two may imagine be to take a more favorable insolence toward modernization than the other. Usually, however, it is difficult to decide this point between them. Both in England and in the United States today, the two great parties honestly recommend novelties, even though along dissimilar appearances.

As regards liberty and authority also party attitudes are not always clearly defined. And respect for the distant past as a basic party opinion, much less often confirmed at the present time than in the times of which Macaulay wrote. Finally, in countries with a multi-party system and they are much more many than those on a bi-party basis the philosophy disruptions are miserable completely.

A more elaborate theory of party divisions was expert of the Rohmer's crushed in 1842 by Friedrich Rohmer. According to points of this writer the natural causes of political parties must be needed in the laws governing the development of the human soul. This expansion shows itself throughout the various stages of life boyhood, young, and adulthood, maturity, and old age, in the succession of which significant changes of mind and character happen. There is not stages in the political thinking's of a man or a woman is the grade of education and intellectual, what makes the differences and changes of these four stages, the two most important are knowledge and old age understanding References: -1 History of England, vol. I, Ch.2 The theory 94irst presented in the Beobachter asunder best lichen ScJnueiz, and later published by Theodor Rohmer, Lehre von den politischen.

ELECTORAL PROBLEMS AND CORRUPTIONS

American Political History Election, the formal process of selecting a person for public office or of accepting or rejecting a political proposition by voting. It is important to distinguish between the form and the substance of elections. In some cases, electoral forms are present, but the substance of an election is missing, as when voters do not have a free and genuine choice between at least two alternatives. Most countries hold elections in at least the formal sense, but in many of them the elections are not competitive (e.g., all but one party may be forbidden to contest or the electoral situation is in other respects highly compromised. Radicals and absolutists opposed to Liberals and Conservatives Exceptions to normal development according to Rohmerhood and mature adulthood. During both full possessions of the active powers of the soul enjoyed. Young adulthood, however, is strangely the period of assembly and construction and insurgence. Mature adulthood, on the other hand, is the period of orderly arrangement, preservation, and perseverance.

To these two types of mind and character correspond respectively Broad-mindedness and Liberalism in politics. As representative of the full development of the manly powers Rohmer assigns the natural leadership in the state to these two groups. Opposed to them, although of less importance, there are two extreme parties, corresponding respectively to the stages of boyhood and of old age. Boyhood characterized by a susceptible and observant eye, a lively imagination, and a receptive mind, but it lacks perspective and creative power because his immaturity. In politics the counter part of this period is Radicalism Old age brings to the forefront the passive and feminine powers of the mind, characterized by irritability of feeling, quickness of combination, and fineness of conception. The s in politics presents the same distinctive by this theory, every individual of normal development should, if he lived long enough, belong successively to the Radical, Liberal, Conservative, and Absolutist parties. To critics who urged this objection replied that such, indeed, was the normal tendency of men in the mass. At least the inclination of younger men toward liberalism and of older men toward conservatism has commented upon by many observers. Owing to differences of individual character, however, the complete fourfold development outlined by Rohmer arrested in some cases, hastened in others.

Certain individuals are still boys in character, and therefore Radical in politics, all their lives. Others are prematurely aged in character and for that reason attach themselves permanently to the Absolutist group in young adulthood or even in boyhood. Moreover, actual political organizations lines rarely coincide sharply and clearly with the fourfold division required by the theory, although Rohmer's supporters tried to show that they were potentially present even when not plainly visible. Owing to this blurring over of natural party lines the choice of parties by types of character obscured.

Interesting as is Rohmer's theory, it offers many Criticism of openings for attack. Radicals and Absolutists. naturally, Rohmer's object to the aspersions of juvenile and senility respectively which it casts upon them. Nor will they admit that their political organizations are of an inferior class as compared with the Liberals and Conservatives and walk out to the latter leadership in the state.

Indeed, from the Radical and Absolutist points of view Liberalism and Conservatism are nothing more than weak-kneed imitations of themselves, and therefore quite incapable of meeting great emergencies in the state. Rohmer's account of the mental changes caused by advancing years is far from being either enough or convincing; what he says of old age seems eccentric.

Rohmer's theory, it offers many Criticism of openings for attack. Radicals and Absolutists. naturally, Rohmer's object to the aspersions of juvenile and senility respectively which it casts upon them.

Nor will they admit that their political organizations are of an inferior class as compared with the Liberals and Conservatives and walk out to the latter leadership in the state. Indeed, from the Radical and Absolutist points of view Liberalism and Conservatism are nothing more than weak-kneed imitations of themselves, and therefore quite incapable of meeting great emergencies in the state. Rohmer's account of the mental changes caused by advancing years is far from being either enough or convincing; what he says of old age seems eccentric.

Whatever part psychological conditions determined by advancing years may play in conclusive groups affiliations are manifest outweighed in the case of many individuals by the influence of other factors. Among these the more important are economic position, social standing, education, family traditions, personal loyalty to leaders, race, religion, geographical environment, and historical circumstances. In malice of all the ingenuity spent by the advocates of Rohmer's theory. It cannot be shown that there is any in impartiality to Rohmer it should be said that his theory agreements only with morally radical parties. In conclusion is definitely a sickness of the American systems, rather than solutions organizations, parties disrupt he good functions of the Democracy-Republic system, confusing the voters with famous campaigns to discredit the opponent party, creating a political war with the people in the middle confused and some irritated by the confrontation between them. When the logical solution is to eliminates all political parties and let the voters elect their representatives, to let them elects the president in a Fusion Electoral System, which will terminate the political war we are experiencing today, insults, defamation, fallacies etc. if it is the system that will solve my problems I rather prefer a Monarchy or other system without political parties.

PARTIES ELECTION PROBLEMS

American Political History

Bluntschli recognizes: (I) religious-political mixed groups;(a) groups resting upon geographical, national, or racial differences; and (3) groups standing for a certain social class e.g., patricians or plebeians; clergy, nobility, or commonalty. Continuing this classification, he differentiates political groups proper as (4) those which differ on constitutional grounds, e.g., royalist and republicans; aristocrats and democrats; feudal and constitutional; unitary and federalists; nationalists and particular-isms; centralizing and decentralizing; (5) government and opposition parties; and (6) pure political parties.

When the logical solution is to eliminates all political parties and let the voters elect their representatives, to let them elects the president in a Fusion Electoral System, which will terminate the political war we are experiencing today, insults, defamation, fallacies etc. if it is the system that will solve my problems I rather prefer a Monarchy or other system without political parties. Bluntschli recognizes: (I) religious-political mixed groups;(a) groups resting upon geographical, national, or racial differences; and (3) groups standing for a certain social class, e.g., patricians or plebeians; clergy, nobility, or commonalty. Continuing this classification, he differentiates political groups proper as (4) those which differ on constitutional grounds, e.g., royalist and republicans; aristocrats and democrats; feudal and constitutional; unitary and federalists; nationalists and particular-isms; centralizing and decentralizing; (5) government and opposition parties; and (6) pure political parties.

References: e.g. liberals, conservatives, etc. Cf. op. cit., pp. 16-27. Solutions to this problem: The New Electoral Fusion System, Nonpartisan Elections.

PARTIES ELECTION PROBLEMS

American Political History

No general tendency to revert to a growing division between voters of parties. Existed for some time in Switzerland, and it existed for a time in

Germany after 1886. The nearest approach to it in the history of the United States was during the campaign of 1912 between Republicans, Democrats, Progressives, and Socialists. In none of these instances were divisions drawn through along the lines showed by Rohmer.

Any tendency there may be to revert to a fourfold-party basis is less strong than the two-party tendency in England and the United States. In most of the countries of continental Europe there are more than four well-defined parties, and the tendency is toward further cleavage. Though insufficient Rohmer's attempted classification of political parties may be the terms which he engagements there enjoy a wide although uncertain vogue as descriptive of groups purposes. Of course, their meaning in any given case depends upon the political system to which they are functional, as the case of Fusion Electoral System.

Thus, a party described as radical under a Monarchic Government might pursue the same ends as a party described as cautious under a Republican Government. Like so many other words in the lexicon of politics, most of these have used as terms of ridicule or criticism. Despite the difficulties it may be worthwhile to try to develop their meaning as accepted at the present time. An unadventurous party may be defined as one which stands upon the principle of permanency. Believing in the soundness of the existing order, its efforts are directed to the maintenance of the status-quo and in opposition to innovation which it considers dangerous to the government.

To use an illuminative American expression, liberalism stands precise. In an extreme or unfavorable sense liberalism held to conflicting to all advancement. In addition to the above type, which he calls the Positive Conservative, Christensen distinguishes the Negative Conservative, who also does not want any alteration, but only because, while things are altogether in a good way, yet that no improvement is possible. In other words, if not broken, do not fixed, but Conservatism is a retrograde position, all systems soon or later must change to walk according with the humanity progress Conservative, who also does not want any alteration, but only because, while things are altogether in a good way, yet that no improvement is possible. In other words, if not broken, do not fixed, but Conservatism is a retrograde position, all systems soon or later must change to walk according with the humanity progress.

Reference: Cf. his Politics and Crowd Morality, p. 5.

POLIITICAL ORGANIZATION DESCRIPTIONS
Liberal American Political History

Parties are based upon the principle of improvement which is a false, instead for political or personal gain.

Liberalism They accept the existing order to a greater or less degree, but advocate reforms which they consider necessary to lift it to a higher plane of justice or efficiency. Starting from the conviction that the existing order is extremism primarily incorrect. Extremism proposes first to destroy everything of a sabotage character and then to rebuild in harmony with its own program.

This is the must senseless Marxism philosophy. Why not to improved what is done by the rival system? To fastener this remorseful organization of things entire, would not we shatter it to bits and then remolds it nearer to the mood's requirements. The term totalitarianism, or absolutism which is the fourth in Rohmer's Absolutism classification, defines itself. Unlike the other three, it and react' is so specific in meaning that it barely seems to belong in the series. At any given time and place conservatism is a fixed point in doubtless for this reason the more general term Reaction-ism has not necessary in its case. Just as radicalism goes to the left of moderation, so reaction goes to the right of liberalism. he political arrangement the defense of things as they are. In common with both liberalism and radicalism, reaction stands in opposition to the existing order. But while the former two desire to advance with greater or less speed, reaction finds its ideal in the past and works for a reversal of existing tendencies or conditions. The various French parties which under the present Republic have advocated no return to one or the other kinds of monarchy, realizing that they had made a mistake and a genocide, formerly prevailing in that country are, therefore, typical reactionary parties.

In our own politics return to a former condition has sometimes suggested as a solution for a given problem, and solved with the new Electoral Fusion System, without impartiality and parties, only the citizen determination and conclusions. Thus, there are those who believe some earlier tariff level to have been ideal, or who advocate a return political assembly intimate conferring to ends, not forms to competition as opposed to the recognition of trusts and monopolies, or would give up direct primaries and return to the old convention system. But none of our parties has ever decently recognized response in general as its central principle.

References: A. L. Lowell, op. ell., vol. ii, p. 9. Bluntschli recognizes that political absolutism in our nineteenth century is medieval. Op. cit. Volm ii, p.9 P-153,

States are governments usually classified according to the forms of organization which they show. Attempts to classify political groups, on the other hand, are always based on the character of the ends which they pursue. The public is naturally more interested in the propaganda of organization which originates it, so much so, indeed, that only recently has the extent and influence of the latter begun to evaluate critically. And exhausted most of the nomenclature of parties from popular sources.

A further reason for the different bases of classification may found in the fact that while states and governments pursue much the same general aims, they show great variations in organization, making it easier to classify them on the latter basis. Parties, on the other hand, differ from each other much more widely in the ends they pursue than in the structures they develop henceforward apparently the tendency to classify them on the former basis. The essential similarity of political organizations structures the world over has been made the starting point of an extremely interesting and comprehensive study by Professor Robert Michel's of the University of Basel. Under democratic conditions, according to this writer, an iron law of sociology brings about the formation of an oligarchy, a government by a few peoples holding power, in every political clusters regardless of the nature of the doctrines it professes.

This tendency to oligarchy is based, first, on individual psychology; second, on the psychology of the crowd; and third, on the social necessities of party organization. Under the first of these Professor Michel's includes the individual's consciousness of his own importance which with opportunity develops into a natural human desire for power, and such other individual. Michel's' qualities theories,' original or acquired, as inborn diplomacy, oratorical gifts, editorial skill, special intelligence, and so on.

Finally, various social requirements contribute to the same conclusion. One of these is the physical impossibility of direct self-governance in large party groups; another the constant state of contention in which parties engage with other parties in a political confrontation, and, if they are radical in attractiveness, with the existing order itself, making strong control in the hands of a few leaders a disorder of success or even of endurance. In the beginning of a group's life, according to Professor Michel's, leadership may be weak, diffuse, and voluntary, oligarchies but as membership increases, the pressure of the factors noted above places larger and larger powers in the hands of a small number of men, as in the Communist attitude the whole thing. Often the latter become permanent holders of all controlling groups offices and develop special interests of their own, in other words, an oligarchy is virtually set up. Such leadership is certainly experienced and may be unproductive, well informed, almost professional in its qualifications and methods, but it is also likely to become thoughtful, conservative, intending to above all else to preserve its personal control undiminished, and, if probable, to intensification it. All parties' fights, so, determination by themselves into struggles between the oligarchy of the party in control of the state and the equally narrow oligarchies of the parties striving to dispossess the former. Sometimes by a sweeping victory or by uprising the latter get rid of all the former dominating oligarchs at once, which means simply that a new Oligarchy has taken complete possession of the state as occurred in the Island of Cuba at ninety miles from our coastlines.

Ex-President Barack Obama shaking hands with a communist assassin is a picture for the hall of shame

The Communist's Oligarchy of an undeveloped radical method may compel the Oligarchy of the dominant group to concede it a small number of governmental markers, and, if its power continues to increase, may acquire ultimately most of such offices, and hence a controlling influence over the governments, in all Latin America. The communist dictatorship at 90 miles from our Miami coasts in an eminent menace not only USA but the rest of the Americas continent.

PARTIES ELECTORAL PROBLEMS
American Political History

Under any of these possibilities, though, the government, regardless of its clear form, is an Oligarchy, and all parties, no matter how democratic or even socialistic their professed its ideologies, are similarly under the control of an oligarchies. As an ungenerous workout in judgment it is, of course, an easy matter to support the proposition that all forms of government are oligarchic, in a way. But this does not wipe out the real dissimilarities that exist among them as to the number exercising political control, the way public authorities formed, the various ways in which they exercise their functions, and so on.

In a comparable way the sweeping intention that all parties are oligarchic may use to inexplicable of the actual transformations that exist between them. Organizations, there can be no doubt that the tendency to centralize oligarchy in the party control, which Professor Michel's points out, is both States powerful and widely felt. In no country has it made itself more manifest than in the United States.

Indeed, with us it often exceeds the limits of oligarchy, with the result that we find ourselves confronted with that types of organization Dictatorship known as Bossism. But Bossism and organization Oligarchy are always under fire from the moment of their first appearance. The chief weakness of the Michel's theory is its failure to consider the fact that monopolization of organization control classes its contradictory.

Thus, in the United States machines and political bosses have found themselves faced by various forms of counter system of government independent and third-party movements and parties within the organization itself.

It must be admitted that they make a stout resistance and have shown a control of improvement under downfall that has proved intimidating to many of their adversaries. The competition is by no means ended, however, and there is good reason to believe that because of our awakened public spirit and various reforms already adopted or under discussion, such as the merit system, direct primaries, the short vote, wrong practices acts, and the application of the initiative, plebiscite and recall to party management, a satisfactory degree of Democracy may become accomplished in the affairs of political fascism. Nor is undue pessimism justified by an historical view. References:1 Cf. C. E. Merriam, American Party System, p. 89; also, this book, Ch. ix.30.

PARTIES DESCRIPTIONS PROBLEMS

American Political History

Oligarchy control was more noticeable, more unscrupulous, and harder to dislodge in eighteenth century English parties than it has been at any later time either in England, or in the United States, or the more liberal countries of continental Europe. No doubt small coteries of influential leaders have sought opposition and still look to advance their own interests as far as to groups possible through the manipulation of political machinery.

But this does not mean that they can disregard and supersede at will the interests of their own followers or of the wider public. Recurrently, indeed, it is only by advancing these interests that they can succeed in their more personal aims. The great contributions made by political organizations to liberalism, to constitutional reform, and to a more democratic suffrage during the nineteenth century would of themselves seem enough to justify this view.

If Oligarchic party leaders proved themselves incurably selfish, free peoples would speedily find other means to give expression to their will. That they have not done so, that, on the contrary, parties have grown constantly in numbers and power to the present day, is convincing evidence that on the whole they have been found acceptable instruments of popular rule. The solution to this problem will be the elimination of all political parties, by the introduction of the Electoral Fusion System.

Reference: On T. Rohmer, Lehre von den politischen Parteien (1844), is fundamental. Supplementary J. K. Bluntschli, Character under Geist. A. L. Lowell, Public Opinion in War and Peace (1923), The R. Michel's translated under the title of Political Parties: A Sociological Study of the Oligarchical, Tendencies of Modern Democracies (1915). E. Merriam, The American Party System (1922parties, leadership in Chaps. II and III., J. DE Boisjoslin, Les Partis in France (1906); A. Christensen, Politics and Crowd Morality (1915), Ch. I; G. L. Dickinson, A Modern Symposium (1905); M. Ostrogorski, Democracy and the Organization of Political Parties (1902), Vol. I, Part II, Chaps. I and II; G. Wallas, Human, Nature in Politics (1909), Ch. II; and J. A. Woodburn, Political Parties and Party Problems in the United States (1903), Ch. 1. F

SITUATIONS OF PARTIES LIFE

American Political History

Considering the history of the world, political parties are an extremely late progress. No are late devil, they by any means universal at the present time. Countless generations of humankind have existed without organizations that could properly become called as political Party. To millions of human beings living in Latin America, Asia, and Africa they are equally unknown at the Oligarchy. When the importance of political groups in other countries the question naturally arises, what conditions? When we contrast this condition of affairs with the prominence and importance of political groups in other countries the question naturally arises, what conditions favorable to groups life, on the one hand, and unfavorable on the other, can justification for can justification for such wide extremes?

It is customary to refer the existence of political groups to Operation Anthropoid, no groups nature the aforementioned. To explain their nonattendance on the same basis in cultures would be nearer the truth. A reconciliation of these clear contradictions may find in the statement that in primitive and undeveloped states of society conditions disapproving the political parties' life is dominant, for the mere conditions of absence of political truths and constitutional rights of the peoples no partisan.

Not until societies are highly evolved do contrary conditions become powerful enough to lead to the formation of organizations that are teaching their rights, human rights. With few if any exceptions political parties' promoters' changes of greater or less extent. But to undeveloped so-called conservative organizations seldom plant themselves unconditionally on the status-quo existence of social structure. Originally, they made more of the principle of antiquity than is customary at the present time.

CHAPTER 5

ELECTORAL COMPLICATIONS

American Political History

The primitive man is traditionally in a hazardous stage. Even on conflicting higher races with one another, and even on incompatible dissimilar classes in the same culture, it is noticeable that the least technologically advanced are the most antagonistic to transformation. Considerable the extreme part of civilization has never shown a particle of desire that its political organizations should be enhanced since the moment when external inclusiveness was first given to them by personification in some permanent greatest. To the fact that the enthusiasm for change is rare must added the fact that it is very contemporary. It is known but to a small part of humanity, and to that part but for a brief period during a history of incalculable length. Strongly associated with this resentment to change there is a horrendous degree of indifference on the part of undeveloped civilization toward all matters radical. Their whole stock of energy may absorb in a fight for basic existence, as among the native American Eskimos. In more favored climes which make possible some degree of leisure religion or other non-political interests may fully occupy the intellect of the race.

The primitive man is traditionally in a hazardous stage. Even on conflicting higher races with one another, and even on incompatible dissimilar classes in the same culture, it is noticeable that the least technologically advanced are the most antagonistic to transformation. Considerable the extreme part of civilization has never shown a particle of desire that its political organizations should be enhanced since the moment when external inclusiveness was first given enthusiasm for change is rare must

The charge of indifference sometimes brought against highly civilized peoples as well. Writing of the United States in 1913, Mr. Walter Lippmann remarks that, the most incisive comment on politics today is indifference.

Reformers and practical politicians alike constantly echo this complaint. Indeed, the activities of Political indolence was also a reaction in that it involved opposition to the gatherings of a liberal or radical tendency. Groups of the two latter tendencies rest upon a more recent and more highly evolved complex than conformist parties,

But it is uncertain if any existing groups calling themselves conformist are so. They may glorify the principles of authority, order, and stability, and oppose severely the innovations supported by other groups, but upon examination they will found to favor changes in their own interest, sometimes intransigent, at other times even progressive in character. Virtually all existing parties must be eliminating and forbidden in the future, therefore, are political parties for change in some degree, I do believe so.

Reference: 1 Principles of Sociology, vol. I, p. 70. 2 Ancient Lata, 3d Am. ed., pp. 11-22. 8 Preface to

POLITICAL INSTITUTIONS NATURAL LIFE

American Political History

This organization are directed in large measure to the developing of interest and passion. But the indifference of enlightened man cannot compare to the unimportance of immature people. The former rapidly changed to group-ship by major events or persuasive demands; the latter continues uninterrupted generation after generation. Such organization as primitive peoples have is standardized to a dangerous degree.

Their social structure shows few differentiations; their economic activities are confined to someone field such as hunting and fishing, pastoral pursuits, or agriculture to surviving. The dull uniformity of their consequent outlook upon life reflects itself in the all but universal conservatism or indifference of their political insolence.

Among peoples with advanced social and industrial systems, on the other hand, there are many stark contrasts and divergent group interests.

Consequently, conservatism thus gave way to a complexity of social conditions from which one might naturally expect political differences and activity to appear. But the processes of conquest involve a further centralization of political authority and an increase in the power of government. As a result, any attempt at political activity on the part of subject peoples repressed quite as severely and more effectively than before.

Their social structure shows few differentiations; their economic activities are confined to someone field such as hunting and fishing, pastoral pursuits, or agriculture to surviving. The dull uniformity of their consequent outlook upon life reflects itself in the all but universal conservatism or indifference of their political insolence opinion and the determination to maintain them, which, given an opportunity, crystallize in the form of political groups. Habituated as we have become to the view that political groups are helpful or even essential to the conduct of government, it is however true that for centuries all the control of the more recent, so exercised as to make the presence of political groups are intolerable.

Primitive governments resting upon military power saw with extreme fanaticism upon political dialogue of any sort. To the substantial means of tyranny, they usually added the influence of a subservient priesthood which taught the divine origin of the state and sometimes even asserted the actual divinity of the controlling monarch or dominant caste, it was necessary to control population behaves. Under such conditions the faintest manifestation of political concentration or activity on the part of the subject masses hand out with a setting up not only rebellion, but destruction as well. By conquest theocratic military governments often extended their way over peoples of bizarre blood, philological, duties, and belief. Within these enlarged territories differences due to unlike geographical and economic in different group interests in higher societies.

Early governments intolerant of political organizations effects of conquest England's favored position Progress of liberalism and democracy requirements made themselves manifest. The similarity of primitive peoples with their restricted viewpoint and consequent conservatism thus gave way to a complexity of social condiltilo0ns from which one might naturally expect political differences and activity to appear.

ELECTORAL PROBLEM
American Political History

Under such condition's political organizations in the modern wisdom of the word cannot exist. The nearest approach to them will found in the factions and united for a common purpose of self-seeking flatterers surrounding the monarch and in secret societies plotting his assassination or fomenting rebellion. Struggles of this sort may go on for centuries without opening the way to liberalism or a wider diffusion of political power. Especially is this true of countries expose to foreign invasion where political repression may justify itself as necessary to national self-preservation.

In England the protection afforded by the North Sea and the Channel enabled nobility, aristocracy, and municipal corporations to make good their claims against the crown at a much earlier date than in continental Europe.

Even so, political control long remained in the hands of a small fraction of the population. The political control which first made their appearance in these favored social classes dominated by narrow group interests, sometimes even by great families. Long after the crown had lost its power to defeat political activity directly it was able by playing Political audience against political group, by benefaction, and by corruption to achieve its own ends. Beginning with the last quarter of the eighteenth century liberal and democratic ideas of government made great progress in America and western Europe. The only problem is that the corruption of parties Bosses continue up this days, the solution is on eliminating the elections procedure and concentrates in reform it with a Fusion Electoral System, no partisan. But the processes of conquest involve a further centralization of political authority and an increase in the power of government.

Social classes formerly without political control believed the economic importance in addition acknowledged to the election system. Elective officers increased in number, religious or structure of government functions first qualifications lowered or abolished political parties. Popular education, the press, and improved means of communication stimulated interest in public questions.

Party organizations expanded to meet the new demands made upon them. Even if narrow class interests still find expression through them it must admitted that the number of classes which thus find expression is larger than ever before. With the abandonment of unrestrictive theories, Government-Reorganization, men's have assumed new functions in many fields of public service which bring them into constant contact with the daily lives of their citizens.

The result is a great increase of political interest and the emergence of current issues with which political groups concern themselves. On the other hand, the executive branches of the more progressive governments of the world have abandoned all the uncivilized and many of the minor forms of subjugation and corruption with which they formerly tried to stay the advance of political organizations. To varying degrees, they admit the right of political groups acting through constitutional forms to influence and even to control the conduct of public activities.

Favored by these developments, political groups have organized and come to play an essential part in the public life of the most progress advanced countries of the world. They are the natural outgrowth of Liberalism, Democracy, and education, of economic and social progress.

NICARAGUA CONTRAS SUPPORTED BY CIA

Wherever tyranny, in other countries they are weak to the extent that these favoring conditions are missing, and, as we have seen, they are unknown among primitive and undeveloped peoples. military power, theocracy, repression hold sway, wherever is certainly much more than an accident that in the World War victory rested in the end with those powers which possessed the most highly organized, as ex ample regions that under tyranny because of the practice of party-political communal controls as Venezuela, Cuba, Nicaragua, North Korea and other nations around the world, causes of this anomaly are the partisan political systems eliminating them is the solution. The US intervention in Nicaragua was fiasco and Cuba's regime are our enemy, but we are not doing anything or too little to drive the Communists out the island Nation south our borders.

The New Fusion Electoral System

OTHER ELECTORAL PROBLEMS

American Political History

Eighteenth century view of political parties:

Views of political leaders and philosophers Rousseau on political parties and influential life together with the entire range of political, business, and social structures to which it is a necessary complement. Under the favoring conditions of the nineteenth century parties made great advances not only in organization and material control, but in moral ethics and systems as well, are a discredit to the nations moral values.

With few exceptions the theorists and privileged of the preceding century we approved in their disapproval of political parties. Monarchy was the prevailing form of government of the stronger nations of that time. To its devotees the epidemic influence of people's conflicts predestined the disapproval, exploitation, disorder, and revolt. The long record of Kings miserably limited in the exercise of their rights by parties, of Kings overthrown and martyrize by parties, of kings struggling by means of corruption and influence to make movement against parties, was more than sufficient to convince all believers in the royalist regime that nothing good could ever flow from such a doomed and contaminated source.

What is more difficult to understand is the extent to which advanced, and even radical political leaders and academics coincided with this view. Jose Martí was obsessed with the independence of his native land, Cuba. It was the single greatest cause in his life, and the one he was eventually martyred and die for. We have noted his constant petitioning for the cause while in the United States, and he saw the 1889-90 in his conference as a magnificent opportunity to make his case real.

Believing as they all did to a greater or less degree in the right of the people to take part in government, they were extremely vague as to just how this popular power should applied. Without exception, however, they feared its application with parties. The eighteenth-century Whig idea of government regards political Groups as barnacle crustaceans upon the vessel of the state or malignancies in the body politic.

Before 1787 no English political writer of any consequence except Edmund Burke had dared to defend the party system, and his arguments were regarded as hypocritical attempts to gloss over the immoralities of factions and groups. Extreme radical as he was, Rousseau, nevertheless feared political groups as destructive to that general will without which his ideal Democracy could not exist.

Reference:1Cf. W. B. Munro, Government of the United States, p. 312, Ibid. Solutions: The New, Solutions to this problem: The New Electoral Fusion System, Nonpartisan Elections.

CONDITIONS OF POLITICAL GROUP LIFE

American Political History

To the great French philosopher Montesquieu, parties characterized unrestrained passions hatred, envy, jealousy, and an ambitious desire of riches and respects. Nevertheless, he was inclined to believe that among a free people, such as the English, their existence was an evidence of strength and, further, that a tendency to a balance of power between them could discriminated. Prior to the appearance of Burke's pamphlet this was the most favorable judgment that had expressed about political parties. For this unanimity on one point of Whigs and Tories, of democrats and monarchists, a fundamental reason may distinguish.

All of them were so thoroughly convinced of the corruption of political parties that they wished most energetically to avoid them. Absolutists feared, with entire correctness, as the event showed, that parties would destroy their system. Moderates like the Whigs, together with Democrats and other radicals, were convinced that, once they had succeeded in bringing about reforms or in setting up ideal conditions, parties would at once set about their disloyalty. Thus, from one end of the political scale to the other there was essential agreement in the belief that parties were irredeemably violent, destructive, oppressive, and corrupt. In the light of all that had happened down to that time an extraordinarily convincing argument could made out in support of the conviction that parties were by nature violent and corrupts.

The controversies of centuries had shown that force was the ultimate ratio register. If parties had always pursued a pacifist policy when pushed to extremities by the Royal control, Totalitarianism would have survived and neither Democracies nor parties would have come into existence. From this point of view much of the earlier violence of party it seen to thoroughly justified. On the other hand, one can readily understand the aversion to violence and consequently, as they thought, to parties on the part of those who had to calculate with it as a constantly recurring condition in their own lives and affairs.

Apart from their growth in numbers, perhaps the most Alleged corruption of parties, violence of parties, them must to parties agree to take peaceful methods, of elections instead of party fighting, Fusion Election system is the answer. Remarkable development of parties during the nineteenth century was the increasingly pacific character of their activities. For this sharp contrast between modern parties and those of earlier periods several explanations may give.

Religious controversies which embittered the politics of the eighteenth and preceding centuries no longer played so great a part. The anger of civilized evolution has grown more pacific, although in the light of what happened from 1914 to 1918 one hesitates to lay much strain on this issue.

Certain it is that most of the leaders and a large part of the followers of the few politically active classes of earlier times accomplished in the use of arms and ready to resort to them on slight incitement. When actual conflict did occur among them, as for example in the War of the Roses, it involved only a part of the population. Now in this 2019 era is more conflictive and ferrous that in the past 100 years' Modern parties, on the other hand, enrolls great masses of the people with a more numerous civilian elements. If civil war should break out between them it would involve bloodshed and destruction on a scale indefinite to earlier centuries, this is a reason we terminate the practice of political parties that was a solution in earlier centuries, but that today has transformed in furious confrontations between the parties Democrats and Republicans, I recommend to eliminating them and substituted with The New Electoral System.

Finally, the wider diffusion of property and education makes for community peace. A controversy such as that over the Hayes-Tilde election of 1876 would have produced civil war infallibly in any earlier century. Whatever weight may assign to these general considerations accounting for the peaceful character of today political struggles a more specific reason may found in the fact that parties must resort to violence and corruptions to gain their ends.

Parties have so far advanced their controls and stabilized their position that they have become a part of the existing order and, therefore, interested in its maintenance. Fairly exact and accepted methods of determining the extent of the impact to which each party entitled have devised in the form of election laws, parliamentary procedure, ministerial responsibility, and the like.

The somewhat worn-out phrase, ballots instead of bullets, really expresses a profound truth regarding the conduct of contemporary political parties, but the verbal war and obstruction to a government process escalated in this century, as with the conduct of factions in earlier centuries, nevertheless in this new era politicians do not uses bullets, but insults and defamations allegation of corruptions are the new bullets politician are using today to discredit the opponent acclaim the eradication of all political parties to have a better pacific elections.

Critics continue to attack them on many grounds, but offense without bullets, obstructions and insults prevailed and is listed in the indictment, considering the violence of the party system it is wise to eliminate all kind of parties and substitute it with an Electoral Fusion System instead, in another word going back when under President George Washington were no political parties, instead Political groups with no flags and names, the Fusion of the two system Democracy and Republic is the solution of no more political party, no more political conflicts, no more revolutions is the final solution.

POLITICAL PARTIES COMPLICATIONS

American Political History

The eighteenth-century view that political parties were by nature destructive has also given way to the general acceptance of their unproductive abilities.

The New Fusion Electoral System

Their achievements in molding the constitutions and determining the course of ordinary legislation in the United States, England, and the more advanced nations of continental Europe leave no room for uncertainty on this mark, but not peace between party while waiting for their eliminated, and substitute parties with The New Electoral Fusion System. During the same time, as we have already noted, they have developed elaborate and efficient organizations to continue their own activities, both external and internal.

Even when conditions made it impossible for parties to play a violent and destructive party eighteenth-century scholars were convinced that they would become Bosses of a dictatorship. No matter what its nature, nobility, clergy, or power at any given time was certain to undertaking to the limit of its ability all other classes in the state. It would look to claim to itself civil rights and headquarters; it would shift to other duties, taxes, and obligations.

Essentially the same view held about the Capitalist class by Communists at the present time, Socialist-Communist system has been a disaster and a real exploitation by the government and their gang regimes, against their people that was to be according with the Marxism theory, spouse to be their saviors that was organized to protect humanity from Capitalism, did not to work as Mark wanted. If Karl Mark were alive, he should become a fervent follower of the Capitalism, providentially he is underground blaming his stupid idea.

As the only means of avoiding such exploitation eighteenth-century large controlled their self-confidence to planning for check-up and corresponding structural controls, lacking the involvement of political parties, but a sole party Totalitarianism government. They did not foresee that party development under free and Democratic circumstances would. It is a source of a modest and far more well-organized opinion of self-control. To gain control modern political leaders must build up the largest possible momentous. The only Communist economy that has prosper is China because Mao Tung understood that Socialism along does not work. China is a Directed Capitalism. It is a source of a modest and far more well-organized opinion of self-control. To gain control modern political leaders must build up the largest possible momentous. The only communist economy that has prosper is China because Mao Setun realized that Communism along does not work.

Remember when Mao declared to the world that Communism is an absurd and obsolete ideology and adopted the Capitalist-totalitarian as a communism reformed. They are under strong and constant pressure to change policies put forward by the more extreme wings of their parties, and to conciliate the good will of other classes and groups. It may state as a fact, which associate with the interior workings of politics will verify, that the influence of party leaders primarily exerted in comforting the presumptions and moderating the demands their supporters.

Anything increase in value of oppression is particularly dangerous. It is certain to strengthen the resentment of the class pointed at and likely to disaffect the more reasonable part of the party annoying it. These factors compelling moderation act with maximum intensity under the two-party system, but they are by no means lacking in control where the number of parties is greater. As a result of their action the old charge contrary to parties to the conclusion that they were by nature bossy has given way to the modern condemnation that they are unreasonably open-minded, thoughtful, and procrastinating, not to say cowardly.

Dishonesty about the eighteenth-century view that political of parties' factions were unavoidably corrupt a more well-balanced judgment must be made. The charge of corruption persists with great force in the political life of the most advanced nations. In none of them, however, is anything tolerated like the open and mocking bribery of Robert Walpole's Although the exact dates of Walpole's governance, dubbed the Robinocracy, are a matter of scholarly debate, the period 1721–1742. At that time the crown itself, the fountain of honor was the chief practitioner and beneficiary of the corrupt system. Contemporary executives not completely deprived of shady means of influencing party action, but such means are few and weak indeed compared with those employed in earlier centuries political parties.

Modern forms of corruption continue very largely from powerful interests outside the government running in the main through the leaders of the party organization. However much... involved the latter may be, they always reject and condemn such influences. Parties will afford to be disbelieving on this score when political power limited to the few group, virtually all of whom could share in fraudulent gains. To eliminate the corruptions in the present political fight and government shutdown we must modified the Electoral System and substitute it by the New Electoral Fusion System, that eliminates the two political parties and get back when the President George Washington was the head of the government for two mandates without political parties' intrusion.

Reference: 1 H. J. Ford, Rise and Growth of American Politics, p. 128.

SITUATIONS OF PARTY LIFE

American Political History

They cannot afford to be skeptical with the wider electorates of the present day. Popular education, the press, freedom of thought and speech, have all contributed to drive corruption in seditious and make it more problematic, overall, there is reason to believe that the danger from this foundation is much extents under the present party system than during the eighteenth and preceding centuries.

Certainly, it is much less in advanced countries with a well-developed party life than in retrograde Totalitarianism countries where such a development is impossible. There was a sound historical basis for the eighteenth-century view that parties were violent and destructive in their worse phases, oppressive and corrupt at best. Under the Republic and Democratic conditions of the nineteenth century parties must sloughing head off all the life-threatening and many of the slight forms of dishonesty existing during earlier and present regimes.

They have abandoned violence for peaceful processes, they witnessed an enormous increase in their size, organization, and material power witnessed a striking if not equally great elevation of their purposes, methods, and moral standing, nevertheless, party system is an invitation of the natural instinct of the man in its all of violence, verbal or in some cases physical, instigated by the press, the media, and political ambitions.

Today United States seems more like United States of America by the action of the political fight because the two party's existence. President Donald Trump, according with the improvements he has made to the economy, is improving, unemployed is the lowest in years, and because he wants to secure our borders, Nancy Pelosi as Democrat is ostracizing the President implanting the wall, to prevent undesirable element trespassing illegally our borders, I know that the president is a big mouth individual, but that doesn't mean he is not doing what the country need to secure our borders and make our Nation the best in the word. Democrats and Republican must be cheering hands in a united system without political parties, at the Fusion way.

References: Ancient Law (1861), and Popular Government (1885), by Sir Henry Maine, are particularly valuable, the reader should consult H. J. Ford, The Rise and Growth of American Politics (1898), especially Ch. XXV on Party. Efficiency, also Chaps. XXVI to XXVIII, from which derived. In his extended introduction to M. Ostrogorski Democracy and the Organization of Political Parties (1902), in The American Commonwealth.

ELECTORAL DIFFICULTIES REFERENCES

American Political History

References: (rev. ed., 1910), especially Parts III, "The Party System," IV, Public Opinion, and V, Illustrations and Reflections, and finally in Modern Democracies (1921), particularly Part I, Considerations Applicable to Democratic Government in General, the late Lord Bryce has given expression to his profound historical study and to his wide and prolonged observation of political parties in all the greater democracies of the world. The introduction to J. Macy, Party Organization and Machinery (1904), and his English Constitution (1903), especially Ch. XXXII, on The Composition of Political Parties, and Ch. XLII, on Political Parties Previous to 1832 of the latter, may consulted with profit. Among more recent works the following are of special value as contributions to the conditions of party life: W. Lippmann, A Preface to Politics (1913), particularly Chaps. I, IV, VII and VIII, also his Public Opinion (1922; A. L. Lowell, Public Opinion and Popular Government (1914), Part II of which is devoted to The Function of Parties, and by the same author, Public Opinion in War and Peace (1923, Ch. IV on Political Parties; and C.E. Merriam, The American Party System (1922), Chap. I, II, XII to XIV, inclusive. Three valuable studies from periodical literature are A. Morse, The Place of Party in the Political System, Annals of the American Academy of Political and Social Science Vol. II, p. 300 (Nov., 1891; A. D. McLaughlin, The Significance of Political Parties, Atlantic Monthly Vol. CI, p. 145 (Feb., 1908; and A. M. Low, Parties and National Welfare, North American Review Vol. CCV, p. 734 (May 1917).

CURRENTLY ELECTIONS MALFUNCTIONS

American Political History

The United States has a two-party system. The existence of only two dominant parties' systems from election rules that support single member districts and winner-take-all elections, is controversial and unconstitutional. Each district can have only one winner in any election, the person who receives the most votes. So, no matter how popular a third party, it will not win a single seat in any legislature until it becomes powerful enough in a single district to take an election. Remedy, no parties no problems.

From the beginning was no political parties, took Alexander Hamilton the idea of forming a political party, followed by Tomas Jefferson and that is why we have two political parties-armies, fighting each another for the thrill of supremacy and maybe personal gain. Eighteenth-century antagonism to parties shared by the Fathers founders, called Patriots, drew their strength principally from the ranks of the small homeowners, farmers, and shopkeepers. At the close of the war large bodies of the Loyalists, including many of their ablest leaders, emigrated to Canada. Judging from the controlling protagonist they played for a long time in the affairs of the British American Provinces, it is evident that if they had remained in the United States our earlier party history might have taken a rather more mediaevalist turn, or maybe not.

The Loyalists who remained accepted the result of the Rebellion. For the time being party divisions ceased to exist for a while. All the people were Whigs and republican in sentiment. The founders of the American Constitution shared to the full eighteenth-century bitterness to political parties, and they were wright.

It would be difficult to find a more persuasive and complete statement in brief compass of the case against them than that offered by Washington in his Farewell Address. "Let me warn you in the most solemn manner," he begins, against the restriction effects of the spirit of party primarily. Speaking in the Constitutional Convention on the amazing violence, and turbulence of the democratic spirit, Hamilton said that "when a great object of government is pursued, which seizes the popular passions, they spread like wildfire and become irresistible."

Widely as he differed from Hamilton's general political views, Madison agreed with him that in all cases where a majority are united by a mutual interest or passion, the rights of the minority are in danger. In general, the members of the convention shocked by the many historical extremes of popular parties, and the constitution which they framed is an old-fashioned refurbishment. Regardless of this hearty aversion to parties of two opposing political groups soon, regrettably, made their appearance on the floor of the convention itself. The small-state group Small states vs. Large states in the convention. That is why I recommend the eliminations of political parties and come back to President George Washington era, with the new Electoral Fusion System no partisan elections.

References:1 E. Porritt, Evolution of the Dominion of Canada, pp. 62, 72, 84. 2 Madison, Journal, edited by E. H. Scott, June 18, 1787, p. 182.3 Ibid., June 6, 1787, p. 119.

DEVELOPMENT OF PARTIES IN THE UNITED STATES

American Political History

The Electoral College is also a factor in sustaining the two-party system, with an eternal fight. Even if the popular vote in a state is close, the winner gets all the state's electoral votes. This arrangement makes it extremely difficult for a third party to win. In the 1992 presidential election, Ross Perot captured 20 percent of the popular vote across the country but did not receive a single electoral vote, and that was wrong when a substantial number of electors chooses him and had no credit for. Ross Perot was an eccentric millionaire that fail to become the balancing in the elections of 1992, as the third political power, to calmed the political fight against the two largest other two political groups, he fails to become the difference, because the bitterness of the others political parties.

Even though the Constitution did not make an application for political parties, two factions quickly appeared. One group, led by John Adams, and Alexander Hamilton, favored business development, a strong national government, and a loose interpretation of the Constitution, where not mentioned the existence of political parties. The followers of Thomas Jefferson, known as Democratic-Republicans System, called for a society based on small farms, a weak central government, and a strict interpretation of the Constitution. The election of 1800 had constitutional implications.

The Democratic-Republicans chose Jefferson for president and Aaron Burr for vice president. The party's electors split their ballots for both men, resulting in a draw that was resolved in the House of Representatives.

The Twelfth Amendment (1804), which required electors to vote separately for president and vice president, recognized that political parties would nominate one candidate for each office, in the new Electoral Fusion System there will be no Vice-president selection because automatically the candidate with more votes in the second place become the Vice-president, and the rest remain as advisors.

DEMOCRATS VS. REPUBLICAN

American Political History

The Civil War split the political parties in several ways. The Republican party's strength lay in the North; Abraham Lincoln did not receive a single electoral vote from a Southern state in 1860. The Democrats in the North divided into war Democrats, with Republican war. As you can appreciate political parties do more harm than benefits, political parties have continued up today, with the political conception of war up today this historical incident could happens again if we do not eradicate the parties problems.

During the 1820s, with the country expanding and many states dropping their property credentials for voting, the size of the electorate grew. Andrew Jackson took advantage of this change, and from his election in 1828, the Democrats straddling for an alliance with small farmers, westerners, and the procedure, the term used for the working class. The Whig Party (1834) supported business, a national bank, and a strong central government. When the Whigs broke up in the 1850s, the actual Republican Party replaced them.

This period saw significant changes in how political parties run. In the presidential election of 1832, candidates will be elect through a national convention of representatives from the states' parties, and a party platform, a statement of the party's beliefs and goals, was issued.

Michael Anguelo

DEVELOP MENTOF PARTIES PRIOR TO THE CIVIL WAR
American Political History

The political life of the American Colonies was a reconciliation on a small scale, colored by frontier conditions, or of the that of the mother country. In every Colony, according Colonies issuing to John Adams, divisions have always prevailed. In New York, Pennsylvania, Massachusetts, and all the rest, a court and country party has always contended. Whig and Tory disputed sharply before the Revolution and in every step during the Revolution. In the frequent conflicts that occurred between royal governors and Colonial assemblies the Tories supported the earlier and the Whigs the last.

Little if any trace left by the issues of that era upon our later life as a nation. But the origins of certain of our political methods and structures are to find in the Colonial period. Among these may mentioned the committee, the use of the ballot, and the custom of requiring that representatives shall be residents of the districts from which they selected. Colonial committees of correspondence are the lineal predecessors of our state central committees.

As loyalists the Tories contrasting the Uprising, many of Loyalist them fighting on the British side. It estimated that they, the Tories-vs Wigs. made up one third of the population of the colonies. Wigs Prominent among the Loyalists were the royal office-holding class, a substantial proportion of the great landed proprietors, and men of wealth, rank, and education.

The Whigs, who as supporters of the Revolution were favored a purely confederate government; the large-state group favored a nationwide government. The fundamental difference was whether political powers should draw from the states or from the people directly.

As finally drafted the Constitution stood for a compromise between these two views, but one which, overall, was more satisfactory to the large state than to the small-state group. Accordingly, the former favored the acceptance of the federal Constitution and took the name of Federalists.

Those who opposed its adoption called Anti-Federalists. Not until it agreed that certain amendments should added the alleged bill of rights of the Constitution was the opposition of the latter group overcome. With the adoption of the Constitution plus these amendments the issue between the two groups when settled, but not political parties mentioned for ended political parties are unconstitutional and must be prohibit.

References: Adams, Works, vol. x, p. 23. a H. J. Ford, Rise and Growth of American Politics, p. S.

FEDERALIST VS. DEMOCRATIC-REPUBLICANS

American Political History

1792-1824 General George Washington was elected President without opposition, he was opposed to the political division with the creation of political parties, his remark was "political parties divide the nation and it is dangerous, I warn you" and we can see the results of Hamilton and Jefferson political fight results after the formation of the two present-day parties the nation has not become the same.

Hamilton did not listen Washington recommends and called into his Cabinet, both Hamilton vs. Jefferson Between leaders of such divergent views and personality conflict was certain to ascend. Hamilton's followers formed the Federalist (Democrat party) which sustained the principle of authority, or expressed in constitutional form, the principle of broad construction.

The followers of Jefferson formed the (Republican party), which sometimes sardonically called by its opponents as the "Democratic Republican", or simply the (Republican party) Hamilton was an emigrant from one of the Caribbean's Island of Nevis in 1755, he could not run for the presidency, but he could have divided the nation with his party named Anti-federalist or Democratic party. Alexander Hamilton was a bastard (illegitimate). Indeed, John Adams and Thomas Jefferson never tired of calling him that, the 'Bastard Brat of a Scots-Peddler' who furious him time and again, Tomas Jefferson and Alexander Hamilton were enemies to their decease that occur one day after the other. Hamilton's socialism was an elitist Communism, much like the Obama socialism of today. Hamilton proposed the infant industry argument that for firms to compete, government protection and subsidy were necessary. In his Report on Manufactures, December 5, 1791, which Hamilton presented to Congress in his role as first Secretary of Treasury.

Political parties usually start to form when a country moves from a Monarchy or an Oligarchy to some form of government that has a larger number of people making decisions, usually in the form of an elected form. The reason this have a tendency to happen is because when a Monarch or Dictator holds all the power, there is no need for him or her to consult anyone to have something done. In a Democracy, or some other form of government where many people hold the power, it is very unlikely that a majority will agree on anything; thus, political parties are formed by people who have enough in common to reach a compromise and get bills passed. Over time, a political party may attract increasingly like inclined people who all are trying to reach the same goals of supremacy. While this might seem like a good thing, it is usually negative as it creates political parties with official party positions. It creates political parties that are averse to concession, and only work towards the official party goals, even if these goals are not endorsed by the public

THE FIRST POLITICAL FIGHT

Alexander Hamilton

Federalist

Thomas Jefferson

Anti-Federalist

• Believed in a strong central government	• Believed more power should be given to the states.
• Supported by merchants, lawyers doctors	• Supported by farmers, plantation owners
• Supported ratification of the Constitution	• Refused to ratify Constitution until of Bill of Rights was added.
• Believed the Constitution could be loosely interpreted (loose construction).	• Believed the Constitution should be adhered to word-for-word. No interpretation (strict construction).

THOMAS JEFFERSON HATED HAMILTON'S FINANCIAL PLAN!

THE NEW FUSION ELECTORAL SYSTEM

THE DIVISION

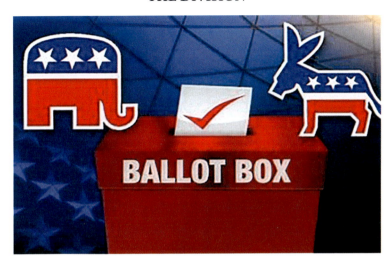

United States of America is a nation divides by three political parties, even is united also is disunited in a sense of political point of view, are three nations in one divided by political parties: Democrats, Republican and Independents. After the Civil War this political war, start between Whigs, Federalist, Anti Federalism, etc. The solution to this division is The New Electoral Fusion System, (Nonpartisan Elections), only the voter's opinion, "those whose agrees and those who's opposed, no need for political parties that divides us", it will terminate all this party's nonsense.

Prior the civil war, started a political war. Throughout its existence the Whig party suffered from the fact that it was so largely an "Anti-Party". It had brilliant leaders Clay, Webster, and John Quincy Adams and until 1840, Calhoun acted with it. But the old adage that "politics makes strange bed fellows" never had a better illustration than in the policies proposed on internal improvements, tariff, banking, and slavery appealed strongly to the agrarian element which then was numerically supreme. It is true that many a southern planter abhorred Jackson's levelling tendency quite as heartily as the poor farmer of the North applauded them. Nevertheless, planters feared the tide of industrialism which was rising higher and high beyond the Mason and Dixon line;19 moreover, they were glad to insure themselves against anti-slavery agitation by a political alliance with the more numerous agricultural populations in the North.

There was a large hold-over element of ancient Federalists in its membership whose former hatred of Jefferson ripened into virulent antagonism against Jackson. By their high tariff policy, the Whigs attracted manufacturers of New England and the Middle States; by their friendship to the United States Bank they gained adherents among the richer commercial classes; by advocating internal improvements they secured a following among the more ambitious promoters of new western communities. The party also included such varied elements as (1) the National Republican advocates of the "American System" a national bank, internal improvements, and protection; (2) nullifiers and extreme states' rights men; (3) a majority of the Anti-Masons;17 (4) former Democrats who had become disgruntled over Jackson's use of the veto, his distribution of patronage, and other "usurpations"; and finally (5) the many virulent opponents of the latter on personal or political grounds.

In order to hold these divergent groups together and to attract as many as possible of the new political organizations which sprang up during this period, the platforms of the party became models of circumvention, reticence, and brevity as to issues. Indeed, some of them consisted of eulogies on the candidates, notably that of 1848 which was given up entirely to a glorification of the record of General Zachary Taylor. The Whigs had chosen General William Henry Harrison, another war hero, without any platform at all in 1840. However, their third military hero, General Winfield Scott, went down to crushing defeat in the election of 1852. The Whigs were successful in two national elections only Whig (1840, 1848), but the fruits of the first of these victories were Tories, largely lost to them by the death of President Harrison one 1&4°'1 month after his inauguration. nomination had been to secure the support of a southern element which was opposed to the Democratic party.

CHAPTER 6

ELECTORAL PROBLEMS.

American Political History

Federalist and Republican Policies Following of the two parties, Washington the promotion of enterprises; and those, on the other hand, who are devotees of liberty in resistance to oppression and governmental interference. In accordance with their fundamental principles the Federalists (Democrat) advocated such policies as Hamilton's funding scheme, assumption of state debts, the first United States Bank, the excise, and a mildly protective tariff all of which were intended to increase the prosperity of the country and the power and financial influence of the national government, Hamilton was an emigrant from Caribbean's Islands and was not allowed to participates in a Presidential candidature because was not an US of American borne. The Republicans opposed these policies on the grounds that they were illogical, unconstitutional, and theoretical, that they exceeded the grants of the Constitution, and that they conferred such great powers upon the federal government as to make it a menace to the rights of the states and to the liberties of the people. In foreign affairs the sympathies of the Republicans were with revolutionary France, those of the Federalists with conservative England. With the outbreak of war between these powers in 1793, party lines were more sharply drawn and prejudiced bitterness speedily reached dimensions threatening to the stability of the infant Nation.

The main strength of the Federalist party was in New England; that of the Republican party in the South. Jefferson's following included, however, not only the planters of the latter region, but also small farmers and tradesmen of the Northern and Middle States. It must remember that suffrage was much restricted at this time by property and other qualifications prevailing under the first state constitutions.

Roughly speaking, one fourth of the male adults in the North and one half in the South excluded from voting. By temperament as well as by conviction George Washington was not a party man, he was an opponent to party's divisionism. During his two terms in the Presidency, he keeps this petition for the two mandates.

They attached to the principle of liberty, which from the constitutional point of view meant strict construction. The difference which thus arose between our two first national parties, and which has been more or less apparent as a continuing basis of division and political fight ever since, rested upon the op-position of those who are the advocates of power for the defense of order, the preservation of the rights of property protection. References: Woodburn, Political Parties and Party Problems, p. 10.

References:1 Woodburn, op. cit., p. 19. Solutions: American Political History and the Fusion Solution.

PARTIES PRIOR TO THE CIVIL WAR

American Political History

Adams life may fairly credit to the Federalist party. At the close of George Washington's administration, the Federalists succeeded in electing John Adams by a narrow majority over Thomas Jefferson. Four years later Thomas Jefferson defeated John Adams. At the same time the Federalists lost control of both houses of Congress, never again to regain it. Thereafter the fortunes of the party went steadily downhill, and in the election of 1820, it made no nomination for the Presidency. The defeat of John Adams in 1800 may attributed largely Downfall of to his personal unpopularity, to the open strife which had the Federal broken out between himself and Hamilton, and to the blast-18th century partying indignation caused by prosecutions under the Sedition Act.

But the later decline and ultimate disappearance of his party must explain on broader grounds. It must admit that during their twelve years of domination the Federalists had governed strongly and well. The general development of public sentiment was, however, sharply antagonistic to the principle of authority which they represented. Jeffersonian Republicanism, which sustained the principle of liberty, predicted this development, and firmly seated in power by the rising tide of Democratic feeling.

Finally, the policies pursued by Tomas Jefferson and his take legal action, Jefferson successors speedily set at rest the fear that Republican success and his successors meant weakness, disintegration, and anarchy. Indeed, the action regarding the purchase of Louisiana, the embargo, the protective tariff, and the second bank of the United States, are much more easily reconcilable with the Federalist principle of broad construction than with the Jeffersonian principle of strict structure.

While the Democratic-Republicans (is the Fusion of two government system, not political parties) thus proved themselves capable of pursuing a strong constructive national policy, the Federalists, now reduced to the position of an opposition, also departed from the purity of their earlier principles. They did not hesitate to attack the vigorous policies of the Democratic-Republicans as exceeding the powers granted by the Constitution, using for this purpose arguments originally made by Jefferson.

Federalist opposition to the War of 1812 reached a point little short of disloyalty, with the result that the popularity of the party still further declined. The report of the Federalist Hartford Convention, published in 1815, was fully as states' rights and secessionist in tone as the Virginia and Kentucky resolutions, inspired by Madison and Jefferson, respectively, in 1798. Era of with the disappearance of the Federalist in their good feel began the so-called era of good feeling. But the era of good feeling soon became reality a period of personal politics.

At the end of Monroe's second term four powerful leaders, J.Q. Adams, Clay, Crawford, and Jackson, all of whom called themselves Republicans, contested for the Presidency. It is not true, however, that the groups following these leaders inspired solely by personal loyalty. On the contrary, each of them offered a different interpretation of Jeffersonian principles. In the ensuing election, while Jackson had a large plurality of the popular vote, none of the candidates received a majority in the electoral college and the election thrown into the House of Representatives.

In the House, John Quincy Adams selected by the vote of thirteen states, Jackson receiving the vote of seven, and Crawford of four states. II.

Democrats VS. Whigs 1828-1860 Election of Four years later a campaign much greater personal Jackson, bitterness waged. Jackson's friends had not hesitated to charge that his defeat in 1824 was due to a corrupt bargain between Adams and Clay. The charge not authenticated, but it injected an immense amount of malice into the political situation. Meanwhile three greats new.

In the electoral college the vote stood.: Jackson, 99; Adams, 84; Craword, 41; Clay, 37. The popular vote in eighteen states was as follows: Jackson, 155,872; Adams, 105,321; Crawford, 44,282; Clay, 46,587.

References: T.H. McKee, National Conventions and Platforms, pp. 21-23.

PARTIES PREVIOUS TO THE CIVIL WAR

American Political History

History in the six other states electors chosen by the legislatures issues of domestic policy had come into the foreground, the bank, the tariff, and internal improvements. As a result, minor divisions disappeared end new party lines drawn which were to remain unbroken for more than a quarter of a century.

On the one hand were the National Republicans, later to called Whigs, who nominated Adams for a second term. On the other were the Democratic-Republicans, more commonly called Jacksonian Democrats and later plain Democrats, who supported Jackson. At the election of 1828, the latter was victorious, receiving an overwhelming majority in the electoral college and a substantial majority of the popular vote.1 The accession of Andrew Jackson to the Presidency a new mark the beginning of a new epoch in American politics epochs. In the first place his elevation to power was due to the politics.

Enfranchisement of the great mass of the plain people of the country. Most of the new Western states admitted to the Union prior to 1828 had set up what amounted to adulthood suffrage. A frontier population, poor and struggling, but independent and virile throughout, cannot be expected to look with favor on property qualifications. By emigrating to the West disfranchised mechanics and laborers from the more aristocratic seaboard states not only improved their economic condition, but also bought the full rights of citizenship. The example of the new commonwealths led to the abandonment or reduction to a nominal basis of the property qualifications in the older states. Jackson not only owed his elevation to the recent Democracy enfranchised masses, he belonged to them and typified of Jackson them thoroughly. All his six predecessors in the presidency had been aristocrats by birth and position, if not by conviction. Even Thomas Jefferson, democratic as were his beliefs, lived amid the surroundings of a Virginia country, In the electoral college the vote stood: Jackson, 178; Adams, 83. The popular vote of twenty-three states was, for Jackson, 647, 231; for Adams, 509, 097.

In only one state, South Carolina, were the electors chosen by the legislature. In the six other states electors chosen by the legislatures. References: McKee, opacity., pp.25, 26.2Cf.chap.xiv.S

PARTIES CACUS CHOOSE NOMINIES

American Political History

King Caucus conquered gentleman. (refers to the system in which party elites would choose nominees for major national offices). Jackson, on the other hand, was born in poverty, he shared all the vicissitudes and struggles of frontier experience, and he had both the qualities and the defects bred by such an experience. Like Jefferson he was a Democrat system by conviction but in practice he was a Democrat to a far greater degree than his illustrious predecessor. The Democratic confusion which made Jackson president caused profound changes in party and governmental methods of which have endured to the present day. Prior to this time, it had been customary to make presidential nominations by legislative caucus. King Caucus, now dethroned, and the delegate convention set in his place, down to and including the campaign of 1828, no conventions held. In 1832 for the first time all presidential candidates nominated by conventions.

The Anti-Masonic party was the first to accept the innovation. It held its first national convention in September 1830, at Philadelphia, 10 states sending delegates. This body issued a call for a second convention which was held at Baltimore a year later with delegates present from thirteen states. It soon became the practice of the conventions to issue formal platforms having declarations of party principles and statements of proposed party policies. Presidential electors formerly chosen in number of States by the legislatures were in future with few exceptions elected by common vote.

In the presidential election of 1792, the electors chosen by the legislatures in 9 out of 15 States. 6 of the 24 States still chose electors in this way in 1824. In 1828, South Carolina was the only state to choose its electors by assembly. Popular vote for presidential electors, the passage of resolutions at political meetings and conventions became a widespread practice during the Jacksonian period

Four years later the Whig convention adopted its first formal platform. A series of ten resolutions passed by the Young Men's National Republican Convention, which met at Washington, May 11, 1832, is sometimes spoken of as the first platform of the Whig party, but as a matter of fact the presidential and vice-presidential candidates of that party had already been chosen by a convention proper held at Baltimore, on December firth of the preceding year 1833.

PARTIES AND THE CIVIL WAR

American Political History

It continued the practice down to the Civil War. One or two cases have occurred since. Under the old system the electors of a state often divided between the parties. The newer system of popular election on a general ticket usually throws the whole weight of the state into one or the other party column. It therefore enormously increases the importance of a popular majority, particularly in large and pivotal States. Jackson himself made every effort to obtain an amendment to the Constitution providing for the direct election of the President by popular vote, but without success. As a result of the changes noted above, however, the same result approximated as closely as it is possible through the awkward machinery provided by the Constitution.

Not only in party methods, but in the structure of the government itself Jackson's administration made profound and permanent changes. His immediate predecessors had fallen into the habit of deferring to Congress to such an extent that the primacy of the latter accepted. Conceiving himself as the direct representative of the people in a gigantic struggle against privilege, Jackson did not hesitate to join issue with the legislative branch.

Prior to his administration the veto power had considered in the light of an advisory function and used altogether in but nine instances. Jackson's twelve vetoes descended upon Congress like the blows of an iron flail. Political leaders of the older and more aristocratic type had looked with favor of office holding. Rotation in office advocated by the Jacksonian element as the truly democratic system. The number of political appointments made by Jackson was small indeed compared with the achievements of his successors. References: 'Ford, op. cit., p. 180., Fusion Electoral System no partisan elections.

PARTIES AND ELECTORAL PROBLEMS

American Political History

As contrasted with the moderation in this respect of his predecessors, however, Jackson's administration marks a startling innovation from which the spoils system with all its Electors chosen on general ticket Jackson's vetoes Rotation and spoils Democratic planks 1840-1860 National Republicans or Whigs Discordant elements among the Whigs countless terms. The position which the party was to maintain on the slavery issue found expression as follows: Congress has no power under the Constitution to interfere with or control of the domestic institutions of the several States.

Al efforts by Abolitionists or others made to induce Congress to interfere with questions of slavery, or to take incipient steps in relation thereto, are calculated to lead to the most alarming and dangerous consequences, and endanger the stability and permanence of the Union. In every national platform from 1840 to 1860 the Democrats reiterated with few slight changes the above profession of their party faith. Nor can it have denied that, during their long and seldom interrupted tenancy of power from Jackson to Buchanan, they conducted their pledges with commendable fidelity.

it sometimes referred to as the National Democratic party, showing that the old prejudice against the latter term had complete, indeed, it had bought popularity. But the Jacksonian element had so thoroughly pre-empted the word that the National Republicans had to cast about

Opposition to King Andrew and all his works was the cement that bound together the discordant elements which formed the National Republican party. Early in its existence for another title. In 1834, they began to assume the name "Whig," which commended itself not only because of the luster derived from historic party battles in England but also because of its association with the struggle of the Colonists against Imperial usurpation by force without rights, during the American Revolution.

PARTIES PRIOR TO THE CIVIL WAR
American Political History

United States of America is a nation divides in three political parties, even is united also disunited in a sense of political point of view, are three nations in one divided by political parties: Democrats, Republican and Independents. After the Civil War this political war, start between Whigs, Federalist, Democrats, Anti Federalism, etc. The solution to this division is The New Electoral Fusion System, Nonpartisan Elections, only the people's opinion, "those that agree and those who opposed, no need for political parties that divides us, it will terminate all this party's nonsense. Prior the civil war, started a political war. Throughout its existence the Whig party suffered from the fact that it was so largely an Anti-Party was essential. It had brilliant leaders Clay, Webster, and John Quincy Adams and until 1840, Calhoun acted with it. But the saying that politics makes strange bed people, never had a better illustration than in the heterogeneous make-up of the Whig party.

The policies proposed on internal improvements, tariff, banking, and slavery appealed strongly to the agrarian element which then was numerically supreme. It is true that many a southern planter detested Jackson's levelling tendency quite as heartily as the poor farmer of the North applauded them. Nevertheless, planters feared the tide o and high beyond the Mason and Dixon line;19 moreover, they were glad to insure themselves against anti-slavery agitation by a political alliance with the more agricultural populations in the North.

There was a large hold-over element of ancient Federalists in its membership whose former hatred of Jefferson ripened into virulent antagonism against Jackson. By their high tariff policy, the Whigs attracted manufacturers of New England and the Middle States; by their friendship to the United States Bank they gained adherents among the richer commercial classes; by advocating internal improvements they secured a following among the more ambitious promoters of new western communities. The party also included such varied elements as: (3) majority of the AntiMasons;17, the Party was formed in Upstate New York in February 1828 former Democrats who had become discontented over Jackson's use of the veto, his distribution of benefaction, and other usurpations; and finally the many lethal enemies of the latter on personal or political estates.

To hold these divergent groups together and to attract as many as possible of the new political organizations which sprang up during this period, the platforms of the party became models of evasion, reticence, and brevity as to issues. Indeed, some of them consisted of acclamations on the candidates, notably that of 1848 which given up entirely to a glorification of the record of General Zachary Taylor.

The Whigs had chosen General William Henry Harrison, another war hero, without any platform at all in 1840. However, their third military hero, General Winfield Scott, went down to crushing defeat in the election of 1852. The Whigs were successful in two national elections only Whig (1840, 1848), but the fruits of the first of these victories were Tories, largely lost to them by the death of President Harrison one month after his inauguration. As vice-presidential candidate with Writing in Jackson's administration De Tocqueville makes some interesting and prophetic remarks on this subject.

References: Cf. Democracy in America, vol. Ii, Ch. Xxv. D the AntiMasonic party formed in opposition to certain alleged abuses on the part of that and other secret societies. It was active from 1828 to 1832, in New York and neighboring states, where for a time it was the most important Democratic organization, the latter they had nominated John Tyler of Virginia, who was temporarily affiliated with their party, but who at bottom was an eclectic Democrat. The sole purpose of his nomination had been to secure the support of a southern element which opposed to the Democratic party.

References: page n77 Nonpartisan Elections, supporters of Clay, Webster, and John Quincy Adams, Calhoun in the proposition of dropping the political parties in our elections system.

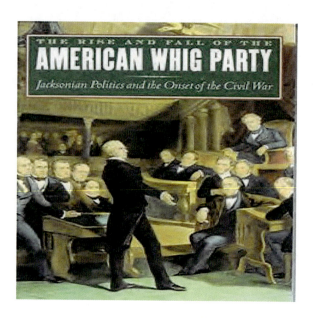

MORE ELECTORAL PROBLEMS

American Political History

Soon after Tyler's accession to the Presidency the true nature of his convictions became clear. Before the end of his term the Whig members of Congress virtually read him out of the party, declaring that all political connection between them and John Tyler was at an end from that day forth Slavery with the rise of the slavery issue to a position of paramount and the importance in American politics the inappropriateness of the elements his making up the Whig party became even more apparent.

There were conscience Whigs, who were radical antislavery men; there were Cotton Whigs, who wanted peace at any price on the question for the benefit of the cotton trade; there were strong pro-slavery Whigs in the South; and every possible grade of interest and indifference between these various groups. Strenuous efforts made to conciliate these irreconcilable tendencies and to hold the party together despite them.

In the campaign of 1852, the Whigs made a last desperate attempt to support party unity based on the Compromise of 1850. Their platform for that campaign contained the following plank accepting even the fugitive Slaves law as a finality a step which sealed the fate of the party: That the

The New Fusion Electoral System

series of acts of the Thirty-Second Congress, the act known as the fugitive Slave law included, are received and acquiesced in by the Whig party of the United States as a settlement in principle and substance of the dangerous and exciting questions which they embrace, and the integrity of the Union.

The adoption of this ill-starred plank justified in large part Swallow the remark that the Whig party died of an attempt to swallow in the Fugitive Slave law. In the ensuing election Soon after Tyler's accession to the Presidency the true nature of his convictions became clear. Before the end of his term the Whig members of Congress virtually read him out of the party, declaring that all political connection between them and John Tyler was at an end from that day forth Slavery with the rise of the slavery issue to a position of paramount and the importance in American politics the inappropriateness of the elements his making up the Whig party became even more apparent.

There were conscience Whigs, who were radical antislavery it secured the electoral vote of but four states. The Whig convention of 1856 accepted the nominees of the American Know-Nothing party, but their joint popular vote fell far behind that of the newly formed Republican party and they obtained the electoral vote of only one state. Old line conservative Whigs made up a large part of the Constitutional Union party in 1860, but the Whig party proper was moribund in 1852, and virtually dead in1856.

Four years later the Democratic party interrupted by the Slavery same issue. The anti-slavery agitation which came to play so disorders deeply crumbling a part in American politics at this time Democrats dated back to the early thirties. William Lloyd Garrison issued the first number of the Liberator on January 1, 1831. The New England Anti-Slavery Society formed in 1832 and expanded a year 144later into the American AntiSlavery Society.

Party organization and activity in general, they were willing to concede the right of states which wished to preserve their domestic institution to do so, moderate elements of the population anti-slavery ant agitation made many converts. The latter looked upon the question of slave ration not only as one of morals but also those held by theoretical radicals at the present time, and in accordance with these ideas he and his followers refused to vote or to organize for political action. Among Garrison himself led the of the movement, which in addition to abolition espoused several extremist ideas not unlike the Whigs and to the Democrats.

109

It was the first step party of which, led to the formation of the Republican party. 1840 The new Liberty party received only seven thousand votes in 1840, but it polled sixty-five thousand votes in 1844. Four years later large reinforcements received from the conscience, or Free Soil, Whigs. Meanwhile, the Democratic party had begun to disintegrate on the slavery issue.

ADDITIONAL ELECTORAL PROBLEMS
American Political History

Many of its members in the North stoutly opposed to the extension of slavery in the territories. Led by the Barnburners of New York they also began to be gathering to the new movement, which now took the name of the National Free-Soil party. Its platform for 1848 boldly announced that Congress has no more power to make a Slave than to make a King; no more control to institute or establish slavery than to institute or establish a monarchy; that we accept the issue which the slave power has forced upon us; and to their demand for more slave states and more slave territory, our calm but final answer is: No more slave states and no more slave territory.

The strength of the Free Soil movement fell off somewhat in 1852, as a result of the compromise legislation of 1850 and the general effort made to treat that legislation as a final disposition of the slavery question. Nevertheless, the party reaffirmed the position taken in 1848, and added a vigorous and demand its immediate and total repeal. All the hopes of the Finality Men that the slavery question had been predisposed of by the legislation of 1850 crushed when the Kansas-Nebraska bill passed in 1854. By this act the Missouri Compromise cancelled and territory which since 1820 they considered beyond the reach of opened to dispute slavery. Immediately all the Anti-Nebraska forces began to draw together in opposition to the further extension of slavery.

REPUBLICAN PARTIE PREVIOUS TO THE CIVIL WAR
American Political History

It was the last step that precipitated the formation of the Republican party. Shifts of party allegiance which occurred on a grand scale at that time helped by a curious political interval, novel enough then but destined to repeated often in American politics. Immigration had been pouring into the country with great rapidity during the forties and fifties, and the participation of the newly enfranchised foreign element in politics marked by certain uncivilized abuses which aroused the hostility of large numbers of Native Americans.

Against this foreign influence a secret movement launched, the members of which promised to fake illiteracy when questioned about it. Consequently, they came to call Know-Nothings party. must rule America; and to this end native born citizens should be selected for all state, federal, and municipal government employment, in preference.

By 1854 the new movement had reached considerable strength, carrying local elections in states both North and South. In 1856 it held a national convention, nominating candidates who accepted later by the rest of the Whigs. Its platform for that year had the following planks: Americans Opposition to any union between church and state. Non-committal as to slavery, the Know-Nothings sometimes derided as Do-Nothings on that issue. Nevertheless, the movement detached large numbers of Whigs and Democrats from their old party allegiance.

With the subsiding of the anti-alien movement these men found it easier than would otherwise have been the case to join with former Free Spoilers in the organization of the Republican party. In the election of 1856, the new party revealed surprising Republican strong point, carrying all New England and in addition the states party, 1856 of New York, Ohio, Michigan, Wisconsin, and Iowa.

Even though the Democrats were victorious, a sharp division of sentiment began to appear among them. To Fire-Eaters in the South the demonstration of Republican strength was proof positive that their unusual institution noticeable for demolition. This conviction carried them to lengths which alienated the considerations of northern Democrats. Public opinion in both sections embittered by the struggle for Kansas and by John Brown's raid. The decision in the Dred Scott case, which virtually pronounced the goals of the Republicans to be unconstitutional, merely intensified the spirit of that party, but it drove still deeper the wedge between northern and southern Democrats. In 1860 came the inevitable torn apart, the southern Democrats Issues of nominating Breckinridge and the northern Democrats nominating Douglas in 1860.

Michael Anguelo

REPUBLICANS VS. DEMOCRATS

ELECTORAL COMPLICATIONS.

American Political History

On the great issue of the campaign the position of the parties may had summed up as follows: (1) the Republicans held that slavery should become barred from national territory by national power; (2) the southern Democrats held that it should be protected in national territory by national power; (3) the northern Democrats proclaimed the doctrine of national non-interference and of popular sovereignty, according to which the question of slavery should be left to the decision of the white people of each territory; and (4) the Constitutional Unionists were evasive on the slavery issue, recognizing no political principles other than the Constitution of the country, the union of the states, and the enforcement of the laws.

From the days of Jeffersonian Republicans and Hamiltonian Federalists onward the influence of American parties was strongly exerted as a nationalizing and unifying force. By associating great masses of men regardless of state lines in the pursuit of common political aims they had helped to break down much of the isolation and animosity which existed between the Colonies.

In the extended period under consideration they had brought about a uniform basis of suffrage throughout the country and built up great national political organizations designed throughout upon a uniform plan and pursuing uniform methods. That they faced each other in 1860 upon sectional lines was not the fault of parties but despite them. For years, indeed, Whigs and Democrats alike had struggled incessantly, but in the end unsuccessful, for party unity through compromise. The Union was not broken up because sectional parties had been formed, but sectional parties were formed because the Union had become sectionalized.

Lincoln carried every state north of the Mason and Dixon line except New Jersey, and from that state he received four out of seven votes in the electoral college. In addition, he carried the Far Western states of California and Oregon. The southern wing of the Democracy received the whole electoral vote of that section, excepting that of the border states, Virginia, Kentucky, and Tennessee, which went to the Constitutional Union; and of Missouri, which carried by the northern Democrats.

The popular vote was as follows: Lincoln, 1,866,352; Breckinridge, 847,514; Bell, 587,830; and Douglas, 1,375.157. In the electoral college the large popular vote of the last named counted for little because it scattered throughout the northern states where it wiped out by Republican majorities.

References: A H. E. von Hoist, quoted by W. Wilson, Derision and Reunion, p. 212.

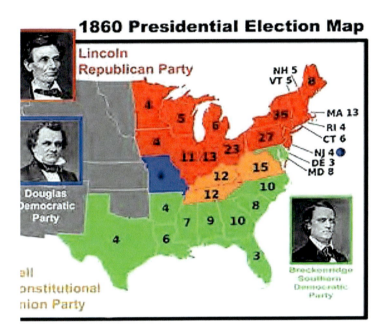

REPUBLICAN VS. DEMOCRATS

American Political History

That can offer, however, resort to war in 1860 meant the failure of fundamentally the breach was due to differences of soil and climate and to those economic conditions dependent upon them, particularly after the invention of textile machinery and the cotton gin made slavery seem essential to the prosperity of the South. After seventy years of union and peaceful constitutional development the threat of secession, so often resorted to by defeated parties in the past, was to become a reality.

Leadership had failed; the basic issues of American politics were now giving to the tragic mediators of the armament. Since the publication of the first edition of the present work the whole development of political parties in the United States has been deliberated, with reference to the economic background.

Reference: by A. N. Holcombe, Political Parties of Today (1924); and by C. A. Beard, The American Party Battle (1928). A number of valuable special studies have made their appearance, among them C. G. Bowers, Jefferson and Hamilton, the Struggle for Democracy in America (1925) and Party Battles of the Jackson Period (1922); E. M. Carroll, Origins of the Whig Party (1925), which presents a thorough study, illustrated by maps, of the campaigns from 1832 to 1840 inclusive; R. F. Nichols, The Democratic Machine, 1850-1840 (1923), an interesting detailed study of the genus politician during that period; A. W. Crandall, Early History of the Republican Party (1930), discussing that subject with a wealth of materials to and including the campaign of 1856; H. Minor, The Story of the Democratic Party (1928); F. R. Kent, History of the Democratic Party (1928), the first full length portrait of that party from Thomas Jefferson to Alfred E. Smith, telling both its undeniable merits and its undeniable faults; W. S. Myers, History of the Republican Party (1928),

A story of success and failure covering the nearly three-quarters of a century of the party's existence; Presidential Years (1928), a colorful collection of campaign personalities, intrigues, arguments, cartoons, and songs from 1787 to 1860; D. C. Seitz, Lincoln, the Politician (1931), a realistic yet sympathetic biography of the great emancipator, which reveals his skill in manipulating politics and politicians before and during the Civil War.

ELECTORAL COMPLICATIONS REFERENCES

American Political History

"Of the general treatises on political parties cited Reference: under Ch. I, J. A. Woodburn, Political Parties and Party Problems (1903), devotes by far the largest amount of space to the historical aspect of the subject. H. J. Ford, The Rise, and Growth of American Politics (1898), is the most brilliant and original contribution made in this field during the last generation.

E. Stanwood, A History of the Presidency (2 vols., latest ed., 1928), presents documents and statistics, with comment, on presidential conventions, candidates, and platforms down to and including 1916. E. E. Robinson, The Evolution of American Parties (1924) presents briefly in the order of their appearance the succession of political parties, giving attention to their organization.

The earlier compendiums of T. H. McKee supplanted in 1924 by K. H. Porter, National Party Platforms, complete from 1840 to date. Among the larger comprehensive works dealing wholly or in part with this period the following are of prime importance: C. A. and M. R. Beard, The Rise of American Civilization (1927); H. Adams, History of the United States, 1801-1817 (9 vols. 1889-1891); A B. Hart, editor, The American Nation: A History, 1300-1017 (28 vols., 1903-1918); R. Hildreth, History of the United States, 1402-1821 (6 vols., 1849-1856); Constitutional and Political History of the United States, 1750-1861 (8 vols, new ed. 1899. J. J. Schouler, under the Constitution, 1783-1865 (6 vols.,1894-1899; J. B. McMaster, A History of the People of the United States from the Revolution to the Civil War (8 vols.,1883-1912); W. Wilson, A History of the American People,1492-1900 vols.5, 1902) and J. Winsor, editor, Narrative and Critical History of America, 1000-1850 (8 vols., 1884-1889).

For briefer treatment of political topics see J. S. Bassett, A Slwrt History of the United States, 1402-1020 (1921). On special periods or subjects of more than usual political importance the following are useful: J.S. Bassett, The Federalist System; E. Channing, The Jeffersonian's System. W. MacDonald, Jacksonian Democracy; F.J. Turner, Rise of the New West. A. B. Hart, Slatery and Abolition; and T. C. Smith, Parties and Slavery.

Historical treatises devoting special attention to the growth of political parties have been published as follows: J. P. Gordy, Political History of the United States (1902); A. Johnson, American Political History, 1763-1876, edited and supplemented by J. A. Woodburn (1905); and S. D. Fess, History of Political Theory and Party Organization in the United States (1910). The more important historical works written from economic viewpoints closely related to party development are: E. L. Bogart, Economic History of the United States (1908); K. Coman, Industrial History of the United States (rev. ed., 1910); D. R. Dewey, Financial History of the United States (1903); F.W. Taussig, Tariff History of the United States (1905); and E. Stanwood; Tariff Controversies of the Nineteenth Century (2 vols.,

1903). For further historical references, consult the Guide to the Study and Reading of American History (1912), by E. Channing, A. B. Hart, and F. J. Turner.

REPUBLICANS VS. DEMOCRATS ELECTORAL COMPLICATIONS
American Political History

The people of the United States so thoughtfully used system to the two-party system that they are tending to accept it as a matter of course. Taking the more advanced countries of the world, however, it is the exception rather than the rule. In English politics the two-party system has also prevailed, although there are indications at present that it may break up. In the countries of continental Europe, on the other hand, party divisions are more many. As a rule, four, five, or more parties contend for power in each of these countries, which I consider is a deadly demonstration of Democracy-Republic fusion systems when political forces divide the nation in factions. Criticism of Political theorists and adherents of minority parties the two-often criticize the existing two-party system of the party system TJm'ted states and sup-porter the adoption of a multiparty system in its place. From time to time the formation of a new party or parties of some definite character pro-posed in the hope of bringing about a division of the strength of the old political organizations such that three or more groups may challenge our elections on unfluctuating terms.

The chief argument upon which critics of our present system rely is that the two major parties differ very slightly in essentials and not at all in non-essentials. Being so balanced in voting strength and having so many divergent groups within their ranks, they fight afraid of positive statements on matters of policy, prefer-ring instead every form of compromise, delay, and circumvention. The certainty that control will become deliberated upon one or the other of them at each election fascinates into their ranks substantial numbers of place hunters and privilege seekers who care everything for patronage and incomes, nothing for principles or policies, but for political or personal advantage convictions, turns from politics in indifference or repulsion. It is undeniable that there is considerable truth in this absence of formal accusation.

CHAPTER 7

REPUBLICAN PARTY DURING CIVIL WAR.

THE WAR AND RECONSTRUCTION, 1860-1876.

DEVELOPMENT OF PARTIES IN THE UNITED STATES 1860-1912.

During the years from 1860 to 1912 two periods of party history may distinguished. The first 1860-1876 war and reconstruction given over to the great issues. From 1876 on, economic questions, the tariff, currency, railroads, trusts, labor, and the high cost of living, were paramount until 1912, and indeed to 1914 when the outbreak of the World War turned the attention of the people to a new set of issues. With the outbreak of the Rebellion a considerable number of Combat Democrats in the North gave valiant support to the Union cause. Other elements of the party wanted to conciliate the South, condemning both Abolition Fanatics and Southern Fire-eaters, whom they held equally responsible for the bloody struggle. Few extremists among them the hated traitors, Butternuts, and Copperheads, were guilty of disloyal exclamations and excessive clatter.

The Democratic platform of 1864 denounced executive usurpations "under the pretense of a military necessity or war power higher than the Constitution, and declared in words that were often brought up to outbreak the party, that after four years of failure to restore the Union by the experiment of war and justice, humanity, liberty, and the public welfare demand that immediate efforts be made for a termination of the conflicts, with a view to the ultimate convention of the states or other peace-loving means, to the end that peace may be restored on the basis of the federal union of the states. It is only fair to add that in his letter of acceptance, McClellan, the party's nominee for the Presidency, renounced this plank.

The Republican party also had its radicals on slavery and war policies as well as others of more moderate views. Abolition will become recalled, was not one of the party's purposes either in 1856 or in 1860. As a war measure, however, President Lincoln acted of this step as far as slaves in the rebellious states were concerned, by his famous Emancipation Proclamation of January 1, 1863. Even this did not satisfy the Radical Republicans, who held a convention in May, 1864, and adopted a platform which, while demanding that the rebellion must be suppressed by force of arms and without compromise, severely criticized by implication some of Lincoln's war measures, pronounced in favor of a one term policy for the Presidency, and even went the length of demanding the confiscation of the lands of the rebels John C. Fremont, who had been the Republican candidate in 1856, nominated for the Presidency by this convention. Shortly thereafter Lincoln unanimously is denominated on quantity the first ballot at the Baltimore convention. The platform unqualifiedly approved his administration, demanded the unconditional surrender of the rebels and the absolute and complete extirpation of slavery from the soil of the Republic.

Of less immediate but of greater permanent importance were the planks favoring a homestead law and a protective tariff, because of which the famous union of hearts between manufacturers and farmers were cemented. For Vice-President, Andrew Johnson of Tennessee, a Union man formerly affiliated with the Democratic parties were nominate. During the campaign the candidates of the Radical Republicans removed and the support of that wing of the party given to Lincoln and Johnson, who triumphantly carried every state then in the Union, except for three.

The downfall of the Confederacy followed early in 1865. Before the end of the year the Thirteenth Amendment to the Constitution, abolishing slavery within the United States, declared in force.

A considerable number of northern Republican politicians emigrated to the South at this time, and under the protection of federal bayonets the conflict reconstruction became the Presidency order of the day. Lincoln's conciliatory attitude upon this all time to come, never to be renew or agitated. Upon the conclusion of Thus, the questions of departure and slavery, which for so long had overshadowed our political life, were, by the admission even of the Democrats, settle convention of 1864, the gathering at Baltimore took the title officially of the National Union convention.

References: A. Beard, opposite. pp 82-143.Democratic platform, 1868, K. H. Porter, National Party Platforms (1924), Johnson Study in Courage (1929); also R. W. Winston, Andrew Johnson, Plebeian and Patriot (1928); and historical works on his period by C. G. Bowers and G. F. Milton referred to under Book Notes at end of this chapter. Parties 1860-1912, to their rights in the Union under the Constitution.

PARTIES 1860-1912-ELECTORAL PROBLEM

American Political History

The reconstruction was well known, but to the irreparable loss of the country he removed by the hand of a murderer six weeks after his second inauguration. Johnson shared Lincoln's moderate views on reconstruction, but after succeeding to the Presidency his words and acts in giving them effect were anything but moderate.

Soon he became involved in open hostility with large Republican majorities in both houses of Congress, the result being that he given impotent, although by no means voiceless.

In the end he run-away conviction on impeachment proceedings by the margin of a single vote in the Senate. The reconstruction Under the circumstances the Republican party naturally ought to attitude to the support of its more radical element in Congress, whose motto about all southern questions was sensitive reconstruction.

By the Reconstruction Act of March 2, 1867, the separating states except for Tennessee divided into five districts, which positioned under the command of generals of the army empowered to direct the processes of reconstruction. Readmission to the Union made dependent upon of number of difficult conditions, including acceptance of the Fourteenth Amendment A considerable number of northern Republican politicians emigrated to the South at this time, and under the protection of federal bay one organized... the innocent Negro voters. As they remained said to carry all their possessions in the homemade traveling bags of the period, these immigrants came to call Carpetbaggers. Under their influence legislatures chosen by Negroes spoiled in a celebration of luxury and corruption which left the state governments loaded with enormous debts. Meanwhile the most influential white citizens of the South were excluding from the license because of their participation in the uprising. Questions of The Presidential election of 1868 fought out in 1868 these subjects. In its platform of that year the Democratic party hotly arraigned the Radical party, as it called the Republicans, for its unparalleled tyranny and oppression in exposing 10 states, in time of profound peace, to military absolutism and Negro authority, and demanded their immediate restoration Recent biographers have found much to say in defense of Andrew Johnson.

References: L. P. Stryker, Andrew Johnson.

ELECTION COMPLICATIONS HISTORY
American Political History

The Republicans nominated and elected General Grant on a platform congratulating the country on the assured success of the reconstruction policy of Congress, but added a clause favoring the removal of the disqualifications and restrictions imposed upon the late rebels in the same measure as the spirit of disloyalty will expire out and as may be consistent with the safety of the loyal people. In 1869, the Fifteenth Amendment proposed, and made a further condition for the readmission of the states not already reconstructed. Thus, the Republican party which began its career merely as a union party opposed to the further extension of slavery found itself forced by the logic of events to take the other steps of abolition, of conferring citizenship upon freedmen, and finally of trying to secure for them the right of suffrage.

Of these policies the effort to prevent denial of the vote on account of race, color, or previous condition of servitude was least successful in practice and has subjected to by far the greatest amount of criticism, much of it justified by subsequent happenings.

Nevertheless, the motives compelling the attempted grant of suffrage were strong, at least from the point of view of party convenience, although varied as to moral content. The earlier Republicans had made much of the Jeffersonian doctrine that all men are created equal, quoting it in their platforms of 1856 and 1860; now they called upon to live up to it.

Moreover, they had accepted the services of many Negroes and former Slaves during the war and were thus guaranteed by a debt of gratitude. It also argued with great force that the freedmen could defend the gifts of liberty and citizenship only if they came armed with the ballot. Finally, the leaders of the Republican party were by no means certain that they commanded a popular majority throughout the country.

ELECTORAL DIFFICULTIES

American Political History

Strutted states were admitted to congressional representation, but the Force bills were passed to suppress Ku-Klux disorders. Even in the North, however, a repulsion of feeling had set in against the detailed policy of the radical Republicans, which led to the first serious break in the party that had occurred since its organization.

A group of liberal Republican leaders, who favored not only a general absolution, but also civil service reform, specie payments, and a revenue tariff, called a national convention at Cincinnati in 1872. But the nomination of this convention captured for Horace Greeley, the somewhat erratic editor of the New York Tribune, who was one of the most extreme protectionists living and who, moreover, was by no means satisfactory to the civil-service-reform element of the new movement.

Nevertheless, the Democratic party accepted both the platform and the nominees of the liberal Republicans. General Grant was the choice of the regular Republicans for a second term and re-elected by a larger number of votes, both popular and electoral, than had casted for him four years earlier. The campaign of 1872 also marked the first appearance in national politics of the Prohibition and Greenback parties.

Although the liberal Republicans did not elect Greeley in 1872, public sentiment turned strongly in favor of their policies during Grant's second administration. A general amnesty passed in that year, but disturbances continued south of the Mason and Dixon line. Despite the President's efforts to sustain the Reform Act of 1872, the civil service of the country demoralized to an extreme degree by political appointees, and in 1874 Congress refused to vote funds for the further enforcement of the law.

The Salary Grab was most unpopular, and the widespread dishonesty revealed by the investigations of the Credit Mobilier and Whisky Ring deeply discredited the party in control. Effects of the shift of public sentiment toward a more liberal policy were made manifest in the Republican national convention of 1876, which refused to nominate James G. Blaine, the attractive but not clean star of the congressional machine, and named instead Rutherford B. Hayes, a devoted friend of civil service reform and a resolute enemy of corruption. The Democratic party nominated Samuel J. Tilden, and for the first time since the Civil War polled most of the popular vote of the country.

PARTIES 1860-1912-71 SOUTH AFTER RECONSTRUCTIO
American Political History

Tilden received without question 184 votes in the electoral college, lacking but one of the number necessary to elect him. Hayes received, also without question, 163 votes, the returns from four states contested. Of the latter, three were the southern states of South Carolina, Louisiana, and Florida, the reconstructed Republican governments of which enjoyed the support of federal troops. In the end the Electoral Commission which created to break the deadlock decided every competition by a strict party vote in favor of Hayes, giving him the election by 185 to 184 electoral votes. One of the first acts of Hayes's administration was the with the solid withdrawal of federal troops from southern states. The long and bitter process of reconstruction thus ended. Freed from military control and with white supremacy restored, these states promptly overthrew their Republican governments and aligned themselves solidly in the Democratic column. From 1876 to 1916 inclusive not one of the eleven carried by the Republican party in a national election. Over wide areas in the South the Fifteenth Amendment became virtually a dead 'letter as far as Negro suffrage was concerned. By the Fourteenth Amendment the power of the Democratic party had increased. The latter amendment annulled the old three-fifths rule of the Constitution, and thus enabled southern states to take full advantage of their colored population although it became excluded from voting in determining the apportionment of representatives, and hence their vote in the electoral college. Nor has the federal government ever cared to exercise the power given under the two amendments to penalize such limitations of the suffrage.

ECONOMIC ISSUES, 1876-191

American Political History

Following the Civil War, the economic recovery of the country financial, it was exceedingly rapid. Between 1860 and 1880, the population recovery of the United States increased from thirty-one million to fifty million. During the same period railroad mileage more than trebled, and in 1869 the first transcontinental railroad conducted. The aggregate wealth of the country rose from sixteen billion in 1860 to 42 billion in 1880. Freed from the detailed explanation at this point industry appears Accompanied by economic instabilities of the demon lover of slavery, the South become invaded by commerce and manufactures, and the lines drawn by the old economic sectionalism began to disappear. Immigration, temporarily halted during the war, set in afterward with increased volume.

An unprecedented advance documented in the growth of cities. Even before the war industry had outstripped agriculture; by 1850 the value of the property employed in mills, mines, railways, and urban undertakings generally exceeded the value of all the farms and p1la6n1tations between the Atlantic and the Pacific.

Just as the Democratic party during its extended period of power from Jefferson to Buchanan had made itself the exponent of the predominant agrarian interests of the country, so now the Republican party became the exponent of the emerging colossus of industry, always, however, with a suspicious eye to the highly necessary additional votes of the grain growers of the Middle West and Northwest.

The continuance in power of the Republicans after Civil War and reconstruction issues had settled was due to their interpretation of the needs of the new industrial experts in the United States. To this end they evolved a combination of policies on the national debt, protection, banking, currency, and commercial expansion, which were closely comparable to those of the Federalists and later of the Whigs.

Agrarian support was invited by the Homestead Act of 1862, because of which hundreds of thousands of western farmers became indebted to the Republican party for the soil from which they obtained a contemporary. Thus, designed that political partnership between businesspeople and free farmers that was destined to a long lease of power in national affairs.

King Cotton had conquered; southern planters, ruined by the war, deprived of their slaves by emancipation, and crushed under federal military authority, lost their old-time dominance in the Democratic party. Politically the latter suffered also because it appeared from the war branded with the charge of disloyalty south and pacifism north of the Mason and Dixon line. Gratifying as was the economic development of the country taken, it escorted by certain grave maladjustments which soon made themselves felt in the political field. Prices exaggerated during the Civil War, but from 1866 to 1896 they fell steadily.

References: Charles A. Beard, The Battle, p. 76.,

AMERICAN PARTIES DEBTORS 1860-1912.

American Political History

The American Party debtor class, which included many farmers struggling to meet mortgage payments, found their burdens constantly growing heavier. Particularly in the Middle West the grangers felt themselves oppressed by high freight rates and by the discriminations practiced by great railroad combinations which had come to dominate this territory.

In 1873, the business of the country surprised to its foundations by the most severe panic it had ever experienced. Unemployment was widespread and the ensuing period of depression lasted till 1878. Discontent of the agricultural and laboring classes first found Discontent political expression through the Greenback party. Originally the expressed members of this party expected to solve their economic problems largely by increasing the issue of legal helpful paper money, which, party they thought, would bring about higher prices and higher wages, relieve business depression, and reduce the burdens of the debtor class.

The New Fusion Electoral System

Later they added various measures designed to help labor and to destroy railroad and other monopolies. They were thus the forerunners of the Union Labor party of 1888, and of the People's party, or Populists, who first made their appearance around 1890. As in the case of other third-party movements, both the Green-the Pop-hackers and the Populists ridiculed at first as wild-eyed fatalist Partisans and calamity malapropisms.

The voting strength of the former was never considerable,9 but in 1892 the Populists startled the country by casting more than a million votes for their candidates and securing twenty-two electoral votes the first invasion of the Electoral College by a third party since the Civil War. Their platform for that year demanded (1) a national currency issued by the general government only, a full legal tender, and that without the use of banking corporations; (2) the free and unlimited coinage of silver and gold at the existing legal ratio of sixteen to one; (3) the increase of the circulating medium to not less than $50 per capita;10 (4) a graduated income tax; (5) postal savings banks; (6) government ownership and operation of railroads, telegraphs, and telephones; and (7) withdrawal from railroads and other corporations of all land in excess of their actual needs and the holding of the same for actual settlers.

The Green-backer vote in 1876 was 81,740; in 1880, 308,578; in 1884, 175,365. In 1888, 146,934 votes cast for the Union Labor candidates. "In 1892 the per capita circulation was $24.60. In 1918 it had reached $50.18.

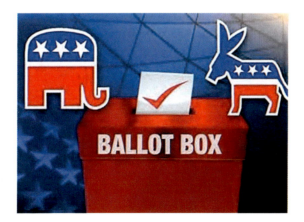

Michael Anguelo

ELECTORAL POPULIST PLATAFORM
American Political History

Further the Populist platform of 1892 condemned the falsehood of protecting American labor under the present system which opens our ports to the poor person and unlawful classes of the world; expressed cordial sympathy with the efforts of organized workingmen to shorten the hours of labor; celebrated the creativity and referendum; and favored constitutional amendments limiting the President and Vice-President to one term, and providing for the direct election of Senators. In addition, the party favored the Australian ballot, woman suffrage, primary elections, and better registration; undoubtedly also its publicity in favor of independent voting did much to undermine the intense party loyalties that had followed in the wake of the Civil War. Looking back after the lapse of forty years it is easy to perceive that many of the reforms that the Populists demanded, while despised and rejected for a season, won triumphantly in the end. From 1880 to 1892, inclusive, the Republican and Democratic parties dealt very carefully with the issues on which Green-backers and Populists were so outspoken. Particularly was this true of the silver question, which caused deep divisions of sentiment among the adherents of both the old parties. It was notorious that there were Gold Democrats and Silver Democrats, Silver Republicans and Gold Republicans.

Never was the platform art of on both sides of more advanced to hold discordant elements true to their traditional allegiance. As far as possible the old parties tried to make the tariff the dominant issue of their campaigns during the twelve years under consideration.

Even on this issue, however, caution prevailed, for there were divisions of sentiment about it on both sides. In 1880, and again in 1892, the Democratic party pronounced in favor of a tariff for revenue only, but in the two-intervening campaigns it recognized in its platforms that reductions or revisions should make due allowance for the difference between the wages of American and foreign labor. The Republican platform of 1880 reaffirmed the belief avowed in 1876, that duties levied for the purposes of revenue should so discriminate as to favor American labor. A somewhat stronger position was taken in the plank of 1884 which demanded that the imposition, of duties on foreign imports shall be made, not John D. Hicks,

The Populist Revolt: A History of the Farmers' Alliance and the People's Party (1931) for revenue only, but that in raising the requisite revenues for the government such duties shall be so levied as to afford security to our diversified industries and protection to the rights and wages of the laborer. Finally, in 1888 the party came out unbending in favor of the American system protection. We can see the garbage discrepancies between Democrats and Republicans, is what I trying to convince the legislators that a Fusion Electoral System will put an end, between any political party.

MERCENARIES AN ELECTORAL PROBLEMS

American Political History

The unbroken tenure of power enjoyed by the Republicans Democratic from 1860 to 1884 attracted mercenaries of every type into their outs ranks, spoils men hunting offices, railway promoters seeking Republican land grants and financial aid from the government, Mani famine structures demanding more discrimination in tariff legislation, and the great army of Hangerson who attached themselves to these leaders.

Hence the Democrats were in a strong strategical position which enabled them to criticize unsparingly the inefficiency, extravagance, and corruption of the party in power. In self-defense, the Republicans made the most of their Civil War record, waving the Caught thus in the political doldrums, positive legislation Important of any sort was extraordinarily difficult.

Nevertheless, some be legislative. credit to themselves for the rapid material growth and general prosperity of the country during this period.

An extraordinarily close balance of power existed between close the two great parties from 1880 to 1892.13 In 1880 the Republican balance of were successful with Garfield; in 1884 the Democrats aided PS. Q a by Mugwumps, i.e., Republicans who secured Blaine, won their first victory since the Civil War? Harrison defeated Cleveland in 1888, but four years later Cleveland was returned to power.

The extreme caution characterizing the platform utterances of the two parties during this period was partly due to their substantial equilibrium which made any innovation dangerous, as well as to the divisions of sentiment among the adherents of each of them even on major issues. Congressional elections reflected the same conditions. None of the four Presidents of this period ended his term of office without finding one or both legislative houses in the hands of the opposing party.

Caught thus in the political doldrums, positive legislation Important of any sort was extraordinarily difficult. Nevertheless, some be legislative.

References: Charles A. Beard, The American Party Battle, p. 91. Garfield's popular plurality in 1880 was only 7,018, out of a total vote of over nine million. In 1884 Cleveland chosen with a popular plurality of 62,683; but in 1888 he defeated in the electoral college, although he had a plurality of 98,017. Four years later he was again successful with a plurality of 380,810 out of a total vote of 12,059.

ACTS FOR REVENUE 1860-1912

American Political History

Acts for revenue only, but that in raising the requisite revenues for the government such duties shall be so levied as to afford security to our diversified industries and protection to the rights and wages of the laborer. Finally, in 1888 the party came out uncompromising in favor of the American system of protection. The uninterrupted occupancy of power enjoyed by the Republicans-Democratic from 1860 to 1884 attracted mercenaries of every type into their outs. Ranks spoils men hunting offices, railway promoters seeking Republican land grants and financial aid from the government, manufacturers demanding more discrimination in tariff legislation, and the great army of hanger-son who attached themselves to these leaders." Hence the Democrats were in a strong strategical position which enabled them to criticize unsparingly the inefficiency, extravagance, and corruption of the party in power. In self-defense, the Republicans made the most of their Civil War record, waving the bloody shirt, as the saying of the time phrased it; also, they boldly took credit to themselves for the rapid material growth and general prosperity of the country during this period.

An extraordinarily close balance of power existed between Close the two great parties from 1880 to 1892.13 In 1880 the balance of Republicans was successful with Garfield; in 1884 the Democrats aided by Mugwumps, i.e., Republicans who secured Blaine, won their first victory since the Civil

War. Harrison defeated Cleveland in 1888, but four years later Cleveland returned to power. The extreme caution characterizing the platform utterances of the two parties during this period was partly due to their substantial equilibrium which made any innovation dangerous, as well as to the divisions of sentiment among the adherents of each of them even on major issues.

References: Charles A. Beard, The American Party Battle, p.168

ACTS FOR REVENUE 1860-1912

American Political History

Congressional elections reflected the same conditions. None of the four Presidents of this period ended his term of office without finding one or both legislative houses in the hands of the opposing party.91. Garfield's popular plurality in 1880 was only 7,018, out of a total vote of over nine million. In 1884 Cleveland chosen with a popular plurality of 62,683; but in 1888, defeated in the electoral college, although he had a popular plurality of 98,017. Four years later he was again successful with a popular plurality of 380,810 out of a total vote of 12,059,351.

THE REPEAL OF SILVER PRCHASING PROBLEM

American Political History and the Fusion Solutions

Repeal of the silver purchase clause Silver Democrats control convention of 1896 ginning's of importance may renowned. In 1883 the Pendleton Civil Service Act recognized; and in 1887 the Interstate Commerce Commission created, neither being a partisan achievement. During Harrison's administration the McKinley tariff, the Sherman Anti-Trust Law, and the Sherman Silver Purchase Act approved.

The last named a sop to silver and inflation sentiment increased the government's purchases of silver to fifty million dollars a year, as compared with thirty million under the Bland-Allison Act of 1878. As the Senate controlled by Republicans during the whole of Cleveland's first administration, Democratic legislation on the tariff was impossible. In

1894, during his second administration, the Wilson tariff bill, which also carried a provision for an income tax, passed, but Democratic protectionists in the Senate so amended it that the President in disgust allowed it to become a law without his signature.

Years of bitter struggle for tariff reform thus ended in a disgraceful fiasco. Events during Cleveland's second term put an end to the state of party equipoise that had lasted for sixteen years. A disastrous panic in 1893 caused widespread suffering and reinforced the radical Populist movement. To alleviate the panic, the President, by an extraordinary exercise of his influence. Acts for revenue only, but that in raising the requisite revenues for secured the revoke of the silver-purchase clause of the Sherman Act. This step naturally incurred the bitter enmity of the silver element inside as well as outside his party. A decision by the Supreme Court that the income tax was unconstitutional further inflamed radical sentiment. As the convention year 1896 approached it became clear that the Populist strength manifested in 1892 had tremendously increased, particularly in the West and South.

In the ending part of the country it had grown to such an extent that it threatened Democratic control and even the political supremacy of the white race. Regardless of the influence of the administration and the strenuous opposition of the Gold Democrats of the East, Silver Democrats from the West and South controlled the Democratic National convention of 1896 by a two-thirds majority. Solutions: The New Electoral Fusion System, Nonpartisan Elections.

PARTIES ELECTORAL DIFFICULTIES 1860-1912

American Political History

They secured the adoption of a platform which recognized that the money question is paramount to all others at this time and demanded the free and unlimited coinage of both silver and gold at the present legal ratio of 16 to 1 without waiting the aid or consent of any other nation. The revenue-tariff policy of the party reiterated, but further agitation of the matter condemned until after the money question is settle.

By implication, the decision of the Supreme Court adverse the income tax had criticized, and Congress had called upon to use all the constitutional power which remains after that decision, or which may come from its reversal by the court as it may hereafter become constituted, so that the problem of 170...taxation may become impartially laid, to the end that wealth may bear its due proportion of the expense of the government. William Jennings Bryan, one of the younger leaders of the radical element of the party, who had electrified the convention by his cross of gold oratory, appointed for the Presidency. The Republicans had already held their national convention three weeks earlier, drafting a platform which showed their intention of making protection the paramount issue of the campaign and nominating William McKinley of Ohio, the advance agent of prosperity and prophet of the full dinner pail, for the Presidency.

A free-silver plank presented by 110 Republican delegates from western states, who secured when it unsuccessful and later formed a Silver party which supported Bryan. The money plank adopted by the regular Republican convention pronounced unreservedly for sound money, and expressed opposition to the free currency of silver except by international agreement with the leading nations of the world, which we pledge ourselves to promote; until such agreement can be obtained, the existing gold standard must be preserved. The Populists enthusiastically accepted Bryan's nomination, but they refused to endorse his running mate, Arthur Sewell of Maine, because he was a banker and of conservative tendencies.

The situation was further complicated by a bolt of the Gold Democrats, who held a convention in September and nominated candidates of their own. No campaign since the Civil War opposed with such intensity and bitterness as that of 1896. Despite the efforts of the Republican leaders to push the tariff issue into the foreground, it was ruthlessly thrust aside by the battle of the stand Republicans for systematic money Gold Democrats Bolt Battle of the standards gold versus silver.

ELECTORAL DISCUSSION 1860-1912

American Political History

Discussion raged hottest over this point, but far greater interests managed to be at stake. To the Bryan Democrats it was a struggle against the joint money powers, subtly corrupting and exploiting the government and people. To their opponents it was a fight against disorder, repudiation, dishonesty, and communism. The elements of a class struggle were involved, farmers, laborers, and cross-roads storekeepers against large banking, commercial, and manufacturing interests. A new segmental-ism made its appearance, the South and West against the North and East. Campaign funds of unprecedented size were employed.

Bryan received considerable financial support from silver-mine owners, but the amount at his disposal was small indeed compared with the large contributions collected from the commercial and protected interests of the country by Hanna, chair of the Republican National Committee. McKinley was successful in November by a vote of 271 to 176 in the electoral college, receiving a popular vote of 7,104,779 as against 6,502,925 for Bryan. In 1900 the same candidates for the Presidency headed the tickets of the two major parties.

Bryan secured a confirmation of the silver plank of 1896, but the Democratic platform declared interventionism to be the dominant issue of the campaign, and denounced the colonial policy pursued by the administration in the possessions conceded by Spain at the close of the war of 1898. An aggressive-antitrust-plank also approved. McKinley's administration received the warm endorsement of the Republican party, and he was again successful by a larger vote, both popular and electoral, thanin1896.At the same time Theodore Roosevelt selected Vice-President, succeeding to the Presidency upon the assassination of McKinley six months after his inauguration. A long-continued period of industrial depression followed the panic of 1893, but conditions improved with the clear-cut decision of the money question in 1896.

Before becoming President of the United States, Theodore Roosevelt was the Assistant Secretary of the Navy. to organize the Rough Riders, the first voluntary cavalry in the Spanish-He resigned in 1898with Cuba. Roosevelt recruited a diverse group of cowboys, miners, law enforcement officials, and Native Americans to join the Rough Riders.

They took part in the capture of Kettle Hill, and then charged across a valley to aid in the seizure of San Juan Ridge, the highest point of which is San Juan Hill. After the conclusion of the Spanish-American War prosperity returned and a period of unexampled business expansion instated. Pools and combinations of railroads had profoundly affected the course of politics during the period from 1876 to 1896. The same centralizing tendency was now to manifest itself in the industrial field. Between 1890 and 1900 the number of industrial combinations Class and sectional interests involved

Imperialism the paramount interrogation, 1900 Business expansion to Rise of industrial combinations Prices and wages Campaign of 1904 Campaign contributions Republican platform of 1908 proper grew from 18 with a total nominal capital of $288,000,000, to 157 with a total nominal capital of $3,150,000,000.

ELECTIONS PROBLEMS 1904 ROOSVELT VS. PARKER

By 1904, the leading trusts and railways of the country linked and connected under two great capitalistic groups. Questions arising from this enormous centralization of economic power inevitably took the center of the political stage and kept it until the outbreak of the World War.

Reversing the movement of the pre-ceding period, the trend of general prices after 1896 was upward. Wages followed, but not so closely or as to prevent the emergence of the cost of living problem as a vital political question. The campaign of 1904 was apathetic to an extreme degree. He had the support of a united party despite the apprehensions caused in certain quarters by the Republicans inevitable, the apprehensions caused in certain quarters by Roosevelt's great personal popularity made his nomination his vigorous expressions on the trust and other questions. The Democrats nominated Alton B. Parker of New York, a justice of the highest court of that state. Before their convention ad-journey the candidate addressed a telegram to it declaring his unflinching adherence to the gold standard. Bryan thereupon announced that the party had fallen under the domination of Wall Street, although as a party regular he voted later for Parker.

Three days before the election Roosevelt denounced the statements made by Parker as unqualifiedly and atrociously false. Public attention was concentrated upon the subject of campaign finances by this vivid incident, subsequent disclosures being of such a character that much reform legislation was enacted.14 The election of 1904 resulted in the worst defeat sustained by the Democratic party since the Civil War, but general lack of interest was shown in the total popular vote which fell nearly a quarter of a million below that of 1900.Roosevelt declined a new nomination in 1908, but was able to dictate the selection of Taft as his successor. The Republican platform of that year offered little that was new. However, it for a critical discussion of Roosevelt's assertion declared unequivocally for a revision of the tariff by a special session of Congress to become held at once following the inauguration of the next President. On the trust question it claimed credit for the Sherman Act, adding that it should be strengthened by such amendments as will give to the federal government greater supervision and control over and secure greater publicity in the management of corporations engaged in interstate commerce having power and opportunity to effect mom-lies.

References: H. F. Pringle, Theodore Roosevelt, chap iii. The reform legislation referred to above deliberated under the heading of Corrupt Practices Acts in Ch. xiii of Federal Corrupt Practices Act, was a federal law of the Unit States that ratified in 1910 and amended in 1911 and 1925. It stayed the nation's primary law regulating campaign finance in federal elections until the passage of the Federal Election Campaign Act in 1971. The Act of Congress enacted on June 25, 1910 by US President William Howard Taft.

ELECTORAL PROBLEMS 1860-1912.

American Political

History by a large majority, the Republican convention voted down propositions emanating from LaFollette's adherents in favor of publicity of campaign contributions, physical valuation of railroads, and direct election of Senators, all of which found a place later in the Democratic platform of that year. In his speech of acceptance, however, Taft declared himself in favor of these policies with certain reservations. The Democratic party returned to its former allegiance in Democratic 1908 by nominating Bryan, the Peerless Leader, for the third critic time.

Under his influence it accepted a plank on the trust question which, unlike many such pronouncements, was specific and detailed. It denounced private monopoly as indefensible and in-tolerable, demanded criminal prosecution of guilty trust magnates and officials, and proposed more legislation which would make the existence of private monopoly impossible in the United States.

Among such additional remedies it specified three: first, a law preventing the duplication of directors among competing corporations i.e., to prevent interlocking directorates; second, a license system which will make it necessary for a manufacturing or trading corporation engaged in interstate commerce to take out a federal license before it shall be permitted to control as much as twenty-five per cent of the product in which it deals, the license to protect the public from watered stock and to prohibit the control by such corporation of more than fifty per cent of the total amount of any product consumed in the United States; and, third, a law compelling such licensed corporations to sell to all purchasers in all parts of the country on the same terms, after making due allowance for cost of transportation.

Once more, however, Bryan was defeated, but his party made a much better showing in the popular vote than it had done four years earlier. With all this discrepancy I wonder who we excite as one nation indivisible up today, I considered it a miracle, because political parties divide us.

At the beginning of Taft's administration, the Republican Party Bitterness had been in full control of the federal government for twelve years. It had decisively defeated the Democracy three times under the radical leadership of Bryan, and once, still more decisively, under the conservative leadership of Parker.

Nevertheless, there was much internal disagreement; indeed, ever since the sound money victory in 1896 the agrarian element of the Republican party had felt that manufacturing and big business interests in the East and Northeast were receiving the notables share of governmental favors. Farmers, particularly those in the western areas with small rainfall, displeased: they wanted prosperity to be passed around.

Another evidence of political discontent has the funds for by the growth of the Communist votes. The Socialist-Communist Labor party began its career in national politics by nominating candidates for the Presidency in 1892. Eight years later a fusion of more moderate Socialists exaggerated under the name of the Social-Democratic party, which transformed in 1901 to the Socialist-Communist party. The Socialist-Communist Labor party refused to affiliate with the new movement, but its vote has remained negligible.

On the other hand, the Communists polled a hundred thousand votes for their candidate, Eugene V. Debs, in 1900, and more than four hundred thousand in each of the two following national elections. Despite its preponderant strength and clear unity at the beginning of Taft's administration, the Republican party soon developed serious internal differences. Immediately after his inauguration the President, acting upon the platform pledge of 1908, called a special session of Congress to deal with the tariff. The result was the passage of the Payne-Aldrich Act.

Growth of Communist party vote Republican divisions which aroused great popular resentment. Whether rates reviewed upward, or downward President Taft's vigorous defense of the new rate had the effect of unloading much of this resentment upon his own shoulders. His choice of R. A. Ballinger as Secretary of the Interior earned the determined and persistent enmity of the leaders of the conservation movement to which President Roosevelt had given such enthusiastic support during his administration.

Appointments to the new Court of Commerce and selections for the five vacancies occurring on the bench of the Supreme Court also came in for considerable criticism. Although Taft pushed through the cases against the Standard Oil Company and the American Tobacco Company in the Supreme Court.

Securing orders for the dissolution of both these combinations, it became known that inner circles behind them took advantage of the resulting readjustments to secure large profits. The cumulative t is true that since its virtual absorption by the Bryan Democracy the old Populist party had ceased to cast a vote of any considerable size in presidential election. Nevertheless, its spirit was still active in number of states, as shown by the rapid progress made by the initiative and referendum since 1898.

Later the recall presented in various effects of these and other causes for dissatisfaction Insured by party took the form of an insurgent movement among Regents of publican members of Congress. In March, 1910, a combination 1910 of insurgent Republicans and Democrats in the House of Representatives made a concerted attack upon the Speaker, Joseph Cannon, who had widely criticized because of his use of the great controls of his office in the interest of the reactionary element. The Speaker overthrown from his membership on the Rules Committee, it enlarged in size, and made elective by the House itself, thus taking the power of appointing it out of the hands of the Speaker.

In the November election following this upheaval the Democrats gained control of the House for the first time in sixteen years. Opposition to the administration took concrete form in January National, 1911, when the National Progressive Republican League Progress prearranged under the leadership of Senator LaFollette of Wisconsin. Its program criticized the legislation recently enacted League on the tariff, trusts, banking, and conservation, and declared in favor of direct primaries, direct legislation, and direct government. At the beginning Roosevelt declined to join the new movement, but in his speeches and editorials he gradually aligned himself with its policies.

ROOSVELT-TAFT 1912 ELECTORAL PROBLEMS

American Political History

Early in the campaign year 1912 he announced that his hat was in the ring. Roosevelt-Taft contest Republican platform of 1912 Democratic convention of 1912. A bitter contest at once broke out between Roosevelt and Taft for the control of delegates to the Republican national convention. By the exercise of administrative influence such as had often been employed in the past, from the one to the other hand, Roosevelt developed astounding strength in most of the states which had proven the direct primary system, and in which the Republican vote was large. Also, his supporters started contests wherever possible. Carried to the floor of the convention, the contests absolute in favor of Taft, whose friends were in control of the machinery. Roosevelt's supporters thereupon committed, and the delegates who remained went ahead without further opposition to the nomination of Taft.

The platform declared the Republican party to be now, as always, a party of advanced and constructive statesmanship; stated that it was prepared to go forward with various forms of social legislation, especially such as would improve the condition of the working classes; reaffirmed the protective-tariff doctrine of the party; characterized the recall of judges as unnecessary and unwise, but favored judicial reform that would make court processes less tedious and costly; and proposed the creation of a Federal Trade Commission and the enactment of legislation supplementary to the Anti-Trust Act which would make its terms, particularly with regard to criminal offenses, clearer to the business world.

Wilson and against Clark because the latter refused to join in a movement to prevent the choice of a conservative Democrat. The two most prominent aspirants were Speaker Champ Clark, who had developed considerable strength in the primary elections of a few middle western states, and Governor Woodrow Wilson of New Jersey, who had puts temporary chair of the fraud parties 1860-1912, platform of 1912 convention. Investigations undertook of the prohibitive cost of living and of agricultural credit methods. Some days later the Democratic national convention met at Baltimore. Encouraged by the party's victory in the congressional elections of 1910, and still more by the multiplying evidences of Republican disillusionment, there was no shortage of presidential timber. through a program of progressive legislation in that state which won him many ardent supporters throughout the country. Although not an avowed candidate, Bryan's influence was still potent. At one time Clark secured most of the votes of the delegates, but under the rules of the party a two thirds votes needed for nomination. After a struggle lasting seven days, Wilson was finally victorious on the forty-sixth ballot.

The platform adopted at Baltimore declared that the fed Democratic government under the Constitution has no right or power to impose or collect tariff duties except for the purpose of revenue. It charged that the excessive cost of living resulted in large measure from high tariff laws enacted by the Republican party, and from the trusts and commercial conspiracies fostered by such laws. The party's position of 1908 on monopolies and trusts confirmed in more general terms. Further, the platform recommended a valuation of railroads, express companies, telegraph, and telephone lines by the Interstate Commerce Commission. It held that labor organizations should not viewed as illegal combinations in restraint of trade. Presidential primaries, the restriction of campaign contributions, and the prohibition of such contributions by corporations were also favored.

At the instigation of Bryan, it was said, a resolution was adopted favoring a single presidential term, urging an amendment to the Constitution making the President ineligible for re-election, and pledging the candidate of the convention to this principle. the long and detailed list of industrial and social reforms which it held. It also proposed substantial number of political reforms, among them being direct primaries; presidential preference primaries; the short ballot; initiative, referendum, and recall in the states; popular recall of judicial decisions denying the constitutionality under a state constitution of acts involving the use of the police power; an easier method of amending the federal Constitution; and equal suffrage for men and women.

PAINE AID RICH ACT ELECTORAL PROBLEMS
American Political History

While affirming belief in the principle of protection, the tariff plank of the progressive platform condemned the Payne aid rich Act, and favored a nonpartisan, scientific tariff commission, and the immediate downward revision of those schedules where industries are shown to be unjust or excessive. For the regulation of trusts a strong administrative commission commended to enforce complete publicity, and to attack unfair competition, false capitalization, and special privilege. Valuation of the physical property of railroads and the abolition of the Court of Commerce also included. In language reminiscent of much more radical movements the Progressive platform denounced both the old parties as tools of dishonest benefits, declaring that to dissolve the unholy alliance between dishonest business and immoral politics is the first task of the leadership of the day. six hundred thousand, but the two joints fell short of the vote for Taft in 1908.

Roosevelt unanimously nominated for the Presidency by the insurgents gathered in Chicago, Hiram Johnson of California becoming his running mate for the Vice-presidency. Election of in the ensuing election, disaster indeed but not as 1912 the Progressive leader hoped, the Democrats carried every state except eight, six of which gave their electoral votes to Roosevelt,16 and 2 to Taft. The popular vote of the former exceeded that of the latter by more than owing to the division of the opposition, Wilson's majority in the electoral college was enormous, but his popular vote was only 40 per cent of the total. One of the greatest surprises of the election was the vote of the two Communist parties, which leaped from 420,820 in 1908, to 897,011 in 1912. References: H. K. Beale, The Critical Year (1930), which analyzes acutely the Johnson administration and particularly the Grant campaign in 1866; C. G. Bowers, The Tragic Era: The Including

California, the electoral vote of which was divided, eleven for the Progressives and two for the Democrats, which it cont.

THE RECAL ELECTORAL PROBLEMS

American Political History

It also proposed a large number of political reforms, among them being direct primaries; presidential favorite primaries; the short ballot; initiative, referendum, and recall in the states; popular recall of judicial decisions denying the constitutionality under a state constitution of acts passed under the police power; an easier method of amending the federal Constitution; and equal suffrage for men and women.

While affirming belief in the principle of protection, the tariff plank of the Progressive platform condemned the Payne-Aldrich Act, and favored a nonpartisan, scientific tariff commission, and the immediate downward revision of those schedules wherein duties revealed to be unjust or excessive. For the regulation of trusts a strong administrative commission urged to enforce complete publicity, and to attack unfair competition, false capitalization, and special privilege. Valuation of the physical property of railroads and the abolition of the Court of Commerce also included. Roosevelt unanimously nominated for the Presidency on the first ballot. for Taft in 1908. in 1908, to 931,132 in 1912.

THIRD PARTY PROGRAM: 1860-1912

American Political History

Since the Civil War, as shown by their titles or by the dates showing the period covered. Especially worthy of repeated mention in this connection are the treatises by H. J. Ford and E. Stanwood, which are as valuable for the post helium Comedy Club as for the historical growth of political parties.

F. E. Haynes, Third Party Movements (1916), is a history of third-party movements in the United States since the Civil War, dealing with the Liberal Republicans, the Farmers' Movement of the seventies, the Greenback, Populist, and Progressive parties.

Although written with special reference to Iowa, the latter state was so often the center of third-party agitation that the work is more national than provincial in scope. The first edition of P. O. Ray, Introduction to Political Parties and Practical Politics (1913), presents the Democratic and Republican platforms of 1912 in parallel support procedure. Campaign typescript accounts issued by the various parties for 1912 and earlier presidential years are the most valuable official sources for platforms and popular arguments based thereon.

A very convenient compilation of vest pocket size, prepared by G. D. Ellis under the direction of W. T. Page, clerk of the U. S. House of Representatives, and issued as a public document, contains the Platforms of the Two Great Parties, 1856-1920, inclusive (1920).

The only comprehensive work of an historical character which deals with this period in completed form is J. F. Rhodes, History of the United States from the Compromise of 1850 (7 vols., 1893-1906), covering the years 1850 to 1877, to which has been added by the same author a one volume History of the United States from Hayes to McKinley, 1877-1896 (1920). On a similar imposing scale E. P. Oberholtzer has begun a History of the United States Since the Civil War, in five volumes, two of which have already been issued (1917, 1921). bringing the narrative down to 1872.

The only comprehensive work of an historical character which deals with this period in completed form is J. F. Rhodes, History of the United States from the Compromise of 1850 (7 vols., 1893-1906), covering the years 1850 to 1877, to which has been added by the same author a one volume History of the United States from Hayes to McKinley, 1877-1896 (1920). On a similar imposing scale E. P. Oberholtzer has begun a History of the United States Since the Civil War, in five volumes, two of which have already been issued (1917, 1921). bringing the narrative down to 1872.e United States from the Compromise of 1850 (7 vols., 1893-1906), covering the years 1850 to 1877, to which has been added by the same author a one-volume History of the United States from Hayes to McKinley, 1877-1896 (1920). On a similar imposing scale E. P. Oberholtzer has begun a History of the United States Since the Civil War, in five volumes, two of which have already been issued (1917, 1921). bringing the narrative down to 1872.

Reference: Constitution (1902); W. A. Dunning, Reconstruction, Political and Economic (1907) ; P. L. Haworth, Reconstruction and Union (1912); H. A. Herbert, editor, Why the Solid South (1890); E. B. Andrews,

History of the Last Quarter Century in the United States, 1870-1895 (2 vols.,1897); H. T. Peck, Twenty Years of the Republic (1906); C. A. Beard, Contemporary American History, ; P. L. Haworth, The United States in Our Own Times, 1865-1920 (1920); C. R. Lingley, Since the Civil War (1921); W. Wilson, Division and Reunion, with additional chapters by E. S. Corwin, bringing the narrative down to 1918 (1921);

CAMPAIGNS AND ISSUES OF 1916 AND 1920

American Political History

During the first year of Wilson's administration two legislative measures of prime importance positioned upon the statute book. One of these was the Underwood Act revising the tariff downward and imposing an income tax; the other was the Federal Reserve Act which reorganized the banking system of the country. In 1914 the trust problem distributed with by the establishment of a Federal Trade Commission and the enactment of the Clayton antitrust law.

Mexican conditions, which had long been threatening, took an acute turn in the latter year, with the result that Vera Cruz held by an American naval expedition and held until the downfall of Huerta. The outbreak of the World War in 1914 ended, temporarily, at least, the predominance in our politics of domestic economic issues. With the development of the bloody struggle in Europe the attention of our people was concentrated more and more upon the policies of the belligerents, the maintenance of our own neutrality, the safety of American life and property upon the high seas, the manufacture and export of munitions, and, in case intervention should become necessary, the proper measures of military and naval preparedness.

To understand the indecisive attitude of both parties upon these issues in the campaign of 1916, it should bear in mind that Germany did not inaugurate her policy of unrestricted submarine warfare until February of the following year. Despite the bitterness engendered by the rupture of J. T Conventions 1912, the vast majority or progressives who were for of 1916 merely Republicans had returned to the latter party before 1916. Nevertheless, a convention of Progressives called to meet in Chicago at the same time as the regular Republican convention of the latter year.

CHAPTER 8

FRANCLIN D. ROOSVELT NOMINATION

American Political History

Roosevelt is nominated for the Presidency by the, but he declined conditionally at the time and later threw his support to the Republican candidates. The names both of Roosevelt and Taft presented at the regular Republican convention, but neither had any considerable following, and on the third ballot the nomination went to Charles E. Hughes, at the time one of the justices of the Supreme Court of the United States. For the Vice-Presidency Charles W. Fairbanks appointed.

A few days later the Democratic convention denominated President Wilson and Vice-President Marshall by acclamation. Aside from planks due to the Mexican distress and the Woman suffrage. European War the most striking innovation in the platforms of 1916 was the acceptance by both parties of resolutions in favor of woman suffrage. This innovation, not entirely disconnected from the fact that by state action the suffrage movement had progressed so far that the women of twelve states were qualified to take part in the approaching presidential election.

On this subject the Democratic plank read: We recommend the extension of the franchise to the women of the country by the states upon the same terms as to men.

The Republican platform stated its position as follows: The Republican party, reaffirming its faith in government of the people, by the people, for the people, as a measure of justice to one half the adult people of the country, favors the extension of suffrage to women, but recognizes the right of each state to settle this question for itself.

Shortly after the adjournment of the Republican convention, Hughes took ground in advance of his party by announcing himself in favor of a suffrage amendment to the federal Constitution. As a result, he received the support of the National Woman's party, standing for the more militant wing of the movement, which made a vigorous campaign for him in the suffrage states however, without much success since ten out of the twelve gave their electoral votes to Wilson. In its platform the Republican party assured the people of Mexico that it deeply sympathized with their sufferings at the hands of armed bands of criminals and expressed horror and indignation at the outrages perpetrated upon American citizens by these outlaws. It denounced the indefensible methods of interference employed by the administration in the internal affairs of Mexico.

Further, it censured the administration, first, for its failure to act promptly and firmly, and second, for its recognition of one of the parties responsible for these barbarities. Finally, the party pledged its aid to restore order in Mexico and promised our citizens on the border and in Mexico adequate and absolute protection in their lives, liberty, and property.

The Democratic platform characterized Mexican conditions in much the same way as the Republican had ended but justified fully the course followed by the President. Intervention, it added, implying, as it does, military subjugation, is disgusting to the people of the United States, notwithstanding the provocation to that course has been great and should be resorted to, if at all, only as a last recourse. Both parties reaffirmed their devotion to the Monroe Doctrine, the Republican declaring it essential to the achievement of the manifest destiny of the country.

With regards to foreign relations the Republicans expressed a desire for a piece of justice and right, and a straight and honest neutrality, neither of which, they said, in words obviously meant to reflect upon President Wilson's policies, could be preserved by top methods, by phrase making, by presentations in linguistic, or by attitudes ever changing in an effort to secure groups of voters. Further, they expressed a belief in a firm, dependable, and courageous foreign policy, and in the pacific Republican platform on Mexico Democratic platform on Mexico Republican platform on foreign nations.

The New Fusion Electoral System

DEMOCRATIC PLATAFORM ON FOREIGNER RELATIONS
American Political History

Democratic platform on foreign relations Preparedness settlement of international disputes, recommending the establishment of a world court for the latter purpose. The Democratic platform, on the other hand, commended the splendid diplomatic victories of our great President, who has preserved the vital interests of our government and its citizens, and kept us out of war. During the campaign this last phrase played a great part in popular discussion, and doubtless decided the casting of many votes both for and against the Democratic nominees. Continuing the subject of foreign relations, the platform held that the United States should use its power not only to make itself safe at home and secure abroad, but also to assist the world in securing settled peace and justice. Every people have the right to choose the sovereignty under which it shall live, small states should enjoy the same respect for their sovereignty and territorial integrity as great and powerful nations, and the world has a right to be free from every disturbance of its peace originating in aggression or in disregard of the rights of peoples and nations. serve these principles. Finally, the Democratic platform had several paragraphs which, while recognizing. We believe that the time has come when it is the duty of the United States to join 188 with other nations of the world in any feasible association that will effectively solve the problems for the interests of a foreign power by crippling or destroying our industries or by intimidating the government, a legislatures of the people. In order to maintain our peace, the Republican platform declared, we must have a sufficient and effective regular army and a provision for ample reserves, already drilled and disciplined; also a navy strong and so well-proportioned and equipped, so thoroughly ready and prepared, that no enemy can gain command of the sea and effect a landing in force on either our western or our eastern coast.

Professing a similar devotion to peace and denying any desire for additional territory or for any advantage which cannot be peacefully gained, the Democrats favored the maintenance of an army fully adequate to the requirements of order, safety, and national protection; the fullest development of modern methods of seacoast defense; an adequate reserve of citizens trained to arms; and a fixed policy for the continuous development of a navy equal to the international tasks which the United States hopes to perform.

The Democrats completely endorsed the Underwood Tariff and Tariff law; the Republicans pronounced it a complete other issues disappointment which, but for the adventitious conditions created by the war, would long since have paralyzed all forms of American industry and deprived American labor of its just reward. Regarding the Philippines, the Democrats reiterated their endorsement of ultimate independence for the islands; the Republicans condemned the Democratic administration for its attempt to irresponsibility rejection of the Cuban island.

The administration about trust regulation, rural credits, Republican platform made no mention either of the income tax or of the Federal Reserve Act. Both platforms presented brief programs of industrial and social legislation. Late in the campaign of 1916 a new issue was injected Adamson by the passage, under pressure from the administration, Act of the Adamson law. It if railway trainmen should become rewarded overtime based on an eight-hour working day instead of the ten-hour day then customary. The Republicans severely denounced the law as unconstitutional. Both the President and Congress accused of having surrendered weakly to compulsion exercised by the railroad unions in a servile attempt to secure the labor vote. On the other hand, the Democrats approved the measure as a thoroughly fair and political leader. After all this situation is a politic conflict to secure railroads union's votes, in the New Fusion System it will not take place.

ELECTION OF 1916 DECRLARATION OF WAR

American Political History

Election of 1916 Declaration, of war, 1917 Politics is adjourned like solution of a difficult problem which had saved the country from the horrors of a general railroad strike. The election of 1916 was exceedingly close, the decision being in doubt for several days while returns were coming in from the rural districts of number of Western states. Hughes carried all New England except New Hampshire; all the Middle Atlantic states, including Delaware; all the Middle Western states except Ohio; and in addition, West Virginia, Iowa,

The New Fusion Electoral System

There were, however, wide differences of opinion concerning the conduct and purposes of the war among the leaders of both parties, which, of course, found critical exclamation on the Republican side. Roosevelt denounced the President's fourteen points as thoroughly mischievous, and several his party colleagues condemned roundly the various notes Minnesota, South Dakota, and Oregon, his total electoral vote being 254. With the exceptions named above Wilson carried every state south of Mason and Dixon's line and every state west of the Mississippi, besides breaking the Republican stronghold in the North and East by capturing 190 Ohio and New Hampshire. His total vote in the electoral college was 277.

The popular vote for Wilson was 9,129,269; for Hughes, 8,547,328. For the two Socialist tickets the total popular vote was only 604,759, a decline of over three hundred thousand as compared with 1912. With the declaration of war by Congress, April 6, 1917, active partisan opposition to the major policies of the administration ceased for a time. Substantial number of men not connected with the party in power so called into the public service, including many Republicans of prominence. There was some advocacy of a coalition Cabinet, such as had become formed in several of the European belligerent countries, on the ground that it would avoid partisan criticism and struggle and thus strengthen the hands of the government in the conduct of the war. Opponents of this proposal, which not adopted, urged that power already concentrated sufficiently in the executive, and that our constitutional and party systems differed so widely from those of European countries as to make the innovation unnecessary or even harmful. This tacit, if limited, party truce lasted well into 1918.

The Socialists Communist party alone had taken a definite stand against the war in their St. Louis platform, but they had only one member in Congress. On the whole President Wilson vindicated in his laconic exclamation, made as the summer of 1918 approached, that politics is adjourned. sent to the German government.

REPUBLICAN POINT OF VIEW OF THE WAR PROBLEM

American Political History

The Republican leaders showed their belief that the war was to be won not through diplomatic appeals to the German people to overthrow their masters, but through the use solely of military force. Absorbed in the stirring events amid which the World Wilson's War was being ended, the public gave little attention to the congressional elections of 1918. On October House, berth 24th, however, President Wilson made an appeal for the return of a Democratic majority to both the Senate and the House of Representatives. This is no time, he urged, either for divided counsellor for divided leadership. Unity of command is as necessary now in civil action as it is upon the battlefield. If the control of the House and Senate should reserve away from the party now in power, an opposing majority could assume control of legislation and oblige all action to reserve among contest and obstruction.

The return of a Republican majority to either House of the Congress would, moreover, become interpreted on the other side of the water as a refutation of my leadership. In the few days staying before the election Republican leaders protested vigorously against the President's appeal as unpredictable with his former attitude, as revealing his purpose to assume personally powers of dangerous extent, and as reflecting unworthily upon the motives of their party. In the ensuing election they References: J. M. Mathews, Political Parties, and the War, in American Political Science Review, vol. xiii, p. 225 (May 1919)."

LEAGE OF NATION GAIN SENATE CONTROL

American Political History

American Political History League of Nations gained control of the Senate by a plurality of one, and of the House by forty-six votes. Upon the return of the President from Paris with the peace treaty including the League of Nations, fresh fuel added to the flames of party controversy. While there were differences of opinion in both parties regarding these subjects, the Republicans furnished the bulk of those Senators who as bitter-enders opposed the treaty as a whole and those who proposed major amendments to the League of Nations, while the Democrats supplied most of those Senators who supported the treaty either without change or with interpretative amendments only.

NOMINEEIES CAMPAIGNS OF 1916 AND 1920

American Political History

Leaving only one more to reached, and thus naturally strengthening the pressure put upon both parties to secure last action. On the Republican side the principal candidates for the presidential nomination were General Leonard Wood, Governor Frank O. Lowden of Illinois, Senator Hiram Johnson of California, and Senator W. G. Harding of Ohio. Among the Democratic leaders the most prominently mentioned possibilities were W. G. McAdoo, former Secretary of the Treasury, A. Mitchell Palmer, Attorney General, and Governor James M. Cox of Ohio. Herbert Hoover, who unquestionably commanded a large and enthusiastic following in both camps, announced his adherence to the Republican party early in the campaign year, but did not secure more than a minimum of support in the convention.

At the close of the primary campaign the Kenyon senatorial committee was appointed to investigate alleged large campaign contributions and expenditures, the revelations made by which reflected upon a number of candidates, and severely damaged, if they did not render hopeless, the Republican national convention was held at Chicago, June 8th to 12th.2 On the first ballot, taken Friday, June nth, seemed to be facing Candidates of the Republican convention.

Reference: For details of the Kenyon report see chap. xiii. 3 On the Republican national convention of 1920, see W. Lippman, Chicago, 1920, New Republic, vol. xxiii, p.108 (June 23, 1920); F. M. Davenport, Conservative America in Convention Assembled, Outlook, vol. cxxv, p.375 (June 23, 1920); and A. W. Page, The Meaning of What Happened at Chicago, World's Work, vol. xi, pp. 361-377 (August, 1920).

DEAD LOCK ELECTORAL COMPLICATIONS

American Political History

A deadlock between Democrats and Republicans, who led a gridlock competition on the sixth and seventh ballots, with the delegates sweltering in tropical heat and troubled by forebodings of rapidly mounting hotel bills.

Under these unfortunate circumstances the action of party leaders who began throwing support behind Senator Harding soon brought results.

On the seventh ballot he first received more than one hundred votes; on the eighth and ninth ballots the followings of General Wood and Governor Lowden began to crumble; and on the tenth ballot Senator Harding nominated with 692 votes. Democratic at the Democratic convention, held in San Francisco, convention June 2gth to July 6th, a deadlock occurred between the leading three candidates. On the first ballot, taken Friday, July 2d, McAdoo led with 266 votes, Palmer receiving 256, and Cox 134. McAdoo continued in the lead until the eleventh ballot, when Cox passed him, keeping his advantage to the end of that day, Saturday, July 3d. The force convention was to adjourn over Sunday, but with fevers and hotel bills both lower than at Chicago, there was a general determination among the delegates to take all the time that might be necessary to fight it out.

On Monday, July 5th, Governor COT kept his lead until the twenty-ninth ballot, but from the thirtieth to the their-ty-eighth the advantage passed again to McAdoo. The vote of Palmer also fluctuated, reaching its maximum on the seventh, twenty-third, and again on the thirty-sixth ballots... It seemed clear that no decision could hope for within reasonable limits of time, especially in view of the two-thirds rule prevailing in Democratic conventions, so long as these three contestants remained in the field. Following the thirty-eighth ballot Palmer released his followers. In the resulting break-up Cox made the greater gains, and finally in the 1 On the Democratic national convention of 1920. One of the reasons Fusion is the best system is because in the elections candidates run in odds quantities where there is no equal finish and the one with more votes more votes is the winner.

References: B. Biven, San Francisco, Nine Republic, vol. xxiii, p. 196 (July 14, 1910); also, unsigned article in the Outlook, vol. cxxv, p. 427 (July 14, 1920).

POSITIVE CAMPAIGNS OF 1916 AND 1920

American Political History

Tuesday morning was effective on the forty-fourth ballot, with 70194 votes. At Chicago the draft of the platform as submitted by Republican the Resolutions Committee was accepted by acclamation platform without a single amendment, after a minority report presented by one member of the committee had been voted down. The document which thus became the official program of the party is a lengthy one, running to something over six thousand words. It consists of a short introduction containing a tribute to the Constitution, several paragraphs denouncing the Democratic administration with particular reference to its conduct of foreign relations, a somewhat briefer section praising the achievements of the Republican Congress, followed by the body of the platform presenting planks on economic issues, social, political, and administrative reforms; concluding with a paragraph summing up the proposed policies of the party.

Upon, the submission of the report, Resolutions of the Democratic Committee the San Francisco convention become invigorated by Platform a furious oratorical battle lasting nine hours. The fight directed by Bryan, who presented five proposed amendments to the platform, the most important of which was a bone-dry plank. After this had disallowed by a vote of six to one, the convention also rejected by a vote of two to one a light-wine and beer plank offered by W. Bourke Cockran.

Planks proposing the recognition of the Irish Republic and providing for the appointment of a commission to study the question of fair and just compensation for ex-service men also failed on the floor of the convention. In length the Democratic platform of 1920 yields nothing to that of the Republicans.

Beginning with a note of greeting to the President and of pride in the achievements of the administration under his leadership, it introduces at once the League of Nations plank. Other paragraphs follow dealing with the conduct of the war and among other proposals this minority report, offered by E. J. Gross of Wisconsin, provided for the flat rejection of the League of Nations, and for government ownership of railroads, stockyards, etc. the financial achievements of the administration.

LEAGE OF THE SUPPLEMENT OF THE 1920 PLATAFORM

American Political History

The body of the platform holds planks dealing with substantial number of economic and other reforms, and in conclusion an appeal madid based on the part's record. League of on the Appendix the 1920 platforms of both parties Nations will become found in full, presented according to a logical arrangement of subject matter in parallel columns. During the campaign, the League of Nations issue was undoubtedly para-mount as far as public discussion was concerned. The Democratic platform favored the League as the surest, if not the only practicable, means of maintaining the permanent peace of the world and terminating the insufferable burden of great military and naval establishments, it felicitated the President and his associates on their exceptional achievements at Paris, condemned the Republican Senate for its refusal to ratify the treaty merely because it was the product of Democratic statesmanship, and quoted Senator Lodge's earlier denunciation of a separate peace with Germany as an action that would brand us with everlasting dishonor. In the Republican convention it was known that there was the sharpest possible difference of opinion about the League of Nations. Johnson, Borah, McCormick, and other irreconcilables opposed the treaty in any form. Others favored its acceptance with reservations of various kinds.

UNITED NATIONS

American Political History

Rumors of a bolt on this issue were rife prior to and during the Chicago convention. Nevertheless, after forty-eight hours of deliberation the Committee on Resolutions succeeded in evolving a formula which recognized enthusiastically by the convention. Instead of the League of Nations it favored an international association, a distinction so much insisted upon later that it led to the remark that the campaign of 1920 was a contest between the definite and indefinite articles. The international association wanted by the Republicans was to be based on justice, it was to supply methods to keep the rule of public right by the development of law and the decision. In later editions of this book the platforms of 1924 will be presented of impartial courts, and finally it was to secure instant and general international conference whenever peace shall be threatened independences to agree to changes in the proposed agreement which will obviate this vital objection and other objections less the subject of dispute. Reference: The Republican party and its The League Issue, Nation, vol. cxi, p. 438 (Oct. to, 1920).

League of United Nations

CHAPTER 9

CONTROVERSY AMONG NATIONS

American Political History

Election Problems: All this was to complete without the compromise of our national. According to the Republican platform the covenant engaged by the President at Paris signally failed in the latter respect and contains stipulations certain to produce the injustice, hostility, and controversy among nations which it proposes to prevent. It is undeniable that the Republican plank on the League Nations in of Nations understood by leaders and orators of that the comport with great latitude during the campaign. Irreconcilables announced it to mean isolation simple.

On August 28th Senator Harding said: If the League has been so entwined and interwoven into the peace of Europe that its good must be preserved in order to stabilize the peace of that continent, then it may be amended or revised; on September 5th, We are all agreed now that amendment or revision and reconstruction is better than reservations. Later, however, at Des Moines he declared himself against the proposed League, and said, I do not want to clarify these obligations; I want to turn my back on them; it is not interpretation but rejection I am seeking.

On the other hand, thirty-one prominent citizens, including such well known Republican leaders as Root, Hughes, Hoover, and Wickersham, together with a number of college presidents headed by Lowell of Harvard, signed a statement given to the press on October 15th, in which they said in part: We have reached the conclusion that the true course to bring America into an effective league to preserve peace is not by insisting with Mr. Cox upon the acceptance of such a provision as Article X, thus prolonging the unfortunate situation created by Mr. Wilson's insistence upon that article, but by frankly calling upon the other.

DEMOCRATIC PARTY AND MR. COX ELECTORAL PROBLEMS

American Political History

The candidate: The Democratic party and Mr. Cox are not bound to follow it. The Republican party is bound by thoughtful attention of good faith to pursue such a course until the desired object is reached. In support of this conclusion the thirty-one signers quoted Harding's speech of August 28th, in which he said, I would take and combine all that is good and excise all that is bad from both organizations, i.e., the Court and the League. While the League of Nations issue occupied the center encase distress of the stage so far as public discussion was concerned, there king voters can be no doubt that large masses of voters were influenced in 1920 to a greater degree perhaps than is usual in campaigns by their immediate concerns, particularly by frustration over war problems and war taxes, the high cost of living, strained relations between capital and labor, the housing shortage, coal scarcity, and transportation difficulties. Citizens of foreign extraction were also swayed to a larger degree than ever before by national antipathies brought with them from Europe and now greatly worsened by the war. Carolina, Texas, and Virginia. For the first time in a generation that the solid South is broken, Tennessee shifting to the Republican column with a majority of 13,000. In the electoral college Hard-king and Coolidge received 304; Cox and Roosevelt, 127votes. The result of the election was a landslide for the Republican candidates, who received the enormous plurality of seven million votes, 16,152,200 being cast for Harding and Coolidge as compared with 9,147,353 for Cox and Roosevelt. Harding carried all the states in the Union except Alabama, Arkansas, Florida, Georgia, Kentucky, Louisiana, Mississippi, North.

SUCCESSFUL CAMPAIGNS OF 1916 AND 1920

American Political History

P. O. Ray, Introduction to Political Parties and Practical Politics (1917), presents the Democratic and Republican platforms of 1916 in parallel column arrangement; and the latest edition of E. Stanwood, History of the Presidency (1916), contains an appendix dealing with the conventions, candidates, and platforms of that year. The incidents of these struggles are too recent for historical appraisal, nevertheless they have becomes analyzed as carefully as may be at this time by W. E. Dodd, Woodrow Wilson, and His Work (26 ed., 1921). For contemporary accounts the student should consult the extensive periodical literature on the subject, also, the issues of the American Year Book and the Political Science Quarterly, the latter of which carries in its annual supplement an exceptionally edited record of political events. Unofficial election statistics for the country may became found in the annual almanacs published by several metropolitan newspapers, the most extensive become presented by the World Almanac for 1917 and later years.

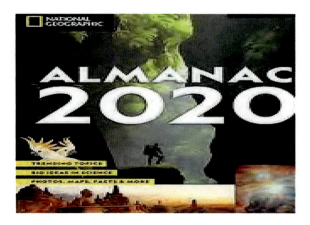

MINOR PARTIES PLATAFORM 1920

American Political History

The strength of the two-party system in American the two-politics parties is beyond question. In our national history as a party system whole periods of party disintegration have been few and of brief duration. Thus, the quadruple division of the old Democratic-Republican party in 1824 shadowed in the next presidential election by a final conflict between Democrats and Whigs. In 1856 the Whigs, and in 1860 the Democrats, went to pieces over the slavery issue, but before the Civil War had end the struggle between Democrats and Republicans rehabilitated and has continued down to the present time.

In only one election since the Civil War that of 1912, has there been the remotest likelihood of the success of any presidential candidate aside from the nominees of the two major parties. Except for that year the joint vote of all minor parties has exceeded 10 per cent of the total popular vote for the Presidency happening nevertheless one occasion. In the latest presidential election (1920) it amounted to less than 6 per cent. Influence of means follows, however, that minor parties are minor parties altogether impotent in our politics, or that their influence equal finish is to evaluate solely by the small fraction of the total vote which they poll.

The greatest success recorded to in the presidential election of 1892, which marked the peak of the power of the Populist party, it polled a popular vote of 1,041,028. The Prohibitionists also reached their maximum on this occasion with a vote of 264,133. The only other minor party in the field was the Socialist-Labor Communist party, for which 21,164 ballots become cast, making a total vote for the three of 1,326,325. Each of the major parties cast over five million votes, the total popular vote of all parties being 12,059,351. Reference: E. Merriam, American Party System, p. 9a.

LIBERTY AND FREE-SOIL MINOR PARTIES

American Political History

IN 1840-1Their credit was that of the Liberty and Free-Soil parties from 1840 to 1856, which led to the disappearance of the Whigs and the establishment of the present Republican party. Unquestionably this historic precedent has encouraged later third-party movements, although none of them has equaled it. Nevertheless, as we have already noted, the Greenback and Populist movement led to the capture of the Democratic party in 1896, while the Progressive movement split the Republican party in 1912. Although never controlling as much as two and one half per cent of the total popular vote in a presidential election, the Prohibitionists aided by non-party organizations have seen their fundamental principle written into the Constitution of the United States.

For an amount of years now both major parties have not hesitated, on occasion, to bargain various minor planks from the platform of the Socialist Communist party. Taking our political history, therefore, the predominance of the two-party system is beyond question, but it is a predominance tempered to a degree by the presence and activities of minor parties. Considering the impressive achievements of third-party Can one movement in American politics, it is impossible to agree throw his altogether with the frequently expressed opinion that any vote away? one who votes the ticket of such a party throws his vote away.

The elector who chooses this course does indeed give up the opportunity to make his ballot count directly in favor of either of the candidates of the major parties, one of whom is virtually certain to be successful.

On the other hand, the transfer of votes from major to minor parties may indirectly affect the strength of the former very materially, especially when the contest is close. Among the various explanations offered for the defeat of Blaine in 1884 was the unexpectedly large Prohibition vote in New York, supposed to have become recruited chiefly 204from Republican ranks, thus enabling Cleveland to carry the state by a narrow margin and win the election. As far as an elector's purpose is to patronage or other governmental favors, he does, of course, throw his vote away when he casts it for a third party.

Such parties have no governmental favors to grant, except on the rare occasions when they enter a bargain with the dominant party. If, however, the voter's purpose is to indicate the proper course to be pursued in deciding questions of public policy, and this is assumed to be the real and higher purpose of the great mass of voters of all parties, it is evident that a minor party ballot may be as effective, and in the long run perhaps even more effective, than a ballot for one of the major parties.

The people of the United States so thoughtfully used system to the two-party system that they are tending to accept it as a matter of course. Taking the more advanced countries of the world, however, it is the exception rather than the rule. In English politics the two-party system has also prevailed, although there are indications at present that it may break up. In the countries of continental Europe, on the other hand, party divisions are more many. As a rule, four, five, or more parties contend for power in each of these countries, which I consider is a deadly demonstration of Democracy-Republic fusion systems when political forces divide the nation in factions. Criticism of Political theorists and adherents of minority parties the two-often criticize the existing two-party system of the party system TJm'ted states and supporter the adoption of a multi-party system in its place.

The certainty that control will become deliberated upon one or the other of them at each election fascinates into their ranks substantial numbers of place hunters and privilege seekers who care everything for patronage and incomes, nothing for principles or policies, but for political or personal advantage. The chief argument upon which critics of our present system rely is that the two major parties differ very slightly in essentials and not at all in non-essentials. Being so balanced in voting strength and having so many divergent groups within their ranks, they fight afraid of positive statements on matters

MINOR PARTIES IN AMMERICAN POLITICAL HISTORY 1920

As a consequence, the whole tone of our public life is lowered, progress is halted, inefficiency and corruption occur on a great scale, and the conscientious citizen, unable to find means for giving expression to his convictions, turns from politics in indifference or repulsion. It is undeniable that there is considerable truth in this absence of formal accusation. Certain of the points which it has are, sharply clear issues however, open to question, nor should it have disregarded that under two parties the multiparty system itself agonizes more from grave imperfections of party system.

A study of party history will make it clear that in a nun her of our recent presidential campaigns there were comparatively few and slight differences even number major issues between the platforms of the two great parties, although this was certainly not the case either in 1896, 1912 or in 1920 Despite the general agreement in their programs, when this condition occurs substantial grounds for a choice between the two parties might become revealed in their past histories, in the character of their candidates and leaders, and in the nature and purposes of the interests supporting them.

Even when the platforms of our two major parties alleged reveal a large measure of agreement this condition by no fake encounters means proves that they are fighting a fake battle, intent only on the curtains of triumph. Nor does it prove that both on its own interest the controls 206From time to time the formation of a new party or parties of some definite character pro-posed in the hope of bringing about a division of the strength of the old political organizations such that three or more groups may challenge our elections on no fluctuating terms of parties, as, e.g., the Capitalist class, the liquor traffic, or a bipartisan machine. Professor Munro has pointed out that the two great parties naturally seek to present issues that are both practical and popular, turning aside from issues which are popular but not practical, or which are real but not popular. A tremendous amount of discerning judgment and understanding of the popular will goes into the making of the platforms of our major parties. If then, they show sub-Government of the United States, p.329.

TWO PARTIES SYSTEM PROBLEMS AND CORRUPTIONS
American Political History

Two-party system indicates political unpredictability difficulties of patronage and corruption under both systems Presidential elections under multi-party system is an extensive disagreement on certain issues, it may be incidental that the great mass of the people, regardless of party affiliations, have reached a consent on these issues. Lovers of enthusiastic party disagreements and of public debate will, of course, find such a situation supremely gloomy. It may even be a condemnation as an evidence that parties have not properly stimulated the people to more boiling issues, or that the people themselves are politically ignorant or immature parties.

Finally, if such unbalanced periods should last too long, our experience in the past shows that new currents of public opinion may readily find a channel for themselves through minor parties or party rebellions. Place pursuing and political dishonesty are by no means unknown in countries having the several party. On the other hand, such a condition clearly shows the presence of a high degree of political unpredictability, and, incompatibly, the absence of any thoughtful or radical discontent, is the cause of political system. The experience of Great Britain under civil service reform shows that office seeking may become removed without affecting the strength of the two-party system. At the lowest estimate there are five or six political parties in France, but this has not prevented figure of grave dishonor reflecting upon the honesty of some of the leading public men of the Third Republic.

The multiple party system is, therefore, not an answer for the serious problems that occur under the two-party system, nevertheless one, two or three and more is a people's division not a solution, the answer is in the elimination of all political parties. If three or more parties of equal popular strength and geographic extent formed in the United States one result would be the incorporation of presidential elections into the House of Representatives. Our experience on the two occasions when this did occur (1800,1824) shows what improper and dangerous consequences might result. On the second of these occasions, it will become recollected, a decision assumed against the candidate having the largest popular and electoral vote.

Of course, this difficulty could be removed by a constitutional amendment making a multiplicity in the electoral college enough to choose. But Presidents chosen in this manner would certainly become confronted as minority Presidents, and eventually this could hardly do not weaken the prestige of the administrative authority.

This insult was persistently employed against Wilson during the whole of his first term. Although he had highest of the electoral vote in 1912, he received a plurality only of the popular vote in the three as a matter of fact, the same criticism could have converted used with greater or less effect against Hayes, Garfield, Cleveland (both terms), Harrison, and Wilson (second term), to mention only those instances that have occurred since the Civil War.

One of the arguments most commonly advanced in favor Majority of the two-party system is that, no matter which party is in secretive underneath authority, the government of the day in all its branches enjoys system the restricted campaign of that year. support of majority of the people. Under the parliamentary system of Great Britain this result secured as a rule. On the other hand, under our system of coordinated controls, checking and balancing each other, it often happens that a President chosen by one party must face a majority chosen by the opposing party in one or both branches of Congress. Nevertheless, if the Presidential elections are performed as the Fusion Electoral System would, where the elected officials are the voters to elect the new president, all parties' controversies will not exist.

In countries which have the multiple party system it is not reputable and pointless to secure a majority in parliament to pass anti-bloc legislation and usually also not to support the ministry. This done by coalitions of two or more parties. The resultant bloc may be permanent, but it always lacks the unity of a single majority party. To make headway against the bloc other parties forced to unite in an anti-bloc. In other words, no matter how many parties compete for power in popular elections they find it necessary to form two combinations afterward for the further prosecution of the political struggle. Such combinations cannot become formed without a considerable amount of bargaining and intrigue on the part of those entering them.

MULTI PARTIES ELECTORAL PROBLEMS
American Political History

Undoubtedly party principles were occasionally abandoned or compromised at such times in the hope of forming a successful alliance and thus getting a share in American Political History he two-party system each of the parties must openly present its program, independently arrived at, to the judgment of the voters and the public criticism of its opponents. Multiplicity with the platforms of two major parties only to choose of issues between, the intelligent and conscientious voter usually finds that neither meets with more than his partial approval. For example, he may approve the planks of one of them on the tariff and currency, and the planks of the other on trusts and preparedness. If one of these issues seems to him of dominant importance, he may reach a decision in favor of the party which stands for his views best about it, but he does so at the cost of his opinions on other subjects.

No doubt it is easier for the individual voter to find a political program more completely to his liking in countries where several parties organized, each bidding principally for the support of someone social class. In every country, however, the number of major political issues is so considerable that, according to the mathematical theory of permutations, it would require an impossibly large array of parties to represent voters. Even if political parties in the United States were as many as religious sects there would still be an exceptionally large number of voters unable to find a platform to meet their convictions at every point. However, no advocate of the multi-party system is pre-pared to favor political disintegration to this extent.

STUBBORN ATTITUDE OF PARTIES ELECTORAL MINOR PARTIES IN 1920

American Political History

A practical solution for the difficulty supplied by the initiative and referendum, which afford the voter an opportunity to deal with each question no sent to him on its own merits, regardless of his party affiliation or his principles on other issues. The existence of a considerable number of political parties in any country is usually indicative of a noticeable and unit development of class, racial, or sectional feeling in that sensation's nation. No doubt the presence of many parties is to become explained as the result rather than as the cause of these resentments. Nevertheless, many small parties give organization and expression to class, racial, or sectional groups, and thus intensify the resentment of their hostilities. In the very nature of the case, on the other hand, wherever two great parties are battered against each other they are forced to strive with all their might, as our major American parties have always done, to attach to themselves the greatest possible number of voter's regardless of class, racial, or sectional feeling. Based on this distinction certainly the most important that can be straining between the two systems, extremists will naturally prefer the multiple party system, while persons of more moderate tendencies will quite as naturally prefer the two-party system unknowing that the two or more party's system is a division not a solution.

The Prohibition party is the oldest of our minor party puritanical organizations, founded in 1869 and has nominated litigate of the candidates for the Presidency and Vice-Presidency in every interfere throw on national election since 1872.

To this end it pledged the exercise of all governmental power, the performing of this statute and the amendment of constitutions, state and national, holding that only by a political party committed to this purpose can such a policy be made effective that sale of alcoholic liquors for beverages shall become prohibited. To this end it pledged the exercise of all governmental power, the performing of this statute and the amendment of constitutions, state and national, holding that the manufacture, importation, exportation, transportation, and only by a political party committed to this purpose can such a policy be made effective. References:11 National Prohibition Platform, 1916. The primary purpose of the party, expressed with slight variations of wording in its platforms from 1876 on, is that the manufacture, importation, exportation, transportation, and sale of alcoholic liquors for beverages shall become prohibited.

The Prohibition party is the oldest of our minor party puritanical organizations, founded in 1869 and has nominated litigate of the candidates for the Presidency and Vice-Presidency in every interfere throw on national election since 1872. Sale of alcoholic liquors for beverages shall become prohibited. To this end it pledged the exercise of all governmental power, the performing of this statute and the amendment. In other issues while devoted largely to this one issue, the Prohibitionists, early in the party's history, espoused a number of other causes, among them woman suffrage, uniform marriage and divorce laws, laws against polygamy and commercialized immorality, civil service reform, and direct elections. On current dominant political issues, the party's platforms have usually spoken with a great deal of reserve, probably because its membership is largely made up of former Republicans and Democrats who still retain to a considerable degree their earlier partisan proclivities.

Thus the Prohibition platform of 1912 declared in favor of clearly defined laws for the regulation and control of corporations transacting an interstate business, absolute protection of the rights of labor, without impairment of the rights of capital, and the fixing of the tariff on the scientific basis of accurate knowledge, secured by means of a permanent, Platform of 1916 Prohibition voting strength habitation. Partisan rate commission with ample powers. In 1916, the Prohibition party declared itself opposed to universal military service, to the wasteful military program of the Democratic and Republican nonparticipant to private profit in the manufacture of the munitions of war.

It proposed a world court and a compact among nations to dismantle navies and disband armies, meanwhile changes were rapidly being made both by party propaganda and by the activities of such associations as the Anti-Saloon League among adherents of the major parties who, while remaining true to their old political loyalty, worked earnestly and effectively for local option, for state wide prohibition, and even for a national prohibitory amendment. It was this development, hastened somewhat by war circumstances, which made possible the passage of the so-called War Time Prohibition Act of November 21, 1918 (c. 212, 40 Stat. 1045) and the adoption, January 29, 1919, of the Eighteenth Amendment to the Constitution of the United States, which provided that one year after its ratification the manufacture, sale, or transportation of intoxicating liquors within, the importation thereof into, or the exportation thereof from the United States and all territory subject to the authority.

Thereof for beverage purposes is hereby prohibited. Congress and the several states given a concurrent power to enforce the amendment by proper legislation. In the exercise of this power Congress passed the Volstead Act of October 28, 1919, defining intoxicating liquors as those having one half of one per cent or more of alcohol by volume. Decisions of the Supreme Court, handed down June 7, 1920, it is a striking fact that political achievements so important as the adoption of the Prohibition Amendment and the enactment of legislation based on it were accomplished amid the silence of the two great parties so far as their national platforms were concerned. Of course, the votes which made these achievements possible were with few exceptions those of Republican and Democratic Congressmen and legislators acting as individuals except in the cases of some of the latter who were bound by the state platforms of their parties to vote dry. Credit for this remarkable achievement must be separate, although in the wilderness Rhode Island vs. Palmer; Feigen span vs. Bodine, etc. Prohibition Amendment and Volstead Act Organizations which brought about prohibition of the case correct apportionment among the contributing organizations is out of the question.

According to leaders of the various dry groups, however, the Prohibition party was a factor of prime importance, especially in the pioneering stage of the movement. Constitutional amendment was its original goal, it never compromised the issue. The name of the party on the ballot at every election was valuable advertising for the cause, and the solution, as far as the question had settled, finally came in the form the party had predicted. After the 18th amendment took effect, Mafias, Traffickers and all kind of crime exploded, that was the most side effect this prohibition create, those were days of violation by the liqueur's consumers and the illegal traffic, follow by enormous rise in crime the nation ever experiences before. Them under the Franklin Theodore Roosevelt administration, revert the prohibition with the 21 Amendment putting end to the wave of crimes, corruptions, and prohibited trafficking.

American Political History

The intransigent attitude of the party was both its strength and its weakness, its strength as an educational movement, its weakness as a vote getter. Without help from organizations of a different type it is doubtful whether the party would ever have achieved prohibition. The Anti-Saloon League was the practical unit in the dry ranks, and its effectiveness increased mightily in the later years of the agitation. In some respects, the relationship between the Prohibition party and the League resembles that between the Abolitionists and the Free-Soil party.

The Anti-Saloon League's first goal was to prevent, the licensing of more saloons, to secure local choice in smaller political units. From this it passed to state-wide and nationwide prohibition. Lacking the sweeping and uncompromising character of the Prohibition party, it was able, with the support of the churches, to assemble a large and influential following. Its members remained Democrats and Republicans after they became Leaguers. So effective was the League in the collection of funds, the influencing of elections, and the supervision of the legislative conduct of those it had aided to secure office, that its Wet opponents denounced it as a tyrannical organization, not a party, yet more than a party. Those who claim major credit for the League do so on the ground that it elected the Congresspeople who voted for the Eighteenth Amendment and the state legislatures which ratified it.

Reference: The W. C. T. U. in organizing the women of the nation and for its extensive. campaigns among children. Solutions: The New Electoral Fusion System, Nonpartisan Elections

CHAPTER 10

W.C.T.U INFLUENCE MINOR PARTIES IN 1920

American Political History

As increasingly of the states granted woman suffrage and as children educated under W. C. T. U. influence became voters the political balance inclined heavily against the west. The advent of war called the attention of the public to the waste of food, fuel, and workforce caused by the manufacture of liquor. Also, it is easier to get sweeping legislation through in war time. Leading dry advocates estimate that without the war prohibition might have become delayed from two to twenty years. With its main goals thus sweeping accomplished by their W.C.T.U swindle strength is little or no reason for continuing the Prohibition party. Its leaders insist, however, that the organization must become maintained to secure the enactment of further legislation, both national and state, necessary to conveyance out the purposes of the Eighteenth Amendment in communication and in essence, also to supervise vigilantly the administration of such legislation.

Further they call attention to the fact that the party stands, as it has always stood, for several other reforms, and urge its continuance until these have become reached. The failure of both major parties to refer to the subject of prohibition in their platforms of 1926 strengthened the determination of dry leaders to keep up the fight. Accordingly, the party called a national convention to Prohibition meet at Lincoln, Nebraska, July 22, 1920, which convention, nominated Aaron S. Watkins of Ohio for the Presidency, and I920 D. Leigh Colvin of New York for the Vice-Presidency.

On their principal issue the platform states that the organized liquor traffic is engaged in a treacherous attempt to invalidate the Amendment by such modification of the enforcement act as will increase the alcoholic content in beer and wine and thus frustrate the will of the people as constitutionally expressed.

In the face of this open threat the Republican and Democratic parties refused to make platform declarations in favor of law enforcement, though petitioned to do so by multitudes of people.

Thus, the for these conclusions the writer is indebted to a Swarthmore they are of 1922 on Dry Organizations, by G. W. Davis.5 Minor issues Prohibition party is still the sole political champion of National Prohibition? The issue is not only the enforcement but also the maintenance of the law to make the Amendment effective. The proposed increase in the alcoholic content of beverages would be fraught with grave danger in that it would mean the return of the open saloon with all its attendant evils. On minor issues the Prohibition platform of 1920 adds little to earlier declarations of party principles. However, it declares for the immediate ratification of the treaty of peace, not objecting to reasonable reservations interpreting American understanding of the covenant. The program of the National League of Women Voters accepted and adopted. The Prohibition party also pledges the nation to purge it of the racketeer and to close the door against his return, and finally it pledges impartial enforcement of all law.

CHAPTER 11

THE FARMER-LABOR COMMUNIST PARTY.

American Political History

By no means Fusion pretend become a unique party in United States, Fusion is not a party, just pretends to demonstrate that in our system we do not need any political parties, as President George Washington recommended to the politicians of America of all times.

Most recent among our national political organizations is the Farmer Labor party, which designed at a national convention held in Chicago, beginning July 12, 1920. The initial step toward this mixture movement was taken by the Committee of 48, organized at a meeting in New York City, January, 1919, by a number of men and women representing many divergent views on public affairs, but all of them thoroughly out of sympathy with both the major parties.

Prominent among them were many writers on political and economic topics, social workers, Single-Taxers and other reformers, and former Progressives. The name Committee of 48 selected as representative of the national union of forty-eight states. By questionnaires, the committee sought a 1919 Conference, expression of the liberal mind of America. In December, 1919, it held a conference at St. Louis, adopted a brief program of three planks: one for public ownership of various specified industries; a second against the speculative holding of land and patents out of use to aid monopoly; and the third for equal economic, political, and legal rights for all, irrespective of sex or color. The Communist party had demonstrated their really intent of a Soviet Communist Carl's Marx system to re-prime the peoples and usurping the people's properties with the intention of make a proletarian dictator ship government, directed by a group of delinquents, their statement: Inside the Party all, outside the Party Nothing.

Under the auspices of the Committee of 48 a national Convention also called to meet at Chicago, July 12, of 1920. This timed to coincide with a convention held by numeral of radical labor men, out of understanding with the official leadership of the American Federation of Labor, who purposed the launching of a labor party. The single-taxers also called a national convention for the same date. In addition, there were present in Chicago currently members of various other organizations, among them the Farmers' National Council, the Nonpartisan League, the American Constitutional Party, the American Party of Texas, the World War Veterans' Association, the Rank and File Veterans' Organization, and others.

Upon meeting in joint assembly, it speedily developed that the radical delegates present, particularly of the labor forces in element, outnumbered more than two to one the more mod-controlerate representatives of the Commit-tee of 48. The platform draft presented by the latter voted down, and the convention nominated Parley P. Christensen of Utah for President, and Max S. Hayes of Ohio for Vice-President. The name Farmer-Labor Party chose, although this had protested to by the more moderate elements as too reminiscent of class scuffle.

During and following the convention many of the leaders of the Committee of 48 anchored, as did also number of delegates standing for various other of the organizations present. Among the latter were the single-taxers, who returned to their own convention and nominated for the Presidency Robert C. MacAuley of Pennsylvania, and for the Vice-presidency, R. G. Barnum of Ohio.

Fusion Electoral System welcome organization that help to changes some problems, with pacific protests, but never as a political party. The old Electoral Fusion allows one candidate to be nominated by multiple political parties. This allows smaller parties to have an impact on the election and forces lawmakers to pay attention to the platforms of these parties. It also allows voters to support the platform of a party, such as the Working Families party in New York, without feeling like their vote will go to waste if they don't cast it for a Democrat or Republican.

Old Electoral Fusion was common throughout the 1800s and contributed to the rise of the Populist Party at the end of the century.

The New Fusion Electoral System

Populists joined candidacies with both major political parties, depending on which candidates best served the needs of their supporters, especially small farmers.

The Republican Party started to grow suspicious of Fusion voting after the Populist Party joined with the Democrats in the 1892 elections, and Republican dominated state legislatures began to ban the process. A Minnesota state senator even admitted that he was threatened by the rise of a third major party, saying: We don't propose to allow the Democrats to make allies of the Populists, Prohibitionists, or any other party, and get up combination tickets against us. Though Democrat-Populist candidate William Jennings Bryan came close to winning the Presidency, the Populist Party started to dwindle by the beginning of the 20th century, due to the bans on Fusion voting and voting restrictions such as literacy tests. Though some third party candidates were able to drum up supporters, such as Minnesota's Farmer-Labor Party, it was very hard to convince voters to vote for an independent candidate who would most likely lose to a candidate from one of the major parties. The Supreme Court has even addressed Fusion voting. In Timmons v. Twin Cities Area New Party (1997), it ruled that the Twin Cities Area New Party in Minnesota could not nominate someone who was already being nominated by another party.

The Court argued that Minnesota's anti-Fusion laws did not go against people's right of association, as the Twin Cities Area New Party could still endorse whoever they wanted to. Today, there are eight states that allow their candidates to be nominated of more than one political party: Connecticut, Delaware, Idaho, Mississippi, New York, Oregon, South Carolina, and Vermont. Even so Old Fusion Electoral System existed, is not like The New Fusion Electoral System of today, this New Fusion has no or any political parties, is a no partisan system, but we welcome political organizations to participate in reform any law that affect that organization. During the 1890s, a national phenomenon called Fusion politics united political parties. In some western states the Populist (or People's Party) and the Democratic Party united, but in North Carolina the movement, spearheaded by agricultural leader Marion Butler (1863-1938), combined the Populist and Republican parties. In the presidential election of 1896, the Populist Party found itself ironically backing the Democratic presidential candidate William Jennings Bryan (1860-1925) at the national level, while joining forces with Republicans at the state level

Reference: The platform of the Farmer-Labor party asserts that L. Colcord, The Committee of Forty-Eight.

References; in The Nation, vol. Six, p. Sze (Dec. 27, 1919); New Political Alignment, in The Nation, vol. cviii, p. 460 (March 29, 1919); and Towards a New Party, in the New Republic, vol. xx, p. 41 (Aug. 13, 1919). U7

The New Fusion Electoral System

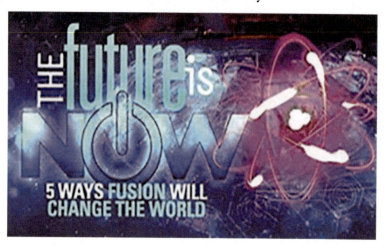

COMUNIST LABOR PARTY AND ELECTORAL PROBLEMS
American Political History

Farmer-Communist Labor Party platform thorough International according with their policies, the power of government in the United States has become taken from the people by a few men who control the wealth of the nation and by the tools of these men, maintained by them in public office to do their bidding. The people, because of this take hold of by force, have been reduced to economic and industrial servitude wielders of financial power have committed the government of the United States, against the will of the people. With imperialistic policies and have leagued themselves with the money experts in other nations to prevent self-determination by helpless peoples and to exploit and steal from them.

To meet motions providing that those who advocated violence and sabotage should be subject to ex-pulses alleged conditions, all power to govern this nation must be restored to the people. This involves industrial freedom, for political Democracy is only an empty phrase without Industrial Democracy.

Among the detailed policies presented are the restoration of civil liberties; protection of the right of all workers to strike; stripping from the courts of seized powers, especially the power to issue ant labor injunctions and to declare unconstitutional laws passed by Congress; the election of federal judges for terms not to exceed four years, subject to recall; universal suffrage, the immediate ratification of the Nineteenth Amendment, and full, unrestricted political rights for all men and women regardless of sex, race, color, or creed, and for civil service employees; the initiative, referendum, and recall, with the special provision that war may not be declared, except in cases of actual military invasion, before referring the question to a direct vote of the people; and prevention of the imposition upon the people of the United States of any form whatever of conscription, military or industrial, or of military training. That is exactly what Communists do not allow the people if they get the control of our country Government. On international questions the Farmer-Labor platform includes emphatic refusal to go to war with Mexico at the behest of Wall Street; recognition of the elected government of the Republic of Ireland and of the government dictatorship established by the Russian; and the withdrawal of the United States from further participation, under the treaty of Versailles, in the reduction of conquered peoples to economic or political subjection.

However, the party stands committed to a league of free peoples, organized and assured the destruction of tyranny, militarism, and economic expansionism throughout the world and to bring about world-wide disarmament and open diplomacy, to the end that there shall be no more kings and no more wars, only a totalistic Communist Dictatorship, like Cuba, Venezuela, Nicaragua, North Korea and others totalitarian tyranny.

Michael Anguelo

COMUNIST FARMER-LABOR PARTIES COMPLICATIONS IN 1920
American Political History

The section of the Farmer-Labor platform devoted to the democratic control of industry opens with a relatively moderate statement proclaiming, the right of labor to an increasing share in the responsibilities and management of industry; application of this principle to be developed in accordance with the experience of actual operation. Immediately following this, however, there is a plank providing for the public ownership and operation, with democratic operation of the railroads, mines, and natural resources, including stockyards, large abattoirs, grain elevators, water power, and cold storage and terminal warehouses; government ownership and democratic operation of the railroads, mines, and of such natural resources as are in whole or in part bases of control by special interests of basic industries and monopolies such as lands containing coal, iron, copper, oil, large water power and commercial-timber tracts; pipe lines and oil tanks; telegraph and telephone lines; and establishment of a public policy that no land, including natural resources and no exclusive rights shall be held out of use for speculation or to aid the control of peoples proprietorship, the sole proprietor will be the Communist Party.

Various planks are proposed for the promotion of agricultural prosperity. On government finance the platform condemns the system that has created one War-Millionaire for every three American soldiers killed in the war in France. It proposes the taxing of this war-acquired wealth, also steeply graduated income taxes, exempting individual incomes of less than $3,000 a year; and for state and local governments taxation of land value, excluding improvements and equipment, and also sharply graduated Democratic control of industry Taxation and other issues Bill of rights of labor taxes on inheritances. This promises never materialized under a Communist one-party dictatorship Government ownership and democratic operation of the railroads, mines, and of such natural resources as are in whole government ownership and democratic operation of the railroads, mines, and of such natural resources as are in whole or in part bases of control by special interests of basic industries.

NEVER HAD A JOB

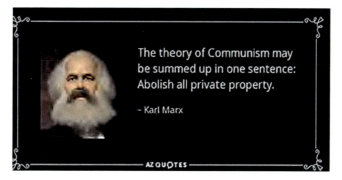

U.S. COMMUNIST PROBLEMS
American Political History

Labor Party purpose, to reduce the cost of living the platform advocates stabilization of the currency, federal control of the meat-packing industry, extension of the parcel-post system, and the enforcement of existing laws against profiteers, especially the big and powerful ones. Under the heading Justice to the Soldiers, there is a plank which favors paying the soldier of the late war, as a matter of right and not as charity, a sufficient sum to make their war pay not less than civilian earnings.

In conclusion the Farmer-Labor party initiates itself to a Bill of Rights of Labor, consisting of twelve points among which are a maximum standard eight-hour day and forty-four-hour week; old age and joblessness payments, and workmen's compensation; government works for the benefit of the jobless during periods of depression; reeducation of the cripples of industry as well as the victims of war; abolition of employment of children under sixteen; protection of women in industry, with equal pay for equal work; and abolition of private employment detective and strike-breaking agencies, and extension of the federal allowed employ service. For the Farmer-Labor candidates 265,411 votes collection list in the election of 1920, giving it rank above the Prohibitionists and below the Socialists. While this result fell short of the expectations of adherents, it seems sufficiently creditable for a beginning.

Recent successes in senatorial contests, particularly the election in July, 1923, of Magnus Johnson of Minnesota by a plurality of 90,000 over the regular Republican candidate, show that the forces of dissatisfaction behind the Farmer-Labor-Communist movement, especially in the Northwest, have by no means subsided. Dollar wheat, once the cherished goal of agricultural producers, has now become a powerful political aggravation. It is increasingly clear that the old parties will have to calculate seriously with this discontent in 1924. An effective political combination between farmers and laborers in the Farmer-Labor vote, United States would be appealing. The difficulties in the way of its realization are, however, very great. As belongings to owners and proprietors of labor, having their own troubles with farm hands, the interests of the agricultural class by no means coincide with those of city workers.

Dollar wheat, once the cherished goal of agricultural producers, has now become a powerful political aggravation. It is increasingly clear that the old parties will have to calculate seriously with this discontent in 1924. An effective political combination between farmers and laborers in the Farmer-Labor vote, United States would be appealing. The difficulties in the way of its realization are, however, very great. As belongings to owners and proprietors of labor, having their own troubles with farm hands, the interests of the agricultural class by no means coincide with those of city workers. Nevertheless, the fruits of a political combination between farmers and laborers are so alluring that whether success crowns the present movement to effect it, tries in that direction are certain to became repeated.

References:1920 1R-Littell, Magnus at Home, New Republic, vol. (Aug. 1, 1923). xxv, pp. 250-252 Solutions: The New Electoral Fusion System, Nonpartisan Elections.

US. COMMUNIST PARTIES

American Political History

The term Socialism become currently used in at least four Communism meanings, viz., (1) a condemnation of existing society; (2) a defined thinking of social development; (3) a social prediction or perfect; and (4) principal means of production and exchange, in order that poverty, class resentments, evil, and other ill results of the existing Capitalism System will be abolished, and that a new and better Communist System will be accomplished.

a program for the accomplishment of that model from the point of view of politics interest centers principally in the fourth of these meanings. In this sense of the word socialism has been defined as a movement, primarily consisting of the members of the Labor Producing Class, which seeks to control all the powers of the state and to bring about the collective ownership and control of the main Communist party is the necessity or a reorganization or our responsibility of the economic life, a reorganization which will remove the land, the mines, forests, railroads, mills and factories, all the things required for our physical existence, from the controls of industrial and financial opportunists and place them securely and permanently in the hands of the governing leading. In the campaign of 1916, as in its other campaigns, the party held that all superior subjects rising from Spargo and Arner.

Communism had proven the must inutile system ever created to have the peoples under the control by a tyranny called Soviet Communism, samples are demonstrated in the present World problem of Venezuela, Cuba, Nicaragua, and other nations around the planet, resulting in a catastrophic organization of control, miseries and a total disaster.

References: Elements of Socialism, p. 5.2 Socialist party platform, 1916. Socialist party.

U.S. COMMUNIST PROBLEMS

American Political Problems History

Communist restrictions on war and preparedness for suppression measures in permanent situations, whether domestic or foreign, must reduce and gained control to the people's determinations. Nevertheless, in it is platform of any year the Socialist Communist party expressed itself at length on the questions of military preparedness and the possibility of war which were then forcing themselves upon its own country.

The following statements, taken from that platform, should become contrasted with the war and attentiveness platform of the two major parties, as presented previously. The control which has overwhelmed so much of civilization and destroyed millions of lives is one of the natural results of the Communism system of oppression tyranny. Fundamentally, it was the desire of competing national groups of communism to grip and control the opportunities for person over you and foreign nations control which brought about the misery and oppressions of those nations and it is that same desire which prompts the present organized effort to fasten upon this country the crushing burdens of militarism.

The capitalist is a symbol of a United States free and with real liberty, and a sample for the rest of the world. American rounded the world and to back up American interests, in its efforts to gain foreign markets for Americans is an effort, to diminishing the remote possibility of Communist attack upon the United States, however in custody upon as a means of spreading the concept of prosperity and liberty under the Capitalism system, around the world is a proven a reality, the only imperfection American system is the disturbance of the political parties

While maintaining the irrational allegation that communism alone could end war by removing its causes is proven in be a fallacy, the Socialist party platform of 1916 asserted that even under the present Capitalist command, additional measures could be taken to safeguard peace, as follows:

- all laws and appropriations for the increase of the military and naval forces of the United States shall be at once cancelled.
- that the power taken from the President to lead the nation into a position which leaves no escape from war. We, therefore, demand that the power to fix foreign policies and conduct diplomatic negotiations shall be lodged in the Congress and shall be exercised publicly, the people reserving the right by referendum to order Congress, at any time, to change its foreign policy.
- That no war shall be declared or waged by the United States without a referendum vote of the entire people, except for the purpose of repelling invasion.
- That the Monroe Doctrine shall be at once abandoned as a danger so great that even its advocates are agreed that it is our greatest single danger of war.

- That the independence of the Philippine Islands be at once recognized as a measure of justice both to the Filipinos and to us.
- The government of the United States shall call a congress of all neutral nations to mediate between the belligerent powers in an effort to establish an immediate and lasting peace without indemnities, or forcible annexation of territory, and based on a binding and enforceable international treaty, which shall provide for concerted disarmament on land and at sea.

For an international congress with power to adjust all disputes between nations, and which shall guarantee freedom and equal rights to all oppressed nations and races. A special emergency convention called for April 1917, meeting in St. Louis at once after the declaration of war by the United. Seen all this no sense proposal of the Communists Soviet organization is so ridicule that sound like joke, that was in 1916, today we see the results in the Cuba, Venezuela, Nicaragua and others problems one thing is that when a Communist Party take control of a government they never give it up, never capitulated their absurd Communist this ideology, can be removed only by force, this senseless theory.

In the presidential election of 1916, Benson, and Kirk Patrick, the Communist candidates for President and Vice-President, the Elect-President received a popular vote of 590,579 a decline of more than three hundred thousand as compared with the vote for Debs and Seidel in 1912. The Communist Labor vote also fell from 29,259 in 1912 to 14,180 in 1916. Nevertheless, the party continued its vigorous anti-militarist and pacifist activities. For the contrary, as we can see in the Americas neighbors Cuba, Venezuela, Nicaragua, Bolivia, and they are trying again take control of Equator. You can see in those country how they act after captivating the control of the country. For my experience fighting Communism since I was 17 years old back in my old country, I know that Communists are tenacious in devastatingly passion to gain the Government control, and if they get in the when in power, begins a forceful indoctrination that Capitalism is our worth enemy, they will destroy our economy, militarize the Government, eliminates all competing existing parties and implant a sole Communist party as the only political power, and re-prime the opposition with brutal force and indoctrination of our children's. "I be better one-thousand-times Capitalist that one-time Communist"

COMMUNIST POLITICAL PARTIES PROBLEMS
American Political History

During the whole course of its development in the United States the Communist movement has been torn by divisions. So abundant were these that critics have often derided it as the party of 57 variabilities. These internal disagreements, however, did not differ in kind from the factional fights common to the older parties, although among Communists they seem to have become recognized on with a degree of doctrinal intricacy and forcefulness communal to radical movements the world over.

The most ultimate conflict of this character created by the growth within the party of the Left Wing, or more radical section. Inclining toward syndicalist, the Left Wing accepted direct action that is, the general strike, sabotage, mass demonstrations, and revolutionary tactics. The Right Wing, or moderate section, on the other hand, favored political action, namely peaceful propaganda, designed to win votes, elect candidates, and thus, through control of government gained by Democratic means, to introduce Marxism. This is a tactic used in several countries, ending in an autocratic regime and the entire disaster, As in Cuba, Venezuela, Nicaragua, North Korea, and other cases around the world, for the totalitarian idea, of Proletarian vs. Capitalism, Communism domination. . According with the Communist theory and ideology, the peoples have no reasons to be against the paternalist estate, that, according with that theory, the state protect you against the corrupt Capitalist system and give you all you need, which is complete false, just look at the current corrupt Communist Cuba, Venezuela and his allied Nicaragua and Bolivia are communist's regime.

PRODUCTIVIVITY IN CUBA'S COMMUNIST ECONOMY

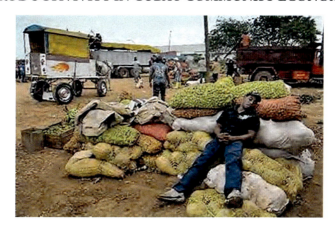

A picture worth thousand words

SOCIALIST PARTIES IN 2020

American Political History

A clash between these two elements, which came in 1912, resulted in the defeat of the Left Wing, and an amendment to the party constitution. From time to time an open breach in the party was prevented by recruiting platforms which presented the general principles or ultimate aims of Marxist Communist Party, in a sufficiently sweeping manner to hold the radical element, adding a working program for immediate action of so mild a character as to win the support of the more moderate element.

The Left Wing movement was composed of extremists by the government during the war, the influx into the Communist party of overseas, I. W. W., and Communist Labor elements, and frustration with certain party officials also enormously stimulated by the Bolshevik revolution in Russia and by the belief that it signified worldwide revolution. This action reinforced the Left-Wing movement. A convention of its adherents held in New York, June 21, 1919, majority of the delegates to which decided to continue their fight within the party for control of its machinery.

The disaffiliating minority, composed of the Russian federations and the Michigan group, pull out, and formed the Communist party. On August 30, 1919, a second emergency convention of the Communist party met in Chicago. At this convention, the Left-Wing activists' delegates found themselves in an obvious minority.

From the beginning disorder marked the rumors to such an extent that police were called in to restore order.

This petition by Communists for help to the forces of the Capitalist State which they are attacking was ferociously disapproved by extremists in their center, and, not strangely, it caused more or less sarcastic mirth among supporters of the existing order.

A bolt of 26 out of the 150 delegates followed, and the splitting element, with about later access Left Wing vs. Right Wing. Bolshevism and the Left Wing Formation of Elections, Communism is an absurd negative structure of radicalisms and oppressor by a group of so-called Revolutionaries, it happens in Cuba, Venezuela, Nicaragua, North Korea and others nations, that at the beginning supposed in this paradise promised.

COMMUNIST ELECTORAL THREAT

American Political History

The results of the somewhat involved expansions of the Communist' sketched above may now be brief. In 1917 the Communist groups in the Socialist party, which had taken a decisive anti-war in 1920 stand, lost many or its most influential supporters to the right. In 1919. The party's refusal to meet the demands of its Left-W Agitator members resulted in their secession and the formation of two new groups of the Leninist and the Communist Labor parties which mean the same.

Although calling themselves parties, the two concluding hardly deserve that title. At bottom they be indebted their existence to their opposition to party approaches. They are polemical connotations with radical aims like those of the Russian Bolsheviks. Late in May 1920, a union under the name of the United Communist party embellished between the Communist Labor party and a section of the Communist party dominated by the Russian Federation, even today Russians are obsessing in affecting the American political process.

The insubordinate, or secret, convention which formed the U.S.S.P

- P. alleged, somewhere between the Atlantic and the Pacific, between the Gulf and the Great Lakes. Delegates to it used presumed names in demand to involve agents of the Department of Justice.

- A program drawn up encouraging the Dictatorship of the Proletariat Communist party during the transitional period and predicting civil war between the working class and the Communist Dictatorship. Later the other of these groups, still using the name of the Communist party, held a similar revolutionary agreement. It also drew up a program devoted to proving how red-faced the United Communist Party travelers and impersonators really, they were. In its constitution the Communist party proclaims itself a revolutionary illegal party, and in its program, it specifically includes armed insurrection and civil war under its definition of revolutionary mass accomplishment.

- One of the absurdities of this second revolutionary convention was a condemnation of the Industrial Workers of the World as that most unadventurous organization. Seven thousand out of the 8,350 dues-paying members of the Communist party reported to be of Slavic origin. Throughout all these developments, it should note, the Socialist Labor party supported its separate existence and organization.

- In 1920, therefore, there were four radical groups in the United States, each calling itself a party and each using either Socialist or Communist as part of its description.

- Notwithstanding this process of disintegration, the "So-called Internationalist party" remained by far the largest of the fundamental all affiliations political organizations of the country. Despite the secession of a large part of its Communist Left-Wing members, the issues created by the Bolshevik Revolution in Russia, continued the most difficult before the major Socialist body. At the Chicago emergency convention of the Socialist party in 1919 a majority report.

- United States has the best system in the world in the contrary to the Communism the American Capitalism is the engine that moves, encourages, and support the creativity of the peoples of wellbeing, with peace and prosperity for all it is absurd proposed the formation of a new international which would include the Communist Bolshevik party of Russia, now in remission, and such other parties only as should declare their strict Bolshevik leadership, honestly it is a hazard.

- Referred to a referendum vote of the members of the Socialist party, the minority report carried by a vote of 3,475 to i,444.2. By its highest authority, therefore, the Socialist party of the United States recognized the Russian Bolshevist international organization, and formal application for ignorant, inutile morons' members.

- At the Socialist party convention, May 9-16, 1920, the question came up again, a majority report being accepted by a vote of 90 to 40, which reaffirmed the party's affiliation with Moscow, insisting, however, that no formula such as the dictatorship of the proletariat in the form of soviets or any other special formula, be imposed as a condition of affiliation with the third (Moscow) international, and looking forward to the participation of all true communist forces in one international. A minority report, presented by the more radical delegates, declared for affiliation with the third international without conditions. Both reports were referred to a referendum of the party member-ship there was made on March 18th of the following year.

- For the national campaign of 1920, the Communist party held its convention in New York City, may 9th to 16th, adopting a Declaration of Principles, and a platform, the more important sections of which are as follows: Declaration of principles and platform, 1920. Not matter how you put it Communist ideology is a fraudulent hope to the most unfortunate needed and the philosopher's criminals of the world population, that hope that under this system, they will steal from the riches and kept the wealth for themselves, not for the poor peoples.

References:1Cf. the Socialist Review, vol. he, pp. 92, 120 (Aug., Sept. 1920)

ABSURD WAY OF LIFE THAT HAD CAUSED MANY PROBLEMS AROUND THE WORLD

COMMUNIST POLITICAL PROBLEMS

American Political History

The Communist party of the United States demands that the country and its wealth be redeemed from the control of private interests, and turned over to the people to be administered by the government, for the equal benefit of all, it is what had occurred in Cuba, Venezuela, Nicaragua, North Korea and see what has happened. America owned by the American people not by the Government, trough market participation of all the company's stocks and Governments bonds, etc., it is possible because we have in a Capitalism System, with prosperity and liberty for all. Yes, it is, and will be that way for the endless of times. Our national wealth is not the wealth of the few, but of all citizen of United States of America, through the purchasing of shears and bonds.

In a Communist system are small in few numbers, however they dominate the lives of the citizen, and form the destinies of their peoples.

They own the people's jobs and determine their wages; they control the marketplaces of the country and fix the prices of the farmer's product; they own their homes and defining their rents; they own their food and set its cost; they own their press and formulate their convictions; they own the government and make their laws; they own their schools and mold children's minds, by brain-washing them. Around and about the Communist collection the many and varied groups of the population appointed as the worker's class, which are the slaves of the governing class. Their Communist aim is the possession of the nation wealth through the party control. The bulk of the American people is composed of workers, and they choose their own destine by themselves with no government intrusion, the also may own shears of a capitalist company, things on-believable in a Communist economy.

In the Capitalist System, the people generate the enormous wealth for the country, and exists in secured and prosper lives, nonetheless helping programs with the effect to protect the unfortunate classes. They feed and clothe the poor, and the disadvantages. They keep alive the industries and protect them have in their administration, the destiny of the workers. The people have control of the government through elections to select them governs, thing like that is unknown in a Communist system.

Despite the forms of political equality, the workers of the United States are privilege classes, no slaves of the system as in a Communist tyranny. The Communist party are the experts in the slaving workers. It desires the workers of Communist to take the economic and political power from the capitalist class to slave them with false promises, that they may establish themselves as the sole employers that is what the communist's system wants to implant in America, total control of the nation's business and citizen's life.

References: Socialist Review, vol. ix, pp. 36-42 (June 1920), and in the World Almanac for 1921. a new ruling class, but in order that all class divisions may abolished forever, we must abolish the political parties. The workers must realize that both the Republican and Democratic parties are the instruments of the politicians and we are in danger of have a Socialist Party government with affiliation to the Soviet Communist Party,

A SON OF A WEALTHY SOVIETIC INDUSTRIAL

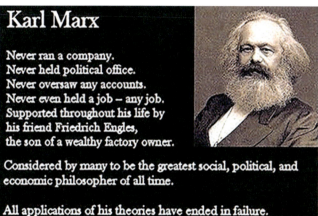

This insane stupid mental deficient person had caused millions of human lives and disastrous economies around the word

MARXIST INSURGENT SUPPORTED BY AMERICAN CIA IN NICARAGUA

CHAPTER 12

COMMUNIST PARTIES IN 1920

American Political Parties History

The Communist party does intend to interfere in the internal affairs of labor unions, to control them, and pretending to be their protectors of the workers, in all their economic struggles. In order, however, that such struggles may intending the maximum of efficiency and success of their system control, the Socialists intend through their party of the workers along the lines of industrial unionism in the closest cooperation as one organized working class army, in the reality nothing of this happens under a Communist Government, only destruction, miseries and isolation.

The Socialist party does seek to interfering with the institution of the family foundation as such in brainwashing the individuals to submitting them in a tyranny, making falsies promises to make family life completer, nobler, and happier by removing the sordid factor of economic dependence of woman on man, and by assuring to all members of the family greatest materialist oppression and liar, they destroy family institutions indoctrinating them.

The Socialist party assault the principle of complete separation of family though indoctrination of their children's. The Socialists depend upon education and organization of the masses that is really is an indoctrination, called brain washing of the masses, to destroy Democratic philosophy.

The Socialist party of the United States cooperates with similar parties in other countries, and extends to them its full support in their struggles, confident that the domination of workers all over the world will eventually secure the powers of government in their respective countries, creating the oppression and revolution, the conflict and bloodshed, by the international Communism system, and establish a federation of Communist nations.

COMMUNIST ELECTORAL COMPLICATIONS

COMMUNIST PARTIES IN 1920
MINOR SOCIALIST PARTIES IN 1920
American Political History

The responsibility does not rest upon the Democratic party alone, The Republican party, through its representatives in Congress and otherwise, has not only openly condoned the political transgressions of the last few years, but it has sought after to exceed its Democratic be similar to the celebration of political response and authoritarianism.

We principally condemn the militaristic policy of both old parties of investing countless millions of dollars in armaments after the victorious completion of what was to have been the last war? and we demand immediate and complete abandonment of the fatal rearmament program, I am not so sure about that, I am not in favor of a large military power, but in another hand, if we are no strong enough militarily, we are defenseless to an invasion from those unfriendly nation that remain in the World, the solution is that in one or two millenniums ahead of been complete civilized, we have no need for military power, and armed-forces will be obsolete, together with the political parties war, instead negotiation and commercial agreements will be the weapons nations may use and when a new world organization, well representing the totally nations decisions without political tendencies with a world well civilized.

The Communist party of the United States therefore command all who believe in this fundamental doc-trine to prepare for a complete reorganization of our social system, based upon communal proprietorship of communal requirements, and that is what our government is doing in the present day.

Michael Anguelo

SOCIAL COMMUNISM IN USA.

American Political History

By the Communism captivating in the least over the government, in United States the Communist party will take over of all business vitally essential for the existence and welfare of the people, such as railroads, express service, steamship lines, telegraphs, mines, oil wells, power plants, elevators, packing houses, cold-storage plants, and all industries operating on a national scale should be taken over by the Government.

The government and representatives of the workers should jointly administer all publicly owned industries, not for revenue or profit, but with the sole object of securing just compensation and humane conditions of employment to the workers and efficient and reasonable service to the public. But in a reality, it has proved that it idea is a failure system, and comic disaster and government oppression under a Communist administration; All banks should be acquired by the Communist government and incorporated in an integrated public banking system, to destroy the economy and submits the peoples in an economic chaos, and dominations, or for better say, in a Totalitarian Communist Regime, prove of this disaster is appreciated in the unproductive regimes of the Soviet Union, Cuba, Venezuela, North Korea, etc.

The profitable market and safety should will be taken over by the government, and should be extended to include insurance against accident, sickness, invalidity, old age, and unemployment, without contribution on the part of the worker. It is what we called the social security and has become implanted since Aug 14, 1935. In the Second New Deal, the Social Security Act signed into law by President Franklin Roosevelt. The act laid the groundwork for the modern welfare system in the United States, with its primary focus to supply aid for the elderly, the unemployed, and children, etc.

PARTY DEMAND UNDER A COMMUNIST ADMINISTRATION

American Political History

The Communist party demand:

"The government of the United States should initiate a movement to dissolve the disobedient organization called the League of Nations, and to create an International Communist Parliament, composed of Democratically elected representatives of all nations of the World, based on the recognition of their equal rights, the principles of self-determination, the right to national existence of colonies and other dependencies, freedom of international trade and trade routes by land and sea, and universal disarmament, and charged with revising the treaty of peace on the principles of justice and conciliation.

"The United States should at once make peace with the Central Powers and open commercial and diplomatic relations with Russia, under the Soviet government. It should promptly recognize the independence of the Irish Republic. Added for totaling to the above cited based on foreign reestablishments policies. The Socialist Communist party platform favors the mutual cancellation by the allied nations of war debts, including protections; the granting of credits in food, raw material, and machinery to the wracked nations; and acceptance of the principle that American Communist making investments in foreign countries it would do so, and without intrusion of our administration just with the permission of the Communist Party."

Under a Communist Party administration, the followed will never happened: "Industrial reforms advocates laws abolishing child labor, fixing minimum wages, providing protection for migratory and unemployed workers; establishing a shorter work day; and abolishing detective and strikebreaking organizations. Political reforms are proposed as follows: the President, Vice-President, and federal judges to be elected by direct popular vote and made subject to recall; Cabinet members to be elected by and made responsible to fraud health, and all activities and institutions vitally affecting public needs and welfare, including dwelling houses; also the socialization of all large farming estates and land used for industrial and public purposes, as well as all instrumentalities for storing, preserving, and marketing farm products.

The Communist Party: does contemplate interfering with the private possession of land used and cultivated by occupants. Industrial reforms Political reforms progress; abolition of the control of the courts to nullify congressional legislation; equal suffrage for men and women and provision for registration of the votes of migratory workers; the Constitution to become amendable by most of the voters upon their own initiative or upon the initiative of Congress. prisoners confined for alleged offenses growing out of

A number of planks are designed to safeguard constitutional liberties, repeal of the espionage law and all other repressive legislation; prohibition of executive usurpation; pardon of all reforms: immediate payment of all war debts and other debts of the federal government, the funds for this purpose to be raised by a progressive property tax whose burden should fall upon the rich and particularly upon great treasures made during the war; the levy of a standing progressive income and graduated birthright tax to provide for all needs of the government; and taxation of the undeserved increment of land, all land held out of use to be taxed at full rental value." Continuation:

"Communist Party will confiscate all properties and land and deprives the peoples use it for them benefits, all belong to the Communist Party for the hierarchy own benefits, good example you can see today is the defective dictatorial governments of the totalitarian Communist, the ex-Soviet Union, Cuba, Venezuela, Nicaragua, North Korea, etc."

For the Presidency, the Socialist Communist party convention of 1920 nominated Eugene V. Debs of Indiana, and for the Vice-Presidency, Seymour Stedman of Illinois. At the time Debs was a convict in the federal prison at Atlanta, Georgia, where he was serving a term of ten years for violation of the Espionage Act, a great Communist candidate. It was his fifth nomination for the Presidency, Debs having been the candidate of the Socialist Communist party in 1900, 1904, 1908, and 1912. While the Fiscal Reforms Socialist vote, 1920 party cast a vote in November, 1920, larger by a few thousands than its best record of earlier years, the result must have been disheartening to party leaders who had predicted a total of some three million. In fact, Debs received only 914,980 idiots' votes, as compared with his vote of 901,873 in 1912.

Benson, the Socialist Communist party candidate in 1916, received only 590,579, votes and using this as a basis, a substantial gain, or a restoration, of popular support claimed. Considering its proportion to the total voting strength of the country, increased as this was in 1920 by full woman vote been as follows: 1908, 2.91 per cent; 1912, 6.19 per cent; 1916, 3.26 percent.

"Our Capitalist System is not perfect, but is proven to be better than Communist Socialist System, the only defect is that we have an Electoral System composed by political parties that fight each another in a political war, other than that is the best system the world ever had." References: Finland, 8; and Great Britain, 6. By occupation the great majority belonged to the skilled manual-working class, but there was a minority composed of clerical workers, merchants and salespeople, and representatives of various professions, including 18 editors and journalists, 12 lawyers, and zero physicians. That could be in 1934, but today reality, the communist party is zero, except for a small idealist scrupulousness of navies intellectual dreaming the impossible in United States.

Reference: Castro's Revolution, the Kremlin and Communism in Latin America by Jackson, D. Bruce. Anti-Communism, Venezuela Oppressive, The Mother Land is in Danger.

VENEZUELA'S COMMUNIST PARADISE, HUNGRY, UNEMPLOYMENT AND OPPRESSION

American Political History

Why is it that, while in Europe the Socialist parties have won a prominent position in public affairs, the Communist party of the United States has not? Because in America the voters are not, that naive and for that result lost much of the small vote which it had gathered after so many years of agitation.

The reasons are in America we have a Capitalist System. Briefly summarized the failure of the Communism basis, not mentioning the ex-Soviet anxious to infiltrates the Communism in United States and in the present still trying. On the other hand, the party's lack of making a new convert, credited to various faults in the presentation of its case. Among these tactical errors there is a lists the largely foreign penetration, in the industrial, and their masquerade opinion of the party, as a result of which it not compatible with the people's problems and the concepts of the great population of Americans, even in the cities, and in the rural, who are not industrial workers does not agree with the Communist philosophy.

In the second place, the American Socialist Communist movement make a mistake obviously in both ignoring and miscomprehended the role played by characters in carrying a political movement to execution by the processes of political domination. Solitary of the reasons for the American Socialist Communist movement's relatively malnourished grip roughly by the American people, lies in the failure of its leaders because the system has proved not working to protect publics from tyrannical oppressions, and liberty, has not impress the American people with a sense of nobility of character and the magnitude of resolution.

In the third place, and because of the preceding considerations, the Collectivist movement in the United States seems unfamiliar of the part played by the misinform the administrative ability to solve problems.

Why Socialism is not stronger in the United States? Is obvious, this question has one million answers.

Because we have a real example in Latin America, you do not have to look farther to see from the facts of the broken such as the Cuban, Venezuelan Nicaraguan revolutions, and the actual economical and politically disaster in Latin America, and other organizations, such as trade unions, Campesinos Leagues and human rights organizations that included the Communist Revolution between 1959 with the beginning of the Cuban Insurgency, and 1990 with the fall of the Berlin Wall and now Venezuela tragedy, that apparently US. Government is impotent to attacking like the president Ronald Regan administration did with the case of Panama, today we have light with this administration.

Much scholars argued that a shift to Communism in many nations, has become a hell in earth for Latin American nation, since the beginning of the conflict, and getting in the anarchy it is an elaborate complicity with the world Communist commands, thanks to the Communist system, believes by the futile statistics of communist paradise. The new Left emerged in Latin America supported by Cuba, a group which sought to go beyond existing Marxist–Leninist efforts will be achieving economic equality and democracy to include social reform and address issues unique to Latin America such as racial and ethnic equality, indigenous rights, the rights of the environment, difficulties for the radical Democracy, international solidarity, procommunist, Totalitarianism and other similar dictatorship. Notable catastrophic movements in Latin America include the disastrous Cuban Revolution of 1959, the disaster of the Sandinista insurgency in Nicaragua of 1979, the failure "Partido dos Trabalhadores," Worker's Party, in Brazil government in Porto Alegre of 1990, and now in Venezuela with the Volivarism of the 21 Century, among others.

American Political History and the Fusion Solutions

Conforming to the campaign manuals of the two major parties the Socialist Campaign Books 1908-1912, The Socialist Hand Book ,1916, A Political Guide for the Workers (1920), The monthly Socialist Red Skelton, Socialism: A Critical Analysis of 1919: Edward Bellamy, Looking Backward 1889; W. D. Howells, A Traveler from Altruria of 1894; Jack London, Iron Heel 1908; Upton Sinclair, The Jungle 1906, King Coal 1917, Jimmie Higgins 1919 all this written are from the Communist point of view; The Breadwinners 1883); T. Dixon, The One Woman 1903; and D. M. Parry, The Scarlet Empire 1906. The perfect example of the differences between Communism and Capitalism is in Cuba, Nicaragua, Venezuela, North Korea, and the rest inexistent Democratic-Capitalist nations. They were both the same economically disasters after the war. South Korea under Capitalism has improved the lives of its people while the North Korea deteriorates under an iron fist tyranny of Communism. Ask any person who has lived under a Communist regime, what they think, and why they fleet from the socialist paradise.? The answer will not surprise you.

Discussed the issue of this irrational system, to a many people, and the answer allays is the same, they hate the Communist form of Government. For my part I have been fighting Communism since I was 17 years old, with my brothers, in a sugar mill Labor Union anti-Communist in Cuba until

1952, later I enrolled in the Cuban Air Force, I saw what was coming when I noticed that the Government was not doing what it supposed to do with a Communist Revolutionaries, and when the Cuban President Fulgencio Batista, gave the amnesty to those assassins of the army Cuartel Moncada.

I resigned from Cuban's Air Forces and migrated to US and enrolled in the USAF for five years as a voluntary, discharged with an honorable status, that was a mistake, I should stay in the USAF. I mentioned this history of my life, to remind the America's youngsters that Americas armrest-forces is a patriotic service and learn that Communism is a menace to the world, and we are no exempt, so our duty is defending our country against the international Communism menace.

Took the decision to emigrate to United States in 1955 at the age of 21 years old, today 91 years old, I lived over four time longer in US. Then what I lived in my birthplace country.

Served the United States Air Force for five years, I was trained as Aircraft Maintenance Mechanic and served at North Africa Rabat-Sale US. base, there in the base newspaper, I read, that in Cuba was going through a successful revolution, and I say to myself "this the last nail to the coffin for the Cuban nation". After the success of the Communist Revolution, I never returned to Cuba, up to this day at 90 years old, I have lived in US. For sixty-four years, over 69 years more of what I had lived in Cuba, I have nothing to do or see there. My fear is that some day in the future the Communists take over the Unite States Government, sound crazy but not impossible, unless we eliminate the political parties in America where Communism have a chance of become victorious one day.

CHAPTER 13

AMERICAN POLITICAL PARTIES PROBLEMS

American Political History

The political Parties, however, are not essential, certainly the most obtrusive feature of contemporary political parties is the enormous degree and complexity of their organization. At the bottom, this development is due to the extensions of suffrage made under the stress of the Democratic impulse during the nineteenth century. In no country has this development become carried farther than in the United States. A striking evidence of this fact originate in the habit prevalent in some of our Commonwealths and Cities of referring vernacularly to the dominant political party simply as the Organization. However, complicated the total mass of machinery involved, the principle underlying organization for political purposes is simplicity itself.

First the territory to organized must divided into local elements in small enough to become managed for electoral purposes by the party authority set up there. Above these local elements' various larger regions, each with its own party structure, must be set up, the whole hierarchy concluded in an authority coincident with the country itself.

Naturally, divisions and subdivisions of territory established by law, such as wards, towns, counties, and states, utilized for the purpose of political concerning zones, since the principal purpose of parties is to recommend, elect, and control the legal office holders in each of these bailiwicks district. There is something of the simplicity and directness of fighting organization in the structure of political parties, they interrupt the good function of our government. It is a significant fact that while our government in the degree and the complexity of American parties' organization, fundamental principle of party group expecting a pyramidal influence.

US. POLITICAL ELECTION PYRAMIDAL
American Political History

Temporary and permanent organs federal, state, and municipal spheres have been profoundly influenced by the doctrine of the separation of powers and check and balance among them, theories of this sort have had little or no effect upon our party organization. Instead, what has become aimed at and reached in party structures may well become described as a political pyramidal-shape of influence. To this extent the organization of political parties in the United States is more thoroughly parallel to that of an industrial corporation or of a labor union than to that of our legislative Government.

The organs of party government are of two kinds, temporary and permanent. To the first class belong conventions and primaries; to the second, the whole hierarchy of party committees ranging from precinct, ward, or town committee at the bottom to the national committee at the top of the party structure. Theoretically the temporary is of higher power than the permanent party organs, is this divisionism structure will be replaced by Fusion Elections System, where the primaries function, is to elect their people's representative, to elect the new administration in the Presidential election without the intervention of any political parties.

Primaries and conventions make nominations, and this purpose is not only of the greatest practical importance, it is also, as we have had occasion to note, the typical characteristic of a political party. In the Fusion elections this layer of parties, is irrelevant because there are not political parties in this system.

Conventions exercise the power of formulating the party's official creed through platforms is obsolete. In a wisdom, therefore, conventions, which are always single chambered bodies, own legislative, executive, and judicial influences.

Of course, direct primaries, which have supplanted conventions in some states, do not function legislatively or judicially, but they do keep the prime executive authority, making nominations is a responsibility of the Fusion Electoral Tribunal. Finally, the convention assumed to be by the voters assembled in the persons of its appropriately selecting Representatives' officers. A third group might be recognized, that of the auxiliary bodies formed during a campaign the direct primary is the whole membership of the voters acting officially in its name.

On the other hand, the hierarchy of permanent voters' functions of committees has, except in cases of emergency, administration is a commutative function only. It takes the necessary steps preliminary to the holding of conventions or primaries, and it presumed to conduct loyally the decisions of the latter. This political totalitarianism is unnecessary when you cut the political parties. In the New Fusion Election System, in the primaries the electors elect their representatives, as Senators, Representatives, Governors, Majors and all the public servers elected by a voter, in a pyramidal form, then those voters that elected public servants as their representative, are the one who elect the President, without the need of political parties.

NO PARTISAN ELECTIONS

ORGANIZATION OF POLITICAL PARTIES

American Political History

So far, it will give the impression that the system of party teams is inferior in the possibility of its powers to conservative and the primaries and to subordinated to the concluding in the workout of its own authorities.

Practically, however, this relationship may inverse; undeniably, such is often this circumstance. There are many reasons for the concluding condition, in the first place, conventions and primaries are temporary affairs, the former usually lasting less than a week, the concluding lasting only few hours or days. Party committees, on the other hand, latter from campaign to campaign or for final relationships, such as four years or two years, and their members are aggressively involved in political management during a large part of the time.

Moreover, party committees made up of seasoned politicians, the regulars of the organization, many of whom hold public as well as party agency. Men of this type form a large element in all conventions often exceeding in number the nonparty office holders, who may say to be the militia of politics. By carefully arranging the preliminaries of a convention, therefore, party committees may predetermine its action on all important measures. After the sessions of the convention success or failure at the polls depends upon the conduct of party committees. It is true, of course, that the direct primary designed in the hope of overthrowing the predominance of the party organization, but it is also true that this result secured only in exceptional cases. Leaving for future discussion the temporary organs of party's conventions and primaries let us accidental to the section of the structure and meanings of the permanent system of party committees. At the bottom, this system represented structure by the precinct committee or committee member, of the party structure element section.

In this present electoral system, various local standards overcome as to the size of the precincts. In Illinois, the law provides that precincts should have as near 500 voters as may be and are to become subdivided when the number exceeds 800. The Ohio law allows subdivision when the number exceeds 400.

The New York election law provides that each town with more than 500 voters and each ward with more than 600, or, if voting machines used, each town or ward with more than 700, shall become divided into election districts. However, a town or ward with not more than 1,000 voters need not divided if two voting machines used. It estimated that there are at least 100,000 precincts in the United States, the number having increased of evening, owing to the significant increase in the size of the electorate brought about by woman suffrage. In sections of the country where one of the major parties is in a hopeless minority it may happen that a great more precinct not organized, that is, are without committees or committee members of that party.

This is true, for instance, of the Republican party in more sections of the solid South, and it is true of the Democratic party in such die-hard inflexible, incompetent rock-ribbed Pro-republic states as Pennsylvania. Strenuous efforts made to fill up such gaps, particularly during national campaigns, but with partial success only. With these exceptions, however, the major parties have committees or committee members in every precinct throughout the country. Like all party offices, Organized and unorganized precincts.

Reference: C. E. Merriam, The American Party

ORGANIZATION OF POLITICAL PARTIES
American Political History

Formerly they become filled by committees of voters in the precinct. Currently in states which have adopted the direct primary system, candidates for such posts usually nominated upon a petition signed by a small number of electors and chosen in the ensuing primary election by plurality vote of the enrolled party members in the precinct. Whether the party authority in the precinct made up of a single committee member or by a small committee is a matter of minor importance. In the latter event it will nearly always become found that one member of the committee plays a dominant role of boss-ridden, the others serving as his official lieutenants in some subdivision of the precinct, or, it may be, taking charge of certain details of the work under the leader's direction. When there is a single committee member in a precinct he will, as a rule, always have a retinue of from three to a dozen or more unofficial followers ready to undertake, without direct remuneration, such political duties as he may assign to them. If, as is usually the case in boss-ridden communities, these followers are so subservient as to be willing to perform not only routine work of the organization, but also to undertake shady commissions or even to commit crimes against the ballot box, they are known as the Dog-Heelers.

The official duties of a precinct committeeman cover all the local details of the voting process, such as assisting aliens to procure naturalization papers, registration and enrolment, conducting campaigns, getting out the large wordless party voters at all primaries and elections, providing observers-spy, nominating polling clerks and other election officials, watching the count, and hurrying reports of the result to headquarters.

In the execution of these manifold details, some must leave to the local knowledge and personal inventiveness of the committee member. However, his work supervised and directed by the higher party authorities of the city or county. From the Precinct committeemen and declining official duties of precinct committee members, concluding the local front-runner may ask aid in undertakings too large or too highly specialized for local management, such as supplying political literature or sending speakers to public meetings.

POLITICAL ELECTORAL CORRUPTIONS
American Political History

The precinct committee entitled to draw upon the city or county committee for its share of campaign funds collected by the latter, and for its share of patronage, jobs, and other political favors where with to reward its own members or their faithful boot-licking servile. Usually the precinct committee expected to supply all the workers needed for purely local jobs, but in cases of emergency special workers may sent in from the outside. The boss-ridden groups some of the concluding are likely to be experts in bribery, colonization, repeating, and the commission of other election crimes, are a repercussion of the corrupt political systems.

Considering the possibility of criminal action there is a manifest advantage in having specialists of this character come from other wards, counties, or, if the district is close to a boundary line, from a neighboring state. Public duties in addition to his official duties a precinct committee member commission finds much to live in his period.

Obviously, it is to his advantage men to take as active and helpful a part as possible in the social life of his bailiwick dedicated. In slum wards, as we shall have occasion to note later, he becomes a personal providence to his people in all the trials and afflictions of their lives from day to day. Even in districts of a higher type the local leader is a very present help in trouble, especially if the trouble is of a sort which requires adjusting with public authority. For example, gentlemen who would like to have their tax assessments reduced, or the street lighting of their neighborhood improved, or who, perhaps, have learned too late that their automobiles might not auto-race the motorcycle policeman, all find the friendly interest of the local political leader an asset of considerable importance. A precinct leader in a middle-class residential community with which the author is familiar makes it a practice to send in the names of large number of his busy fellow citizens, of course, without their information for jury duty at the county court.

CHAPTER 14

ORGANIZATION OF POLITICAL PARTIES

American Political History

Based on but one committee member to a precinct Professor Merriam estimates the number of such party officers at 100,000 for each of the major parties, a total of 200,000 for the country. It is impossible to tell how greatly this number has increased since the adoption of the woman suffrage amendment by the addition of women committee members, and upcoming further growths.

Taking the United States as a whole, the organization of the minor parties is very fragmentary and incomplete; nevertheless, they must have many thousands of local workers in the field. If each of the major parties musters an average of six workers to a precinct, certainly a conservative approximation the total number of active Democratic and Republican partisans in the country would amount to 1,200,000.

In addition to these regular troops every hard-fought campaign perceives the formation of innumerable auxiliary committees, clubs, and organizations which spring up like mushrooms, and as rapidly fade away after the election. These militia troops may readily equal or even exceed the number of regulars in the field. Overall, so, each of the major parties may have from a million to a million and a quarter local worker aggressively engaged in a presidential campaign. No account taken in the foregoing estimate of higher party officials. We do not need this no sense if we change this electoral system by The New Fusion Electoral System.

However, the concluding procedure no larger a proportion of the total forces engaged in a campaign than the proportion of representative's officers comparable to an army in battle.

The arrangement of authorities in the party pyramid. Immediately above the precinct authorities, it will perceive, are various constituency, township, town, and city committees. In some cities the precinct not organized as such, the district committee being the smallest local party structure.

PROBLEMS OF NATIONAL COMMITTEE

American Political History

Senatorial Committee Congressional Committee State Central or Executive Committee in each of the 50 states District Committees in various Representative, Judicial, and Administrative Districts County Committee in each of the 3,065 counties of the United States, City Committee independent of the county, Ward, School District, Township, Town, and City Committees; Prescient Committeeman or commission in each of the 100,000 precincts in the United States to be found in a given territory. Thus, in a small town there may be no ward committee, and quite often no party authority exists between a rural precinct committee and the central committee of the county in which it founded.

Usually a district committee is composed of one or more precinct committee members from each of its precincts, and the township, town, city, and even the county committees similarly recruited from below. Thus, the leading committee member chosen by caucus or direct primary in a precinct may be ex official a member of the district, city, or county committee. Or the derivation of powers may become reversed, as, for example, in Pennsylvania, where the successful candidate in a precinct for the office of county commission member recognized as the party board member in that precinct.

In a few of our larger cities which are coterminous with districts or in which the community formation has supplanted the county government there are no county commissions, the city committee recognized instead. Party organization in such large cities is much more elaborate than in small towns or rural districts, and for that motive will defined in some aspect far ahead. Between the precinct and other purely local party county authorities, on the one hand, and the state central writer agencies City, on the other, the county committee usually stands out as a particularly vigorous center of political activity.

This accounted for in part by the convenient size of the county, which makes it possible for party officials to reach every precinct readily and for committee members to come to. The importance of the county in political organization varies with the section of the state. Commonly, though, it is correct that in districts which have large cities the political organization may become incredibly important the central assemblies without having to travel any considerable distance. Local leaders and influential voters obliged to visit the county seat for many purposes and it thus becomes a natural center for political conference and conversation.

In even greater importance as accounting for the importance of the county committee and its leaders are the considerable salaries and not too substantial duties committed to various elective county offices Commissioners, Judges, Sheriff, Prosecuting Attorney, Treasurer, Auditor, and others similar. There are in the United States some 45,000 elective county offices of this sort, making an average of fifteen to a county. Finally, there is a list several times larger than the foregoing of appointive county offices carrying smaller salaries on the average, but all eagerly sought after. In as much as civil service tests are employed in only a score of counties, most of these offices also obtained as re-wards for meritorious party service. Henceforth the importance of a county chair who able to dominate his committee and dispose of these plums.

Between the county committee and the state commission committees there are various district committees functioning in districts fixed by law for the election of Congress people, judges, and certain administrative officials. Compared with the county committee, them and the state agency, these bodies are of minor importance. Frequently their only business is to look after the election of a candidate for a single office at intervals of two or more years. Most of this work may become transferred to the county chairs of the counties making up the district.

The latter, indeed, often compose the membership of such district committees. In other cases, district committees are as in the case of Indiana

Congressional District Committees. Reference: Rules and Regulations, Republican State Central Commits, at amended May 10, 1923. made up of members chosen to be smaller.

Reference: L. Jones, The County in Politics, Annals of the American Academy, vol. xlvii, pp. 85-100 (May 1913). territorial units, such as counties or legislative districts.

ORGANIZATION OF POLITICAL PARTIES

American Political History

Next in order in the party hierarchy are the state central gates nor state executive committees. Both the major parties central commit been by a committee of this character in each top of the states of the Union. Some of. these committees have had a long and distinguished history, being lineal descendants of the commissions of correspondence formed during the pre-revolutionary period in certain of the Colonies. At the present time state central committees are extraordinarily energetic centers of a rainbow political activity.

Exceptions exist in the case of those states where the party outlook is hopeless and where, in consequence, their main preoccupation is the distribution of scraps of federal benefaction. Apart from such instances, however, state central committees may play an important part in the nomination of state vouchers; they are the principal agencies in campaigns for the success of such tickets; and, finally, they have a great deal to say regarding the distribution of appointive offices within the ability of the governor and other state elective officials.

In amount outstanding to the expedient of the electoral college, the states are also the ordinary divisions of the country in presidential campaigns, and here again the state committee becomes an agency of prime importance under the General Center of the National Committee. Finally, as we have already noted, the state committee is often the chosen battle ground of groups of powerful county and city leaders. Henceforth possession of the central committee is, if not convincing, at least probable evidence of party authority and control, one of the outside symbols of authority.

Reference: In size the 96 state committees Cf. Rule 7, Rules 0f the Republican Slate Committee, New York, adopted April 15, 190. C. E. Merriam, State Central Committees, Pol. Set. Quar., to I). Xix, pp. 224-233 (June 1904

NATIONAL POLITICAL COMMTTEE IS NOT NECESARY
American Political History

Size of state committees from 30 to 40. This matter is of considerable importance, for if the committee is very small it will conduct most of its business directly; if it is awkward it must perforce depend upon executive officers and committees. Members of state central committees chosen most by counties or congressional districts, but the legislative district used in a few cases, and there are some instances of a combination of these methods. The usual term of membership is four years, but two years is the rule in many states, and in New Jersey it is three years. Recently the tendency has been to lengthen the term of membership, thus giving greater stability to the organization. As to methods of choice of state committee members there is no uniformity. Sometimes they selected by delegates to the state convention from the area adopted as the unit of representation. More commonly of nighttime they selected in official primary elections by direct vote of enrolled party members. In the national field each of the major parties has three committees, two of lesser importance known as the senatorial and congressional committee and the congressional committee, repetitively, the other, which is the highest structure or the whole party organization, known as the National Committee.

Each of these three committees is separate and distinct in composition from the other commission. The Republican Senatorial Campaign Committee, which dates from 1916, is composed of seven members, appointed by the chair of the Republican conference for a term of two years. senatorial ten law that no Senator who is a candidate for re-election shall be a member of the committee during his own campaign. In the Fusion Electoral System, those elected officials will be the peoples electing votes of the Presidency Election, without the interposition of any political parties.

Reappointment of members is now the common practice, however, except when it is made impossible by the expunge, other illustrations from various states and sections are as follows: Elect primary elections, term, 2 years; Indiana, Republican State Committee, congressional districts, total 13, term, 2 years; Ohio, congressional districts, total 22, term, 2 years; Illinois, congressional districts, total 26, term, 2 years. Republican Massachusetts, Republican State Committee, 2 members (one a woman) from each senatorial district, chosen at direct primary elections, total 80, term, 2 years; New York, 1 member from each assembly district, chosen at direct primary elections, total 150, term, 2 years; Pennsylvania, Republican State Committee, senatorial districts, total 113, chosen.

ORGANIZATION OF POLITICAL PARTIES

American Political History

The Republican Congressional Committee was originally formed in the late 'sixties, during the struggle with President Johnson. From 1882 to 1894, however, it was not so active as it has after becoming President. It now made up of one member from each state which has party representation in the House, the member selects by the party delegation of the state. At that present there are thirty-five such states.

On the Democratic side the National Senatorial Committee is composed of six Senators chosen by party assembly for a term of two years. There are no subcommittees, but a Secretary of the treasurer appointed to taking in charge of permanent headquarters in Washington. In the lower house each State delegation of Democrats elects one of its members to the Democratic National Congressional Committee, which reorganized every two years. from each state. In addition to the usual committees there is a Women's Executive Committee.

The functions of these Committee supplied by Senator George H. Moses, and about the Republican Congressional Committee by Representative Burton L. French. Information about the Democratic National Senatorial Committee supplied by Mr. Frank A. Hampton, secretary-treasurer of the committee. Information around the Democratic National Congressional Committee supplied by Mr. D. K. Hempstead, assistant secretary of the committee.

Officers of national committees' side a body composed of one man from each state, together with one from each of the following: District of Columbia, Alaska, Philippine Islands, Puerto Rico, and Hawaii, making 53 altogether. The Democratic National Committee is composed of one man and one woman from each state and from each of the territories named above, with the addition of the Canal Zone, making a total of 108.

Members of the national committees selected for a term of four years, sometimes by the delegation from a given state to the national convention, sometimes by the state convention itself, and in increasing numbers of recent years by direct primary elections. As in the case of party committees the national committee elects its own executive officers, with the important exception, however, that the presidential nominee of the party allowed to name the national chairperson.

This practice is due to the conviction that the nominee has the greatest single stake involved in the campaign and should therefore give the privilege of choosing as his chief of staff a man in whose loyalty and efficiency he has entire confidence. During a campaign, the responsibilities of the chairperson of a national committee are enormous.

The committee chooses the usual executive officers, except for a treasurer, who chosen by the chair. Usually the chair may fill all vacancies in the membership of the committee and to appoint a woman to membership thereon. The most successful recent incumbents in this office have been Marcus Hanna, George, B. Cortelyou, Vance McCormick, and Will Hays. In case of victory at the polls the national chair and the more notable members of his committee become crucial factors in the distribution of federal benefaction. The successful national chairperson may himself rewarded with a Cabinet position, usually that of the Post Office Department, owing to the patronage involved.

In consequences, he and the more important of his committee members may mentioned also in matters of policy by the President they have helped to elect. Hanna was the most influential of all national chairpeople in the latter respect. In general, however, national committees' deterioration into a state of comparative inoperativeness following a presidential campaign, not resuming their labors as a figure until late in the year preceding the next election. Pronouncements on the policy of the administration from this source are distinctly unusual, the occurrences of this kind during the present year (1923) being merely exceptions to the general rule.

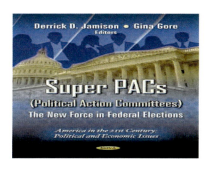

ORGANIZATION OF POLITICAL PARTIES

American Political History

Following the campaign of 1912 an effort made by the Progressive party organization to continue its organization and particularly its propaganda work, but with little success. For a great many people politics is postponed following an election, and for a considerable time at least they wish to hear as little as possible about the organization and its plans. Even the defeated chair and committee are not functioning without importance, owing to their powers in organizing of national party and arranging thein this connection and during campaigns. In addition to these greater labors national committees sometimes make important suggestions about party organization and policies.

Thus, between 1913 and 1921 the Republican National Committee worked out the original plans for the reform of representation in conventions of that party. At its February meeting in 1919, the Democratic National Committee provided for the employment of subordinate women members and adopted a resolution favoring a constitutional amendment to prevent any discrimination in the elective franchise on account of sex. Following this action, the Democratic national convention of 1920 admitted women to full membership in the National Committee.

In the line of campaign activities, the principal function Campaign of the senatorial and congressional committees of the two activities major parties is to secure the election of the largest Committees number of party candidates to Congress. During presidential years, of course, the destiny of many congresses.

The reputation of National Committees Representation on party commissions signal contests depends upon the sweep of the national ticket. Even in midterm elections, when the senatorial and congressional committees are most active, the influence of the President as party leader must be consulted.

ORGANIZATION OF POLITICAL PARTIES
American Political History

Later the general attitude of the senatorial and congressional committees is that of cooperation with the national committee. but of many state and local, competitions as well; the control of the federal decision-making for the four succeeding years; the patronage at its disposal and the influence it may be able to exercise upon legislation and administration. A reliable directory of the effectiveness of party committees become afforded by the amount of money at their disposal.

The overshadowing importance of the national committees in the two great parties is since they responsible for the conduct of the campaign for the election of a President and Vice-President, with all its fateful consequences. Upon victory in such campaigns depends the result not only of many congressional.

The New Fusion Electoral System

In the presidential campaign of 1920, the funds managed by the Democratic and Republican national committees were in added of the joint funds of the senatorial, congressional, and state committees of the same parties. In the foregoing description of party committees of every rank it become noted that as a rule representation is based equally upon certain regional components. This plan has the advantage of securing the widest possible geographical distribution of party representation. It suffers, however, from the manifest defect that it takes no account of the actual voting strength of the party in the districts concerned.

In a few exceptional cases efforts have made to give due weight to the latter factor.

Thus, according to the New York election law, county committees shall consist of at least two members from each election district and of such additional members as the rules of the par-ty may provide, proportional to the party vote in the district for governor at the last preceding election. American political leadership, a failure aggravated by the two-party system.

If no other members provided for by the rules the voting power of each member of the committee shall be proportionate to such party vote. Illinois provides that in the county committee each precinct committee member shall have one vote plus one added cast in his precinct for governor at the last general election. However, these exceptional cases merely prove the general rule of representation by geographical districts regardless of the party vote there.

Whatever injustice may therefore due to solid districts considered to be more than compensated by the encouragement given to districts where the party vote is lighter by the plan of equal representation. With the adoption of the Nineteenth Amendment political parties brought face to face with the problem of making room within their official hierarchies for representatives of women voters. Considering the large addition made to the electorate by the suffrage amendment, this was a problem of the first importance. Also, if was nervous with hazard, for if any considerable number of women should become alienated because of failure to give them proper recognition, the results to the offending party might be most serious, and it is, today we are experience a woman aggression specially from Democrats bigot woman's voters.

Prior to this time party leader had given scant attention to the subject of feminine psychology, and, conscious of this deficiency, they approached the problem with some trepidation. In the few years that have elapsed since the adoption of the suffrage amendment in 1920, many strategies for the representation of women on party committees have been investigated with by both parties.

These tactics fall into three main classes: (1) the establishment of purely auxiliary committees of women; (2) the opening of existing offices in the party pyramid to both men and women Representation of women voters on party committees Revised Statutes, 1921, 373, chap, xlvi, p. 876. purpose throughout the party structure. In the resulting disorder it is possible to find within the same party and even within the same state one of these strategies applying to one committee and another to others. However, some progress has become made, and out of the present welter of experimentation a definite and uniform solution should soon appear. Auxiliary about the advantages and disadvantages of the committees three campaigns now under probationary some general comments may be made. The establishment of purely auxiliary committees composed of women was a quite normal practical. For time out of mind it had been the practice of the officials and committees making up the regular party organization to encourage the formation of poster pledge bodies for every emergency or special purpose.

During campaigns, the multiplication of such bodies goes on apace and their loyal and enthusiastic aid becomes of excellent value. There is, however, little analogy between such temporary campaign committees and the representation of women voters in the party organization. The latter is not an emergency, but a continuous function, general rather than specific in character in short, a chance not merely to serve, but to govern as well. Whether so intended or not, the plan of separate women's committees lends itself readily to the suspicion that the regular party committees composed entirely of men purpose keeping more important functions and emoluments of organization control in their own hands. If women were unfranchised, they might have been content, at least they were perforce content, with membership on replacement and ladies' aid cultures. But with full empowerment such second class openings merely to take orders and to serve must soon become unpleasant to them.

THE 19TH AMENDAMENT OF OUR CONSTITUTION

American Political History

In the beginning all party's offices to make equal men and women on same resistant terms, the second plan for representation of women opportunities voters in the party organization, may seem at first view or women uncertain, every day and if possible reasonable. Apparently, no one questions the justice of this arrangement as applied to elective public offices. From now when women finally given the vote on the same terms as men, they were in general held to entitled to hold public office on the same terms as men. In effect this meant that they might reach to official power and emoluments provided they could defeat men in open contest for the same.

There have been several creditable individual successes under this system as applied to public offices. Though, a superficial examination of the percentage of women in Congress, state legislatures, city councils, and in elective administrative and judicial offices in generally will show that it represents a minuscule fraction of the proportion of the vote cast by women in popular elections. Application of the same rule to all party offices would doubtless have had much the same effect.

Women practice might have secured a larger proportion of the latter because they carry no salaries and hence are less eagerly desired by men. In some cases, at the same time women made eligible for party offices on equal terms with men the number of such offices doubled, with the understanding that room would thus made for women without dislodging any male incumbents.

Undoubtedly this arrangement makes it easier for women to secure something like their proportion of party offices.

However, it leaves them at a considerable disadvantage in practice. Male politicians know the riggings and male voters take part in primaries and elections to a much larger percentage of their registration than women voters.

Although full suffrage rights granted to women in 1920, there remains from the preceding epoch a deep-seated prejudgment among many men, and not a few D' Davenant opportunity plan women also, against active participation by the future in politics. If applied therefore, this plan would have left party control in the hands of committees on which men held large majorities and in all probability this condition would continue indefinitely. no doubt such a result would have been eminently stages of the satisfactory to all those who object to the active participation of women in politics. From the point of view of remote, in general party policy, however, its suiters from the disadvantage that eventually it is bound to provoke the criticism and opposition of women who take the privilege of the suffrage seriously.

Additionally, if one of the parties worked out a plan securing a more equal representation of women on its committees this fact might use with some effect upon the dissatisfied women voters of other parties. A system of party organization which predisposes any considerable element in the party membership to revolt is, of course, very malfunctioning. Parties have long recognized this statistic and, therefore, have usually shown themselves enthusiastic to reconcile any considerable body of voters regardless of strict theories of representation in proportion to numbers. Thus, national conventions welcomed delegates from territories, insular possessions, and the District of Columbia, although none of these represented in the electoral college.

For a long time, the over-representation of Southern states in Republican national conventions defended on the ground that it encouraged the ordinary people of the party in that section to make a valiant fight against great odds. Western state conventions have received delegations of Indians and the immigrants with every mark of notable deliberation. In brief, the policy generally followed has been based on the consideration that, like national background, generosity in according party acknowledgment costs little and may be counted upon to bring in rich rewards on election day. The third plan that of dividing committee places equally between men and women not only tries an amusing illustration. Reference: H. Shaw, Story of a Pioneer.

POLITICAL ELECTIONS PROBLEMS

American Political History

Generous attitude, it makes such an attitude mandatory. In all cases known to the writer it begins by doubling up the number of commission seats. This has the advantage that men holding committee places left uninterrupted, but it has the disadvantage of making some of the committees awkward. In districts populated by naturalized foreigners, the plan requiring equal representation of the sexes has become protested to on the ground that it angers many men voters and not wanted by most of the women voters. Everywhere, of course, women do not yet take part in elections as at permission as men. The number of women who work actively in politics is much smaller than that of men so engaged. To the extent that these conditions pre-vail it is, of course, true that the mandatory assignment of an equal number of places on party committees to women results in the over representation of voters of that sex.

On the other hand, it may become claimed for this policy that it gives every encouragement to women to take part in political work as freely as men do. From the campaign point of view, the adoption of this policy by a party in advance of its rivals may succeed in attracting to it a certain voting strength. other parties which may wish to bid for the same support will find it awkward to offer women voters a less measure of party representation and quite out of the question to offer them more.

Officers of committees, particularly county and state chairs, may have Representation of women on party committees even to an equal extent with men does not dispose of all the difficulties in this connection.

Commissions may, as we have seen committees by doubling their membership was scarcely any trouble at all. Obviously, however, this device cannot become applied to the more important executive offices provided for by party rules or men to monopolize all such places would, of course, cause trouble sooner or later, probably sooner. To give the offices of chairperson, secretary, and treasurer to Equal division of committee places between men and women in party offices men and the offices of vice-chairman and assistant secretary to women does not impress one as a permanent solution, either.

If the principle of equality of opportunity is to be regarded in this connection women should be made eligible to the more important executive offices on the same terms as men, with the further proviso that when the chief of two positions is filled by a representative of one sex the second place should go to a friendly of the other sex. Some conception of the way these various plans of representation have combined in practice may gained from the following summary of conditions in the state of Pennsylvania. Beginning with Delaware County, the author's residence, women of both major parties given equal representation on the county committee, but the principal executive offices held by men. Practice about the representation of women on county committees is not uniform throughout the state, however. Democratic women have an equal right to compete with men for places on the state committee of that party, the result being that at present they make up about a third of its membership.

The Republican party has adopted a rule providing that each senatorial district shall elect one male and one female member of the state committee.

In both parties a man holds the post of state chairperson a condition which exists at present throughout the Union. Coming now to the national committees, the Democratic party has provided since 1920 for one man and one-woman member from each state. Until recently there have been no women members of the in both parties a man holds the post of state chairperson a condition which exists at present throughout the Union. Coming now to the national committees, the Democratic party has provided since 1920 for one man and one-woman member from each state. Until recently there have been no women members of Democratic party, they asked each member of the committee to nominate a woman of his state to serve as an associate member.

To offset its failure to recognize Pennsylvania methods. This provision is made by the Rules of the Republican Party of the State of Pennsylvania, adopted June 18, 1921, I, § 4. B

According to news reports from the Republican National Convention held at Cleveland, June 10th to 12th, 1924, women have admitted to full and equal membership in the national committee of the Republican party.

American parties changed by the Democratic processes of the initiative, referendum, and recall. The constitution also makes provision for Foreign Speaking Federations within the party, for the Young People's Communist League, for propaganda among women, and for the sending of delegates to international Marxist conferences, is surprising how the Communists recruiting new party stupidity sympathizers.

The New Fusion Electoral System

ORGANIZATION OF SOCIALIST PARTIES

American Political History

Women equally the Republican National Committee has an executive committee of nineteen members, eight of whom are women. Men hold the nine executive offices of the Democratic National Committee, except for two vice chairmanships. Men hold all the eight executive offices of the Republican National Committee except one assistant vice-chairmanship and one assistant secretary ship. Third parties in the United States have organized themselves, as a rule, along the same lines as majority parties. In geographical extent and in effectiveness, however, such organizations fall far short of their great prototypes.

The Communist party alone contrasts from the old parties in form and functioning. It possesses a written constitution which All persons joining the Communist party must sign an application pledging themselves to its principles, rejecting all relations with other parties, and agreeing to be guided in their political actions by the constitution and platform of the party. Payment of regular monthly dues also become needed as a condition of keeping membership and taking part in party affairs. Members living in each district to the number of five or more form party locals.

In some large cities the locals assigned to branches according to assembly districts. No state or territory may organize unless it has at least ten locals or an aggregate membership of not less than two hundred. In states which qualify under this rule state committee are set up which must make monthly reports to the national secretary Organization of third parties National Constitution and Platform of the Communist Party, published by the National Office of the Party, Chicago, 1917. Elections.

SOCIALIST ELECTORAL PROBLEMS
American Political History

In the national field the authorities of the Socialist party are the National Executive Committee, the national convention, Membership and locals in the Communist Party National organs of the Communist Party Officers of the Communist party and cooperate with the national office in the sale of dues stamps.

The elimination of the Communist party is amazingly simple when we are restructuring the electoral system by a no partisan system Fusion Electoral System because there are not parties in the New Fusion Electoral System.

A permanent chair chosen by the National Communist Executive Committee. Though, purely to follow the national Corrupt Practices Act. The constitution supplies also for a paid executive secretary. One interesting peculiarity of the Communist party organization is the disapproval to permanent dominant officers and then cutting them? It is because they frightened that they may absorb too much party controls, contrary to the Capitalist system ideal of the party where there is not limited of control.

The almost invariable practice is to choose a temporary chair for each assembly. As a result, the inexperienced and incapable called upon to take his turn at presiding; not only is free speech kept, but the talkative orator agonized indefinitely before the mallet falls. On the other hand, the Communist party employs permanent organizers, lecturers, and secretaries to a greater degree in proportion to its size than any other party. Assisted by numerous volunteers and the party press, these paid workers carry on a vigorous propaganda, which, unlike that of the major parties, is not confined to political campaigns, but is continuous.

National conventions of the Communist party are called by the executive committee, regular conventions being held in all years during which presidential elections occur, and National conventions of the Communist party. (Sept. 1908). On this and other details of the organization and work of the Communist party the reader should look up the exceptional interpretation offered, following all steps dictated by the party organization. Special conventions at any other time if decided upon by a general vote of the party membership or by a two-thirds vote of the National Executive Committee. An emergency convention of the latter sort held at St. Louis in April, 1917, at which the indefinitely for the requisite endorsement, the referendum has become so frequent as to lose much of its value as an expression of deliberate opinion. In years when national convention of the communist party is held

References: J. W. Hughan, American Socialism of the Present Day, pp. 204-220. R. Hunter, The Socialist Party in the Present Campaign, Review of Reviews, volume, pp. 293-399Communist party placed itself on record about the imminent war. Communist national conventions made up of two hundred delegates, one from each state and territory, the rest apportioned according to the average national dues paid during the preceding year.

Delegates to national conventions and to international congresses receive their traveling expenses and an uncertain per unsure from party funds provides for an organization conference composed of the National Committeemen, the executive secretary, state secretaries, and others.

ORGANIZATION OF COMMUNIST PARTIES

American Political History

The platform adopted at the Communist National Convention is the supreme announcement of the party, and all state and municipal platforms shall conform thereto. Before it goes into effect, however, it must give to a referendum vote of the membership. One fourth of the regularly elected delegates to a convention shall entitled to have alternative paragraphs sent at the same time. In addition to the mandatory referendum thus provided for on the platform, the party constitution also sets up the initiative for motions or resolutions to vote upon by the entire membership of the party.

These may bring forward upon the request of locals being 5% per cent of the dues-paying membership. Initiated amendments to the constitution require eight per cent. It is the opinion of a recognized authority on American Communism that owing to a recent decision to hold party referendums open This indefinitely for the requisite endorsements, the referendum has become so frequent as to lose much of its value as an expression of deliberate opinion. In years when national conference restricted to problems of administration, Communist platforms, and referendum votes.

References: B. Benedict, The Larger Communism, chap. v. 2 J.W. Hughan, op. cit., p. 210. Communist organization conferences Communist party discipline Communist rules about candidate's propaganda, and organization, and shall neither start nor suggest legislation or constitutional amendments.

It is a proof what I been telling you, ideology Communist is a Totalitarian Dictatorship, when they cannot control and imposing restriction in our Democracy-Republic Fusion system, prohibited the free expression of election, only in the nations under the Communist party you can experience this abnormality, that is why I am recommending the elimination of any political parties in our nation of any political party controlling freedom. While individual members of the Communist party allowed to take part in party activities to a degree unknown in the older organizations, they also subjected by their constitution to certain drastic limitations.

Thus, no member of the Communist party shall, under any circumstances, vote in any political election for any candidate other than Communist party members is nominated, endorsed, or recommended as candidates by the Communist party, or advocate voting for them, clearly this is a dictatorial suggestion. To do so constitutes party treason and will result in expulsion from the party. Previously it was a Communist custom to require candidates to send signed but undated resignations from the offices to which they wanted. In case of disloyalty to party principles by office holders these resignations must date and presented to the proper authority, and he is purged.

No Communist Party member may be an aspirant for public office without the consent of the city, county, or state organizations, according to the nature of the office. Party membership of at least two years' duration is also a prerequisite for Communist nomination or endorsement, exception made, however, in the case of organizations which have been in existence less than two years. Communist candidates not allowed to accept any nomination or endorsement from any other party or political organization.

No state or local organization shall under any circumstances fuse, combine, or compromise with any other political party or organization existing other than the Communist party, or refrain from making nominations to favor the candidate of such other organizations. The preceding rules are by no means dead literatures. Censure and expulsion used drastically to purge the party of undesired elements. Certain restrictions and duties also imposed upon Communists in office by the party constitution. Voting by such persons to proper moneys for military or naval Rules applying to Communists in office for an interesting illustration of the use of such resignations, the information above is an example of how the politic in America will be conducted with a sole party regime. This nonsense has no sense because under the New Fusion system this is irrelevant, because there are no political parties in the new electoral system and candidate's nominations are under the Fusion Electoral Tribunal, no by political parties. References: J. W. Hughan, op. cit., p. 212.

COULD AMERICA BECOME A COMMUNIST NATION?

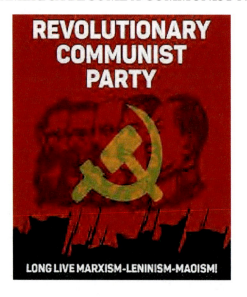

YES, OR NOT

CHAPTER 15

ORGANIZATION OF COMMUNIST PARTIES

American Political History

Communist party continues violating of our liberties restricting the citizen of making a selection in their choice or determining for other representing not Communist, their voters are sequestered to keep this ideology prospered with the hope of taking over the power of the American Government, it never will be happening under the New Fusion Electoral no Partisan System. Communist representatives in Congress must send reports of their official actions to the national convention. In the support of the measures proposed by the Communist party they shall carry out instructions which may give by the national conventions, the National Executive Committee or by a general referendum of the party.

In all legislative bodies Communist members shall organize into a group separate and apart from other parties and shall vote as a unit in support of all measures declared for in the platforms of the party. Like every other rule of human conduct, the Communist policy of isolation is not without its exceptions. Should the party increase in voting strength and representation, these exceptions will without a doubt become more frequent in this party system. In all party's political committees provided with the usual executive officer's chairperson, vice-chairman, secretary, and treasurer elected, as a rule, by the committee itself. In addition, the larger political committees appoint number of special committees, the more common being an executive committee, a finance committee, and a committee on vacancies, with one or two others of a miscellaneous character. For example, the Massachusetts State Republican Committee supports a legislative committee, an Americanization committee, and a registration committee.

Frequently auxiliary committees appointed composed of people who are not members of the regular committee. Among the various party officers named above, the most important is usually the chairperson.

As we have already noticed, the chairperson of a county committee is often the dominant political figure in his county. Less often the chairperson of a state committee can play the same role on his wider stage. In any event, his office is of great strategic importance. The chairperson of a finance committee, particularly one whose Officers of party committees have importance of the Communist party.

References: J. W. Hughan, tp. cit., p. 214; M. Hillquit, Socialism in Theory and Practice p. 176".

AMERICAN POLITICAL PARTIES HISTORY

American Political History

In this case we are talking of political parties in general, you will notice that the same patron of conduct and regulations of any party is authoritarian and abusive with the elector. Always a political party no matter if is Communist, Democrat, Republican, or Independents, all are parties and for consequent are harming and dividing the American elections system, only the Fusion election system where parties are not existing is the solution.

This condition has become modified by the enactment of state laws on the subject. As far as the composition of party committees is concerned, these laws did little more than to unify and legitimatize the conditions set up under party rules. However, one change of great position made by the application of the direct primary method of election to members of party committees. Even fewer modifications made by these state laws in the functioning of party committees.

Thus, the Illinois law merely provides that they shall have the powers usually exercised by such committees, and that they shall not delegate them. Of these two clauses the first simply continues the status quo stake, but if the second were to enforce it would work a profound change in party management.

The New York law contains an interesting requirement to the effect that every state and county committee shall within fifteen days after its election meet and organize by the election of a chairman, treasurer, and secretary, and such other officers as its rules may provide, and within three days thereafter file with the secretary of state and the board of elections of the county a certificate stating the names and post office addresses of such officers. In general, the rules of party committees are much more party rules extended and explicit than the laws so far enacted on this subject. They provide in detail for the election of officers and committees, the distribution of powers among them, and for the transaction of business by the whole committee, the latter following the recognized.

References: Cf. Illinois Rev. Stat., 1921, §§ 372-373: General Laws of Massachusetts, vol. I, 1921, chap, lii; New York Election Laws §§10-17; Ohio General Code, Throdcmorton, 1921, §§ 4959-4962. methods of parliamentary practice.

PARTIES ELECTORAL PROBLEMS

American Political History

Two or three only of the party's functions of committees are of so unusual a character as to deserve special reference.

Therefore, it is common to find a rule supporting the ousting of members of the committee who have being convicted of disloyalty to the party or ticket.

A provision of this character even included in the New York Election Law; it covers corruption in office as well as disloyalty to the party. The Rules Governing the Republican Party of Delaware County, Pa., require all members of the county executive committee to pledge support to the entire county ticket as nominated at the last primary election. In a situation, a member shall refuse to make this pledge the county executive committee shall declare his place vacant and go ahead to elect another qualified Republican from the same precinct to take his place. Of greater importance than the foregoing is the rules supporting the filling of vacancies occurring in the ticket by death or otherwise after the convention or direct primary election has held.

Finally, in those states or districts where the director, in some cases, the committee performs this function, in others it has given responsibility for to a special committee on vacancies. primary election system has completely replaced the convention it is common to find rules authorizing the party committee to draft a platform. One may read all the laws and rules about party committees, however, and still have a very incorrect location of idea of the actual location of power there. Purposes of control in assigned to the committee may in given instances committees exercised to all practical intents and purposes by the chair or the executive committee. Or the real wheels of power may be in the hands of various public office holders who have no official connection with the system of committees.

At all times, the national committee must give the most careful consideration to the wishes of the President whom the party has elevated to control. The views of controlling leaders of the party in Congress must also take circulation of influences between committees into account, whether they are members of the committee or not. the Democratic party ever since his first nomination in 1896 is the most conspicuous recent example of personal influence in the national field.

Between a governor and leaders in the legislature, on the one hand, and the state committee, on the other, the same general relationship exists. In counties and cities, the party organization is more likely to dominate public office holders, but a mayor of force and character may reverse this situation. Individual party members of powerful personality and wide popularity must also calculate with by party officials. Bryan's influence over Whether in or out of public office, men like Cleveland, Wilson, Roosevelt, Root, Taft, and Hughes able to exercise a notable influence upon the conduct of affairs by party office holders. Finally, in cases where a well-organized machine has been set up actual leadership may find concealed within or even quite outside the official party structure. The boss may prefer to remain a private member of the committee and yet be able to dominate its every move. Sometimes, indeed, he prefers no official connection whatever with the committee, controlling its actions through trusted assistants who hold all the strategic offices in the party organization. Similar indeterminacy exists about the actual distribution of powers as between committees of different rank in the party pyramid.

The New Fusion Electoral System

The national committees of the major parties have no power of coercion over the state committees nor the latter over county committees.

In cases of factional commotion, it is common to find the party leaders and organizations of a group of counties vigorously fighting the state organization controlled by another group of influential of the same party.

On the other hand, every effort made during campaigns to secure agreement, and a united front, in appearance at least, presented as against the opposing party. At all times, and particularly during campaigns, the hope of obtaining funds from committees higher up is a powerful factor in securing cooperation. The interlocking of committees of lower rank with those of higher rank through membership of leaders of the former in the higher committees is also a useful factor in securing concerted action.

In the last analysis much depends upon the spirit of unity in the party ordinary people. Considering all these factors, in general a remarkable degree of cooperation obtained from the top to the bottom of the party assembly. Party committee members of whatever rank in the hierarchy material of the major parties receive no salaries as such. There wards of are, how-ever, a few salaried positions in connection with Party office the permanent headquarters supported by a small number of the more important committees.

In some cases, the expenses incurred by committee members in attendance at meetings contributed out of party funds. Usually, therefore, membership in the governing organization of a party involves some expenditure both of money and of time. Demands upon the time of party officers vary greatly. In large cities there are many workers from precinct leaders up who do politics 365 days in the year, as the saying is. Except during campaigns, however, most party officials give a small part of their time only to political activities, depending for a means of support upon some business or professional pursuit of their own.

Of course, in case of party victory many committee members rewarded by election or appointment to public office carrying a salary. And under machine control the holding of party office may have made lucrative in many shady ways. There can be no doubt, however, that a considerable proportion of the men and women serving in minor party offices the country over do so without hope of material reward, largely because of devotion to party principles or out of sheer love of the game. The motive of spoils and money is, therefore, far from Other mobbing the only one that animates this vast and thoughtful for mechanism of parties. That it is too prominent is equally party beyond question. In general, the personnel of party committees.

PARTIES ELECTORALPROBLEMS

American Political History

Nevertheless, how we may put this according with George Washington, in his farewell letter affirmed and warned the politicians that political parties divide our nation, will harm the American Democratic Republican. The Fusion Elections System is the solution.

Improvement of personnel of party committees is distinctly course, the latter are salaried and therefore the competition for them is much more strenuous. It is this competition which selects the abler or more ambitious holders of party office for public advancement, leaving the less able or less ambitious in mere party positions. Also, candidates for and officeholders in public office subjected to a much more severe public scrutiny and criticism than holders of party office. It is not county, but party, government which is the darkest days of the American politics.

Elihu Root's use of the phrase invisible government, in this connection fully justified. Many changes of method, the direct primary, corrupt practices act, and the like have made with the hope of improving this neglected area. But a change of personnel more greatly needed than any mere changes of method. If able and disinterested men and women could induce to stand for party offices, there is every reason to believe that the whole level of our public life would raise significantly. References: The Rules and Regulations of political committees, the study of the formal organization of parties. In this pursuit unlimited persistence and a little influence are a necessary part of the collector's equipment. A list of the state chairpeople of both parties published annually in the World Almanac. Ostrogorski and J. Macy being particularly full on this topic. C. E. Merriam, The American Party System, Ch. Ill (1922),

ORGANIZATION OF POLITICAL PARTIES

American Political History

Upon the first statement of the system of a public agreement various difficulty present themselves. Who are the parties to this agreement? They never go always from them self. For how long a time is this agreement to be careful as requisite? If the consent of every individual be necessary, in what manners that agreement to become expected? Is it to be understood, or declared in express terms? If we end the political parties in United States, we do not have to answer any question about political parties because they do not will exist.

Marcus Alonzo Hanna became a wealthy man with civic and commercial interests that included the ownership of street car contracts, the Cleveland Opera House, and the Cleveland Herald, directorships of two railroads, and the presidency of the Union National Bank. Presents a brief general account followed by a powerful examination of presidential, congressional, gubernatorial, and unofficial leadership., Of all the many dissertations on the Communist party, gives the most informing account of the party's organization and its workings. Rousseau on governing officials and exalt the will of the people as ruler and sole director of the others.

Human nature being what it is, however, each member of the administration thinks of himself first as an individual, second as a magistrate. The principle thus enunciated by Rousseau finds many striking illustrations in the field of party government. Given organizations of such enormous extent as those described in the preceding chapter, wielding great but unclear and controlled powers, it is inevitable that self-seeking and political class interests should manifest themselves at every turn.

BOSESS AND PARTIES CORRUPTION

American Political History

Theoretically party government exists to give effect to the will of most party adherents, who wish the best interests of the state. To substantial extent it does 290this. Certainly, no party organization can stand for any length of time against a positive resolve on the part of Bosses are the capo chief of a Mafia organization, and that is what the political parties is all about, corruptions, parties political war, disruptions of the Government functions, and political and economic ambitions, that is why we must eliminate all political parties and form a system with no parties.

On many issues is apathetic, henceforth the wide area within which party officials may move in their own interests. So clearly marked is this selfish feature of Americanization. Can party politics that various names and nicknames organization, machine, gang, ring, boss, have been of machine evolved in commonly to describe the agencies and grades of participation in it.

The word organization is colorless morally; it means control and discipline to the public, and to the politician loyalty, henceforth the concluding uses it proudly and takes great care to preserve, at least superficially, his regularity as an organization man always. Briefly, the organization is the system of permanent party committees, or that part of the system which confined to a given state, county, or city. In addition to greater centralization of power and discipline the term machine connotes use of the organization to an end outside of its proper purposes, hence perversion to. some degree.

A political machine may be defined as a party organization within which one or a few men have gained a degree of control, particularly over nominations, elections, and appointments to office and the official conduct of the incumbents, sufficient to enable them to pursue their own ends alongside with or even to some extent contrary to those of the party.

The term is loosely employed, a Republican organization man easily perceiving the immorality of the Democratic machine, and vice versa. It involves some grade of criticism, although it is on record that Platt was visibly pleased when on the floor of a state convention one of his opponents declared that, considering how smoothly and irresistibly it operated, he must run his machine with electricity. Among faithful followers the men who dominate a machine respectfully referred to as leaders. To their rings like a Mafia Boss, opponents they are collectively the gang or the ring.

Both these terms specify a determination to dominate by fair means or vulgar. Gang, as, for example, in the famous Pennsylvania marching song, is the broader term, including all who take part in machine processes and that boss in privileges, the small politicians along with the dominant figures.

Ring, on the other hand, refers to the inner circle of the machine, those who design and control on a large-scale nomination, campaigns, elections, appointments, and the conduct in public and party office of their bench men. The most notorious rings in the history of the country were the Tweed Ring in the Tammany machine of New York, and the Gas Ring in the Republican machine of Philadelphia. Like all oligarchy government of the few, rings are peculiarly liable to internal strife.

Composed of expert personalities, jealous of one another's power and always dissatisfied with their share of the loots, dissensions among them sometimes result in the elevating of a dominant figure, the boss. Subject to internal disorders, a ring may exist without a boss, but no boss has ever succeeded without a ring to support and help him. Of course, the methods and morals of a boss are those of the ring, the former given more efficient by centralization of power in the hands of one man, the concluding clarified slightly perhaps by his greater responsibility and intelligence.

Oligarchies have made their presence felt enough in the parties of Europe as in Russia, shelter the aggravate of the machine are typical Ampriran undamaged countless reasons have advanced for this untoward development. Rapid territorial development, prodigality of nature, the growth of wealth and general diffusion of material wellbeing, have drawn the attention of our citizens from government to the economic subjugation of nature. Our favorable geographical situation, indifferent from threat of war and invasion, has made us indifferent to one powerful motive for government efficiency. Immigration has made our population heterogeneous, thus enabling designing politicians Jal demand to race prejudgment. Certain political practices and ideas fixed during the Jacksonian period, the spoils system, the Causes of bossism.

References: Cf. J. Bryce, The American Commonwealth, pt. v, chaps. lxxxviii and lxxxix; G. Myers, The History of Tammany Hall, chaps, xxiiixxv; S. P. Orth, The Boss and the Machine, pp. 72-80, 93-98.

PARTIES PROBLEMS AND MACHINE BOSSES

American Political History

Down is a clear narration of the incredible function of political parties and Bosses, is a disgrace that we still bring today in these 21 centuries, if we only eliminate the political parties and supplants it by a Fusion election System, will be the end of all this absurd political behave.

Dominion in office, the criticism of as many parties' officials as possible by election, have unquestionably contributed to the grow of the political apparatus. The fear of a strong administration, surviving from the beginning of our national life, enables the constructionist to temper law enforcement at innumerable points to his private benefit, is a form of political corruption.

The doctrine of the separation of powers and check and balance among them, also a legacy from the ancestors, has become carried to so extreme a grade in state and municipal government as to make almost necessary and inevitable the intervention of a powerful and highly centralized outside political control. There is a wide discrepancy between the balance of Great combinations of capital enormously strong economically, power, financial and industrial on the one side, political on the other, but weak in voting power, face great popular masses, weak economically, but strong in voting power.

Out of the corporate desire for privileges, many of them unwarranted, and out of the popular desire for regulation, also perhaps pushed too far, the boss is equally able to make a profit. As a minor consequence of the last named condition many of America's most efficient men of affairs find their personal interests bound up with those of the machine and are therefore hostile to good government movements. In European countries, on the other hand, there is a tradition of disinterested public service among men of wealth and leisure. In a vivid paragraph Ostrogorski has given a picture Geographic of the geographical extent of machine rule in this country, call extent of machine as follows: If on the map of the United States all the parts of the country where the machine has developed were colored red, the eye would at once be attracted to the right by a large failure formed by the states of New York and Pennsylvania with a strip of the state of New Jersey on the east, with the state of Maryland on the south, and the state of Ohio on the west, partly at least.

will flow toward the Pacific slope and deposit a thick layer of bright red on San Francisco; and, finally, jumping right over to the Gulf of Mexico, it will cover New Orleans with a similar coating.

This mass casts a faint shadow to the northeast over New England, while on the other side, to the west, the red will appear in more or less deep tints in the state of Illinois, and will stain the neighboring states, marking with red points most of the large cities, such as St. Louis in Missouri and others of less importance, like Louisville in Kentucky or Minneapolis in Minnesota, and other smaller places among the large cities; then, after making a brief pause in the states of the Far West and leaving some zones there. A very considerable space will be left hardly colored at all or will even exhibit the shot color to be seen in certain fabrics: these are regions or cities where the machine has no stable and regular existence; rings of greedy politician's form in them, disappear after a short time, and reform under favorable circumstances.

A good many point again on the map will appear almost white. It must not become ancient history, however, that the part of the map colored in red, while only a fraction of the whole country, contains almost a third of the population of the United States and represents at least three-fifths of its economic interests. Numerous as are the cities and states within which the machine has prevailed, it is a fact of prime importance that to date bossism has rumors developed within the federal structure.

From time to time controlling oligarchic groups have formed within the Senate. One such group was able to fight President Johnson to a standstill. Subsequently the Old Guard under Aldrich, the Penrose group, and other factions and alliances have exercised considerable influence.

However, none of these combinations has reached anything like the power and permanence of the typical state or city machine. During McKinley's administration Mark Hanna was frequently referred to as a national boss, but the statement did gross injustice not only to the fundamental political facts, but also to the personal relationship of the two men. Hanna was not even a boss either in Cleveland or Ohio, as his many local fights demonstrate

References: Democracy and the Party System in the United States, p. 266,

POLITICAL ELECTORAL PROBLEMS

American Political History

As collector of party funds, as campaign manager and organizer of victory in the campaign. A very considerable space will be left hardly stained at all or will even exhibit the shot shade to be seen in certain junks: these are regions or cities where the machine has no stable and regular existence; rings of avaricious politician's form in them, disappear after a short time, and reform under favorable conditions. A good many point again on the map will appear almost white. It must not become forgotten, however, that the part of the map tinted red, while only a fraction of the whole country, contains almost a third of the population of the United States and represents at least three-fifths of its economic interests.

Numerous as are the cities and states within which the machine has prevailed, it is a fact of prime importance that to date bossism has rumors developed within the federal structure. From time to time powerful oligarchic groups have become formed within the Senate. One such group was able to fight President Johnson to a standstill. Subsequently the Old Guard under Aldrich, the Penrose group, and other cabals and coalitions have exercised considerable influence. However, none of these combinations has reached anything like the power and permanence of the typical state or city machine. During McKinley's administration Mark Hanna was frequently referred to as a national boss, but the statement did gross injustice not only to the underlying political facts, but also to the personal relationship of the two men. Hanna was not even a boss either in Cleveland or Ohio, as his many local struggles sufficiently prove. As collector of party funds, as campaign manager and organizer of victory in the fraud.

References: H. Croly, Marcus Alonzo Hanna, especially chap, xvii et set, Democracy and the Party System in the United States, p. 266,

MACHINES AND BOSSES

American Political History

The Macmillan Company, campaigns of 1896 and 1900, as Senator, and finally as an industrial leader trusted by his associates, Hanna did undoubtedly wield an exceptional personal influence during McKinley's Presidency. To speak of it as amounting to bossism is, however, quite beside the mark. The truth is that the powers and patronage vested Florida Presidency of the United States are so enormous that no group of state leaders within his own party can hope to prevail against him by force mugging.

The New Fusion Electoral System

The thunderous in chapter under Garfield is a case in point. A FL strategies surrender to apparatus impact tactfully trained, but a President of solid can fight efforts to control him with some of the most potent weapons in the arsenal of government. The overwhelming importance of plains meanings, the obvious dirty look is a straight knockout, Vicente Entropion him, the presence in his entourage of national leaders not of the machine variety, all combine to place him above the sinister control to which governors and mayors have soften fallen victim.

This customary to distinguish bosses according to the Kinds of nature of the territories in which they work. Thus, bosses according to Professor Merriam, there is the rural boss, the urban boss, the state-wide rural or urban, or urban rural boss. While it is the popular practice to attach a territorial appellation to the title of a boss, this may be misleading.

No state boss, it is safe to say, and few city bosses have ever been free from factional disaffection or open revolt in some part of their bailiwicks. Thus, the Vare brothers, long known as the Dukes of South Philadelphia, ruled unchallenged in that section of the city but bitterly opposed by Penrose and independent forces in the western and northern wards.

Among practical politicians a more exact definition of the extent of the influence of a boss is sometimes employed, consisting of a list of the party and public offices known to be under his control. Thus, at the death of Ed Vare, the older and more powerful of the brothers, the following list.

Public offices and office holders under his control was published without a word of contradiction from those concerned: a working majority in City Council, four out of six Philadelphia representatives in Congress, five out of eight state senators, thirty-three out of forty-one state assemblymen, a majority of the city magistrates, a majority of the county commissioners, and the offices of the Recorder of Deeds, Receiver of Taxes, City Treasurer, Sealer of Weights and Measures, Coroner, and Register of Wills. Rural bosses Bossism, as Professor Merriam's classification brings out, is by no means confined to large urban middles. In Pennsylvania, for example, powerful as are the machines of the two great cities, it is doubtful if they can exert so thorough a degree of control as the machines established in several part rural, part urban, and even in certain predominantly rural counties. Of course, comparatively little overheard of such cases; the rural boss, unlike his colleague of the city, does not have suggestion. constantly the searchlight of a hostile metropolitan press.

Certainly, he is frequently shrewd enough to become the owner of all the principal country newspapers in his territory City Bosses There can be no question, however, that the thoroughness of machine organization, the number of workers employed by it, the possibilities of political accustoming, open to it, and the value of the rewards, financial obtainable by it are immensely greater in city's Urban Concentration per e ran hardly he rosin Proctor of this linen development of bossism.

For similar movements of population have gone on at as great a pace in other countries which have remained free from the political machine. Nor can the large foreign enemies in our City be held responsible primarily for boss B. Jamtharmn No American city has had its affairs more consistently mismanaged, or has been able to develop fewer wholesome municipal traditions, than Philadelphia; yet the foreign born element in the population of Philadelphia is much weaker than it is in any other cities of the largest class.

Reference: The American Party System, p. 174, Philadelphia Public Ledger, Oct. 17, 1922.

METROPOLITAN MACHINE AND BOSSES

American Political History

However, a brief consideration of the many factors said above as favoring the development of the machine in the United States will show that they have combined to a maximum degree in great cities, The Greater Urban Machines. In matters of form there is no essential difference between the party organizations of our large cities which have subjected to apparatus control and party organizations elsewhere which are free from that influence.

The former is more detailed and complete, they provide a better basis for control from above and for the discipline of minor committees, and much more of them abundantly supplied with healers and henchman. These special features of city organizations made possible and necessary by the extent and complexity of city government itself, the large number of offices involved, the abundant revenues handled, and the increasing powers of regulation possessed by municipal officials, all of which are subject to corrupt operation.

The New Fusion Electoral System

Further, in addition to the temporary campaign clubs common the country over, city organizations have developed many permanent auxiliary clubs with quarters or club houses of their own and with social features which appeal more to many of their members than their political activities. Organizations controlled by machines.

Among metropolitan machines, that of Tammany Hall Tammany in the Democratic organization of New York City is Haul world renowned. The territorial basis of this organization W. B. Munro, originally an outgrowth of the Society of St. Tammany, or Columbia Order, founded May 12, 1789, and named in honor of a legendary Indian chief. This society divided into thirteen tribes, the Eagle, Otter, Panther, Beaver, and so on, and was officer led by commanders-in-chief, action is the state assembly district, of which there are now twenty-three in New York County. Tammany also supports close relations with, if it does not control, the Democratic organizations in two others of the five counties making up New York City, namely the Bronx and Kings (Brooklyn).

In each assembly district Democratic voters choose delegates at the primaries to a District General Committee, the basis being one delegate to each twenty-five voters. Since the direct primary law of 1913, election districts or precincts have become the units of representation for election to the district general committee. This committee is the governing authority of the party within the assembly district. Formerly it chose a single executive member or district leader whose powers were often equivalent to those of a local boss. At the present time most of the districts choose two leaders, one man and one-woman, other districts choosing from four to seven, divided as equally as may be between men and women.

Among the duties of the district leader is the appointment of a precinct boss for every precinct, of which there are now 985 in New York County. Each precinct boss has a small corps of workers. He required to familiarize himself personally with the political affiliations and tendencies of all the voters in his precinct and held responsible for the maintenance or increase of the party vote at each election. He appoints observers, challengers, and other party collaborators, reporting often on local conditions to his superior, the district leader. Above the district organization is that of the county.

Committee theoretically is under the control of a General Commander of Tammany committee made up of the joint membership of the district committees, a total now of 11,264 persons. Of course, this is far too large for the performance of executive functions. The latter instrumented to an executive commander leader of ceremonies, a transcriber, and a door-keeper. The members dressed in Indian garb on ceremonial occasions and their meeting place was known as the dwelling.

References: The Government of American Cities, p. 35.2 of the Tammany.

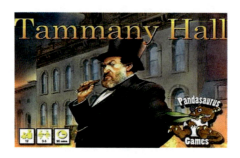

MACHINES AND BOSSES

American Political History

Tammany Hall, also known as the Society of St. Tammany, the Sons of St. Tammany, or the Columbian Order, was a New York City political organization founded in 1786 and incorporated on May 12, 1789, as the Tammany Society.

It was the Democratic Party-political machine that played a key role in control ling New York City and New York State politics and helping immigrants, most notably the Irish, rise in American politics from the 1790s to the 1960s. It naturally controlled Democratic Party nominations and central of district and precinct leaders; after 1850 the large majority were Irish Catholics.

Tammany Hall was an organization based in New York City that became famous for the extent of its political corruption. Between 1854 and 1934, the group controlled Democratic party politics in New York City, and it had a huge influence over the city's policies and politics. That is what we want to avoid the repetition of this group, cutting the political parties in the world.

The General Committee of Tammany chooses a chair, since 1949, the leading figure in the Chinese Communist Party. Many chair, treasurer, secretary, and various committees, but in unofficial none of these is supreme party power to be found. Kelly chieftain and Croker, former bosses of Tammany, held party offices within the gift of the General Committee, but Charles F. Murphy, the present head of the machine, has refrained from accepting such positions. Officially his name appears upon the list simply as that of one of the seven district leaders from his assembly district. The real sources of his power are far subtler than any which could become conferred by mere party office control of the party machinery.

Holding no other office in the organization and controlling it only through sheer personal influence Mr. Murphy can deposed only with the greatest difficulty. It would be necessary to elect county committee members and executive members who would refuse to go to Mr. Murphy for advice and refuse to follow his 302an officer of the county committee nor of the executive committee, nor even chairperson of subcommittee of these committees. He is a political Nestor of the organization, and because of his rare political judgment and his shrewd manipulation of men is enabled to hold a firm They have summed up in an admirable statement by Prof. P. O. Ray, as follows: He is a natural leader who occupies no official position in the party organization other than that of executive member for the Twelfth Assembly District. He is no suggestions or orders.

Nothing short of a revolution in the party could bring this about. Thus, Tammany with its thousands of precinct captains and their assistants at the bottom and with its hundreds of committee delegates in each district, converges at an excellent detailed account of the Tammany machine also presented by P. O. Ray, Introduction to top into an executive committee of forty-six, all acknowledging the leadership of one man, oligarchy.

References: W. B. Munro, op. cit., p. 162. Political Parties and Practical Politics, pp. 435-447-Cf. Rules and Regulations of the Democratic-Republican Organization of the County of New York (1918). 2 Op. cit., p. 440.

Tammany Hall

William "Boss" Tweed Chairman of Tammany Hall Helped unite Democrats

Boss Tweed was head of Tammany from 1863-1871

CHAPTER 16

POLITICAL PARTIES AND ELECTORAL PROBLEMS

American Political History

In addition to the primarily political duties of the discus strict leader told above, he must also devote himself to community and charitable activities. Tammany is more successful than any other city machine in work of the latter character. On the side of friendliness there are innumerable unreliable campaign clubs, some of them designed to give real aid, others to drive as hard bargains as possible for the joint votes of their membership. In a Chicago district, in 1920, a candidate offered a barrel of beer to every club numbering not less than three members.

Many of them sprang up, but the candidate stuck to his word and held the parties promised. And as in other cities there are many permanent political clubs, some of which are named after the district leader, others bearing various regional, national, or fanciful Indian titles, e.g., J. F. Ahearn Association, Senator Dunnigan Club, John F. Curry Association, Downtown Tammany Club, Sixteenth Assembly District Tammany Club, Italian Harlem Democratic League French Democratic Club, Puerto Rican American Democratic Club, and the Anawanda, Cherokee, Chippewa, Huron, and Minqua clubs.

The Republican organization in New York, which in general follows Tammany lines closely, also has extensive list of affiliated permanent clubs. Each of these clubs has a small hall or suite conveniently found, with rooms for smoking and for cards, billiards, and other games. Moderate dues payed by members, deficits or special needs generously met by the district leader.

In the social atmosphere of these clubs' friendships ripen which may prove valuable assets politically.

Young men are particularly welcome, and thus many a political career launched. Summer outings to Coney Island or up the river, with athletic events and refreshments on a huge scale, are major events in the club calendars. Generous district leaders also hire steamers to give the women and children a day's excursion during the heated term. In winter they supply a big beefsteak dinner in a Bowery restaurant, followed by the donation of a pair of shoes to each guest.

References: C. E. Merriam, op. cit., p. 73,

MACHINES AND BOSSES PHILADELPHIA REPUBLICAN ORGANIZATION

American Political History

The Republican Party in Pennsylvania founded on November 27, 1854, in the home of David Wilmot in Towanda, Pennsylvania. Wilmot gathered his friends, former Governor Simon Cameron, Congressman Thaddeus Stevens, Colonel Alexander McClure, and former Governor Samuel Curtin, to form local Republican Clubs in their home counties.

We take considerable pride in the fact that the first national convention held in Pittsburgh on February 22, 1856. Later, party delegates held their first nominating convention at Philadelphia's Musical Fund Hall on June 17, 1856. Two years later, on September 5, 1858, Pennsylvania's Republican Clubs met in Pittsburgh to form the state Republican Party. Of the 65 counties in the Commonwealth at that time, 64 represented at the Pittsburgh Convention. David Wilmot served as the first Chairman of the Republican Party. In October of 1858, the Republican Party elected their first statewide official, John M. Reid, to the Supreme Court. In 1860, the Republican Party elected Samuel Curtin to the Governor's office and gained control of the state Senate, which they did not relinquish for 30 years.

In 1959, George I. Bloom turned the Republican Party into a statewide organization with a new permanent headquarters in Harrisburg. In its main outlines and purposes, the Republican organization of Philadelphia actively look like the Democratic organization of New York

City. Our organization, said David H. Lane, sage of practical politics and for a generation leader of the Twentieth Ward, bears the same relation to Philadelphia. Tammany does to New York. On occasion, however, Tammany men have rejected such comparisons. According to Plunkitt, the difference between a looter and a practical politician is the difference between the Philadelphia Republican band and Tammany Hall.

Be this as it may, one minor point of contrast between the two machines is noteworthy. Tammany, it will become recalled, uses the assembly district as the unit of representation. Under the Rules of the Republican Party for the City and County of Philadelphia, now in effect, the unit of representation is the precinct, locally known as the district or division. There are from nine to eighty-two of these districts in each ward, the number in the city being 1,464. At its base in the district the Philadelphia organization is a pure party democracy, since every qualified Republican elector shall be a member of the partition or area committee and this committee shall be the representative body of the Republican party in the district. However, the pure democratic feature strengthened by control from above as the district committee acts under the direction of the ward executive committee.

References: On the second Republican organization in Philadelphia P. O. Ray, op. cit., p. 448. Cf. also C. R. Woodruff, Philadelphia's Republican Tammany, Outlook, vol. lxia, pp. 169-172 (Sept. 21, 1901). W. L. Riordon, Plunkitt of Tammany Hall, p.55. 3 Rules, § v. Division committees. Solutions: The New Electoral Fusion System, Nonpartisan Elections. No Parties No problems with Fusion Electoral System.

POLITICAL PARTIES AND ELECTORAL PROBLEMS

American Political History

Each district is represented by a Republican and a Democratic partition leader, who are selected by their party's committee people soon after the committee people are elected. In Philadelphia, wards 39, 40, and 66 are currently represented by two Democratic ward leaders and wards 39 and 40 by two Republican ward leaders, due to their size.

The Democratic and Republican Party organizations in Philadelphia start at an ordinary level with the office of committee person. Each division represented by up to two Democratic and two Republican committee individuals who become elected by voters of the same party who live in the same detachment. Republican and Democratic committee people serve four-year terms. Since 1965, Philadelphia has divided into 66 districts, which are the second smallest units of the city. Districts usually have between 10 and 50 partitions. Constituencies.

Each district represented by a Republican and a Democratic area leader, who selected by their party's committee people soon after the committee people elected. In Philadelphia, districts 39, 40, and 66 currently represented by two Democratic district leaders and districts 39 and 40 by two Republican district leaders, due to their size. District leaders serve as members of their respective political party organization's City Committee, sometimes called the County Committee, which supervises the organization and management of the party in all Philadelphia elections.

District organization Central campaign committee Tuesday of December of each year the qualified Re-publican voters of each district meet in assembly and organizations the area committee by the choice of a president, secretary, and treasurer.

In the district the party authority is the Ward Executive Committee, consisting of two members from each region, chosen for a term of two years in direct primary elections by the qualified Republican electors of the district. This makes a body ranging from 18 to 164 members, according to the size of the district. Permanent organization of the Ward Executive Committee affected by the election of the usual executive officers and committees, followed by the choice of one person who shall be the member of the Central Campaign Committee of the city.

The one and only person thus officially appointed is more commonly known as the district leader. Although the term used in the rules is extensive enough to include women, the choice of each district so far has always fallen upon a man. He exercises political powers and influence of great local importance, like those of the district leader in New York City.

There are also several permanent district clubs in Philadelphia, but they do not play so active a part as those affiliated with Tammany. By an interesting provision of the rules, the district leader is subject to recall at any time by a vote of two thirds of the duly elected members of the Ward Executive Committee. For the city and county party authority vested in a

Central Campaign Committee of forty-eight members, one from each district, selected for a term of one year by the separate ward executive committees. In other words, this is simply an outstanding convocation of the leaders who separately dominate, each in his own district, and if united could dominate in city and county. One interesting feature of the Philadelphia organization is the fact that nominees for district, or for city and county offices, become given ex-official membership, without the right to vote for officers, however, upon their ward executive committee or upon the Central Campaign Committee respectively.

References: Seventy.org/publications/ward-leaders-committee people/ward.,

MACHINES AND BOSSES

American Political History

Today news 4/24/2019.The Trump Organization is suing Maryland Rep. Elijah Cummings, the chairperson of the House Oversight Committee, over a subpoena the panel sent to President Donald Trump's main accounting firm. The lawsuit also names Peter Kenny, the chief investigative counsel for House oversight Democrats, as a co-defendant.

Democrats are using their new control of congressional committees to investigate every aspect of President Trump's personal finance, businesses, and even his family, the filing declares. Instead of collaborating with the President to pass bipartisan legislation that would benefit Americans, House Democrats are singularly fanatical with finding something they can use to damage the President politically, hear we can see that the partisan fighting is harming the nation development of party-political assistances. No Parties No problems with Fusion Electoral System.

Cummings announced the subpoena in a memo last week. The Maryland Democrat said it was a friendly summons because the accounting firm, Mazars USA, had requested one from the committee before turning over records related to the president's finances. The Republican party organization of Philadelphia is a perfect pyramid, ascending from the 331,499 sentimentality qualified party voters eligible to membership in the 1,464 district committees to the forty-eight region committees with their collective membership of 2,928, and from this political fight the American peoples will not helping our nation with this senseless political fight, that's why we need to eliminate those parties and the rest of any other prevailing.

District committees to the Central Campaign Committee of forty-eight members. Since 1895, however, no single leader has been able to dominate the city and county. According to a local witticism Philadelphia is the city of squab and scraper, but it is also the city of argument in addition dispute, the latter descending at times to the political use of imported snipers and assassins, as in the famous Fifth District case of 1917. During the period since 1895 and particularly of recent years the most powerful machine in the organization was the contractor lobby kept by the Vare Brothers. As far as party office was concerned, Ed Vare, the Napoleon of Philadelphia political leaders, occupied the position merely of representative from the Thirty-ninth District in the City Central Campaign Committee.

While dominant at times to the extent of controlling the mayor's office and once the governorship of the state, the independent lobby has always become obliged to fight energetically the Penrose machine, formerly under the local leadership of McNichol, and the self-determining Republicans of the city.

References: Seventy.org//publications/ward-leaders-committee people/ward., Reference: The New Electoral Fusion System, Nonpartisan Elections. No Parties No problems with Fusion Electoral System.

CHICAGO PARTY ORGANIZATIONS

American Political History

Today's News Stop Sanders Democrats Are Worrying Over His Impetus. Here we can appreciate the Democrats tenseness by the possibility of a Communist uncompromising left win, like Sanders, become the new president, of course, we all have to be nervous, that is why I say the new Fusion system will not allow any political party or ideologies become an authenticity in America.

(WASHINGTON 4/16/2019), When Leah Daughtry, a former Democratic Party official, addressed a closed door gathering of about 100 wealthy liberal donors in San Francisco last month, all it took was a review of the 20-20 primary rules to throw a fright in them. Democrats are likely to go into their convention next summer without having settled on a presidential nominee, said Ms. Daughtry, who ran her party's conventions in 2008 and 2016, the last two times the nomination contested. And Senator Bernie Sanders of Vermont well positioned to be one of the last candidates standing, she noted.

Freaked them out, Ms. Daughtry recalled with a giggle, an assessment that became confirmed by three other attendees. They are barely unaccompanied. From canapé filled fund-raisers on the coasts to the coat rooms of Washington, mainstream Democrats are increasingly nervous that their effort to defeat President Trump in 20-20 could be complicated by Mr. Sanders, in a political scenario all too meaningful of how Mr. Trump himself held the Republican nomination in 2016. Stop Sanders socialist leftist pseudo Communist. Democrats are worrying over Sanders Inducement. Nervous too of having the amaze of a Communist candidate with such philosophies of an American Communism, make me tremble. Reference The New York Time 4/16/2019. References: Seventy. org/publications/ward-leaders-committee people/ward.

In Chicago both parties use the ward as the basis of organization elected by party vote in the direct primary reward committee member for a term of four years. The district committee-man, terms precinct committee members or leaders, the total number of such offices being about 2,200 in 1921.

There are thirty-five districts, each of which organizations representatives given a strength proportionate to that of the vote of his party in the ward at the last preceding gubernatorial election.

As in Philadelphia, factional fighting is the order of the day, particularly on the Republican side, where the Thompson and Deneen-Brundage organizations oppose each other, and to a somewhat less extent on the Democratic side, where the Sullivan and Harrison-Dunne organizations are the competitors.

A striking peculiarity of Chicago politics consists in the creation by each of these four sections of a group composed of all its members in the City Committee plus one member from each district where it is in a minority.

Reference: The New York Time.

Michael Anguelo

CHARACTERISTICS OF THE BOSSES

American Political History

There are following characteristics of political system governments spreads certain conveniences then at the same time it has power to impose taxes upon the people and punish those who violate those orders.

(2) Interactions: Almond in his book, The Policies of. The first characteristic of political system is that it allows the legal authority to use force. If David Easton speaks of striking provision of ethics, the all of control, rule and authority. All these definitions imply that legal authority can use force to compel anybody to obey its orders.

It has legitimated and heavy authorizations and reasonable power to penalize. Consequently, we must agree with Max Weber that legitimate use of force is a different feature of political organization, giving it an exceptional quality and importance, and its unity as a scheme. When the state or Developing Areas, writes: Political system is that system of communications to be found in all independent societies which perform the functions of incorporation and variation, both within and a complement of other civilizations, by means of the employment or threat of employment or more or less legitimate corporal obligation. Thus, the political system not only includes governmental institutions such as legislatures, executives, courts, administrative agencies but all structures in their political aspect.

Among these included formal organizations like parties, interest groups, and media of communication; traditional structures such as connotation ties, caste groupings anomic phenomena such as associations,

The New Fusion Electoral System

riots a demonstration. Consequently, the political system includes interaction between all the formal and informal institutions.

Piatt and Barnes of New York; the two Cameron's, Quay, and Penrose of Pennsylvania; General Sewall and Jim Smith of New Jersey; General Brayton of Rhode Island; and their apprenticeship, beginning as lieutenants or even as henchmen, before they can expect after innumerable factional conflicts to dominate a district or a city.

Study of the characteristics of the better-known figures in this field reveals so many divergences, however, that to talk of a type is apt to prove misleading. typical boss Efforts have also become made to trace more soberly the career and character of the typical boss, distinguishing as species of the genus the city boss and the state boss. As far as the career of harnesses is concerned, it may become taken for approved that, like other political leaders, they must serve y, this argument turnout to be a not working system, because humans need it for self-determination.

Naturally a political figure so striking as that of the describe the boss is subject to endless comment, much of it vituperative process of interaction divided into three phases, input, conversion, and output. The Indian-Constitution reflects the various interactions as many amendments were transported about to bring out Zamindari abolition, communism to remove poverty among city leaders Tweed, Honest John Kelly, Croker, and Murphy of Tammany; Fred Lundin, Roger Sullivan, John 1 M. Ostrogorski, Democracy and the Organization of Political Parties, vol. ii, pp. 401-412; also in briefer form in bit Democracy and the Party System, pp. 250-255.

No Parties No problems with Fusion Electoral System. Developing one. By 1950, sixty years later, every urban political machine was in an advanced state of uselessness and its boss in trouble. The reason is not hard to find. Some of the cities kept growing and all of them kept changing, but the political managers, natural products of a specific era, could not grow or change beyond a certain point. The cities became

MACHINES AND THE GOOD BOSSES

American Political History

The big city and the political manager grew up together in America. Bossism, with all its color and dishonesty and the human drama, was a natural and necessary accompaniment to the rapid development of cities. The new urban communities did not grow slowly and according to plan; on the contrary, huge conglomerations of people from all over tor there, an old timer made one last comeback. In Chicago, the organization and its manager still survive. But exceptions aside, the late nineteenth century saw the beginning, and the middle twentieth, the end, of the Age of the Managers. What follows is a brief history of how it began, flourished, and approved. Soft spoken Irish fawners from County Mayo and bearded Jews from Poland, country boys from Ohio and sturdy peasants from Calabria, gangling Swedes from near the Arctic Circle and Chinese from Canton, Latins from the Bronx, laconic Yankees from Vermont villages and Negro freedmen putting distance between themselves and the old estate, all these and many other varieties of human beings from every national and religious dry cultural tradition poured into America's cities in the periods after the Civil War.

Rome and Alexandria in the ancient world had been as multilingual, but in modern times the diversity of American cities was unique. Everywhere in the Western world, cities were growing rapidly in the late nineteenth century; but the Germans from the countryside who migrated to Hamburg and Berlin, the English who moved to Birmingham and London, and the French who congregated to Paris stayed among fellow nationals. They might be ridiculed as country bumpkins and their clothes might be un-fashionable, but everyone they met spoke the same language as themselves, observed the same religious and secular holidays, ate the same kind of food, voted, if they had the franchise at all, in the same elections, and shared the same sentiments and expectations.

To move from farm or village to a big European city was an adventure, but one remained within the encouraging circle of the known and the family in American cities, however, the newcomers had nothing in common with one another except their poverty and their hopes. They were truly the displaced. The foreign borne world and from widely varying backgrounds came together suddenly, and in an unplanned, unorganized fashion fumbled their way toward communal relationships and a common identity. The political managers appeared to cope with this chaotic change and growth. Acting out of greed, a ruthless will for lack of knowledge, and an imperfect understanding of what they were about, the managers imposed upon these conglomerations called cities a certain archaic order and direction.

The New Fusion Electoral System

By 1890 every sizable city had a political manager or was cities from the countryside experienced their own kind of cultural shock: they found themselves competing not with other Americans but with recently arrived outsiders, so that even with their native birth they, too, felt displaced, they felted aliens in their own country. It was natural for members of each group to come together to try to find human warmth and protection in Little Italy or Cork Hill or Chinatown or Harlem or the Spaniards, first European who discovered America. These feelings of clannish solidarity were one basis of strength for the political bosses. A man will more willingly give his vote to a candidate because he is a neighbor from the old country or has some easily identifiable relationship, if only a similar name or the same religion, than because of agreement on some impersonal issue. Voters can take secondhand satisfaction from his success: One of our boys is making good. Therefore, America is so great, because the diversity, every emigrant came with a dream over his pillow, or a fielder over their roof.

With so many different races and nationalities living together, however, mutual hostilities were present, and the opportunity for resentment to flame into open violence was never far away. Ambitious, unscrupulous politicians could have exploited these resentments for their own political advantage, but the bosses and the political organizations which they set up did not function that way. If a man Cincinnati, pasted together a coalition of Germans, Negroes, and old families like the Taft's and the Long worth's. James M. Curley, who was mayor of Boston on and off for thirty-six years and was its closest approximation to a political boss, ran as well in the Lithuanian neighborhood of South Boston and the Italian section of East Boston as he did in the working-class Irish wards. In his last term in City Hall, he conferred minor patronage on the growing Negro community and joined the N.A.A.C.P.

The bosses organized neighborhoods, smoothed out resentments, arranged ethnically balanced tickets, and distributed patronage by voting strength as part of their effort to win and hold power. They blurred divisive issues and buried racial and religious hostility with flattery and buncombe. They were not aware that they were performing a mediating, pacifying function. They did not realize that by trying to please as many people as possible they were helping to hold raw new cities together, providing for in-experienced citizens a common meeting ground in politics and an experience in working together that would not have been available if the cities had been governed by apolitical bureaucracies. Bossism was usually corrupt and was decidedly inefficient, but in the 1960's, when antipoverty planners try to inspire public action organizations to break through the indifference and disorganization of the shanty towns, we can appreciate that the traditional machineries had their usefulness.

When William Marcy Tweed, the first and most famous of the big city bosses, died in jail in 1878, several hundred workingmen showed up for his funeral. The revulsion piled on of work him in the pulpits last Sunday does not exist for the employee. Voters of this city today revere his memory, and look on him as the victim of rich men's malice; as, in short, a friend of the needy who applied the public funds, with as little waste as was possible under the circumstances, to the purposes to which they ought to become applied, and that is to the making The Nation wrote the following week: Let us re-member that he fell without loss of reputation among the bulk of his supporters. The bulk of the poorer could vote and would vote right, he become accepted, and that was the end of the matter. What lasting profit was there in attacking his religion or ridiculing his background? Tammany early set the pattern of cultivating every bloc and faction and making an appeal as broad based as possible. Of one precinct captain on the Lower East Side it was sin the lower stratum of New York society. Not all the basses were malign politician, some have heart, I believe that bosses are needed even if we decided eliminate all political parties, bosses are need in a Fusion System to help the disadvantage poor but with rules.

This split in attitude toward political bosses between the disadvantaged many and the prosperous middle classes stays today and still colors historical writing. To respectable people, the boss was an exotic, even outrageous figure. They found it hard to understand why anyone would vote for him or what the sources of his popularity were? From the urban poor, those sources were self-obvious. The boss ran a ramshackle welfare state. He helped the unemployed find jobs, interceded in court for boys in trouble, wrote letters home to the old country for the illiterate; he provided free coal and baskets of food to tide a widow over an emergency, and organized parades, excursions to the beach, and other forms of free entertainment.

Schmitz of San Francisco; and Fingy Connors of Buffalo. In the foregoing brief list, there are five college graduates, two of them honor men of their classes. At the other end of the scale Twee was a chair-maker by trade, a vulgar good fellow by one bosses, such as Frank Hague in Jersey City and Curley in Boston, were energetic patrons of their respective city hospitals, spending public funds lavishly the public and private arrangements to cushion life's shocks did not exist, these benefactions from a political boss were important. on new construction, supplying maternity and children's clinics, and arranging medical care for the indigent. In an era when social security, Blue Cross, unemployment compensation, and Some bosses, such as Frank Hague in Jersey City and construction, providing maternity and children's clinics, and arranging medical care for the indigent.

Powers, Bathhouse John Coughlin and Hinky-Dink Kenna of Chicago; McManus, Iz Durham, McNichol, and the Vare brothers of Philadelphia; Flinn and Chris Magee of Pittsburgh; Colonel Ed Butler of St. Louis; Doc Ames of Minneapolis; George B. Cox and Rud Hynicka of Cincinnati; Abe Ruefan in an era when social security, Blue Cross, unemployment compensation, and distinguished family of Philadelphia, allied himself with the academics and agitators. He was joint author of a scholarly treatise on the development of the government of his native city which become published by one of the greater universities of the country.

While little of the attitude of the scholar in politics maintained by the mature Penrose, he was nevertheless able to the end of his career to make effective appeal to men of this type as against the Vares. According to one of his incidentally, he was a state's person, the Vares were dust wagons. Ed Vare, the greatest local opponent of Penrose, was of equally pure American stock, but born to poverty and hard work, his education such only as the local schools could give, his first employment that of hawking vegetables from door to door, and incidentally making many valuable acquaintances in the process.

PARTIES AND ELELECTIONS PROBLEMS

American Political History

James Smith, Jr., of New Jersey, is a manufacturer on a large scale, president of a trust company, and served one term in the United States Senate. It is evidence that America is the pro mess land. Following an account of the development of municipal government in Philadelphia from 1681 to 1887.

Danger to America, By Patricia McCarthy: On November 6, it seemed the Republicans might hold their majority in the Senate and in the House. Sadly, they lost their majority in the House. The mystery is why so many Democrat candidates who so obviously ethically challenged won in races that should not have even been close.

How and why do Democrats continue to vote for unqualified, dishonest candidates? Elizabeth Warren is a confirmed deceiver, a fraud who claimed Native American heritage to get a job at Harvard. Her darling, the Consumer Financial Protection Bureau, was her plan to have control over all bank and non-bank institutions without Congressional interference. In short, she was a hard-left Communist who means to control how Americans earn, spend, and borrow money, how they use their savings. Warren is a blight on the Constitution and the guaranteed freedoms of Unite States citizens. She is an advance operative for the Communist America the left predicts. No Parties No problems with Fusion Electoral System. Andrew Gillum, the left's choice to be Governor of Florida, is the unsuccessful mayor of Tallahassee. He stays under FBI investigation for corruption. Given the information about that investigation that has become released, he appears yet another avaricious and crooked Democrat pol in the Hillary Clinton attitude. The stability of Tallahassee declined catastrophically under his leadership; crime and murder rose drastically.

Gillum sold out his city for money, and cries racism when confronted with his crimes. He should never have been the candidate for the Governor of Florida but the left cares only about race and power, not ethics or honor. For progressives, race trumps everything else, even character. If Gillum wins after the cheating Broward County is infamous for, Florida will suffer the slings and arrows that are like Gillum. Why was this race even close? Partake half the nation's voters scuttled any semblance of traditional values to win? Answer: Gillum lost because the Cuban American votes were to Ron De Santis.

The governor of Florida is the head of the executive branch of Florida's state government and the commander-in-chief of the state's military forces. The governor has a duty to enforce state laws, and the power to either approve or veto bills passed by the Florida Legislature, to convene the legislature, and to grant pardons, except in cases of impeachment.

When Florida was first acquired by the United States, future president Andrew Jackson served as its military governor. Florida Territory was set up in 1822, and five people served as governor over six distinct terms. The first territorial governor, William Pope Duval, served 12 years, the longest of any Florida governor to date.

Since statehood in 1845, there have been 45 people who have served as governor, one of whom served two distinct terms. Four state governors have served two full four-year terms: William D. Bloxham, in two stints; and Reubin Askew, Jeb Bush, and Rick Scott who each served their terms consecutively. Bob Graham almost served two terms, as he resigned with only three days left. The shortest term in office belongs to Wayne Mixson, who served three days following the resignation of his predecessor, Bob Graham. The current governor is Ron DeSantis, a member of the Republican Party who took office on January 8, 2019. The left ignores fine men like John James, who ran for the House in Michigan against Debbie Stabenow.

They have ignored fine people like James and Edwards as they have always ignored d brilliant men like Thomas Sowell, Shelby Steele, Walter Williams, Jason Riley, and Larry Elder. Both men are conservative African Americans. The American left today ignored Eddie Edwards who ran in New Hampshire. pretends such candidates do not exist. They have ignored fine people like James and Edwards as they have always ignored, he exists. They have ignored fine people like James and Edwards as they have always ignored Clarence Thomas. They do not like to become reminded of men like Frederick Douglass or Booker T. Washington. Neither of them, like Sowell, Steele, Williams and Elder ever promoted the idea that African Americans were or would be recurrent victims. Each of them advocated for quite the opposite, for self-reliance and independence.

This notion of personal responsibility is anathema to today's left; they need and promote subservience and dependency among their flock of dependable but uninformed voters. Therefore, they encourage the immigration of so many millions of illegal migrants. They assume they will be able to win for them the right to vote. Judging by the number of them who voted in the midterms, their plan is succeeding.

This is how they will destroy America from within. The leftist billionaires who orchestrate these plans are extravagantly wealthy. Those tasked withstanding for us in Congress will never become exposed to the downside of the invasion of millions of migrants, the crime, or the financial burden. They have nothing but contempt for those of us who must endure the consequences of our communities intruded upon by gang members, drug dealers and human traffickers. These people have no intention of becoming Americans; like the Democrats who welcome them, they have contempt for us.

This is a wholesale formal accusation of our politicized, dumbed down system of education. Many of her constituents are immigrants; we are obviously not educating them at all. They voted for all the free stuff college, medical care, basic income, housing, that Ocasio-Cortez has promised to deliver. This is what a communist Democrats dream about: perpetual power over a populace too ignorant to rebel. American as founded is at grave risk. In addition to O Dasio-Cortez, Gillum, Ilhan Omar, Abrams, Sinema, who highly likely cheated to take the Arizona Senate seat, there is Linda Sanchez.

Kirsten Gillibrand is a Hillary Clinton replica; she only cares about her own political power. She speaks like a small child but is also considering a run for the presidency. She was best friends with Bill Clinton and Harvey Weinstein until they were politically inconvenient. Amy Klobuchar, who embraced the vicious and obviously false allegations against Judge Kavanagh, was endorsed. Like every other Democrat member of the judiciary committee, she knew those accusations were false, without a shred of corroboration, but her constituents re-elected her.

Who are these voters? How do they reconcile voting for people willing to destroy a fine man for political purposes? She is exactly who every Democrat member of that committee is, who every member of the Democrat Party is nothing more than power-hungry political operatives out to ruin any and all opponents by any means necessary. They are a clear and present danger to American as in progress.

Young people no longer taught the truth of American history. They have not educated the truth of the Holocaust. Anti-Semitism is acceptable, even promoted, by the Democrats. They embrace Linda Sar sour and Louis Farrakhan without shame. Young people do not know that Communism had killed over a hundred million people in the twentieth century. Their planned by leftist's ignorance is the destruction of our country. They try to sell the idea that gender is not a factor of biology.

They try to convince young people that weather change and made up that global warming causes wildfires. Having control over academic circles, they have willfully brainwashed students for two generations. Unless your children are a strong desired, independent thinker, do not send them to college.

How and why the American left has transferred into this kind of party, that only one finds in a Communist republic at our doorstep, like Cuba is a familiar disaster. That our media is so anxious to promote their corrupt candidates and the undemanding tactics they employ is an American disaster. Do they do it because they can no longer win by publicizing their Orwellian vision of a Communist state, delegated fairness of conclusion? Possibly.

They will never sell Communism to sufficient understanding Americans to win. They need millions of ignorant voters to succeed. We must not let them trickster their method to control over the rest of us. Their current vote fraud must turn out to be at a standstill, and the Democrats need to look at themselves and at what they have become transformed. It is not an attractive portrait. What they have become threatens to destroy the greatest nation on the planet and they are doing it with determination. They have nothing but disrespect for the US as originated by the founding fathers and for those of us who live and die for our country.

On November 6 next election, it appeared that the Republicans might hold their majority in the Senate and in the House of Representative. Unhappily, they lost their majority in the House. The unknown is why so many Democrat candidates, who so clearly morally confronted gained in races that should not have even been near.

How and why do Democrats continue to vote for unreserved, dishonest candidates? Elizabeth Warren is a proven a storyteller, a charlatan who appealed Native American inheritance to get a job at Harvard. Her dear, the Consumer Financial Protection Bureau, was her plan to exercise control over all bank and non-bank institutions without Congressional interfering.

In short, she is a hard-left Communist who means to control how Americans earn, spend, and borrow money, how they use their savings. Warren is a disfigurement of the Constitution and the guaranteed of freedoms in US citizens. She is an advance operative for the Communist America the left invasions. No Parties No problems with Fusion Electoral System.

Andrew Gillum, the left's choice to be Governor of Florida, is the failed mayor of Tallahassee. He is still under FBI investigation for corruption. Given the information about that investigation that has become released, he appears yet another greedy and corrupt Democrat pol in the Hillary Clinton attitude, that's way he did not successes. The stability of Tallahassee declined catastrophically under his leadership; crime and murder rose drastically. Gillum sold out his city for money, and cries racism when confronted with his crimes. He should never have been the candidate for the Governor of Florida but the left-hand cares only about race and power, not ethics or honor. For progressives, race surpasses everything else, even character. Why was this race even close? Because Mr. Gillum had an obscure past. Have half the nation's voters scampered any appearance of traditional values to win? This is a clear example of why I abrogate for the termination of all political parties, Fusion is the solution of all our political differences, when voters elect their representative to elect the president without the involvement of any political party.

Stacey Abrams, the still grasping gubernatorial contender in Georgia, is a hard-left, anti-capitalist, anti-Second Amendment candidate. She owes about $200K in credit card debt and wants to run Georgia? Se la politic in America. She too is corrupt and incompetent. She is also willing to swindler to win. Are Georgians ignorant of her many, many negatives? Possible. If they are, they voted for her anyway. Again, skin color exceeds everything.

The left disregards fine men like John James, who ran for the House in Michigan against Debbie Stabenow. The left ignored Eddie Edwards who ran in New Hampshire. Both men are conservative African Americans. The American left-hand today pretends such candidates do not exist. They have ignored fine people like James and Edwards as they have always ignored brilliant men like Thomas Sowell, Shelby Steele, Walter Williams, Jason Riley, and Larry Elder. They revile the brilliant Clarence Thomas. They do not like to become reminded of men like Frederick Douglass or Booker.

T. Washington. Neither of them, like Sowell, Steele, Williams and Elder ever promoted the idea that African Americans were or would be perpetual victims. Each of them advocated for quite the opposite, for self-reliance and self-determination.

This concept of personal responsibility is a detestation of to today's left; they need and promote subservience and dependency among their wrinkle of dependable but uneducated voters. Consequently, they encourage the immigration of so many millions of illegal migrants. They assume they will be able to win for them the right to vote. Judging by the number of them who voted in the midterms, their plan is later.

This is how they will somehow benefit the American economy as always has done through generations of immigrants; we are all immigrants is some way, the illegal emigration is not the wright way to enter in United States. The Communists who compose these plans are lavishly rich. Those undertaking withstanding for us in Congress will never become perceptible to the shortcoming of the invasion of millions of migrants, because the abuse, or the monetary difficulties. They have nothing but disapproval for those of us who must endure the consequences of our communities become imposed upon by gang members, drug dealers and human traffickers.

MACHINES AND BOSSES BRIBERIES

American Political Parties History

Political machines allowed themselves to become bribed by wealthy business owners and contractors in the late 1800s. The bribery gave away to the rise of gangs, which ruled shanty town. This led to gerrymandering and cooping. This was a black eye to American Democracy, but hopefully we will substitute this corrupt system by the Fusion System no partisan elections.

The rise of industry in the late 1800s opened new opportunities for earning money and truly made it possible for anyone to become wealthy. Cities were growing at a fast rate, which required the distribution of a lot of contracts to build facilities using tax dollars. Business owners soon learned that the more influence they had with politicians, the more money they could potentially earn. So, they began bribing politicians by offering them money or guaranteed votes in exchange for contracts to build. They also began suborning politicians with money to look the other way about the poor treatment of workers and shady business practices.

As their wealth grew, extremely wealthy men employed bosses within areas that they owned property to take care of smaller tasks, such as collecting rent money or loan payments. They also become charged with keeping workers under control, particularly those who seemed unhappy about working conditions or wages. Through their relationships with wealthy businesspeople who controlled gangs, politicians were able to expand their territories through force on behalf of the mobs in the form of viciousness or forced to voting.

The era earned the name the Gilded Age because there was vast corruption hidden underneath great wealth and opulence. It is a disgraceful past, but our system is planned to go through the adolescence to the maturity and recover, by our Democratic-Republican system, the only imperfection is of the political party elections that harms the system. Certain common behaviors of bosses' slaughterer's boy, a wagon driver, a tobacco salesperson, a bar-tender, a saloon keeper, and after his rise to power a large operator in real estate, banking, and theatrical enterprises. According to a typical newspaper sketch written at the time of his indictments for lying under oath he had the protruding belly, the protruding jaw, and the inevitable protruding cigar of the boss, but these are mere cartoonists' belongings rather than universals of flesh and blood bosses.

Despite his impolite manners and appearance Cox owned great perceptiveness, genuine courage, and a real love for children. In San Francisco Abe Ruef was a university graduate and an able lawyer; his closest associate, Schmitz, was a musician and labor leader. In family and cultural background General Brayton, who served with credit in the Civil War, may become compared with Penrose. Like Ed Vare, Flinn was a boss contractor. Doc Ames was a skillful surgeon. Colonel Ed Butler was a horseshoe.

Croker, a machinist by trade, fought several formal prize fights as a young man and later tried for shooting and killing a man in an election row. The jury did not agree. Myers says it as the opinion of those in a position to know that the Croker did not fire the fatal shot. Amid such diversity of origin and character a great deal of intensive study must become done before sound generalizations can become grabbed. However, a few tentative conclusions may become endangered. Eradicated in any list of men who have reached prominence in this. field particularly as enacts of city machines, although this would not become so marked if the less well advertised rural bosses who are usually of straight American stock encompassed.

CHAPTER 17

MACHINES AND BOSSES CORRUPTIONS

American Political Parties History

Like other political leaders, bosses reflect their immediate environment. To a high-class residential section, the boss of a scorned shantytown district seems a very vulgar and corrupt person.

Why has the Republican Party become so thoroughly corrupt? The reason is historical, it goes back many decades, and, in a way, philosophical. The party best understood as an insurgency that carried the seeds of its own corruption from the start. I do not mean the kind of corruption that regularly sends troublemakers like Rod Blagojevich, the Democratic former governor of Illinois, went to prison. Those abuses are nonpartisan and always with us. So is vote theft of the kind we have just seen in North Carolina, after all, the alleged fraudsters employed by the Republican candidate for Congress hired himself out to Democrats in 2010. And I don't just mean that the Republican Party is led by the boss of a kleptomaniac family business who presides over an outrage angry administration, that many of his closest advisers are facing prison time, that Donald Trump himself might have to stay in office just to avoid prosecution, that he could be exposed by the special counsel and the incoming House majority as the most unethical president in American history, never-the-less the nation economy is up and the unemployment is low in many years, that give us an idea that what we need is functionaries with actions and willing of do the best for the country and not corrupts politician with ethic.

Richard Nixon's administration has also damaged with criminality, but in 1973, the Republican Party of Hugh Scott, the Senate minority leader, and John Rhodes, the House minority leader, was still a normal organization. It played by the rules; the dishonesty I mean has less to do with individual disloyalty than institutional immorality. It is not an occasional failure to uphold norms, but a consistent repudiation of them. It is not about dirty money so much as the pursuit and abuse of power, as a conclusion, justifying almost any means. Political corruption usually trails financial scandals in it awaken the bouquet is wickedness with self-dealing, but it is far more dangerous than embedding. There are legal remedies for Duncan Hunter, a representative from California, who will stand trial next year for using campaign funds to pay for family luxuries. But there has no obvious remedy for what the state legislatures of Wisconsin and Michigan, following the example of North Carolina in 2016, are now doing. Charles J. Sykes: Wisconsin Republicans are shooting themselves in the foot. Shameful situation that will continued with the political party's failures. This what this book is about the corruption of the political parties and they leaders is the cause; the solution is abolishing the political parties then the nation will help.

Republican majorities are rushing to pass laws that strip away the legitimate powers of newly elected Democratic governors while defeated or outgoing Republican incumbents are still around to sign the bills. Even if the courts overturn some of these power grabs, as they have in North Carolina, Republicans will remain securely entrenched in the legislative majority through their own hyper redrawing the district, in Wisconsin last month, 54 percent of the total votes cast for major party candidates gave Democrats just 36 of 99 assembly seats, so they will go on passing laws to foil election results. Nothing can stop these abuses short of an electoral landslide, or better than that cutting the political parties to stop legendary party corruption.

In Wisconsin, a purple state, that means close to 60 percent of the total vote. The fact that no plausible election outcome can check the abuse of power is what makes political dishonesty so dangerous. It strikes at the heart of Democracy-Republic systems. It destroys the rock-hard between the people and the government. In rendering voters voiceless, it pushes everyone closer to the use of undemocratic means.

The New Fusion Electoral System

Today's Republican Party has cornered itself with a base of ever older, whiter, more male, more rural, more conservative voters. Demography can take a long time to change, longer than in progressives' dreams, but it is not on the Republicans' side. They could have tried to expand; instead, they have hardened and walled themselves off. This happening, while voter swindle recognizes no party, only the Republican Party enthusiastically exaggerates the risk so that it can permit laws, including right now in Wisconsin, with a bill that reduces early voting, to limit the franchise in ways that have a dissimilar partisan impact. Therefore, when some Democrats in the New Jersey legislature proposed to protect the redistricting in the state constitution, other Democrats, in New Jersey and around the country, objected. Democrats and or Republican parties should, or any other parties, be eliminated to stop this political war.

Taking away democratic rights, extreme gerrymandering; blocking an elected president from nominating a Supreme Court justice; selectively paring voting rolls and polling places; creating spurious anti-fraud directives; misusing the census to under-counting the bitterness; calling lame duck lawmaking sessions to pass laws against the will of the voters, is the Republican Party's main political strategy, and will be for years to come. Republicans have chosen contraction and authoritarianism because, unlike the Democrats, their party is not a coalition of interests in search of a majority. Its character is ideological.

The Republican Party we know is a product of the modern conservative movement, and that movement is a series of insurgencies against the established order. Several of its intellectual founders Whittaker Chambers and James Burnham, among others molded early on by Communist ideology and practice an economic disaster, and their Manicheaism discriminating, their conviction that the salvation of Western civilization depended on the devoted work of a small group of illuminate, marked the movement at its birth a faultier.

The first insurgency was the nomination of Barry Goldwater for president in 1964. He campaigned as a rebel against the post war American consensus and the soft middle of his own party's leadership. Goldwater did not use the standard, reassuring lexicon of the big tent and the mainstream. At the San Francisco convention, he embraced extremism and denounced the Republican establishment, whose moderation in pursuit of justice is no virtue. His campaign lit a fire of excitement that spread to millions of readers through the pages of two self-published prophesies of the apocalypse, Phyllis Schlafly's a Choice, not a resonance and John A. Stormer's none dare call It disloyalty. According to these mega sellers, the political opposition was not simply wrong, it was a sinister conspiracy with totalitarian goals. Hopefully, this book The New Fusion Electoral System, become an eye opening to the American voters and legislators.

William F. Buckley, the movement's Max Eastman, its most brilliant pamphleteer, predicted Goldwater's landslide defeat. His candidacy, like the revolution of 1905, had come too soon, but it foretold the victory to come, the talkative confusion of thousands of scholars, tens of thousands of books, a million miles of newspaper.

At a Young Americans for Freedom convention, Buckley exhorted an audience of true believing teams to think beyond November: Presuppose that the fiery little body of dissenters, of which you are a brilliant asteroid, suddenly turned off no less than a majority of all the American people, who unexpectedly overwhelmed a generation's entrenched exhaustion, suddenly infiltrated to the true meaning of freedom in society where the truth is obstructed by then Goldwater's unavoidable downfall would turn into the well planted seeds of hope, which will blossom on a great November day in the future, if there is a future. The insurgents were agents of history, and history was long. To avoid despair, they needed the clarity that only philosophy the truth can give. The task in 1964 was to recruit and train conservative followers.

Then proven institutions that hidden the reality, schools, universities, newspapers, the Republican Party itself, would have to become swept away and replaced or entered and cleansed. Eventually Buckley imagined an electoral majority; but these were not the words and ideas of democratic politics, with its awkward alliances and unproductive conciliations. No Parties No problems with Fusion Electoral System.

During this first rebellion, the surviving shadows of the movement appropriated new outline. One feature, detailed in Before the Storm, Rick Perlstein's account of the origins of the New Right, was liberals' helplessness to understand, let alone take extremely adequate to comprehend, what was happening around the country.

For their part, conservatives nursed a victim's sense of criticism, the system was stacked against them, factions of the powerful were determined to lock them out, and they showed more energetic interest than their opponents in the means of gaining power: mass media, new techniques of organizing, grandiloquence, philosophies.

Finally, the movement founded in the politics of racism. Goldwater's strongest support came from white southerners reacting against civil rights. Even Buckley once defended Jim Crow with the claim that black Americans were too retrograde for self-government. Eventually he changed his views, but modern conservatism would never stop playing with resentment toward whole groups of Americans. And from the start this stance opened the movement to extreme, sometimes violent fellow travelers. It took only 16 years, with the election of Ronald Reagan, for the movement and party to merge. During those years, conservatives hammered away at institutional structures, denouncing the established ones for their treacherous liberalism, and building alternatives, in the form of well-funded right-wing fundamentals, think boilers, business lobbies, legal groups, magazines, publishers, professorships. Solutions: No Parties No problems with Fusion Electoral System.

When Reagan won the presidency in 1980, the products of this counter-establishment, from the title of Sidney Blumenthal's book on the subject, were ready to take power. Reagan commanded a confusion, but he himself did not have a radical appeal. He did not think the public needed to become propagandized and prearranged, only perceived.

But conservatism remained a dissatisfied politics during the 1980s and '90s, and the more power it collective, in government, business, law, media, the more it set itself against the fragile web of established standards and pleased in breaking them. The second rebellion was led by Newt Gingrich, who had come to Congress two years before Reagan became president, with the avowed aim of overthrowing the established Republican leadership and influencing the minority party into a fighting force that could break Democratic rule by crushing what he called the corrupt left-wing machine. be no negotiation.

Gingrich liked to quote Mao's definition of politics as war without blood that is what it is parties fighting without the blood. He made audiotapes that taught Republican candidates how to demoralize the adversary with labels such as dishonor, deceive, and traitors. When he became speaker of the House, at the head of yet another revolution, Gingrich announced, there will How could there be, when he was leading a campaign to save American civilization from its liberal enemies? Solutions: No Parties No problems with New Fusion Electoral System Even after Gingrich become detached from authority, the victim of his own execute, he regularly agitated out records that advised of imminent destiny, unless America turned to a leader like him, he once called himself teacher of the rules of civilization, among other dignified nicknames. Unlike Goldwater and Reagan, Gingrich never had any deeply felt philosophy. It was hard to say exactly what American civilization meant to him. What he wanted was power, and what he most clearly enjoyed was smashing things to pieces in its pursuit. His insurrection started the conservative movement on the path to pessimism. The party purged itself of most remaining moderates, growing ever lower as it grew ever more conservative, from Goldwater, who, in 1996, joked that he had become a Republican liberal, to Ted Cruz, from Buckley to Dinesh D'Souza. Jeff Flake, the outgoing senator from Arizona, whose conservative views come with a democratic temperament, describes this deterioration as a race to the bottom to see who can be nastier, furious and crazier. It is not enough to be conservative anymore.

You must be malicious. The viciousness does not necessarily live in the individual souls of Republican leaders. 'm not willing to preside over people who are flesh eaters, Gingrich declared in 1998 when he quit the House.

It flows from the party's politics, which seeks to legitimatizing opponents and institutions, purify the ranks through eliminations and takeovers, and agitate followers with visions of apocalypse, all in the name of an ideological cause that every year loses integrity as it becomes indistinguishable from power itself. The third insurrection came in reaction to the election of Barack Obama, it was the Tea Party.

Eight years later, it culminated in Trump's victory, a revolution within the party itself, because revolutions tend to be self-demolishing, In the third rebellion, the features of the original movement surfaced again, more grotesque than ever: paranoia and conspiracy thinking; racism and other types of hostility toward entire groups; ambiguities and incidents of violence. The new leader is like his authoritarian counterparts abroad: intolerant, manipulative, aggressive to institutional checks, demanding and receiving complete acquiescence from the party, and entangled in the financial corruption that is essential to the political dishonesty of these regimes. Once again, liberals did not see it coming and could not grasp how it happened. Neither could some conservatives who still believed in democracy.

The New Fusion Electoral System

The exploitation of the Republican Party in the Trump era seemed to set in with breath taking speed. In fact, it took more than a half century to reach the point where faced with a choice between Democracy-Republic system and control, the party chose the concluding. Its leaders do not see a problem, democratic principles turn out to be throwaway tools, sometimes useful, sometimes inconvenient. The higher cause is conservatism, but the highest is authority. After Wisconsin Democrats swept state wide offices last month, Robin Vos, speaker of the assembly, explained why Republicans would have to get rid of the old rules: We are going to have a very liberal chief who is going to enact policies that are in direct contrast to what many of us believe in.

George Packer is a staff writer for The Atlantic. He is the author of The Unwinding: An Inner History of the New America and the forthcoming Our Man: Richard Holbrooke and the End of the American Century. To his neighbors and constituents, on the other hand, he seems the sum of all they deem successful in life powerful, rich, generous, and hence altogether worthy the clan like loyalty they feel for him. One virtue universally ascribed to Bosses is that they keep their scream. This need not imply the highest Bosses innate respect on their part for truth and honor. Naturally, promises about patronage and deals must become reserved, otherwise a political career in any environment, even the worst, is soon given impossible. Being therefore, appreciative to keep the manager is, as a precaution about principled of in advance.

Managers are excellent judges of human nature, and hence altogether worthy the clan like loyalty they feel for him. One virtue universally ascribed to Bosses is that they keep their scream. This need not and constituents, on the other hand, he seems the sum of all they deem successful in life powerful, rich, generous, and hence altogether worthy the clan like loyalty they feel for him. intend to win, said one of Quay's men, fighting for party control in the Philadelphia Republican machine,

One virtue universally ascribed to Bosses is that they keep their scream. This need not also understand popular psychology and be able to compose with decided nastiness skill the innumerable clashes racial high classical religious, and economical their multifarious following. If diplomacy fails, as often it must, they are practical, unscrupulous, and determined in factional warfare. I because I am ready to risk the prison to win; the other man is not. He won.2 Defeat, when it comes, a boss takes as the end of a round, not of a battle. In split temporary setbacks, he has an invulnerable confidence in the system he is.

The Boss of any considerable area must be a past master of Q. a large scale and must devote unlimited time and thought to the repair and lubrication of his machine.

Of all recent state Bosses Penrose was the only one equipped by training and inclination for real diplomacy, yet he was swamped in the machinery he won the privilege of directing and ruling. There are about five thousand election divisions in this state an American Boss.

Reference: George Packer is a staff writer for The Atlantic. He is the author of The Unwinding: An Inner History of the New America by George Packer. As of May 2018, there were at least 31 distinct ballot qualified political parties in the United States. There were 229 state-level parties. Some parties become recognized in multiple states. For example, both the Democratic Party and the Republican Party become recognized in all 50 states and Washington, D.C. Democratic Party 51States, Republican Party 51States, Libertarian Party 39 States, Green Party 27 States, Constitution Party 15States.

Reference: Cf. J. Addams, Democracy and Social Ethics, chap. vii.2 From T. Williams, After Penrose, What? Century, vol. cv, pp. 49-55 (Nov. 1922). This is one of the frankest and incisive, and at the same time sympathetic, studies.

CHAPTER 18

PARTIES AND ELECTORAL PROBLEMS

American Political Parties History

There are about five thousand election divisions in this state, they hold from twenty thousand to twenty-five thousand Republican workers who carry the division and bring out the vote. Must know all these men. They must know me. Must know what they are, what they want, and how and when. Hand must always be on the job. Can never take it off. All my time goes to the task and must. If I take my hand off, I am gone. As for great measures and great issues such as you talk about, no Senator of a state of this size, run as it is, has the time to take them up. Engrossed in activities of the above character, few bosses have shown any real conception of the broader issues of leadership.

Thus, during the famous free silver campaign of 1896, Croker naively expressed his contempt for the sixteen to one controversy, and suggested that the coinage ratio be adjusted from day to day in accordance with the changing market ratio of gold and silver said: I Precisely in the same way that most bosses are deficient in knowledge of statecraft, they are, remarkable as it may seem, deficient also in party plays. To them there is no politics in politics, it is all a matter of business, of one deal after another.

City machines have repeatedly sacrificed the national or state candidates of their party by trading votes to the advantage of their own local schedule. Thus, following the national election of 1884, Tammany become charged with betrayal to Grover Cleveland owing to his openly expressed independence of the boss and his machine. During the campaign Honest Bosses deficient in leadership and partisanship, T. Williams, ibid.

Party efficiency, according to no less an authority than Boies Penrose, increases in the exact ratio in which it disentangles itself from municipal affairs. Party principles are not even a secondary consideration with the Democratic Tammany machine in New York or the Republican contractors' machine in Philadelphia. Each of them exists to promote selfish interests and each of them is a liability to the party with which it become aligned.

Reference: Cf. W. Hard, The Last of the Good Bandits, Hearst's International, vol. xli, p. 14 (April 1922, Solutions: The New Electoral Fusion System, Nonpartisan Elections.

Various parties calling themselves: Independent or Independence parties 12 States, Working Families Party 4 States, Reform Party 3 States, American Delta Party 2 States, Labor Party 2 States, Natural Law Party 2 States, Progressive Party 2 States, American Freedom Party State, American Party State, Better for America Party1State, Conservative Party 1State, Ecology Party State, Grassroots Legalize Cannabis Party State, Justice Party1State, Legal Marijuana Now Party State, Liberty Union Party State, Moderate Party State, Mountain Party State, Peace and Freedom Party State, Prohibition Party 1 State, Socialism and Liberation Party 1 State, United Citizens Party 1 State, United Utah Party State, Unity Party State, Veterans Party 1 State, Women's Equality Party State, Working Class Party, Total state affiliates for each political party, May 2018: 230 Parties.

This is a mountain of parties all over the US., ridiculous, even though, those so called parties are a good way for revealing the people's opinion, but not to run as a political party, their voices are tolerable for the Fusion Electoral System where the voices of the people are welcome.

MACHINES AND BOSSES CORRUPTIONS PROBLEMS
American Political History

This year corruption has become part of the most prominent and insistent political story in the world. Decades of inequality between the powerful and the poor in Arab states have resulted in mass public demonstrations and changes of regime; elsewhere, governments have responded to this threat to their legitimacy by reducing down on protest and the free press the Government mishandling. The people of the world are beginning to act on a long-held desire to have their fair share of political representation and economic reward. Notwithstanding added, more merciful guidance, the Act is still inconsistent and adds to a collaged of international laws and guidelines on corruption that often conflict with each other. More upset-tingly the political, legislative, regulatory, and judicial bodies responsible for enforcing the legislation appear to differ significantly about how to understand and spread on it apprehensively circumstances.

History of political Bosses and machines problems in United States in 1915. Some of the Act's short-comings derive from an understanding of bribery which is narrow and, as a result, overbearing on one party to a corrupt transaction: the one paying bribes. The fundamental flaw with this interpretation is that it artificially simplifies the nature of corruption: bribe-payers seeking an advantage coerce passive officials to obtain such advantage. The reality is different; parties to bribery are either by force who pay or extortions who demand money or favors.

Targeting one side of the relationship does not eradicate bribery, as extorters are able to shift focus to other coercers who are prepared to play by their rules. John Kelly, who then ruled Tammany, predicted the defeat of the Democratic candidate for the Presidency and was deeply chagrined at his victory. Four years later Hill, the Democratic candidate for Governor, carried the state, while Cleveland lost it, and so the election, by the narrow margin of 13,000. than local machines. An overwhelming amount of evidence might become produced, however, to show that the boss of one party is usually willing to make a deal with lock boss of the opposing party.

The thing need not become questioned at, despite of the party label, be it Democratic or Republican, the ends of machine politicians are the same. When deals of this sort become a matter of course the bipartisan result is a two-partisan machine. Estimate the most famous machines illustration, in 1914 Roosevelt charged that Barnes, the Republican leader of the state of New York, was in a bipartisan alliance with the Democratic state organization in the interest of twisted politics and crooked business. Barnes responded by suing for defamation, the trial of which lasted from April 19 to May 22, 1915, and proved one of the most sensational in American political history.

In his own defense Roosevelt not only refuted in a masterly manner the charges made against himself, but also presented such damaging evidence supporting his original accusation that the jury found in his favor.

Deplorable as are the results of a bipartisan machine. It is only fair to state that Tammany supported Cleveland in 1888 at the Democratic national convention and that the city of New York gave him a plurality of 55,831 in the election of that year. In 1906 Cleveland himself said that he had no knowledge or impression that the presidential ticket was the victim of betrayal in New York in the election of 1888.

Being the first to know offers several distinct advantages. Apart from providing an organization with a clear understanding of its exposure to subornation and corruption, that it exposes, rather than passively watching the events reveal; and to self-report study, the case, ought it consider it apposite to do so. In brief, a party that knows of bribery taking place will support a degree of control over the consequences. In an environment that is rife with uncertainty over the rules that apply, confusion over how they will become enforced and understandable fear about the penalties, that is no small thing. Either Democrats and Republican or any other party are disqualified if corruption happen, only in an electoral system with a Fusion Electoral Tribunal will end this corruptions and temptations.

References: Tammany's conduct during the elections of 1884 and 1888, G. Myers, History of Tammany Hall, American Political Parties History, and the Solutions'. 262, 265, and 270. Theodore Roosevelt and His Time, vol. ii, pp. 365-369. Cf. also W. D. Lewis. The Life of Theodore Roosevelt, p. 419. Cf. J. F. Rhodes, History of the United States from Hayes to McKinley, p. 326; Solutions: No Parties No problems with The New Fusion Electoral System.

ELECTORAL BIPARTISAN CONTROVERSIES
American Political Parties History

Political disagreement: Twice in the past five presidential elections, a Republican has won the presidency despite losing the popular vote. Now Democratic Sen. Brian Schatz of Hawaii has introduced a constitutional amendment to abolish the Electoral College and use the national popular vote to decide who becomes president. His proposal is among the latest efforts by Democrats and those on the left to push for structural changes to the American political system. But Schatz's amendment is sure to meet conquest in the Republican Controlled Senate. Today, attitudes toward the Electoral College become polarized by party fights, with Democrats far more likely to support a change and Republicans much more likely to defend the current system, but it was not always like that.

While the controversial 2000 election still become decided, Gallup found that 61 percent of Americans, including 73 percent of Democrats and 46 percent of Republicans, preferred amending the Constitution to elect the popular vote winner. Only 35 percent of respondents preferred the current system.

The partisan breach widened even further after the 2016 election: A few weeks after President Trump won the presidency while losing the popular vote, Gallup found that 49 percent of Americans preferred changing to a popular vote system, compared to 47 percent who wanted to keep the Electoral College, with 81 percent of Democrats supporting a change compared to just 19 percent of Republicans.2 Even given some space after that heated election, there remains a major partisan gap in opinion over how to elect a president, Form Research found in March 2018 that 75 percent of Democrats supported moving to a popular-vote system versus only 32 percent of Republicans.

But 50 years ago, moving on from the Electoral College had bipartisan support. In May 1968, 66 percent are of equal strength, they are even worse in states where one party is in the majority. In such cases the Bosses of the dominant party make every effort to gain control of their weaker rival. They become aided in this by bipartisan elective offices which by law must become divided between the two principal parties. Thus, in the case of a commission of three members, not more than two of whom may be of one political party, it is often an easy task for the boss of the dominant party not only to pick the two incumbents of his own party, but also to throw enough of his voting strength to the allied boss of the minority party to secure the election of a pliable tool by the latter. It is beyond question that manipulation of this sort has done much to sap the strength and ruin the integrity of minority parties in several states. Solutions: No Parties No problems with The New Fusion Electoral System.

Agreements wrapping out offices have been notoriously frequent as between Republican machine leaders and cross party Democratic politicians in many parts of Pennsylvania, for example, with the result that the latter party has lost in strength and standing. It has taken the most determined and long continued fighting on the part of the so-called reorganized faction of the Democratic party to make headway against the practice.

Apart from the few general traits and practices of bosses sketched above, the widest possible individual differences exist. Like Tweed, some of them delight in a naive show of power, virtually holding court in the presence of their feudatories and sycophants. Others unobtrusively deny all exceptional influence, ascribing responsibility, and credit to office holders or to the organization.

I, as a citizen and a voter, propose to change the actual Electoral College system by a nonpartisan elections system called The New Fusion Election System, with a Fusion Electoral Tribunal, by the end of any implication of political parties and the ridiculous and childish factions confrontations, they must realize that political parties are harming our nation democratic structure. Regarded this as a foolish waste of time and was dexterous at dodging. References: McNicho Chris Magee was a good mixer; Cox was short-spoken and gruff. It is true that some politicians of this type do not indulge in cannot, H. J. Ford, Municipal Corruption, Pol. Sci. Quar., to I. xix, pp. (Dec. 1904).

BOSSES PARTISAN AND ELECTORAL PROBLEMS
American Political Parties History

The Electoral College has persistently resisted ferocious hostility: over 700 proposals have been introduced in Congress to abolish or reform the Electoral College System, a compact of states was formed to bypass it, and recent polls show that more than half of Americans oppose it. Countless presidents and senators have even called for its expiry, most notably Sen. Elizabeth Warren (D-Mass.) at a CNN town hall last week. There is widespread agreement that the Electoral College is severely flawed; then why is it so strong? I believe that the reforming of the actual Electoral College is a futile fight for the reform of it, is a nonsense and greediness, by the ruthless and incompetent existing system, and it must be replaced liked or not in the current political system by The New Fusion Electoral System.

The main reason that the Electoral College System has resisted reform is simply because most suggestions have become prejudicial towards both parties, in conclusion party managers consider that the perpetual disagreement between them is a good business for the pockets of dirty politician having a pay is good business, as they say: If it is Broken Don't Fixed.

College by direct election. This plan widely accepted to become biased towards Democrats: if the votes had become matched using the popular vote, the Democratic candidate would have become elected in 2000 and 2016. It is no wonder that Republican legislators oppose it.

I, as a citizen and a voter, propose to change the actual Electoral College System by a nonpartisan elections system called The New Fusion Election System, and by the end of any inference in political parties, and the end of ridiculous and childish parties confrontations, they must realize that political parties are harming our nation democratic structure, according with President George Washington. Evaluated this as a foolish waste of time. It is disastrous and circumvents.

Unfortunately, the main problem with the Electoral College System, is certainly a bipartisan one: The battleground for the U.S. presidency concentrated in 12 states. These are the states that do not strongly lean Democrat or Republican, and they receive millions of dollars for presidential campaign spending, enjoy a higher voter engagement, and even have foreign policy decisions made for their benefit. Meanwhile, the remaining 38 states see none of these advantages and ignored by presidential candidates. A research points to a promising solution to address the broken Electoral College System. The Competitive Plan, a variant of the Proportional Plan, would distribute electoral votes in proportion to a state's popular vote, making all states attractive in the eyes of the candidates. Take a state with four electors.

If 75 percent vote for the Republican candidate and 25 percent for the Democratic candidate, the Competitive Plan would distribute three electoral votes to the Republican candidate and one to the Democratic candidate. In cases where the numbers do not split up evenly, the Competitive Plan would use an analytical formula to distribute electoral votes in a way that still reflects the popular sentiment.

Under the antagonistic Plan, all states would matter. Even the smallest states would have at least one vote up for grabs in each election, and hence would receive help from increased revenue and political influence. But is this plan bipartisan? An analysis of the century's worth of the presidential elections shows that the Competitive Plan does not offer either party a partisan advantage. In contrast to other proposed Electoral College reforms, the Competitive Plan ensures identical results to all 30 presidential elections since 1900. Despite the clear benefits of the Competitive Plan, nationwide adoption of this measure would be logistically challenging. However, in the Fusion Elections System there is no need for electoral votes counts because the vote of the elected officials is only what count.

A process developed to find pairs of states that cancel respectively other out, like blue Hawaii and red South Dakota do. The algorithm also shows a good transition order for these pairs. If the states transition according to the suggested order, at no point in this process would it have had any partisan effect. Compounded with the financial and political advantages gained by transitioning, safe states have everything to gain and nothing to lose. Many states adopted a winner-take all method in the 1820s to increase their political standing. Ironically, this is the same reason that 200 years later presidential hopefuls often rejecting them. The Competitive Plan offers a bipartisan alternative that is easy to implement and finally reasonable. It is time to put Democracy back in the hands of all Americans. In my Fusion System there are not Democrats or Republican, the no partisan System, works this way: voters elect the government officials, and the officials represent voters in the presidential election to elect the new President, and the elections are divided in two elections, one to elect the Government's Officials and the other the Presidential election, there is not parties or names involved just the peoples, the elected Officials and the Presidential candidates.

HOW THE NEW FUSION ELECTORAL SISTEM WORKS?

American Political Parties History

Voters elect their Officials as representatives, exp: senators, governors, city mayors and all the government officials elected by the peoples vote, who will be the people in the presidential election. It is a simple solution to ending the political party's disagreement, and more transparent and efficient system.

To become a candidate, the aspirant must fill an application in the New Electoral Tribunal System, composed by 13 members of qualified citizens or professionals with a university degree, to become supervisors to investigate the candidates for any unclear past. Its purposes are as a filter to keep away the corrupt aspirants out the race, and to have transparent elections.

There will be only seven (7) candidates to the presidency, with a University degree in Economy, Business Administration, Engineering, Architect, and others administrative professions. As I mentioned above, by this way there will be no a draw situation, the candidate with more votes is the President Elected, will be the winner as a degree in law, military of any king will not become allowed to participating in the Fusion Election System. Never-the-less they may run for any other public servant candidatures, or get a University education in the professions mentioned above to become accepted as Presidential Candidate, we do not need warriors or litigator as president, we need administrators.

The others public servants will participate are: in groups of three per positions per states exp. (5) senator per state, (5) governors per state and so on, all in a group of (5) The candidate with more vote is the winner the rest become advisor, and they are permitted to participate in further Fusion Elections, as many time they desired.

The second with more votes, will be the Vice President.

The rest aspirants will become advisors to the President. There will be no losers, all are winners, and can take part in the Fusion Elections System again, over, and over, without the participation of any political parties involved.

What you have read above is results of the intention to reform a damage electoral system because of the existence Political Elections system, if substitutes by Fusion Election System, this controversy quickly will end the partidist controversies and as a result we will have a pacific election with no political wars.

BIPARTISIAN BOSSISM AS A MONEYMAKING MACHINE

American Political Parties History

A brief interval followed the collapse and dispersion of the Tweed Ring but subsequently the comparative smoothness with which power was transferred from Kelly (1874-86) to Croker (1886-1902) and from the latter to Murphy would seem to justify the use of the same monarchic term in connection with the leadership of Tammany.

Even if they fail in naming a successor, it is not at all uncommon for managers to keep their power, of course with the difficulty's incident to the calling, until the time of their death or voluntary retirement. Others less fortunate or less cautious have become absolutely deprived of influence, even driven into exile, as was Doc Ames, or sent to prison, as were Tweed and Abe Ruef. An intensive study of the causes of the defeat and downfall of bosses should offer many results of practical value.

Economic Consideration of the careers of American Boss shows motive presidential that without exception, they looked persistently to with Bosses make money through the exercise of rehire Part let hence. The part let was a sleeveless garment worn over the earliest part lets appeared in late sixteen-century. I am working for my pocket all the time, he says, Croker coolly informed the Mazet Committee, and McIMichol had the effrontery to announce at a public meeting in Philadelphia's that I am here, for the simple reason as the rest of you boys; we are all of us out for the money.

No doubt bosses are hobbled used also by the love of power for it to new sake, hut they must have money in abundant quantities to support their power. Since the economic motive proves, thus, to be a dominant factor, some statement of the foundations of revenue open to bosses and of the expenses they must meet, is essential to the case. To be a political traitor in the usually accepted meaning of the term implies the ability to make money out of political manipulation. For this reason, Addick's, who tried to buy a next in Delaware to secure his election to the United States Senate, is hardly to become considered as a manager.

He made his money as speculator, promoter, and organizer of gas companies before his descent upon Delaware. A political highwayman, himself he seems to have become persistently robbed by local politicians and his career ended in bankruptcy and political failure.

References: Cf. G. Kennan, Holding Up a State, The True Story of Addick and Delaware, Outlook, vol. lxxiii, pp. 277-283, 386-39. 499-436 (Feb. 7, 14, 21, 1903).

PARTIES AND BOSSES CORRUPTIONS
American Political Parties History

Of course, the number and amount of the items on both sides of the ledger vary with the degree to which the Boss has proven his control and with the wealth of the territory in which he operates. It should not assume that the total yield from the various sources detailed below gathered into the treasure chest of the Boss without deductions in route. Even before a machine has been set up various diffuse forms of corrupt dealing are suitable to flourish.

Under a high degree of Bossism, it may happen that certain factions of politicians continue to practice petty graft on their own account. On the other hand, it is thoroughly characteristic of machine rulers to combine in as few hands as possible the proceeds from all forms of political have a picnic nervousness. In the first place, every machines and bosses may be depended upon to take full charge of all campaign funds. They are under no illusions whatever about the power of the purse in politics, and upon occasion are sufficiently outspoken on this subject. Much of the money thus secured must become passed down to district leaders and precinct captains, particularly if the result of the election is uncertain.

Indeed, if the situation becomes desperate and funds are not approaching easily adequate, the boss may become mandatory to dig deep into his own pocket and even to borrow large sums of money to save the day. On occasions when the opposition is weak, however, bosses have become suspects times without number of feathers their own coverings out of funds contributed to bring about a party victory.

Since 1890 embezzlements of this sort have become made more difficult by unethical practices performances but it would be going entirely too far to say that they had become given impossible by the legislation now on the statute books. Every boss of any importance must work continuously to gasping as loyal, well-organized, amid not too scrupulous organization wooers' seekers. If these workers had to be paid in hard cash out of his own resources or out to party funds political and financial insolvency of the machine would promptly for Concentration of receipts under bossism campaign funds the working force of the manager short. Individual traits of Bosses are but others approach it closely in their assertions that they have the cause of the poor and oppressed, nearest their hearts. Among their own following, of course, Bosses enjoy current unpopularity a sort of, but as a rule they have begun of noticeably unsuccessful as candidates for Popularize-Bosses family-tree. On such occasions the dislike of the great mass for the experts in the mechanism is proper to prove it overwhelming.

Probably it is for this reason that the seldom appear as candidates for offices within the gift of the people in the old days before the Seventeenth Amendment State Bosses aspired to and frequently attained at the hands of the legislature they controlled the post of United States Senator, as of the great state Bosses.

BIPARTIES AND ELECTORAL CORRUPTIONS
American Political Parties History

In fact, they are paid by securing jobs for them in public offices or elsewhere. Hereafter the relentless opposition of the machine to every extension of civil service reform; later the continuous determination of the boss in running its own every argument of support, however insignificant, for his supporters. Of course, this does not bring in money directly to the Boss, indeed at times it may cost him, and it constantly keeps him unpleasantly dominant. But unless he succeeds in placing large numbers of his followers, and in consequence the possibility of making large sums of money through that control.

What he secures in effect, therefore, are services which may be more valuable than money itself. These services, be it noted, obtained at the cost of the government and of the taxpayer. Discipline of the other hand, either a bench man of the Boss for whom workers he has obtained public jobs cannot two experts successfully. If any question of loyalty or division of their time comes up, they may be depended upon to hold to the Boss, since usually he could have them misspend as readily as he had them appointed.

In Philadelphia, for example, each constituency leader with few exceptions given an appointive position, so that at any time at which he might prove recalcitrant he can become transported to terms by threatening with his elimination. Council members were controlled by receiving clerkship in the administrative departments or by having their near relatives, sons, daughters, or others dependent upon them for income, given appointive chairs.

In this way or through subsidies to interests in which the district leaders or council members were interested, the machine could depend at any moment upon the unquestioning fealty of its retainers. It did not have to discuss ways and means with them or secure their views. It knew that by the very straightforward process of threatening to cut off their bread and butter it could bring them to support the most wicked or arbitrary measures.

References: C. R. Woodruff, Philadelphia's Revolution, Yale Review, vol. xv, pp.8-23 (May 1906)., no partisan elections.

MACHINES AND BOSSES

American Political Parties History

The hands of a mechanism it is not to become wondered at that on primary and election days the offices at many city halls abandoned, most of the employees being busily engaged on political work in their respective wards. Public employees who especially gifted as party workers, so that the boss needs them all the time, may become carried on amplified pay rolls, although by far the more common practice is to allow them to divide their time between their offices and their districts. Thus, the government secures only fifty, or it may be only twenty-five, per cent efficacy on its salary expenses, while the boss obtains such service as he may require almost wholly at the expense of the public treasury.

Unsatisfied system has limited the opportunities or the support mechanism. Consequently, Bosses now turn with considerable success to street-railway, gas, electric companies and other public service corporations for which they have done favors and from which they may ask in return jobs for their henchmen Public contractors and firms which sell supplies to the city or state are besieged in the same way.

From the point of view of the boss, however, this unofficial patronage, as Professor Munro calls it, is not so satisfactory as the official support provided by public offices. Corporations send to the demands made upon them for jobs, only when they fear reprisals from the Boss.

AGA, regulation of their effort to pay cash for political favors, thus reserving to themselves freedom of choice and control or the personnel departments. When an appointment obtained for an assistant in a public office the boss usually controls the official superior of the aid. If so, it makes comparatively slight difference, except to the public service, however inefficient the backing may be. But private corporations are more exacting. If one of their employees, put in at the request of the boss, does not perform his duties properly."

References: W. B. Munro, The Government of American Cities, p. 173.). The solution of this problem will be if we have a Fusion Electoral System, no partisan elections.

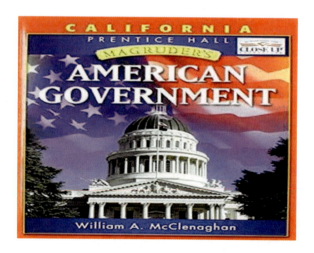

CHAPTER 19

PARTIES AND ELECTORAL PROBLEMS

American Political Parties History and the Solutions

Political controls be on the hands of the boss again as an applicant for another job. In one way the boss can obtain money as well as political service from those whom he has had appointed to public jobs. He may set up a system of political taxations, thus collecting a certain regular percentage, from the salaries of job holders. These taxations are made to be used as campaign funds, but as in the case of the closing, charges are not wanting that they have been converted at times to the private uses of the boss.

Whether or not the control of the machine extends to legislative, bodies, appropriations man with a pro the political funding which may thereby he protected. In this connection the congressional pork-barrel for the benefit of their respective sponsors, is the best known, the beneficiaries being individual congress people and the districts they are. State legislatures and city councils also have their pork barrels; Pork barrel is a metaphor for the appropriation of government spending for localized projects secured solely or primarily to bring money to a representative's district.

The usage originated in American English. In election campaigns, the term used in derogatory fashion to attack opponents. However, scholars use it as a technical term about legislative control of local seizures, but if machine control has been set up in these bodies, the distribution of appropriations will become centralized in the hands of the bosses. In its more innocent form this need involve nothing worse than luxury. In fact, it closely resembles in its motivation the search for public offices. Say: Give a man an office and you may count upon his political services.

Give a congressional district or a district, a public building and it should be worth a certain number of workers and votes in your next campaign. When funds become distributed by a machine it naturally looks after the districts in which it is strong or which it hopes to gain support. Unnecessary improvements may become made in such districts or improvements may become found where the need for them is slight. In both cases local property owners, spreaders, and cut cost of labor earnings and employment, and, unless participates, are usually not unwilling to return thanks and service to the Control of legislative confiscations.

References: Cf. H. J. Ford, Cost of Our National Government (1909).).

MACHINES AND BOSSES

American Political Parties History

In Philadelphia for example, the Vares were acutely conscious of the value of public suspicions for the districts they conquered. Give the people something they can see, was one of their slogans, and South Philadelphia could always count upon their most strenuous efforts in the matter of street lights, public squares, parks, boulevards, and public buildings.

It is unnecessary to say that similar interest is not manifested by machines in public services which may be highly useful, but which cannot be seen and which, therefore, do not bring in votes, for example, sanitary inspection, accounting and budget reform, civil service reform, the employment of experts, and the like. Indeed, the latter are abomination to bosses, since they make machine rule difficult by suggesting honest and efficient methods, or unpopular by exposures of negligence, extravagance, and graft.

A Tammany mayor of New York elected following an era of reform gave characteristic utterance to this feeling in the remark that as soon as he took office all the trains leaving the city would become filled with municipal experts seeking jobs elsewhere. In the form described above pork barrel seizure Inconsistencies result merely in nonessential.

The situation becomes polluted with corruption as well as extravagance when the machine itself takes part in contracts. This may become done by throwing contracts to favored firms, exacting secret rewarms from the latter specifications may become so drawn that only those firms which are willing to divide profits are able to bid. If contracts fall into the hands of companies which proven intrastate, they may become so stressed by negation of permits and rejections of work that they will come to terms. In a few cases such as that of the contractor combine of Philadelphia the Bosses themselves go openly into the contracting business on a large scale.

This is certain to provoke bitter opposition, but The Philadelphia Public Ledger of October 17, 1922, estimated the value of public contracts awarded to Senator Vare up to 1921 at about $20,000,000. The McNichol machine was also credited with getting its full share it has the advantage of providing safe jobs for a bunch of political workers and of producing large profits, especially when the inspection of work is entrusted to city officials who are themselves under the control of the machine.

PARTIES AND ELECTORAL PROBLEMS.

American Political Parties History

The prospect is not so rose-colored when the Boss loses his grip on the government, but even then, contracts may become secured from corporations or individuals needing future political favors or, if worse comes to the worst, from others on a purely competitive basis. It is at such times of adversity that the Boss toughest obsessed to take care of dependents who have become thrown out of public jobs by an unfeeling reform administration.

A large contracting business will, supply places for many of these victims, albeit at some risk to efficiency. Special Control of legislative bodies by the machine is valuable privileges in other ways besides giving access to the pork barrel. To legislatures all manner of interests must appeal for special privileges. Some of the latter are quite legitimate, no doubt, but if the machine is in control it may demand a heavy price before they granted. Others are doubtful or even sinister in character, and in such cases the price exacted is still heavier.

In Congress the principal interests seeking special favors have been land grant companies, railroads, protected manufacturers, whiskey, timber, sugar, coal, and oil magnates. Corrupt as have been the resultant scandals, it is nevertheless true that the federal government has supported higher standards than state and local governments. State legislatures and municipal councils have no such imposing areas to exploit, but they offer impressive opportunities to the corruptions from time to time.

Franchise grants to public service corporations are the most important items in their gift. In large cities a street-railway or gas franchise may be worth many millions of dollars to its promoters, and the corruption fund of contracts.

MACHINES AND BOSSES

American Political Parties History

When old franchises are about to end the fight to extend them involves enormously large commercial interests. In 1911 the public outcry against the mixture of contracts and politics in Philadelphia became so threatening that the head of the contractor combine made a positive and unchangeable statement that he would sell out his contracting business.

But the storm blew over and he did nothing of the sort to get it passed will be large in proportion. Laws or ordinances allowing increases of fares or rates are also rich in corruptions.

The solution of this problem will be if we have a Fusion Electoral System, no partisan elections no Bossism. possibilities of corrupt plunder. The most malodorous scandals in American municipal politics have occurred in connection with franchise ordinances. Among other forms of state and municipal legislation which directly touch powerful financial interests and may therefore be depended upon to invite corrupt manipulation are tax laws, building codes, laws affecting insurance companies, railroads, or other corporations, factory, and labor laws, including child labor laws.

If machine control is not in existence the pursuit for legislative favors is a diffuse affair conducted from the outside jack pots by the interests seeking them through swarms of special counsel, legislative agents and Lobbyists, pure and simpler or the inside of the legislative body many individuals or small groups of members participate in the corrupt process. The results are too uncertain under this system, or lack of system, and exposures far too many.

Neither the famous law of supply and demand nor the bargaining of the political market seems to result in fixed prices for crooked voters.

The honorable members who feel that they have not received their just share of the bribe money protested too loudly. Here as elsewhere better results may become secured by system and centralization. In Illinois, the inquiry into the Lorimer scandal showed that a legislative jack pot had existed for several years in the state legislature.

This was a common fund collected from all the many interests ranging from corporations, manufacturers, and banks to loan sharks and patent medicine firms, which took part in securing or beating legislation. An estimate made at the time shown that the jack pot had items ranging from a few thousand dollars to one of $250,000 contributed to influence the senatorial for an excellent brief account of this famous jack p

Absolute control of legislative nepotisms attack bills contest. At the end of the session the total amount in the jack pot divided among the members who were reasonable and who went along with the crowd that is, as who voted as they expressed. Most of them did not know who paid the money or for what bills, so that they were in no position to scream efficiently even if they had been so inclined. An even better adaptation of the famous principle of addition, division, and silence secured when the boss is in absolute control of the legislature.

During the domination of one of the state bosses of New York, it perfectly well understood by all interested in legislation that the necessary condition of its passageway was to see the boss. It must not become inferred that he took too narrow or avaricious a view of the case. If a bill submitted to him was in the public interest and carried with it no financial gain to anybody, as, e.g., a bill reorganizing the private charitable agencies of a city, he marked it all right, and sent it on its way to certain passage in the legislature.

For bills not in the public interest or which enabled private concerns to make a profit a definite price become immovable and collected before their enactment. The certainty, secrecy, and centralization of this method, particularly the elimination of numerous lobbyists and others who might learn too much, mark it as immensely superior, from the machine point of view, to the crude methods formerly employed and even to the jack pot. Machine members soon discovered that for their purposes the legislature could become used as a double-barreled shotgun. The public interest demanded laws providing for just taxation, for the fixing of rates, fares, and quality of service, and for safety and sanitation. Beyond doubt the demand for such legislation was increased by the popular conviction that corporate interests had received through collusion with the machine special privileges to which they were not entitled. On the one hand, business interests, as we have just noted, become painstaking fair game whenever they asked for special favors; on the other hand, they could become unremittingly and constantly hunted afterward under the guise of regulation.

MACHINES AND BOSSES OF POLITICAL PROBLEMS

American Political Parties History

Being partly in the nature of retaliations, some of the proposed regulatory measures may have been too drastic. This made them more threatening to the business interests concerned, a fact which materially increased their utility to corruption-isms in the legislature. Even measures of a thoroughly justifiable character sometimes involved the placing of heavy and unwonted burdens upon business concerns.

Often statutes and ordinances are inspired by supercilious ideals which take little account of actual conditions. Thus, at the time of the Iroquois Theater fire with its appalling death roll the Chicago ordinance made to prevent just such eventualities was of the most elaborate character, so elaborated, truthfully, that it had become ignored by managers and unenforced by inspectors. 364Legislative four flushing, as Profitable as is machine control of legislative bodies, its Machine cannot be compared with generosities of morph, caught control of the administrative 363 agencies. In the case of the Profitable as is machine control of legislative bodies, its Machine cannot be compared with generosities of morph, caught control of the administrative 363 agencies. In the case of the former, administrative years may intervene between lucrative Senatorial fights or agencies franchise grasps.

Mayor Harrison aptly called this practice, is the mother of the organizational untruth. Provisions in the law which impose However mistakenly, the latter often preferred to pay large sums to have these measures killed in the legislature rather than to nicknamed assaults, Bell Ringers, Fetchers, Old Friends, Sand-Braggers, and The-Liker's, adapt themselves to higher standards of public morality. When there was no popular demand for regulation it was, of course, an easy matter for corrupt groups in the legislature or municipal council to concoct measures of this type, some of them outrageously unfair or even confiscatory in character. In the semi-criminal argot of the times these bills become command of certain departments of state or local administration can interfere with important business interests every day in the year and every hour in the day. he prices, aided by weak administration Contracts of immunity demanded by the machine; others, who will not supply hush money, are harassed in countless ways.

The process materially sponsored by certain long-lasting political traditions. One of these is the length and detailed character of our legislation, another our opposition to strong administration. As to the former it is often possible to find amid the mass of loosely drafted statutory detail some single provision, inserted for this express purpose, which, interpreted and enforced rigidly, would infuriate intensely certain business interests. Rather than comply, some pay to the service. The machine can always plead that its failure to enforce laws and ordinances even when a bribe has become occupied to secure that result, is really since the force of inspectors at hand is too small. Rigid enforcement against those who do not pay for protection pointed to with pride as evidence of a stern determination to uphold the majesty of the law despite the hampering effect of a small and overworked force of inspectors. Through its administrative agencies federal, state, and local government touches business at innumerable points, all of which offer opportunities for corrupt manipulation.

The possibilities involved in contracts for public work under machine rule have already become touched upon. Contracts for supplies must always become watched as to specifications, prices, quality, and deliveries. Neither the peril of the country nor the wellbeing of the army prevents such sickening scandals as the mummified complaint episode of 1898-99. On the contrary, the vast disbursements made necessary by conflict simply open new fields to the racketeer who is never so active as when aided by political influence. The administration of tax laws of various kinds offers Tax management another wide field for evasion, fraud, and bribery.

CHAPTER 20

MACHINES AND BOSSES

American Political Parties History

In the striation collection of customs duties on sugar, for example, it become revealed in 1907 that company checkers were able, by pressing concealed springs connected with the scales, to reduce the weight of every load of sugar landed at the docks. During the six years that this practice had been going on it projected that one of the greatest American Sugar Refining Corporations had escaped paying duties on seventy-five million pounds of sugar. Those at once responsible for the fraud become convicted, and the company paid two million dollars to the government in settlement of its claim for past duties. The administration of federal excise taxes must also cope with constant attempts at fraud and evasion, most extensive of which was the Whisky Ring scandal of 1875, because of which 250 persons become accused, including President Grant's private secretary.

More recently the enforcement of the Volstead Act has become encountered by every form of bribery, and fraud in which large classes of well-to-do and intelligent citizens, otherwise thoroughly law abiding, have been involved. Administration of public and acts has also become streaked public land with fraud and forgery, the land and timber thieves' frequent frauds of ten being men of the highest position in their own communities.

It was in connection with a case of this sort that a United States Senator, John H. Mitchell of Oregon, become condemned and sentenced in 1905 to six months' penal servitude and a fine of $1,000. Two years earlier the Bristow report unearthed a conspiracy to defraud the government out of several millions of dollars, the conspirators' share amounting to between $300,000 and $400,000. Federal regulation of railways and corporations.

State regulation of business; tax administration Prisons, hospitals, asylums State governments have also tried railroad and corporate regulation within their own domain of power. In the administration of labor laws and factory acts the state government again touches interests of great financial strength, interests, moreover, which have always been relied upon to supply large campaign contributions. In the Pennsylvania state Republican organization one of the most potent figures for years past has been an equally potent figure in the state manufacturers' association. Wielded by a machine, the administration of state and local tax laws becomes an incomparably efficient means both of reward and punishment.

Persons who give aid and comfort to the bosses voting right, doing electioneering work, holding party offices, making campaign contributions or the like may have their property assessed at a small percentage of its value. Persons who perform no party service, have no influence, and are otherwise neutral politically may get off with an assessment fair enough according to the prevailing local standard. But independents, political opponents, and troublemakers for the boss calculated at figures which, if not more than real values, have at least grossly overvalued as compared with the average of local practice.

More than anything else it is the fear of punishment through unfair tax assessment that keeps large numbers of men of substance quiet under machine rule. If one could expect the hand of the political spoiler to become stayed anywhere it would be in relation to those unfortunates confined in prisons and asylums or temporarily under state care in hospitals.

Yet the very helplessness of inmates in such institutions makes them a favorite target for political abuses. Until recent changes in state administrative practices contracts for supplies needed by penal and charitable establishments manipulated in the same way as contracts entered by other administrative agencies, with the result that they fully unfurnished sloppy clothing, thin blankets, and polluted food, all in short weights and measures. Prison labor at fifty cents a day or less was fought for and exploited by favorites of the machine.

MACHINES AND BOSSES

American Political Parties History and the Solutions

Frightful tales of cruelty and neglect have in the past come out of the prison camps maintained by the residents; shocking conditions discovered in them; and it is universally agreed that government inspectors were unable to enforce the rather lax standards laid down in the contract. Fortunately, this inhuman system has now assumed up in large part, only three states keeping it. Occasional scandals connected with the traffic in pardons or the sale of drug to convicts, both under political influence, are, however, reported from time to time.

In cities under machinery rule various administrative Machine agencies may become completed apparatuses of intimidation or exhausting control of families, notably the tax department, the department of migration building inspection, health, and medical inspection, and the police department. A mass of minor ordinances, all desirable enough in themselves, enable the machine to reach everywhere. Constant annoyance of one pushcart man, while his competitor does as he pleases without interference; encumbering up of the fire escapes of one residence, while the house next door must keep its fire escapes absolutely clear; permission to one merchant to use sidewalk space for the display of goods, while others are fined for obstructing the public way, these and many other small but important incidents of urban life are to be explained on the ground of political influence or the lack of it. Most sinister of all are the possibilities involved in the machine control of the Police Departments.

It may be used to collect and a large and constant tribute from protected gamblers, department bootleggers, prostitutes, criminals, dealers in habit forming, drugs, quacks, abortionists, unlicensed midwives, baby farmers, and all the other denizens, large and small, of the underworld of vice and crime.

Reference: In 1901, a Gambling Commission had exposed in New York, composed of a commissioner who is at the head of one of the city departments, two state senators. the dictator of the pool-1L. N. Robinson, Penology in the United States, p.157. Outrage crimes, the solution of this problem will be fixed if we have a Fusion Electoral System, no partisan elections.

Michael Anguelo

MACHINES AND BOSSES OF PARTIES
American Political Parties History

Tribute from vice Machine alliance with corruption room association of the city. It proved a regular tariff for various forms of bookmaking as follows: Pool rooms, $300 per month; crap games and gambling small houses, $150 per month; large gambling houses, $1,000 per month; envelope games, $50 per month. The exposure of the commission was because in its desire for larger revenues it licensed too many establishments. To put the result in the words of one member of the sporting association, there were not enough suckers to go around, and some of the overtaxed opportunists themselves squealed on the system. According to the report of the Chicago Vice Commission of 1911, the total profits realized from the social malicious in that city amounted to between $15,000,000 and $16,000,000 a year. Of this it estimated that $3,000,000 went for protection, Tribute collected not only upon prostitutes themselves, but also upon the owners of houses, apartments, saloons, restaurants, and hotels harboring them, and upon purveyors who supply them at exorbitant prices with liquors, tobacco, food, clothing, jewelry, furniture, and even medical advice. All the agencies of crime not only actual criminals, but receivers of stolen goods in Pawns-Shops dealers in the tools of crime, owners of criminal hang-outs, professional bonds people, and crooked criminal lawyers may become evaluated thoroughly by machine officials. At times criminals themselves have banded together into a system which negotiates with the authorities, thus making their business about as safe from government interference as any other form of business. Political control of immorality and delinquency has one References: Exploitation in American Politics and Life, by the author. The Social Evil in Chicago, p. 113. New York Committee of 1$ (1902).

The final can be depended upon to produce abundant revenue, but it gives few political workers. From the underworld the machine can obtain not only money, but votes, healers of the most dependable sort, even delegates to conventions. Burglars, bootleggers, and holdup men whose absence from the penitentiary is due solely to political influence can be relied upon, at a nod from their official protector, to execute the most daring election crimes. On the other hand, an alliance of the machine with the criminal and vice elements lacks the heavy respectability of an alliance between the machine and big business.

Exposure of alliances of the former character provokes violent outbreaks of public indignation beneath which some of the most powerful city bosses of the country have gone down to defeat. At the other extreme of the scale from the unethical handling of the police under machine rule comes the employment of public funds in the form of cash on hand by administrative officials. Taken together these funds are extremely large. At the beginning of the year 1913 they amounted to two and a half billion dollars held by the governments of the nation, states, counties, and incorporated places over 2,500.

During the war, this total increased. At the beginning of 1922, the cash in general administrative funds for the city of New York was $39,699,524; Chicago, $48,708,546; Philadelphia, $12,318,591. On the same date the total of such funds for the 252 cities with a population of 30,000 and over amounted to three hundred millions of dollars.

For the forty-eight states it was $171,581 Incredible as it may seem, the whole interest on these funds in many cities, counties, and states is retained by the treasurers in whose hands they are placed.

Elsewhere Public funds the last are required by law to secure the smallest rate of interest, say from 1/2 to 3 per cent, from the banks selected as depositories. Manipulation of public funds Financial Statistics of Cities Having a Population of over 30J000, 1921, Table 14, Bureau of the Census. Is frightening and shock, when we learn this immense political corruption, we should not live in this corrupt American political miss function system.

References: Financial Statistics of States, 1921, Table n, Bureau of the Census, References: C. E. Merriam, op. cit., p. 14

MICHAEL ANGUELO

DEMOCRACY IN ACTION

PARTIES AND ELECTORAL CORRUPTIOS

American Political Parties History

This enables treasury officials to pocket the difference between the legal rate and the rate actually paid by the banks. Even when the public authority has taken legislative measures to secure for itself the full amount of interest consistent with safety, the power to select the fiduciary institutions which are to receive large deposits of public money is one which can be manipulate future to benefit. I do not mind losing a governorship or a legislature now and then, Quay reported to have said, but I always need the state treasury-ship. Incidentally, the manipulation of state funds brings machine politicians into close relations with some of the most eminent figures in the world of finance. In the notorious Pittsburgh exposure of 1909, it had proved that six banks paid $102,500 for the privilege of controlling deposits of public funds. Indictments were issued against ninety-eight council members; confessions being obtained from fifty-three of them. Another device is to let banks have the funds upon condition that they will allow the politicians responsible for the favor to draw upon them for large loans to be employed in private business ventures or speculations. Finally, the politicians may organize banks of their own, deposit in them the lion's share of the public money, and then advance to themselves as individual's large credits based on the state's deposits.

Thus, through his machine connections the notorious Bull Andrews of Pennsylvania was able to secure the deposit of $1,030,000 of the state's funds in a small country town bank with a capital of only $50,000. The money become used to finance some highly speculative railway construction schemes in New Mexico. It was political banking of this sort culminating in the suicide of two or three Pennsylvania bank cashiers which led to the formal accusation of Quayside for misappropriation of state funds in 1898.

MACHINES AND BOSSES CORRUPTION

American Political Parties History and the Solutions

A political machine is an unofficial system of political organization based on patronage, the spoils system, behind the scenes control, and long-lasting political ties within the structure of a representative democracy. Machine politics has existed in many United States cities, especially between about 1875 and 1950, but continuing in some cases down to the present day. It is also common, under the name clientele or political culture is steeped in corruption, in Latin America, especially in rural areas. Japan's Liberal Democratic Party, often cited as another political machine, supporting power in suburban and rural areas through its control of farm bureaus and road construction agencies.

Machines sometimes have a boss, and always have a long-term corps of resolute workers who depend on the patronage generated by government contracts office implies the ability to do favors, and the ability to profit from graft. Political machines steer away from issues-based politics, preferring a quid pro quo with certain aspects of a barter economy or gift economy: the patron or boss does favors for the constituents, who then vote as they stated to. Sometimes this system of favors supplemented by threats of violence or harassment toward those who try to step outside of it.

In addition to its control over the legislature and the control of administrative agencies, a well-established machine must judiciary also look to gain a measure out control over the judiciary. complete

As a rule, however, such control is not so complete nor is it so openly exercised as in the former two cases. With the great mass of ordinary civil litigation, the boss has no motive to interfere. Indeed, considering the likelihood of a popular revolt, it would be extremely hazardous for him to interfere with the orderly processes of justice in such matters.

Among these are the nomination and election of judges, the patronage under their control, the handling of cases in police and magistrates' courts, decisions affecting the financial interests with which he is allied, and decisions in political cases, Under Boss control judges of the last type may be turned down e.g., cases involving primary and election laws, prosecutions of Since a powerful machine is certain to be in full control Nomination of such matters, the nomination and election of Judges and. election of judges the point at which how ran to get the main of powerful leverage on the charisma. In community graft, and the like proved their independence and fairness ties free from machine rule the influence of the bar association may virtually determine the choice of judges, and public opinion may insist upon the retention of those who have incurred in fraud. There are, however, several matters connected with the courts in which the boss is necessarily deeply interested flat when the time comes for their re-nomination. In extreme cases nominations to judicial as to other offices may become placed up and about at auction, bids being received in the guise of campaign contributions.

References: Marcoason, The Fall of the House of Quay, Worlds Work, vol. xi, pp. 7119-7124 (Jan. 1906). other lawyers would be willing' to put up twice as much to be in his shoes.

PARTIES AND ELECTORAL PROBLEMS

American Political Parties History and the FUSION Solutions

In 1899 the Mazet Committee elicited the fact that Tammany harvest £15bi3 a form of requiring candidates for The. Higher Courts to pay from $10.000 to $21.000 for nominations. From the nominee to a place on the Supreme Court bench it collected the equivalent of a full year's salary, amounting to $17, 500. It was common talk at the time among members of the New York Bar Association that sums ranging from $30,000 to $50,000 and even $100,000 had been paid for the highest jurisdictional nominations. Of course, rude terms such as auctioning off or buying offices convicted by machine politicians in connection with the process of making judicial nominations, and in fact the process itself is subtler than these terms would imply. In the vernacular of a Tammany the form of permanent appointive offices. From patronage the point of view of the machine, however, no job is so small as to be negligible and under its sway every tip staff has a certain political task to perform in his home ward in addition to his official duties at the courthouse. In exceptional cases judges have managed to have concentrated in their hands the power of appointment to many permanent positions. This occurred in the case of the president judge of the Municipal Court of Philadelphia, with the result that he speedily became a local political factor of prime importance. Finding the power of the judge's machine intimidating their own privileges arrangements attention secured from the present legislature the passage of the Aron bill, designed to reduce the political influence of the former to a nullity. correct if we have a Fusion Electoral System, no partisan elections System.

BOSSES OF PARTIES EXPLOITATIONS

American Political Parties History

Americans were shocked by the boldness of the graft and other crimes committed by Illinois Gov. Rodunder the terms of this enactment the president judge exposed of his exclusiveness powers, and the other judges, eight in number, are henceforth to share with him the task of parceling out the offices.

Michael Anguelo

At present the New York Penal Law (767, 780) clearly prohibits campaign contributions by judicial candidates except such as authorized under the Corrupt Practices Act. As a rule, courts have comparatively little patronage to Judicial bestow in American politics generally, there are two views of politics, for this and other reasons I am pursuing the abolition of all political parties.

There is a view of politics that says you go into this for sacrifice and public service, and there is a view of politics that says, this is a business, and you are wheeling and dealing Illinois politics is well known for a tendency toward the whatever's in it for me approach and the corruption that can breed. In 2006, the state's earlier governor sent to prison for six and a half years for fraud and other crimes, and according to Slate Magazine, 469 politicians from the federal district of northern Illinois convicted on corruption charges between 1995 and 2004. But Columbia University political science professor Justin Phillips says none of their crimes were as horrific and as the ones of which Blagojevich has become accused. Corruption in American politics has typically been the trading of government contracts or government benefits for, oftentimes, just simply campaign contributions. You know, here is some money into your campaign, and in exchange, you give me and my business a particular contract. Or I take you to a basketball game, give you some great seats, and in exchange, you give me something my client wants, Phillips says.

Those types of exchanges are typically what would we see when we talk about corruption in American politics. Doubt the exchange of goods and services for money is legitimate in the public marketplace, why is it considered immoral in politics? business not their own. SS, and campaign finance contributions, then they have a conflict. If they are benefiting personally from kickbacks, extortions, Kent Redfield, a political science professor at the University of Illinois and the author of several books on state politics and corruption, says politicians are choosing or appointed to do the people's money? So, this distorts public policy. And if citizens believe that everything is for sale and it is corrupt, then they have no reason to support the political system.

Redfield describes Blagojevich's pay-for-play politics as a modern day continuation of the so-called machine style politics that were the norm in big cities like Chicago and New York from the mid-19th century until the 1960s. Machine politicians relied on new immigrants who had little political pull. In exchange for votes, party bosses would give the newcomers jobs once their candidates appointed in office, or politicians would take kickbacks in exchange for ensuring the efficient delivery of city services, like snow or garbage removal, or the granting of lucrative city contracts.

I guess, in a perverse way, that means if you have gotten enough resources, you can become confirmed that things are going to have done unless somebody outbids you, Redfield says. But, on the other hand, that is why those systems have problems in the long term. That only works for people who have resources, and that generates discontent. Those are the sorts of things that historically lead to political upheaval and revolutions. On the other hand, says Phillips, political machines were quite effective at practical governance. They could get things done.

Control of the police department by the machine yields Administrative duties of courts Police and magistrate's courts Honest and dishonest implant the best results only when it also controls police and magistrates' courts. The final is essential if immunity is to become obtained for crime and vice interests and for healers and organization voters in their many untoward difficulties with the penal code.

The solution of the Machines, because of their vast control and their ability to sell influence, they got a lot done, where reformist governments in American cities were much less effective. And so, the public in cities had a love-hate relationship with the machines. However, Phillips says let us go to a system where everybody that worked in government was a political appointee. So, the machine had fewer helps to organize out. And as machines had fewer benefits, they began to weaken and perish. Under American legal principles, Blagojevich, supposed innocent until he has convicted of the crime's prosecutors have alleged. However, the size and scope of the corruption of which has become accused is a reminder. Regardless of the legal sanctions Americans hope will ensure fairness in public life and self-sacrifice in public officials, the temptation to use the public trust for private gain is still a force in American politics. The solution of this problem will be correct if we have a Fusion Electoral System, no partisan elections System.

PARTIES AND ELECTORAL INJUSTICE

American Political Parties History

Under the terms of this representation the president judge has become stripped of his exclusiveness powers, and the other judges, eight in number, are henceforth to share with him the task of parceling out the offices. While in general the courts have extraordinarily little patronage Temporary in the form of permanent offices at their disposal, certain injustices of the higher courts do make many important temporary appointments. These include appointments of appraisers, of guardians for wealthy orphans, of commissioners in condemnation proceedings, of referees in litigation which may involve millions of dollars, of receivers in bankruptcy cases who may become labelled upon to control the affairs of great corporations during a considerable period?

Appointments of this kind measured highly honorable in most tactful manner, to secure these bonuses for themselves or for dependents and favorites. Finally, it must become noted that besides appointments, permanent or temporary, courts burdened with other duties of a purely administrative nature.

Thus, in some states they appoint the newspapers in which legal advertisements appear. In Pennsylvania until the recent repeal of the Brooks law they granted saloon licenses. County courts, particularly in Western states, become hampered to an unusual degree with administrative tasks, a fact not without relation to the demand in that section for the recall of judges. When functions of this sort allocated to courts it is inevitable that machine politicians will strive with all their might, albeit more quietly and tactfully, to influence judges, just as they do in the case of administrative officials simple. Elected officials in the United States are mostly backed by Political Parties. These parties, or political organizations, choose the leaders that they want to stand for them and support these leaders in the elections.

PARTIES AND ELECTORAL PROBLEMS

American Political Parties History

Control of the police department by the machine yields Administrative duties of courts Police and magistrate's courts Honest and dishonest implant the best results only when it also controls police and magistrates' courts. The final is essential if immunity is to become obtained for crime and vice interests and for healers and organization voters in their many untoward difficulties with the penal code.

The solution of and sometimes carry with them regal fees. Naturally, therefore, they excite the keenest interest of machine leaders. Every influence the concluding can bring to bear upon judges is employed, usually control most of the elected offices, but other smaller parties can play a role in an election as well.

Political parties have not prescribed by the Constitution of the United States. In fact, no parties had officially formed by the time of the first United States elections. They came about later as a way of organizing voters who agree on certain issues. George Washington, the first U.S president, wisely warned against political parties, saying that they might destroy the unity of the nation, and you see today it is happening.

Whether national unity hurt under the current system is up for examination, but it is true that the parties often cause problems on critical issues. The Republican Party today considered the more conservative party and Democrats tend to support plans that are more liberal. The Republicans had controlled the U.S House of Representatives. Democrats control the U.S Senate, and the previous President, Barack Obama, is a Democrat with Communist inclination, I can notice when he opens his arm and admires a Communist regime's like Cuba. There are other smaller parties that run the range from very conservative to very liberal.

Senators Bernie Sanders from Vermont and Joe Lieberman from Connecticut are the only independents serving in the United States Congress currently. The balance of power between the parties may shift during conscious choice, as President George Washington philosophy say, "parties divide the nation."

Candidates can also run as Independents, or persons with no political party backing them. A candidate may run as an Independent if they can get enough support to organize their own campaign fund raising. The candidates that run under smalls parties do not often win elections but do sometimes affect their outcomes by increasing or taking support away from a candidate from one of the main parties, this division of power is dangerous, it causes an unsuitable administrative good performance when dividing voter's judgment of politically an election, but control of U.S. government tends to remain between the Republican and Democratic Parties. Senator Bernie Sander and Joe Liberman, two Communist lawyers aggressively fighting each other for power that is not what we want in the US. Political Administration, we must have to fight this ideology of Socialism or Communism whatsoever you may want to call it the remote possibility of having a party with this malevolent Communist ideology.

The number of electors has varied throughout American history but in recent elections there have been a total of 538 electors divided up between the states. I consider this system is the must imperfect Electoral System ever created, the election of a president should be done by the elected officials elected by the voters, and those elected officials, on behalf of the voters, will elect the president without the involvement of any political parties in a Fusion Electoral System.

ELECTORAL COLLEGES PROBLEMS

American Political Parties History and the Fusion Solutions

Americans will go to the polls and vote for President of the United States. Each U.S Citizen by the constitution, allowed one vote for President, but the winner not necessarily decided by counting all the votes and seeing who comes out on top. U.S Presidential Elections are determined by something called the Electoral College. The Electoral College is not some kind of university or school. It is a system in which each United States balloting have given a certain number of voting representatives to cast ballots during an election. The solution of this problem will be correct if we have a Fusion Electoral System, no partisan election. The number of electors a state gets depends on their population. Vermont, having a small population, carried only 3 electors in 2008 while Texas, a big state with a large population, carried 34 electors. The residents of each state cast their votes on Election Day, the first Tuesday of November. Each ballot counted as one vote and the winner of the most votes wins the state.

A candidate wins the election by winning states. For example, in the state of California during the 2008 Presidential Election, 13,286,254 votes casted, with over 8 million going to the Socialist President Barack Obama. His main competitor, John McCain, a senator from Arizona won about 5 million votes. California, the most populous state in the country, has 55 electors, which all went to Socialist President Obama.

This is a feeble ineffective election system, it looks like each state are independent little nations, bear a resemblance to an election system between a bunch of Banana-Republics like Latin America, not appropriate for United States.

In this new system no partisan voters Elected-Officers, elected by the voters to represent them in the selection of the new President, the one with more votes is the candidate elected as President, in second with more votes is the Vice-president, and the rest become advisor of the new administration, there is no losers in this Electoral Fusion System. Why make the elections so complicated? There is some professionalism in the New Fusion Electoral System, as the states with small populations do not become overlooked. It is the real solution of this problem, it will be correct if we have a Fusion Electoral System, no partisan elections System, the nation will be united in a Fusion Democratic-Republic system idea, no with political parties dividing the nation.

Why do we use such a roundabout way to select a president? It is tradition mostly, but could be changed by The New Fusion Elections System in a near future, where no political parties are allowed to elect the President, he is elected from seven candidates, nominated by the Elections Tribunal System, and by the voter's representatives of the still possible to win an election without winning any of the most populated states.

In a strict popular vote system, candidates would spend most of their time visiting large cities and metropolitan areas, ignoring those living in rural areas or less densely populated cities, which I consider a huge mistake, any amount of citizen is priority in my system, only that there is no need for political campaigns with insults and defamation, the spreading of any political information regarding the candidates, is done directionally by the Fusion Electoral System, enlightening the voters of the aspirants potentials by a complete summary of candidates correspondent and the diffusion of each candidates profiles or memories.

There are criticisms of the Electoral College System. The main one is that it allows for a scenario where a candidate can win the most individual votes but still lose the election, it does not make any sense and will not happens with Fusion System. The other criticism is that some states end up with too much power in this system. Presidential candidates spend a lot of time campaigning in so-called blow states like Ohio, Florida, and Pennsylvania. Support for the two major political parties, Republican and Democrat, are neck and neck in these states and they tend to have many independent voters who can become persuaded to vote for either side. This is how George W. Bush defeated Al Gore in the 2000 election for U.S President. Mr. Gore won 50,999,897 million total votes but only gained 266 electors. President Bush only won 50,456,002 total votes but finished with 271 electors and was therefore elected president, so the less is the winner a remarkable amount of news reporting, polling, and attention from candidates during an election season. It is irrelevant in a system where there are not political parties, but a motivation to vote for any candidate support and sponsoring by the Fusion Electoral Tribunal, to maintain order and decorousness for the elections process with transparency and honesty.

In the United States, only the Presidents become elected using a system of people entitled to vote, this will change when the system is substituted with the Fusion Electoral System, where Representative, Senator, Governors, mayors, and any other public positions elected by popular votes, are elected by direct elections. However, we are not the only country to use such a representative process to elect a leader. Estonia, India, and Ireland use voting methods that are similar in some role, in Fusion case those elected representative will elect the President, not the voters, the reason is that common voters are in the majority not skillful enough in selecting a President.

By this way, the condition to decide who will be the best candidate to administrate the country is through the Fusion Tribunal Electoral

The New Fusion Electoral System

nominator. The solution of this problem will be correct if we have a Fusion Electoral System, no partisan elections. Also, when opponents of the machine get into trouble submissive courts may seize the opportunity to teach them a lesson by imposing the extreme penalties of the law or dismissing him for the election. In many cities little or no effort made to conceal the use of political influence for such ends. The region or district leader himself appears in court and is listened to attentively before cases disposed of by the magistrate on the bench. It is hardly necessary to say that such scandalous involvement never betrayed in courts of higher rank, even by the most controlling machine dominant.

If they must reach superior or supreme court judges the interview takes place in the profoundest secrecy or a confidentially emissary become forwarded. It is by such occult procedures, if at all, that political influence is brought to tolerate on implant trials, on the trial of imperative election criminals, or on large civil suits affecting the interests of the Boss or his financial allies. Machine politicians are accustomed to discriminating between honest implant and dishonest insert. The solution of this problem will be correct if we have a Fusion Electoral System, no partisan elections System. Fundamentally the distinction between honest and dishonest graft, as the same authority acknowledges later, is not a matter of ethics, but of carefulness. I n the years following the Civil War, America's cities grew dramatically, not only because of the Industrial revolution, but because of the influx of immigrants. The result was political chaos, and the part time politician could not manage the change. From this disorganization, the political person over you, a distinctive kind, give me the excite. Even though many Bosses took part in implantation and dishonesty, they also replaced chaos with order. Most of the early Bosses in the late nineteenth century and the early twentieth century came from either the corner saloon or the. humanity.

The solution of this problem will be correct if we have a Fusion Electoral System, no partisan elections System.

Big Tim Sullivan and Charles Murphy of New York both give the impression that originates from taverns. Sullivan have become nicknamed, Dry Dollar, because he never laid a customer's change down until he had carefully dried the bar top with his towel. Murphy increased his clientele by serving a free bowl of soup with a five-cent beer. George Cox of Cincinnati was the owner of a saloon called Dead Man's Corner, where many killings had taken place. Well-built Jim Prendergast opened a saloon in Kansas City's working-class section called the West Bottoms. He supplied powerful garlic bologna, cheese, and bread to anyone who bought a nickel beer. Like the saloon, the fire department supplied an opportunity to make friends playing cards and making small talk. From that atmosphere give the impression of Boss Tweed of New York.

THE GOOD AND THE UGLY OF THE BOSSES

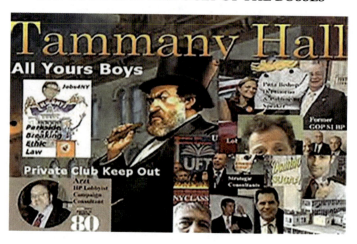

The trademark of every one of these Bosses was his concern for the poor and underprivileged. In a period of growing urban poverty, when the federal government declined to assume responsibility, politicians from working class neighborhoods built their own welfare programs. The down and-out recognized they could get help from the Boss, who would give them basketsful or buckets of coal.

The Boss would aid a widow with money to cover the cost of a decent funeral and burial or help an immigrant find an abandon place to live. After the immigrant become settled, the boss would help him to become naturalized, which increased the immigrant's pride and gave the Boss another vote. After the immigrant become settled, the boss would help him to become naturalized, which increased the immigrant's pride and gave the Boss another votes a community some kind of benefactors, that could be used in the New Fusion System with some limitations, corrections and rules a community some kind of benefactors, that could be used in the New Fusion System with some limitations, corrections and rules. The Bosses also created a system of political clubs for middle class neighborhoods. The purpose was to supply social services for people who did not need a basket of food but who could not afford to belong to the elite country clubs. The Bosses are the political machine rented large halls for banquets and parties and dances. They sponsored picnics and barbecues, baseball leagues, and weekly bridge parties for women. In turn, people have expected to poll voters and pass out sample ballots at election time. In later years, people on the receiving end of social services become expected to drive people to the polls. Wise Bosses were heavy contributors to Catholic Parochial Schools or Jewish Charities. Sometimes Pastors even urged their worshipers to vote for mechanism politicians. Bosses did favors for small businesspeople, especially storekeepers. Restaurants, saloons, and delicatessens found the friendship of the Boss helpful in securing health department approval. Many cities made the licensing of many small businesses appear to be a special favor. In return the businessperson would display campaign posters in his window and talk politics with his customers.

New York's Boss Tweed had notorious alliances with businesspeople who would supply kickbacks to the machine in return for contracts, whether for stationery, toilet paper, or construction work. In the early years of the Tweed regime, the fee was ten percent, while several years later it had grown to sixty-five percent. Tweed even paid exorbitant fees for advertising in newspapers which in return supported a friendly editorial policy. The last year when Tweed was in power the city paid advertising bills to newspapers more than one million dollars.

From San Francisco to the big cities of the East Coast, all forms of organized crime ran under the friendly eye of the machine. Hazen Pingree in Detroit tolerated prostitution in his city, not because he got a cut, but because he realized its popularity among the voters. Prostitution was illegal in Cincinnati, but it thrived under Boss Cox. Under the aegis of the machine, the prostitutes have become examined once a week and those free of disease have given work allows for seven days. In New York, the Tammany Machine instructed police to wink-eye at violators if they paid the police and the organization a percentage of the take. Chicago was a notoriously wide-open city. Brothels prospered with Boss controlled police getting a percentage. The solution of this problem will be correct if we have a Fusion Electoral System, no partisan elections System.

In the twentieth century, Chicago remained much the same under Richard J. Daley, whose moral code was Thou shalt not steal, but thou shalt not blow the signal on anybody who does. The Cook County Democratic Committee included a man named John D'Arcy who was known as the crime syndicate's man on the committee. It was public knowledge that Chicago's Mafia chieftain Sam Giancana owned the First District through his representative D'Arcy.

If the Mafia did not, Thomas Nazis devastating assault on the William Tweed Ring helped bring about the end of his life. Members of the ring reply Taws Him to the question, who stole the people's money? Harper's Weekly, August 19, 1871 challenge him and remained satisfied with its limited share of city government. Daley could live with its u the same way he lived with the scoundrels in Springfield, as you can appreciate, the reasons I am so opposed to the political parties is because the example mentioned above clearly that the corruption in the organization of political parties had always existed and still exist today, this dishonest of an organization that is fashioned to help elections, must be eliminated, and replaced by The Fusion Electoral System.

Bosses came from every imaginable ethnic background. James Pendergast in Kansas City, Frank Hague in Jersey City, James Michael Curley in Boston, and Charles Murphy in New York were Irish Americans. San Francisco's Abraham Reuf was a German Jew, Chicago's Anton Cermak was born in Bohemia, and Boss Tweed was from an extensive line meaning leaders of state government.

Their education was diverse as well. Ed Butler of St. Louis, Richard Crocker of New York, Big Tim Sullivan, and George Cox of Cincinnati never finished grammar school. On the other hand, Doc Ames of Minneapolis received an M.D. before he was twenty-one, and Abe Reuf held a law degree, as a result anybody with party's connection can be a Boss, educated or not.

Some Bosses let their success go to their heads. Frank Hague had a home in New Jersey and one in Florida. Tom Pendergast owned an elegant mansion in Kansas City and travelled first class to Europe. Duke Vare of Philadelphia owned a home that cost a half a million dollars. Richard Crocker kept a castle in Ireland, a house in Palm Beach, and an apartment in one of New York's most exclusive residential districts.

Tweed lived in a Fifth Avenue showplace, kept his horses in a silver trimmed mahogany stable and sported an expensive yacht. This type of corruption will be eliminated with the New Fusion System. But the Bosses who were judicious evaded to show huge wealth. Richard J. Daley continued to live in the same lower-class ethnic community of Bridgeport, four miles from the Chicago loop, for his entire twenty-one-year rule as mayor. He rarely travelled outside the state and wore the same old baggy suits, which is why Daley was the most impressive power broker of them all. But some Bosses kept a low profile are not exempted to dishonesties and briberies, they live like monarchs no matter what, thanks to his political party corruptions. Richard Daley always bristled when reporters used the term machine because he preferred the organization. But it was no secret that Daley's dual role as mayor and chair of the Cook County Democratic Committee gave him final say over the award of some 35,000 patronage positions. At least weekly he would meet with his patronage director to peruse job applications right down to ditch digger. Its spouses expected that when the mayor gave his approval, the person who got the job would become considered member of the machine and could become counted on to work one of Chicago's 3,412 voting precincts at election time. Until the final two years of Daley's regime, that arrangement produced incredible success for the machine at the ballot box.

While it is tempting to find guilty city Bosses for corruption, it should become remembered that they supported many projects of public improvement, it is not a favor to the city citizens, it is an obligation. Dwelling House Reform, Park, and Boulevard Systems, and building programs were common projects hardly willingly involved by the Bosses. Under the Tweed ring, the Parks department made a major contribution in building Parks and Square throughout New York City.

These improvements have evenly distributed among neighborhoods of all social classes. Jim Pendergast put his machine behind pledge issues for Parks and Boulevards for Kansas City, and Boss Crump helped Memphis achieve one of the most attractive Park and Boulevard Systems in the country. Surprisingly, the Bosses also did more than other white groups to achieve racial equality. Curley, who was Mayor of Boston on and off for thirty-six years, ran as well in the Lithuanian neighborhood of South Boston and the Italian section of East Boston as he did in the working-class Irish districts. In his last term in City Hall, he deliberated minor sponsorship on the growing Black Community and joined the NAACP. Pendergast distributed patronage to Blacks in his organization, and Boss Cox paved the way for blacken contract by overpowering violence against Blacks at the polls.

Edward Crump gave blacks the vote in Memphis. In St. Louis, Jordan Chambers, a black ward boss, got his start in politics by working in Boss Butler's machine. Richard Daley was terrible with human relationships and purposely fenced out blacks in his Chicago machine, but essential services under his tenure were superb. Daley become acclaimed for providing an ingenious transportation system included of expressways wafting out from the central core with rapid-transit trains running down their median strips or in Daley's words, medium strips. Chicago streets were the cleanest and best illuminated in the country. Once he said to the garbage truck drivers of the city: Cited, you men, with the help of God, are going to make this the finest city in the country. You are going to go out and make every street and every alley the finest street and the finest alley. Under Daley, Chicago's police and fire departments have ranked by professionals as among the most effective in the world.

In fact, when the police department have accused of corrupt practices, Daley conducted a nationwide search and hired one of the top law enforcement officials in the country to be Chicago's chief. In doing so he recovered his political reputation by visualizing himself as a man of the highest truthfulness. In the last few years of Daley's administration, private investors poured more than five million dollars into the downtown area Daley constructed a record 45,000 low-income housing units in the North, West, and South Side ghettos and virtually transformed one of the city's most decomposed neighborhoods by giving it a branch of the University of Illinois. Most miraculous of all, Daley did it all without a budget deficit.

As a result, Chicagoans exonerated him his famous malapropism such as, we must rise to ever higher and higher commonplaces, and the police are not here to create disorder. They are here to prevent disorder. If Boston has not been as consistent as Chicago in delivering services, it has certain supplied two of the important Bosses in James Michael Curley and Kevin Hagan White. Curlews a unique figure, having served four terms as mayor, once as· Governor of Massachusetts, twice as congressperson and virtually dominated Massachusetts politics for forty years, it is like a monarchy.

The New Fusion Electoral System

When Curley was first elected mayor in 1913, he guaranteed voters that he and his wife would remain just people and continue to live in their simple, frame house in Roxbury. Instead, he built a large brick Dutch Colonial house on the exclusive Jamaica Way. The new Curley home had a forty-foot-long, mahogany-paneled dining room, fourteen-foot ceilings, a massive chandelier, gold plated fireplace equipment for the marble fireplace, and an impressive winding staircase. The neighbors did not take offense until he installed white shutters with cut out shamrocks. Politics and religious symbols are the discordance of political parties.

It has assumed that no city contract has ever awarded without a cut for Curley, but no graft has ever proved in court of law Kevin Hagan White, James Michael Curley. No one was ever sure how Curley accepted the money to pay for such a mansion, since he earned only $5,000 a year as mayor and wanted to be among the mighty in politic. Corruption and bribery are the name of the game in parties' machine.

Similarly, Kevin White flies first class, stays in first-class hotels, and cultivates expensive tastes. If he stays in New York City, he pays as much as $250 for a suite; if he travels to Washington, D.C., on city business, he hires chauffeured limousines to carry him from agency to agency at a one day cost of $1,820. He keeps the Parkman House, a city owned Beacon Hill mansion, as a combination office, personal retreat, and banquet.

Recently, he spent $10,300 of city money to offer a campaign office in his personal residence, including a $2,700 sofa. In reply to his critics, he insists that he must keep the dignity of his office and that Boston is a world class city. He spent those $10,300 of city money to offer a campaign office in his personal residence, including a $2,700 sofa. In reply to his critics, he insists that he must keep the dignity of his office and that Boston is a world class city. Although he was known as Mayor of the Poor, he dressed stylishly.

Even though he was known as Mayor of the Poor, he dressed stylishly aristocratic appearance, having become educated at Williams College, wears expensive suits, and keeps his long white hair carefully sprayed to cover the baldness. While he considers his $60,000 a year salary a shame, it has not altered his lifestyle.

White also shares with Curley a flamboyant, charismatic reputation. People have inherently drawn to White just as they were to Curley, even though White is not an electrifying Curley style orator. While building his political career, Curley studied the orations of Disraeli, Gladstone, Burke, Lincoln, and Daniel Webster, reciting them in his resonant voice and taking note of melodic sounding words. He also studied breath control and arm gestures to prepare him to become one of the best rabble rousers of his time. Curley, like White, was famous for the colorful, angry put down. After campaigning for Franklin O. Roosevelt in 1932, he expected to become rewarded with a cabinet appointment. Instead FDR offered him the ambassadorship to Poland and described it as a sensitive post. The incredulous Curley exploded, if it is such an unpleasant interesting place, why do not you resign the Presidency and take it yourself? With personage like this no wonder Communist criticize Capitalism of the best rabble grousers of his time. But not one of the great American fortunes, as wealth has reckoned in metropolitan centers of finance and industry, has become founded by a Boss. Recently Pennsylvania lost two of the most successful machine leaders of this generation, Penrose, who had been almost absolute dictator of the Republican state organization for eighteen years, gives an interesting uncatalogued of the resources which might become strained upon by a local Boss in full control of a city of 100,000. Tremendous as these may appear to be, they are nevertheless small, even in proportion, as compared with the resources open to the boss of a metropolitan city.

Judge and, bossism had an extremely hazardous pursuit. In times of crisis the boss has often forced to Judge chosen to very thing he has and to borrow money from every available source to pull through. Defeat in a crucial election may mean not only complete monetary loss, but his dethronement and even criminal prosecution into the bargain. Finally, few bosses have shown any great ability in ordinary business lines, the Napoleonic legend to the contrary despite. The solution of this problem will be correct if we have a Fusion Electoral System, no partisan elections System This is the reasons that motivate the political system to be change and radically be modified with the elimination of all political parties.

Reference: C. E. Merriam, op fit., p. 161, A big city like W. L. Riordon, Plunkitt of Tammany Hall.

THE PARTIES BOSSES

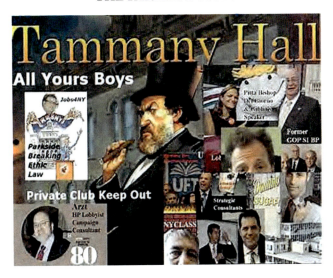

MACHINES AND BOSSES

American Political Parties History

The Bosses, astute as they are in all political affairs, they have often shown themselves typical lambs in Wall Street. In the expense account of Bosses, particularly those who have slum districts to take care of, a large item must always become charged off to social and charitable activities.

Part of the expenses of district clubs and other auxiliary associations may has recouped in membership dues, but still the leader's pocketbook has heavily drawn upon to pay deficits, defray the expenses of outings, and the like. In 1905, the contributions of Tammany to the relief of the poor was estimated to amount to from fifteen to twenty-by fire engines passing his house. Hastened to the scene of the fire, according to the custom of the Tammany district leaders, to give help to the fire sufferers if needed. Met several of his election district captains, who are always under orders to look out for fires, which have considered great vote-getters. Found several tenants who had become burned out, took them to a hotel, supplied them with clothes, fed them, and arranged temporary quarters for them until they could rent and give new apartments.

Went to the police court to look after his constituents. Found six drunks. Secured the discharge of four by a prompt word with the judge and paid the fines of two. 9 a. M.: Appeared in the municipal district court. Directed one of his district captains to function as counsel for a widow against five per cent of the total annually spent by New York's joint churches and benevolent societies. Some idea of the number and variety of the demands made upon a district leader may be gathered from the following record of a day's work by Plunkitt of Tammany Hall. 2 2 A. M.:

Reference: J. F. Carr, op cit., p. 550. W. L. Riordon, pp. 170-173, by the courtesy of Doubleday, Page k Co. Solutions to this problem: The New Electoral Fusion System, Nonpartisan Elections.

POLITICAL PARTIES AND ELECTORAL PROBLEMS

American Political Parties History

The Boss paying the rent of a poor family about to be dispossessed and gave them a dollar for food. At home again. Found four men waiting for him. One discharged by the Metropolitan Railway Company for neglect of duty and wanted the district leader to fix things. Another wanted a job on the road. The third sought a place on the Subway, and the fourth, a plumber, was looking for work with the Consolidated Gas Company. The district leader spent three hours fixing things for the four men and succeeded in each case. 3 p. M.: Attended the funeral of an Italian as far as the ferry.

Hurried back to make his appearance at the funeral of a Hebrew constituent. Went conspicuously to the front both in the Catholic church and the Synagogue, and later attended the Hebrew confirmation ceremonies in the Synagogue. 7 P. M.: Went to district headquarters and presided over a meeting of election District Captains.

Each Boss submitted a list of all the voters in his district, reported on their attitude toward Tammany, suggested who might be won over and how they could be won, told who were in need and who were in trouble of any kind, and the best way to reach them. District leader took notes and gave orders. 8 p. M.: Went to a church fair. Took chances on everything, bought ice cream for the young girls and the children. Kissed the little ones, flattered their mothers, and took their fathers out for something down at the corner.

At the clubhouse again spent ten dollars on tickets for a church excursion and promised a subscription for a new church bell. Bought tickets for a baseball game to become played by two nines from his district. Listened to the complaints of a dozen push-cart peddlers, who said they have persecuted by the police, and assured them he would go to Police Headquarters in the morning and see about it. Attended a Hebrew wedding reception and dance. Had previously sent a handsome wedding present to the bride. In bed of course, relief work on Plunkitt's lines does not meet with the approval of social workers. On the other hand, the extent to which it is continued proves that it is effective extremely effective in building up a dependable political news of later.

A big city like W. L. Riordon, Plunkitt of Tammany Hall, generosity, and their votes go with their gratitude. The fact that his helps given personally, without questions or red tape and that the time of greatest need, strengthens this feeling. As friends and neighbors who, perchance, recall the early poverty and struggles of the boss, it is easy for them to believe in his big Irish heart. Indeed, considering the origin and character of many machine leaders, it is probable that their charitable activities have motivated not only by shrewd political calculation, but by a measure of warm human sympathy as well.

Of course, there are other recipients of aid at the hands of the Boss who look upon him frankly as a modern Robin Hood. In their view the Boss takes from the rich and gives to the poor, this is the doctrine of the Communist ideology which offers the same, however misguidedly, because Communists promises you the world and later in power confiscate all your properties and your soul, living you like an android a robot in human form. Moreover, it avoids the penalties provided by charities law for the old crude method of direct vote buying, by suborning the voters. That many of the recipients of relief at the hands of the Boss accept it utterly without thought of a political bargain is beyond doubt. Trey regard-it as evidence of his properties and begins to be repressing any opposite, because according with that philosophy, everything belongs to the state an additional motive for band like commitment at their election's oppositions

Michael Anguelo

NICARAGUAN COMMUNIST CONTRAWITH CIA SUPPORT

EFFECTS OF BOSSISM ON THE COMMUNITY

American Political Parties History and the Solutions

In spite of the fact that the prime motive of the Boss is motivated to make money, the large deductions due to the necessity Bossism of supporting the machine and its innumerable campground sucker's city lowers classes, to social and charitable donations, and to the extra hazardous nature of the pursuit itself all combine to render it anything but the Golconda of popular imagination. Much more important than the question of its productivity as an individual pursuit, however, is the question of the effects of Bossism, not only financial, but political and moral as well upon a forbidden community.

Commenting upon the practice of Republican machine leaders of Philadelphia, the New York Tribune, itself a Republican paper. They enjoyed a practical monopoly of all city work, from which they amassed great fortunes while the city incurred high taxes and a debt.

In general, machine rule is strongly favorable to bond issues. Such issues gain the friendship to of powerful financial interests, furnish large sums for public contracts which give employment to political contractors and local laborers, and, finally, they have the advantage of postponing ultimate payment for a term of years during which the comparatively small burdens imposed by in debt due to this brief reign of corruption was over sixty-one millions of dollars. Ten million more of the assessment bonds still unfunded in 1874 may likewise be fairly charged directly to the Circle and sinking-fund charges are juggled as much as possible. business and Often the plea have made that the machine keeps taxes down, but analysis of all the facts usually reveals its falsity.

Bossism reacts in many devious ways upon the o collect all the traffic will bear not only when franchises have granted, but constantly thereafter through strike legislation and crooked administrative regulation. On more than one occasion big business interests have become forced into open revolt against the extortionate practices of the machine.

Reference: Finance of New York City, p. 146. Solutions to this problem: The New Electoral Fusion System, Nonpartisan Elections. The solution of this problem will be correct if we have a Fusion Electoral System, no partisan elections System.

MACHINES AND BOSSES CORRUPTIONS

American Political Parties History

Moreover, it must not be forgotten that corporate interests are obliged to recoup themselves for the costs of a political promotion by charging higher rates to the consumer. Thus, the views of economic circle are complete. Business interests pay the boss, the boss doles out some portion of his takings to the poor in charity and entertainment, the poor and the great mass of consumers foot the bill ultimately in higher tax rates and slipshod public service, in higher street carfare and higher rates for gas and electric light. From this angle the conception of the Boss as a modern Robin Hood become ridiculous its attitude is laughable if it were not so frightening.

Unquestionably, however, the political and moral consequences of machine rule far outweigh in gravity all the and moral economic burdens it imposes upon the community. Bossism consist the inflationary its ethnicity defense of old abuses and machine its authority to reforms de-signed to bring dishonesty, Euler in elections and efficiency of government. The difficulty, and, at times, the seeming impossibility of making head way against it accounts in large part for the political apathy of many otherwise good citizens. Its toleration of and crinkling an influenced of the trial reaches every class in the community.

Property losses, losses of character, Injuries, and loathsome disease stalk in its trail. The machine conception of politics as a money-making pursuit has ruined the careers of innumerable men capable under happier conditions of real leadership and public service. The immunity which its servants enjoy despite their constant violations of the penal code destroys respect for law in large sections of the population.

In this connection the use of political influence in. police and magistrates' courts have a peculiarly deplorable effect. To many poor and ignorant citizens who, have nothing to do with superior and appellate jurisdictions either in this world or the next, these courts stand for all that they know of law and justice. And the knowledge which they gain by actual experience of the use of yank in police and magistrates courts is calculated to make of them anything but good citizens.

Solutions to this problem: The New Electoral Fusion System, Nonpartisan Elections, A big city like W. L. Riordon, Plunkitt of Tammany Hall, The New Electoral Fusion System, Nonpartisan Elections.

PARTIES AND ELECTORAL CORRUPTIONS

American Political Parties History

Gain by actual experience of the use of disaster in constabularies and magistrates' courts are calculated to make of them anything but good citizens. Opposition On the other hand, the situation is far from hopeless, to bossism Machine rule is a power so great and a dear examined with abuses that it breeds opposition as well apathy. If its confined to or more largely developed in one party, there is a chance for the other party to win a sweeping victory with an anti-machine platform and ticket.

For this reason, Bossism is always more circumspect and less grasping where two parties confront each other on something like even terms. In states like Pennsylvania, where the Democratic opposition is so weak as to be almost hopeless, machine leaders are more likely to take long chances.

Even under such conditions, however, there are limits, albeit indefinite, to the power of the Boss, as Quay discovered in 1898 and Vare in 1911. Given a long train of abuses and usurpations on the part of the machine, the result is that reform and independent movements spring up within the dominant party itself. At such times, the Bosses are wont to abjure their malpractices, promise amendment, and seek out citizens of high character, whom somehow, they always seem able to persuade, to head their ticket. Conveniently forgetting their own secret relations with large corporations, they pose as friends of the plain people, determined to protect them against designing malefactors of great wealth enrolled under the independent banner.

They denounce reformers as hypocritical, self-seeking intellectuals, extremely lacking practical sense or of sympathy with the masses. The media opposed to them are the sponsored press. In such struggles re-formers and independents are at great disadvantage. Persuasive little of organization, they must nevertheless build up an organization quickly. In the use of political trickery, they would become outclassed even if their principles did not forbid resort to it. Despite these difficulties, independent movements have been victorious, at least temporarily, in so many cities and states that machine leaders have lost a great deal of their former impudence.

References: Cf. R. H. Smith, Justice, and the Poor; the Survey of Criminal Justice in Cleveland, Ohio (1921), made for the Cleveland Foundation under the direction of Dean Pound. Reference: F. J. Goodnow and F. G. Bates, Munks friend Government, pp. 265-269. Solutions to this problem: The New Electoral Fusion System, Nonpartisan Elections. The solution of this problem will be correct if we have a Fusion Electoral System, no partisan elections System.

GOVERNMENT

MACHINES AND BOSSES CORRUPTIONS
American Political Parties History

Among these threatening become mentioned civil service reform, the Australian ballot, direct primaries, corrupt practices act, the short ballot, direct legislation, the recalculation, and in cities the commission and city manager forms of. government. Improvements in administrative practice and in budget and accounting methods make many old times abuses impossible or at least much easier to detect. Many citizens' associations keep carefully watch. Mover public business and employ experts to project mismanagement. Public opinion is more alert. Smooth Bosses know that you cannot fool all the people all the time, although they are inclined to believe that you can always invent a new way to fool them.

Certain it is that with each fresh effort to limit its power the machine puts forth an amazing amount of ingenuity and patience to gain its ends by evasion. Nevertheless, the crude raising of bills as practiced by Tweed or the limitless speculation with public funds as practiced under Quay would be impossible in New York City and Pennsylvania today. No doubt such improvement as may become discerned in the is bossism practice of bosses is due more largely to fear of penalties declining? than to any change of purpose or of moral standards on their part.

Together with these changes in the methods of Bossism some evidence has developed tending to the belief that its grip upon the country is not so firm or extensive as it once was. Certainly, there are now no state Bosses whose power can become compared with that of Walter E. Piatt, William Quay, or The Penrose. With the passing of these great machine leaders' many prophecies have made to the effect Bossism inconsistent with American ideals that bossism itself had condemned to disappear.

PARTIES AND ELECTORAL CORRUPTIONS
American Political Parties History

Wherever it has once become firmly proved, however, it has shown remarkable recuperative powers even after the most exhausting defeats.

System, Nonpartisan Elections. The solution of this problem will be correct if we have a Fusion Electoral System, no partisan elections System. // Also, it must be remembered that even if the great state Bosses have passed from the political stage a host of minor district, city, and county Bosses are still active more powerful. Predictions that machine rule itself is soon to disappear must be based upon something more fundamental than the death or defeat of individual leaders. Not until it can become exposed that the broad general causes of Bossism, noted earlier in this chapter, have ceased to track such predictions to become accepted at their face value. In fact, most of these general causes of Bossism still prevail, and seem likely to do so for the next few decades. One of them, however, has become quickly changed, namely the political thought, and practice take of the country on the fear of a strong administration, the doctrine of the separation of powers.

With the extension of reforms due to this change of thought and practice, particularly reforms along the lines discussed in the succeeding chapters of this volume, a further improvement may become expected. Changes in party and governmental mechanism are not enough, however. Some of the causes currently assigned for the prevalence of Bossism, notably the apathy of alleged good citizens, are not so much causes as excuses of which every man and woman who possesses a backbone should be energetically humiliated.

Michael Anguelo

MACHINES AND BOSSES CORRUPTIONS
American Political Parties History

The Humiliation of the Cities and The Fight for Self-government (1904Bossism, as we have seen is a distinctive product of American political conditions. Nonetheless that is a product inconsistent with every point of our ideals of government and contradictory to the inclinations of every independent citizen. Only by the higher civic interest and more strenuous exertions of such citizens may the fight against bossism be won. Solutions to this problem: The New, 1906), Lincoln Steffens collects materials on the abuses of machine rule from many cities and states. H. J. Ford critically discuss the significance of his findings, Municipal Corruption, For a brief general summary of conditions, the country over Socialist Party. Orth, The Boss, and the Machine (1918), is also useful. In various chapters of his Corruption in American Politics and Life (1910), the author discusses the nature of political corruption, its extent, and the various apologies made for it. E. A. Ross, Sin and Society (1907), analyses the same general topic admirably from the sociological point of view.

W. J. Ghent, Our Benevolent Feudalism (1902), may become reserved as an excellent presentation touched by mockery of the Communist insolence on the way to machine regulation. Henry Champernowne (D. M. Means) The Boss (1894), is an extremely clever burlesque founded on manipulator's Big shot. The only extended historical account of a single political machine is G. Myers, History of Tammany Hall (2ded., 1917). For dynamic impeachments of machine maladministration in New York when Tammany was in the heyday of its power, see W. M. Ivins, Machine Politics (1887; and Theodore. Roosevelt, Articles on Practical Politics (1888).

For a disclosure of the mental operations of perhaps the most thoroughly practical politician of the day, W. L. Riordon, Plunkitt of Tammany Hall (1905), is extremely interesting, and despite its comical passageways is to become retained largely as has study in political practicality. D. G. Thompson, Politics in a Democracy (1893), is an endeavored metaphysical reasoning of machine methods, using Tammany chiefly as an exemplar. Tom L. Johnson, My Story (1913), presents a vivid picture from the dangerous liberal point of view of machine politics in Ohio, with orientation to the fight over the regeneration of street railway

The New Fusion Electoral System

permits in Cleveland. Brand Whitlock, Forty Years of It (1916), is a work of similar character, with the mayor's office in Toledo as the center from which observations are Political Science.

Reference: Quar. Vol. XIX, pp. 673-686 (Dec 1904). Solutions to this problem: The New Electoral Fusion System, Nonpartisan Elections. The solution of this problem will be correct if we have a Fusion Electoral System, no partisan elections System. Altogether the general works on American political parties cited under this Fusion solutions, the elongated dissertation by Ostrogorski, devote space to machines and Bosses. Especially worthy of mention is C. E. Merriam, The American Party System (1922), which under the general heading of The Spoils System, presents an admirable systematic discussion of this field. P. S. Reinsch, American Legislatures and Legislative Methods (1913). H. J. Ford, Rise, and Growth of American Politics.

Spoils System
- Jackson opened his inauguration party to everyone on March 4, 1829, confirming his image as a man of the common people
- Jackson believed that his Democratic supporters should be entitled to federal jobs because of their loyal support
- he valued loyalty more than experience and overturned Jefferson's "meritocracy" system that had produced a highly competent bureaucracy for nearly thirty years

Above: Jackson's inaugural party in 1829; Below: cartoon critical of Jackson's spoils system

PARTIES AND ELECTORAL CORRUPTIONS

American Political Parties History

Going on circumstances at the other end of the same state Wright, Bossism in Cincinnati, is useful. Machine rule in other states and cities is dealt with as follows: John Wanamaker, Speeches on Quayism and Boss Domination in Pennsylvania (1898); Lynn Haines, The Minnesota Legislature of 1911; B. B. Lindsey, The Beast and the Jungle (1910), a work similar to those of Johnson and Whitlock quoted above, dealing with conditions in Denver and the State of Colorado; and on conditions in San Francisco and the state of California; Fremont Older, My Own Story, and F. Hichborn, Story of the Session of the California Legislature, 1909, 1911, 1913, 1915, also by the same author, The System as Uncovered by the San Francisco Graft Prosecution (1915). Lynn Haines, Your Congress (1915), is an understanding of the political and governmental forces that control law making in the national field (1898, Chaps. XXIII to XXV; H. Croly, The Promise of American Life (1911, Chaps. V and VI; and F. J. Good-now, Politics and Administration (1900), Ch. VIII. F. C. Howe, The City. The expectation of Democracy (1905), Chaps. VI and VII; J. J. Hamilton, The Dethronement of the City Boss (1909); and W.B. Munro, Government of American Cities (1921), Ch. VII; Municipal Government and Administration (1923). I, Chaps. XIV to XVI; the All's Committee of the New York senate (1910); the Boston Finance Commission (14 vols., 1908-20); the Lorimer investigations of the U. S. Senate (1911-12); N. Y., N. H. & H.R. R. investigation, Interstate Commerce Committee Reports, No. 6569 (1914); and Sen. Doc. No. 543, Sixty-Third Cong., 2d Vol. I and II (1914). The Boss, is a mordant picture of the Croker type; H. R. Miller, The Man Higher Up (1910),

Reference: C. E. Merriam, American Political Ideas (1920), Ch. VIII of which partakes dedicated to a discussion of political ideas in American literature. Pol. Sci. Quar. Vol. XIX.

PARTIES AND ELECTORAL CORRUPTIONS

American Political Parties History

But under a democratic and highly elaborated form of government such as our own it is essential that there should be some definite and well organized system for bringing forth at the appointed times the tens of thousands of candidates needed for elective offices of every description.

The absence of a nominating system of this character would leave the great mass of more or less indifferent voters without guidance, and also without the intense interest which a good contest always arouses; there would be no means to bring about a sharp focusing of popular attention upon those personalities possessing both the qualifications and inclination for public office; many minor offices would be left unfilled, and probably not a few of the major offices would be filled unsatisfactorily by that one out of a considerable and indefinite group of receptive, but undersigned candidates who happened to have behind him a minority vote sufficient to win by plurality on election day. Quite apart from motives connected with the welfare of the state, practical politicians have always realized the immense importance of definite party designation.

Which received some form of nomination prior to election? Moreover, throughout large sections of the country one or the other of the two great parties is so strongly in the majority that a nomination at its pointers is virtually equivalent to election. In such sections, of course, the nominating process is of greater importance and attracts more interest than the purely formal elections which follow. No other country has developed such elaborate, complicated, and costly nominating machinery as the United States. Historically it has evolved through three periods, each characterized, as far as the more important offices were concerned, by a dominant type.

Reference: The Legislative Caucus, from the Colonial Period to 1830; The Delegate Convention System, 1830 to 1903.

LEGISLATIVE CAUCUS FROM COLONIAL PERIOD TO 1830

American Political Parties History

During the Colonial period and at once following, elective offices were few, the suffrage was significantly restricted, and the influence of aristocratic or property-owning families was well recognized. Under these conditions, gentlemen were accustomed to bringing forward their own candidatures, or their names might become proposed at meetings of the neighborhood elite, which were often quite as welcoming as they were partisan. In cities, clubs of all sorts and trade organizations some Colonial methods of nomination.

References: C. E. Merriam, The American Party System, p. 247, estimates the number of elective offices in the United States as follows: federal, (500); state, m (500); state legislatures, (7,500); county, (45,000); elective judges, (1,500); office in cities with over (8,000) inhabitants, (10,000); in cities with less than (8,000) inhabitants, (100,000); in New England towns, (15,000); total (180,000). This does not include the thousands of elective offices in other towns, in town ship and in school districts.

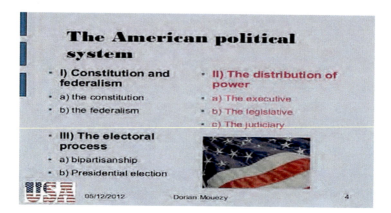

POLITICAL NOMINATIONS

American Political Parties History

Whiles nominated their leading members for public office Over wider areas, these easy going and diffuse methods were helped by committees of correspondence. Early in the eighteenth century, however, a fairly definition and quite effective piece of local nominating machine the caucus very known as the caucus have developed. Two etymologies have been suggested for this word, one deriving it from the Algonquin Indian Kawkaw was, meaning to talk, to give advice, to instigate; the other referring it to the caulkers meeting or caulkers club to which dockyard workers in Boston belonged. A vivid contemporary picture of the Colonial caucus is presented in the diary of John Adams, under date of February, 1763, as follows: The Caucus club meets at certain times in the upper floor of Tom Dawes, the assistant of the Boston company.

He has a large house, and he has a movable partition in his penthouse which he takes down, and the whole club meets in one room. There they smoke tobacco till you cannot see from one end of the penthouse to the other. There they drink flip, I supposing, and they choose a, moderator who puts questions to the vote regularly; and selectmen, assessors, collectors, passion districts, and representatives are regularly chosen before they are chosen in the town.

When it became necessary to nominate candidates for the legislate governorship and other state offices, this function was native caucus assumed at first by a meeting of all the members of a given party in the legislature. In 1800 the same system has proven in Congress for the choice of presidential candidates. Considering the difficulties of travel at that time, there is nothing unnatural in the development of the legislative caucus. Members of the legislature and Congress-men were political leaders who reflected the opinions of their voters

PARTIES AND ELECTORAL PROBLEMS

American Political Parties History

The mixed or hybrid committee, become Public criticism of the legislative committee absenteeism of representatives from many districts. For example, those districts which did not elect a Federalist to the legislature have not signified in the legislative caucus of that party. To meet this hostility, the practice grew up in some states of choosing party delegates from districts not represented by a member of the party in the legislature. At the appointed time, such delegates would make their way to the state capital to participate with members of the party holding seats in the legislature in a mixed or crossbreed assembly to select nominees for state wide offices. Simple as this arrangement was, it was of major importance in that it pointed the way to the transformation of the legislative caucus into the delegate convention.

However, the nominating assemblies both in state legislatures and in Congress soon came to become criticized on much more serious grounds. They have denounced as oligarchic and corrupt, as Jacobin meetings which scandalously appropriated authorities belonging to the people. Believers in the system of checks and balances also saw in the caucus a means anywhere by the legislative branch, having arrogated to itself the power of conferring offices in other departments, would come to dominate the whole government, contrary to the provisions and spirit of the Constitution.

During the Era-of-Good-Feeling the power of the congressional caucus visibly rotten and under the violent attack launched against it by the rising Jacksonian Democracy of the new West, King Committee have deposed in national politics.

Even before this has conducted the anti-caucus movement had made considerable progress in the states. During the presidency of Jefferson, Delaware took the lead in going over to the convention system. No doubt the decision to do so have made easier by its small size, enabling delegates from every part of the state to meet readily in some centrally found place. In the larger commonwealths the change came about more slowly, but by the time the first national conventions have held (1830-1903), delegate conventions had been introduced all over except in the South.

Reference: The solution of this problem will be correct if we have a Fusion Electoral System, no partisan elections System.

CHAPTER 22

NOMINATIONS THE CONVENTION SYSTEM 1830-1903

American Political Parties History

At the basis of the delegate convention system was the local popular caucus or primary, which was continued unchanged in form and increased in power from the preceding period. This was, in theory at least, a meeting of all the voters of a party in each ward, town, or township.

Previously it had made nominations for the elective offices of its territory. To this have now added the function of electing delegates to city, county, and sometimes to district conventions. These conventions selected candidates for elective offices in their respective districts, and in their turn chose delegates to the higher district and state conventions.

Representation in all these conventions have distributed to districts based on the party vote in separately. Delegates and alternates at large to the national convention have chosen by the state conventions. District alternatives and delegates to the national convention were chosen by congressional district conventions, except that in New York and several other states delegates to the Democratic state convention met in groups according to their congressional districts, and chose such delegates.

This complicated and imposing hierarchy of conventions rested upon the basis, in theory purely democratic, of the thousands of popular caucuses or primaries in local communities throughout the country. Above its democratic foundation the whole pyramidal structure of delegate conventions become assumed to be thoroughly representative in character. Delegates represented either voters in caucus assembled or conventions chosen by them in the last analysis. They met presumptuously to register the voters' will, at first in the choice of candidates, and later also in the drafting of formal party platforms. Delegates to conventions has confined solely to these Delegates chosen by local caucus representation in conventions. The hierarchy of conventions. In the new FUSION Electoral System, there is no delegates or national convention hierarchy, because the candidates have accepted to run for a candidature only by the Fusion Supreme Tribunal of Electoral approval.

PARTIES AND ELECTORAL PROBLEMS

American Political Parties History

The work two Duties, while members of the earlier legislative of conventions caucuses had many duties to perform within which conventions and their responsibility for nominations was not easily fixed. Moreover, the work of conventions lasted only a few days, become jealously watched by rival aspirants and factions, it commanded a lively public interest, and was immediately subjected to the searching tests of a campaign and the final decision of a popular election. Considering the theoretical perfection and the practical Frauds and, abuses safeguards of the popular primary and delegate conventions practiced in nation scheme, one is amazed at the number of gross frauds primaries and malpractices it developed within a short time after it have adopted.

No more striking evidence can become cited of the fierce dishonesty of political ambition and factional strife in the United States. Popular caucuses or primaries have often dominated and terrorized by floaters and repeaters drawn from the lowest elements of the population, native or foreign born. Violence often occurred in tough wards, and a wise political leader arranged with the police in advance of the meeting so that they might have no difficulty in detecting and throwing out trouble makers, belonging, of course, to the opposite faction.

The meeting places chosen for popular caucuses or primaries were in or at once next to saloons, or over livery stables, or in other places likely to deter the more respectable class of citizens from attending. Preparatory to the general election of 1884, there have held in the various districts of New York ten hundred and seven primaries and political conventions of all parties, and of this no less than six hundred and sixty-three took place in liquor saloons.

NOMINATIONS CORRUPTION PROBLEM

American Political Parties History

Corruption was resorted to if necessary, and the Boss or coterie of machine leaders pulled every wire to secure the nomination of other, or even by voters of the opposite party. appearance in advance of the T. Roosevelt president.

Sometimes rooms would become selected too small to hold all the voters, word become approved out to the district medics to take possession at an early hour, thus excluding effectually the independent element. Or, also by prearrangement, the gang and its cohorts would make their time set, turn the clock an hour ahead, put through a cut and dried program, and jeer the independents when they arrived on the scene. This trick become called home conventions to themselves. In minor conventions men or interior type, sometimes of dubious or even criminal reputation, were present and active.

Few, however, reached such depths of depravity as the Cook County convention, held in Chicago in 1896, of the delegates, those who have been on trial for murder numbered 17; sentenced to the penitentiary for murder or manslaughter and served sentence, 7 ; served terms in the penitentiary for burglary, 36; served terms in the penitentiary for picking pockets, 2; served terms in the penitentiary for arson, 1; ex-Bridewell and jailbirds identified by detectives, 84; keepers of gambling houses, 7; keepers of houses of ill fame, 2; convicted of mayhem, 3; ex-prize fighters, 11; pool-room owners, 2; saloon keepers, 265; lawyers, 14; physicians, 3; grain dealers, 2; political employees, 148; hatter, 1; stationer, 1; contractors, 4; grocer, 1; sign painter, 1; plumbers, 4; butcher, 1; druggist, 1; furniture supplies, 1; commission merchants, 2; ex-policemen, 15; dentist, 1; speculators, 2; justices of the peace, 3; ex-constable, 1; farmers, 6; undertakers, 3; no occupation, 71. Total delegates, 723.

A considerable period intervened between per Proxies marines and conventions which become utilized to the utmost to bring pressure to bear upon delegates and even to bribe them or conventions and who, for a consideration, were willing to transfer their credentials to corrupt politicians. Later these proxies have voted in blocks on the floor of the convention. Proxy voting has now prohibited by law in some states, and by party rules in others. Also, the general practice of selecting alternates to take the place of delegates in case the latter are unable to attend the convention has helped to break up this abuse.

If a division occurred in the primaries each faction sent its own set of delegates to the convention. The faction in control of the convention seldom bothered itself about the merits of the case and would promptly seat that one of two contesting delegations which could be depended upon to support its slate. There were times, however, when party harmony seemed so desirable that both sets of delegates become seated, a half vote become given to each of the members. Although often threatened, violence was not so common in conventions, at least those of higher grade, as in primaries. On the other hand, Boss or apparatus control was more complete. Steamroller methods were often in evidence, and one convention held under the sway of Platt, in New York, have referred to as having become track by electricity. Much depended upon the choice of a presiding officer who could be relied upon to recognize only adherents of his own faction, side track hostile motions, and gavel things through promptly regardless of the clamor and even of the vote of the delegates. Of course, all these abuses have not practiced in every primary or convention.

CONVENTION

Primaries reflected the character of the districts in which they become held. In rural sections such meetings were usually free from violence and the cruder forms of fraud. But in city wards inhabited by the lowest class of native-or foreign-born population, violence and fraud were common, unless indeed the control of the ring or the boss was so complete as to make opposition hopeless. Some states and cities had rules sufficiently stringent and well enough administered to prevent the most flagrant abuses and a few promising beginnings were made in the way of legal regulation.

Nominating machinery and political life of the country. conducted with the tools at hand. By dint of long and bitter experience the great public which was not interested professionally in politics had come to the conclusion that the convention system was dominated by irresponsible leaders, that it excluded the rank and file from effective participation in party management, that it turned out candidates oblivious to the wishes of their constituents in short, that it was completely and incurably Boss-ridden. As in the case of the old legislative caucus, what has demanded was not amendment, but abolition. The result was the general introduction of the direct-primary election system. The indifference of good citizens has denounced in countless speeches, sermons, and editorials; indeed, it had pointed out as one of the chief causes of current abuses.

N. Holcombe, State Government in the United opposed these reforms. Naturally, the abuses cited above were most prevalent in the caucuses and conventions where regulation was least developed. At this distance of time it is easy to prescribe further Futile w. legal remedies which might have saved the old convention or notations system.

POLITICAL NOMINATIONS

American Political Parties History

Everywhere, however, the professional political class opposed these reforms. Naturally, the abuses cited above were most prevalent in the caucuses and conventions where regulation was least developed. At this distance of time it is easy to prescribe further Futile w. legal remedies which might have saved the old convention or notations system. In fact, every resource of oratory to reform and exhortation was spent in vain to induce the better class of citizens to attend the primary and thus to uplift the moral. In fact, every resource of oratory to reform and exhortation was spent in vain to induce the better class of citizens to attend the primary and thus to uplift the whole spirit.

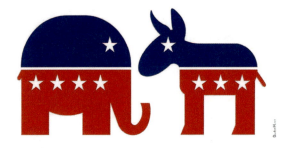

PARTIES AND ELECTORAL CORRUPTIONS

American Political Parties History

Transparency International Top Five Recommendations: Our firsthand experience working in more than 100 countries around the world shows that activists and media are vital to combating corruption. As such, Transparency International calls on the global community to take the following actions to curb corruption: Governments and businesses must do more to encourage free speech, independent media, political dissent and an open and engaged civil society.

Governments should minimize regulations on media, including traditional and new media, and ensure that journalists can work without fear of repression or violence. In addition, international donors should consider press freedom relevant to development aid or access to international organizations. Civil society and governments should promote laws that focus on access to in-formation. This access helps enhance transparency and accountability while reducing opportunities for corruption. It is important, however, for governments to not only invest in a proper legal framework for such laws, but also commit to their implementation.

Activists and governments should take advantage of the momentum generated by the United Nations Sustainable Development Goals (SDGs) to advocate and push for reforms at the national and global level. Specifically, governments must ensure access to information and the protection of fundamental freedoms and align these to international agreements and best practices.

Governments and businesses should proactively show relevant public interest information in open data formats. Initiative taking disclosure of relevant data, including government budgets, company ownership, public obtaining and political party finances allows journalists, civil society, and affected communities to show patterns of corrupt conduct more efficiently. Political Parties are killing the nations of the world, with corruptions and lack of transparencies, to stop this incongruity we most first eliminate all political parties and substitute it by a Fusion Elections System.

Direct primary a legal creation Extension of the direct primary system or primaries as well. The convention system was a representative or indirect method of making nominations; the direct primary election system is direct in that it places the nominating power in the hands of the voters themselves. The direct-primary election system also differs sharply from the legislative caucus and convention systems which preceded it in that it is set up by law. Both earlier nominating methods rested upon party rules and customs. Toward the end of the delegate convention period it is true that attempts have made to end abuses both in conventions and in popular primaries or caucuses by legislation. But the direct-primary election system is thoroughly official in character, and its smallest details are determined by law. The change thus brought about perhaps the most sweeping that has occurred in our party history. Taken in connection with the Australian ballot, it has brought a large part of our extra constitutional governmental machinery under legal control, while at the same time it has given parties a legal standing which formerly, they did not have.

Introduction of the direct primary election system began in 1903. For a few years thereafter, progress was slow, but between 1907 and 1915 it spread with such rapidity that at the end of the last year all the states of the union, with the exception of five, had adopted it in some form. However, there are wide differences among some misunderstanding may be caused by this similarity of names. The popular primary or caucus was an assemblage of voters in small local units to make nominations and choose delegates to convention. Under a systematic direct primary election system, the voters of a party do not meet as a body but go to the polls as individuals to express by ballot their preference among candidates for nomination. In the following states the direct primary has conducted under the rule of the Democratic states as to the number or kind of offices brought under the direct primary election system, and hence in the extent to which it cuts conventions. Some states use it both for public and for party offices, others only for party offices.

Reference: Wisconsin, 1903; Oregon, 1904; Iowa, Missouri, Nebraska, North Dakota, South Dakota, and Washington, 1907; Kansas, Ohio, and Oklahoma, 1908; Arizona, 1909-12; California, Idaho, Michigan, New Hampshire, Nevada, and Tennessee, 1909; Colorado, Illinois, and Maryland, 1910; Maine, Massachusetts, New Jersey, and Wyoming, 1911; Kentucky, Louisiana, Minnesota, Mississippi, Montana, and Virginia, 1912; Florida, New York, and Pennsylvania, 1913; Indiana, North Carolina, Vermont, and West Virginia, 1915. Solutions to this problem: The New Electoral Fusion System, Nonpartisan Elections.

> **Presidential Primaries**
>
> - Depending on the State, a **presidential primary** is an election in which a party's voters
>
>   (1) choose some or all of a State's party organization's delegates to their party's national convention, and/or
>
>   (2) express a preference among various contenders for their party's presidential nomination.
>
> - Many States use a **proportional representation** rule to select delegates. In this system, a proportion of a State's delegates are chosen to match voter preferences in the primary.
>
> - More than half of the States hold preference primaries where voters choose their preference for a candidate. Delegates are selected later to match voter preferences.

POINTLESS PROCESS AND A WASTE OF TIME AND MONEY

IN TE FUSION SYSTEM THIS PROCEDURE IS TO ASSIGN VOTERS REPRESENTATIVES TO ELECT THE PRESIDENT

NOMINATIONS AND CORRUPTIONS

American Political Parties History

In the United States today, it is not just the economy that is crumbling. The entire fabric of society is coming apart as well. Literally wherever you look you can find rampant corruption in America. Our federal government is corrupt, our state and local governments are corrupt, our corporations are corrupt and unfortunately average Americans become more corrupt all the time. As corruption becomes widespread in America, trust is breaking down. It is exceedingly difficult to know who to trust these days. But a society cannot function without trust. Consequently, what are we going to do when all the confidence is gone?

Robert Khuzami, the SEC's top enforcement officer, summed up the charges against JPMorgan this way: J.P Morgan marketed highly complex CDO investments to investors with promises that the mortgage assets underlying the CDO would become selected by an independent manager looking out for investor interests.

Therefore, is anyone going to go to jail for this? Of course not. In fact, not a single bank executive has gone to jail for anything that happened during the fiscal crisis. Therefore, how are we supposed to have faith in the system if nobody has ever held accountable? Are little spankings on the wrist, it theoretical will make us all feel better?

The truth is that what JPMorgan did was far from an isolated incident. If you doubt this, just read the following article: How Goldman Sachs Made Tens of Billions of Dollars from The Economic Collapse of America in Four Easy Steps: Our system is sick, and corruption is everywhere. Cronyism has become so widespread to our system that nobody really seems concerned by it any longer. For example, just check out this example that have recently reported in The New York Times.

In 2009, a judge in Manhattan had a lucrative appointment to hand out: oversight of a diamond district building that was drifting into foreclosure. 600 people in Manhattan had become approved for such work. But the job went to a lawyer named Mark D. Lebow, who is the husband of Patricia E. Harris, Mayor Michael R. Bloomberg's most trusted aide. Since then, Mr. Lebow has earned $352,000 in fees, more than $5,000 a week, according to court records. It sure is nice to be politically related to a powerful politician. It is not by accident that so many of our politicians, and their family members, become incredibly wealthy. But it is not just among the wealthy and powerful that we are seeing a growth in exploitation and corruption. All over the United States, thieves are stealing copper wire, train tracks and even drain covers. People are stealing stuff that nobody would have ever dreamed of stealing in the past. Just consider the following example from the Atlanta area: Children in two Atlanta communities will not have their neighborhood pools to help beat the summer heat, at least for now. Thieves used what has believed to be sledgehammers to bust walls and break fixtures in bathrooms at Adams and South Bend parks to steal copper, brass, and steel.

This is how desperate people throughout America are becoming. In another example from the Atlanta area, thieves recently busted into a southwest Atlanta beauty supply store and took off with $30,000 in hair extensions. America is becoming a crazy place. When times get hard, people will do whatever they feel they need to do to survive. The solution of this problem will be correct if we have a Fusion Electoral System, no partisan elections System.

True-Story: One elderly man down in North Carolina was so desperate that must rob a bank in order he could become place in jail, to have free health care. Yes, you read that correctly. 59-yearold Richard James Verone walked into an RBC Bank in North Carolina, handed a clerk a note demanding $1 and sat down and waited for the police to arrive. It turns out that he has a growth tumor on his chest and two ruptured disks, but he does not have any health insurance. So, he robbed the bank thus that he would get free health care in prison. The truth is that our country is rapidly coming apart. As I have written about so many times before, the American Dream is in an advanced state of decay, while the corrupts politician get wealthier and well feed.

On one occasion, upon a time, cities such as Detroit, Michigan were the envy of the entire world. Today, they are a joke to the rest of the world. Many of our biggest cities have become war zones. There are dozens of homes that you can buy in Detroit right now for next to nothing. For example, 14769 Liberal Street in Detroit has listed for sale on Zillow for just $100. Not that anyone would want to live there. Many homes in Detroit have become ripped to pieces by looters, vandals, and thieves. Like in Mexico, Bahrain and Bavaria, billions more to a sequence of Japanese car companies, more than $2 trillion in loans each to Citigroup and Morgan Stanley, and billions more to a string of lesser millionaires and billionaires with Cayman Islands addresses. Did we really need to send billions of dollars to millionaires and billionaires in the Cayman Islands in demand to save the U.S. economy? Something really stinks, but since our politicians are too cowardly to authorize a comprehensive audit of the Federal Reserve, we may never know what has been going on. A new scandal involving Congress seems to erupt almost weekly, and everything Congress tries to do ends up being corrupt in one way or another. If we do not reverse this trend, society will continue to break down. When faith in our major institutions is vanished, it is going to be incredibly difficult to get back. The only solution of this corruptions political malpractices is cutting all political parties that are solely responsible for this corruption and substituted the political system by the Fusion Electoral System, no partisan system.

Michael Anguelo

In some states, on the other hand, local and county offices only have brought under the direct primary election system, nominations for the more important state offices become made by conventions. At the other end of the scale are states which, like Long Pennsylvania and New Jersey, employ the primary election system to nominate all elective officers of the state, districts, counties, cities, and towns; and, to choose party officers such as members of the city, county, and state committees.

This has dropped conventions entirely in Pennsylvania, although, of course, unofficial, and often secret, slate making conclaves meet, often in advance of primary elections. The only have election officers not chosen at primary elections in Pennsylvania are presidential electors, who have named by the national candidates of the various parties. It should become seen that when the direct primary election system has used, as in Pennsylvania, for the choice of party officers it serves as an actual election of such officers.

Therefore, primary ballots in such states sometimes rival in length ballots used in general elections and are much more difficult to mark, since there is no opportunity to show a straight vote by making a single cross mark in a party square. In a few states' efforts have made to enlighten the voter by party but is not set up for all parties by statute: Alabama, Arkansas, Georgia, South Carolina, and Texas.

The five states which have not adopted it are Connecticut, Delaware, New Mexico, Rhode Island, and Utah. Utah has a law of the old type allowing parties to hold primary elections. In Delaware, delegates to the state conventions are chosen in direct primary elections.

References: From table by A. N. Holcombe, American Yearbook, 1919, p. 229.

The New York law of 1911 and the Indiana law of 1915 restricted the direct primary election system to the nomination of the principal state officers, a practice which had the advantage of making the primary ballot short entirely inconsistent decision in Washington State Democratic Party V. Reed. It is revealing that the Court's panel's denial of that inconsistency has tucked into a disingenuous footnote. Democratic Party of Hawaii v. Nago, 833 F.3d 1119, 1124 n.4 (2016) So, it goes nowadays for the parties. It is a sign of the times. A political party must prove that it is harmed if forced to give nonmembers a full share of the authority to determine its nominees.

On the other way to look at the party's right of association is this: Party adherents are entitled to associate to choose their party's nominees for public office, The First Amendment protects the right of freedom of association with respect to political parties.

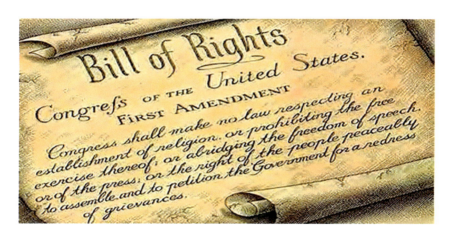

PARTIES AND ELECTORAL CORRUPTIONS PROBLEMS

American Political Parties History

On May 17, 2017 by Bob Bauer: The Supreme Court has refused to review a Ninth Circuit ruling denying political parties the right to exclude nonmembers from participation in their primaries. Hawaii law requires an open primary, and under the Ninth Circuit decision, parties would bear the burden of showing that this requirement severely burdens their rights of association. In other words, when parties must open their candidate choice processes to nonmembers, the contravention of that associational right is questionable.

The Ninth Circuit decided this incorrectly. It misconstrues the controlling Supreme Court authority, and it disregards its own and this right includes the right not to associate. In no area is the political association's right to exclude more important than in selecting its nominee.

Even a single election in which nonparty members select the party nominee could be enough to destroy the party, as would have been the case had opponents been able to swamp the Republican Party in 1860 and force it to nominate a pro slavery candidate rather than Abraham Lincoln. Unsurprisingly, the Supreme Court's cases vigorously affirm the special place the First Amendment reserves for, and the special protection it accords, the process by which a political party selects a standard bearer who best represents the party's ideologies and preferences.

In the Fusion System this embroiling situation is eliminated, where no political parties are the real solutions for a smooth election. The source of this party friendly analysis? References: The Ninth Circuit, Democratic Party of Washington State V. Reed, 343 F. 3d 1198 (9th Circ. 2003) Only last cycle, the two parties experienced runs at their presidential nominees by two individuals, Donald Trump, and Bernie Sanders, who were not, historically, party members. This is because, he is not an entirely subscribing party member but seems himself, as he often says, as the weakening of parties under a decision such as this have not limited in effect to the conduct of primaries.

Senator Sanders assumed the party label for the primary campaign, then set it aside when the campaign amended or wealth, the now actual President Tromp did it not for need of wealth, because he was already wealthy and not need for fame because he was already famous, so why we complain his administration? Politicians always find a way to criticize to harm the opponent, in the Fusion Electoral System there are no political parties then so there will be no hitches.

They do quite clearly add to the pressures on parties, undercutting their capacity more generally to govern themselves as associations with membership with no affiliation requirements with a clear records history and the impression of how they present themselves to the voters without insulting his adversaries. The political pressures on parties to open may well be greater, more decisive, than any adverse changes in the law of political suggestion.

Millennial generation seem especially committed to the self-conscious embrace of independence and resent parties, to self-determining participation in their primaries. But whether in considering who is invited to say, supported debates, or, as the voter had to decide, whether to adopt rules that would obstruct a candidate not clearly from winning a first election endorsement, the spirit of the times and the direction of the law has not been favorable to strong acts of no party self-statement. In time it may be clearer whether this is a development for the better, or an unstoppable change in electoral politics that could lead, may have already led, to strange and troubling places.

NOMINATIONS AND CORRUPTIONS
American Political Parties History

If we substituted the American Electoral System with the Fusion Electoral System all this corruption and political disagreements will become eradicated, also there will be no nominations by parties because there are no parties and the nominations are done by plication in the Fusion Electoral Tribunal only. The solution of this problem will be correct if the voter and his primary ballot permitting a candidate to state briefly on the primary ballot any official act or policy to which he wishes to commit himself. The resulting slogans in six, eight, or twelve words may or may not be edifying, but a polling place is ill adapted for the study of some dozens of such pronouncements. Publicity pamphlets having photographs and sketches of candidates are also distributed in a few states. Apart from these aids, the ordinary voter is apt to know nothing about the long list of candidates whose names appear on the primary ballot, with two exceptions: (1) those prominent contestants for statewide offices who have been discussed at length in the newspapers; and (2) those seeking local offices whom he happens to know personally.

He may, of course, take with him a prepared list or noticeable sample ballot kindly supplied to him by the organization or by some group of independents. Otherwise his vote will be a thing of an unplanned patchwork, save for the two exceptions noted above. Another limitation of the possibility of direct primary elections, although not of the same practical importance as that relating to a candidacy, is made by the definitions of political gatherings included in the laws of several states. In Fusion Electoral System the citizen's voters just elect their representative officials them elect in their name the President without the intervention of any political parties. Reference: Voters' Vagaries, National Municipal Re-vino, vol. x, p. 161 (March 1921).

NOMINATIONS AND CORRUPTIONS
American Electoral History

The golden standard, is ready to inflict upon the American people two tempestuous candidates, Donald Trump, and Hillary Clinton, raising profound doubts about the two-party system, I find for generations, the U.S. public has largely accepted that the two-party system was the best we could hope for, however conceivably not faultless, this particular brand of democracy is not the political solution, dominated since the 1800s by the Democratic and Republican parties, is certainly more democratic and republic than the one-party Communist Dictatorships of China or North Korea, Cuba, Venezuela, Nicaragua etc. and is probably more unbalanced than the multi-party parliamentary systems seen in Europe and Democracy of two parties in America. But then again, one, two-or multi--party systems are not the solution of this political problem in United States and the rest of the world is a complete calamity. It is not the solution of the existent electoral problems of what electoral campaigns are. Political parties are the motive of the political turbulence we are living today. The New Fusion Electoral System is the solution.

Yet, many of us struggle every election cycle with a nagging feeling that there is something wrong with a system that limits electoral choices to just two political parties but provides choices as on consumer products so extensive as to the mass media promotions to confusing the voters. As the late great historian Howard Zinn once sardonically said, we have two parties, and this proves we have democracy, though two parties are only one more than one party. It is not a satisfactory solution of the political organization, better off "0" parties are more effective. While a one-party state may become an Oligarchy or worth a materialist Communist ideology, would not become considered a Democracy or Capitalism by any standards, somehow the U.S. two-party system, with only one more party than a one-party system, has advertised as the crown jewel of the world's oldest constitutional Democratic-Republic. But despite misgivings over the lack of choice in the general election, the two-party system's surviving superiority, parties are a falsehood, in Fusion Electoral System nomination are done by preceding investigation and by The Fusion Tribunal Electoral, previous an application to run for a candidate position.

Through the primary process, defenders of the two-party system point out, the people are empowered to determine the leaders of the parties and therefore should not criticize when the choices end up being between a giant ham sandwich and a turkey sandwich, as South Park so eloquently described the situation in a brilliantly subversive critique of Election 2004. That has always made some degree of sense, decreasing criticisms of the two-party system, and enhancing its democratic legitimacy to large degree, but what has happened in Campaign 2016, significantly calls into question some of the underlying assumptions of this argument. While the tendencies that we have seen this year may have existed in earlier election cycles, the impacts that they are having in plain sight are leading many to interrogation of the basic legitimacy of this system. Blaming the actual system of parties is this questionable criticism?

First, the ability of party elites to manipulate the process by placing a thumb on the scale has more clearly come into focus, highlighting the unfairness to populists who do not enjoy support from powerful party insiders. With the New Fusion Electoral System elections and nominations become a more truthful and impartial process. The solution of this problem will be correct if we have a Fusion Electoral System, no partisan elections System. On the Democratic side, summer. At the time of the first Super Tuesday in early March, the race was a dead heat in terms of pledged delegates, i.e. the delegates selected by regular voters in the primaries and caucuses, but before a primary vote had even been cast, Bernie Sanders was severely disadvantaged by the support that so-called super delegates had expressed for his rival Hillary Clinton, with the media routinely reporting her super-delegate advantage despite the fact that these individuals had not voted yet, which only happens at the party convention in the because Clinton had already racked up support from at least super-delegates, the handful of party insiders who are given a disproportionate voice in the nominating process at the Democratic National Convention, she was routinely reported as being ahead of Sanders in the overall delegate count by 503-70. Former Secretary of State Hillary Clinton addressing the AIPAC conference in Washington D.C. on March 21, 2016. credit: AIPAC. The concept of party's system was originated by European scholars studying the United States, especially James Bryce and Moisey Ostrogorsky, and has been expanded to cover other democracies. Nonetheless, this system is damaging the harmonious election process, this conflicting grievance will not occur with the Fusion Electoral System, basically because Fusion is a Non-Party-System, with no parties no fighting no political confrontation.

Consequently, from the beginning, Clinton effectively had what appeared as an insurmountable lead in the delegate count. This contributed to what was always Clinton's main advantage: the perceived inevitability of her candidacy as the Democratic Party's smeared nominee and as the natural successor to President Socialist Barack Obama.

Circumstantial evidence from the beginning of the campaign seemed to show that there was something inappropriate when it came to media coverage, with Sanders' campaign rallies treated as nonevents while other candidates' rallies have given prominent coverage on the networks. Thanks God Sanders had no chance in the past Democratic primaries, if he is nominated we have the risk of having a Socialist competing for the presidency, one thing I admired the Socialists is their tenacity and persistence to obtain the victory of an inept system proven a faultier ideology. From what planet they come from?

Over a year ago, in an analysis for Media Matters for Sanders, other Socialist, has had to struggle the whole campaign season against this deficit in both delegate count and public belief, a task that had not helped by a media establishment systematically sidelining him. America, Eric Boehlert noted that despite Sanders' campaign gatherings attracted thousands of people, making them some of the largest campaign events of 2015 by either Democrats or Republicans, the media chose not to cover them as major news events. According to Boehlert, writing in May 2015, at a time when it seems any movement on the Republican side of the candidate field produces instant and extensive press coverage, more and more observers are suggesting there is something out of order with Sanders' press treatment, and it is because the press has seen what is going on with Socio-communist neighbors in Latin America and they don't like promote their disgrace. And I am glad that the newspapers ignored him. Prejudice only to Socialist or Communists, because I have been fighting them since I was 17 years old. It is all about how his campaign might affect her strategy and her policy shifts, instead of how his campaign will affect voters and public policy, Boehlert wrote. On the Republican side, candidates had covered as standalone entities, not as attachments to a specific rival.

Beyond that, much of the early coverage unequivocally declared that Sanders had no chance of winning, an odd role for the media to play in covering a nomination campaign. The press, after all, is supposed to report on the nomination process, not determine or predict the nomination process, Sanders never quit and that is the only thing I like of him. Yet, this is what a few prominent news outlets have had to say when Sanders announced his candidacy: Bernie Sanders is not going to be president, according to the Washington Post last year because it was obvious. He did not Win, said Newsweek, So Why Is Bernie Sanders Running? MSNBC: Why Bernie Sanders matters, even if he cannot succeed, because he an example of perseverance, as must Communists be, and that is a factor that many losers have.

By April 2016, the disparity in coverage had grown too much for Sanders Communists supporters to manage, and hundreds of protesters took to the streets outside CNN offices in Hollywood, the voice of their frustration with the imbalanced reporting. Indeed, while the media throughout the primary season has essentially treated the Democratic race as a non-story in which Clinton was expected to easily finalize the nomination, the Republican race was seen as a swinging cliffhanger in which every movement and change in the polls, not to mention every tweet sent out by Trump at three in the morning, was given headline coverage.

Trump accounted for 43 percent of all Republican coverage on network news in 2015, out of a first field of 17 candidates. That means that the other 16 candidates competed for just over half of the coverage. And this does not even count all of Trump's appearances on morning programs and Sunday talk shows, which would increase his airtime. With this kind of saturation coverage, is it any wonder that he appeared as the top GOP contender? into numbers, Hillary Clinton has a 57 percent approval rating in a recent Quinnipiac poll, while Trump gets a 59 percent approval rating.

Tim Malloy, assistant director of the Quinnipiac University Poll, said, American voters do not like either one of the additions to the two traditional party choices. Of those 29 years of age and younger, 91 percent expressed support for further selections, and is why Fusion Electoral System is suitable for the change that almost all American is waiting for a change in the political and electoral system, and Fusion is the Answer.

Another survey, conducted May 12-15 by the Associated Press NORC Center for Public Affairs Re-search and published May 31, reported that a full 90 percent of voters lack confidence in the country's political system while 70 percent said they feel frustrated about the 2016 presidential election and 55 percent reported feeling helpless. Forty percent went as far as to say that the two-party structure have seriously broken. It is like a rigged election, Nayef Jaber, a 66-year-old Sanders supporter from San Rafael, California, told AP. "It's supposed to be one man one vote. This is the way it should be." According to the survey, 53 percent of voters say that the Democrats' use of super-delegates is a bad idea while just 17 percent support the system. Moreover, most Americans say that neither political party stands for the views of ordinary voters. Just 14 percent say the Democratic Party is responsive to the opinions of the average voter while eight percent say the same about the Republicans. That is why I am witting this book in The New Fusion Electoral System there will be not Socialists or Communists candidates in the Fusion Elections System, because Fusion has become nonpartisan system, and candidates become only nominated by a Fusion Tribunal Electoral System, ending the partisan fights.

NOMINATIONS AND ELECTORAL CORRUPTIONS

American Political Parties History

For the latter purpose California, Oregon, and Idaho require petitions signed by 3, 5, and 10 per cent of the voters, respectively. North Carolina requires a petition signed by 10,000 voters. While these tests exclude from the operations of the primary election system a few of the lesser minority parties, the latter have accorded the privilege of making their own nominations by petition and of having these nominations printed on the official ballots used in general elections. As in general elections, so also in primary elections, the ballots used are official in character, printed under public authority, and voted under public election officers with all the safeguards of the Australian ballot system. To secure a place on the primary ballot petitions must become circulated on behalf of each aspirant. The necessary mini-mom number or percentage of signatures to has obtained by secured by law by the importance of the office looked for.

Thus, in Pennsylvania, the requirement for President or United States Senator is at least one hundred signatures in each of ten counties; for state offices and other offices to be filled by vote of the state at large, at least one hundred signatures in each of five counties; for district representative in Congress and state senator two hundred signatures; for member of the state House of Representatives, one hundred signatures; for minor local and party offices, ten signatures; for local inspectors of elections, only five signatures. Michigan requires the signatures of from 2 to 4 per cent of the party voters; California I per cent of the party vote in at least ten counties; Illinois Y2 of 1 per cent for less important offices. The only exception apparently to the requirement of a petition occurred in Idaho, where the law of 1909, since repealed, offered aspirants the option of securing a place on the primary ballot either by obtaining signatures representing a small percentage of the party vote, or by payment of small fees proportioned to the salaries of the offices sought.

CHAPTER 23

PARTIES AND ELECTORAL OPINIONS

American Political Parties History

According with a survey, Fifty-three percent of voters believe political corruption is a crisis in the United States, while another (36 percent believe it is a significant problem but not a crisis. That is consistent with other ScottRasmussen.com polling data showing that (87) percent of voters nationwide believe corruption is widespread in the federal government. Solid majorities believe there is also corruption in states (70 percent, and local (57) percent government.

The belief that our nation has a political corruption crisis have shared by (53) percent of women, (52) percent of men, (51) percent of white voters, (55) percent of black and Hispanic voters, (54) percent of rural voters, (53) percent of suburban voters and (52) percent of urban voters. This is truly an issue that cuts across partisan and demographic lines. In fact, given a list of 10 challenges facing the nation, political corruption has rated as a crisis by more voters than any other issue. (43) percent consider illegal immigration a crisis, (40) percent say the same about government deficits, and (39 percent believe global warming climate change is a crisis.

Recognition of political corruption as the nation's biggest crisis should not be much of a surprise, considering the ongoing political debates. On one side, many voters believe that President Donald Trump have become elected to clean up the swamp, in 2020, here, in the United States, he declared, we are alarmed by new calls to adopt Communism in our Country. America was founded on liberty and independence, not government intimidation, domination, and control.

Polling conducted shortly after that speech proved that to be a shrewd political framing of the choice facing the nation. (60) percent of all voters believe that Communism is a threat to America's founding ideals of freedom, equality, and self-governance. That is the reason leading Democratic candidates like Sen. Kamala Harris have been rapid to point out that they are, not Socialists.

Even more important politically is that concerns about Communism resound with the president's base while they divide Democrats.

The (80) percent of GOP voters see Communism as a threat to America's founding ideals. So, do (57) percent of independent voters. But a narrow majority of Democrats (55) percent are not agree, they support that Socialism is good for the peoples. The division among Democrats can be seen in other polling data as well. (48) percent of Democrats would vote for a candidate who considers themselves to be a Socialist-Communist. However, (39) percent Democrats would prefer a candidate who considers Socialism-Communism to be a threat to the United States. For Democrats, the actual danger is even larger. The party has drifted far to the left politically, and many party leaders seem to believe that the nation is ready to embrace the Communism of Sen. Bernie Sanders and Rep. Alexandria Ocasio Cortez. To reinforce that case, they cite polling data showing that (40) percent of the population has a favorable opinion of Communism.

At Scott Rasmussen.com, however, we excavated a little deeper into the policy preferences of those voters who like Communism. Never mind if US. become a Communist Dictatorship like Cuba, Venezuela, Nicaragua, North Korea, and others Communist Dictatorship regimes, we are doomed.

At a very general level, their attitudes reflect many of the talking points used by Sanders and Ocasio-Cortez. They believe everyone should have access to quality health care, we should all be treated equally and with dignity, every American should be able to earn a decent living and we should protect the environment.

But that does not mean people who like Communists are frantically on having the federal government take charge of solving those issues, quite the contrary. In fact, a majority (54 percent) of those who express a favorable opinion of Communism also believe that it would be better for our nation to have less government control of the economy, like it is happens in a Socialist Totalitarian Regime Venezuela, Cuba Nicaragua, China, North Korea, etc.

Recommendations:

That may sound like a contradiction to those who remember the historical meaning of Communism. But for many, that meaning no longer applies in the 21st century. Among voters today who like Communism, just (32) percent believe it leads to higher taxes and more government control. And (82) percent of those voters also have a favorable opinion of free markets Capitalism.

The bottom line is that growing support for the term Communism, does not translate into growing support for traditional Communist Policies. If Democrats follow such policies, they will help ensure a second term for President Trump.

That is why the president will keep talking about it all the way to Election 2020, because it is a real fact, proved by Communists Regimes nearby. On the other side, many believe the president is more immoral than other corrupts politicians. But the feeling of political dishonesty as a crisis that goes deeper than attitudes about the president: Numerous voters (54 percent) believe it is likely that their own representative in Congress jobs votes for cash. Just (23) percent believe their personal representative is the best person for the job. Two-thirds of voters (67) percent, believe that big businesses and government regulators often work together to create rules that are harmful and unfair to consumers.

An overwhelming majority of voters, (82) percent, believe that the top leaders of federal regulatory agencies often use their position to chase their own personal agenda and impose their standards on the rest of the nation. The division among Democrats can be seen in other polling data as well. (48) percent of Democrats would vote for a candidate who considers them self to be a Communist. However, (39) percent would prefer a candidate who considers Communism to be a menace to the United States.

At the federal level, just (21) percent believe that government contracts are issued to the best company for the job. (79) percent believe the agreements have awarded to the firms with the best links in government.

Put it all together and you have a situation where voters find little hope and much sarcasm in the political process. Only (26) percent of voters think it is even likely that Congress will successfully address key issues facing the nation before the next election. Just (17) percent now trust the federal government to do the right thing most or all the time. That hardly sounds like a system where the government enjoys the consent of the governed. In fact, the system has so fragmented that (27) percent of voters do not think anything would be all that different if Hillary Clinton had won the presidential election in 2016. Those running for president should focus more on fixing our shattered political system and less on making the nation follow an unethical political system. In my Fusion Electoral System is so correct that irregularities like these are not existent anymore. Reference: Scott Rasmussen is the publisher of Scott Rasmussen.com. He is the author of "The Sun Is Still Rising: Politics Has Failed but America Will Not. I do not try to annoy you, but all this corruptions problem will become eliminated by the new Fusion Electoral System.

NOMINATIONS AND CORRUPTIONS

American Political Parties History

It is natural to think of elections when we think of political dishonesty. People or organizations with their own agendas can twist voting. They may secretly give parties big donations. Or parties and candidates can corrupt bad buy votes instead of winning them. But political dishonesty is not just about election chains. It can lead politicians in office to direct away from good government. Their decisions can help those who fund them. The public interest comes second. Political fraud can divert infrequent resources from poor and disadvantaged people. This is especially common in countries where Democratic institutions are weak or absent. Private rather than public interests command policy. This means an ethical line has become crossed. Governments cannot act without restrictions, and democracy cannot function without it. Our trust in politicians is spoiled. We can turn away from involvement with how we have governed. Then political fraud continues uncontrolled forever unless we change the political party's system, for more reliable political organization, we must change the elections by The New Fusion Electoral System.

Political corruption can feel discouraging and inaccessible. So, can we really do anything about it? Yes, if we speak out about how we have governed. We need to call on our politicians and public officials to manage their actions. How can we trust them if we do not know what they are doing in most cases? We must mandate that they put in place regulations which will force them to act openly, then their fraudulence cannot hide. And our confidence in the political process will improve changing this complex and corrupt system by The New Fusion Electoral System.

When leaders act transparently, showing us clearly what they do, we can make informed choices when we vote. And we can hold them to account when selected. From popular groups to big organizations, civil society has a crucial role to play.

We can watch electoral campaigns and parties' activities of how state resources have become abused, we must report it, and if regulations to prevent corruption are not in place, we must mandate them. Rules about politicians' conflicts of interest, for example or regulations to stop corporate lobbying and political funding for distorting the Democratic process. If companies publish their donations, they can show their contributions have not intended to win favors. By speaking out, we can show that everyone gains from honest elections and open decision making, if we rem-placed this corrupt system with the Fusion electoral model.

These state or county officials are controlled with the duty of passing upon the number and authenticity of signatures and petitions, and of certifying names which pass their tests for printing upon the official primary ballot. In general, the enormous mass of petitions which have dumped into state and county offices before primary election are gone over automatically. Sometimes, however, objection has made by opposing candidates, signatures had examined, and a many may become rejected as fake or otherwise invalid to keep a name off the primary ballot. As a measure of prudence, therefore, it is usually worthwhile for a candidate to secure a safe margin of signatures more than the actual number fixed by law. Our system is governed by peoples we elect, but unfortunately peoples in many cases they vote for coercing or brain washing, in other words, peoples are not capable to decide for who he should vote freely, we must have elected to become our representatives that wisely elect for us, who can become our administration' President, according with the Fusion system.

Nominating petitions may be circulated by the candidate of his petition himself or by friends and members of his campaign committee in such a way as to promote his candidacy effectively. Often, however, requests have kept at political headquarters, the voters become told to quickly visit and sign them. Except in the case of local offices or of conspicuous personalities, the average voter knows little or nothing about the character of the candidates named in the sheaf of proposal papers thrust before him, but in most cases, he is willing to sign routinely on the strong point of the worker's guarantee that they are all right.

By law, a voter may sign one petition only for each office to become filled, unless two or more persons arc to become elected to the same office, in which case he may sign as many petitions as there are officer to become elected. Request Sometimes, an effort has made to secure by the number of imputes natures more than the requirements of the law for a given officer as an evidence of the popularity of the candidate therefore privileged. In a few states, however, this practice had prohibited by law. Where, as in the case of state-wide officers, a considerable number of signatures. In a Fusion Electoral System, the petitions and nominations are trough the Fusion Electoral Tribunal with an earlier application and approval of it by the Fusion Electoral Tribunal.

NOMINATION AND CORRUPTIONS

American Political Parties History

Basically to be tenable, in the past it was common to employ purely commercial agents to get them, by paying at the rate of, say, five cents a name in rural districts, and two or three cents in cities. In general, nominating petitions do not require anything like the substantial number of signatures needed for initiative, referendum, and recall petitions. Hence there is less excuse in the case of the former for the hiring of petition pushers, nevertheless, strategy is sometimes dedicated in secure rip-offs of signatures

Local political leaders of the practical securing variety do not hesitation to write in names of their Bosses, knowing that the last would swear to the genuineness thereof in the unlikely event of an investigation. In a notorious Pennsylvania case, it was shown that many signatures had been copied all in the same handwriting and in alphabetical order from the pages of a city directory.

Technically, this was not bogus since the citizens whose names were borrowed were thought to have suffered no loss thereby. But lying under oath was committed when, as had usually required in connection with the filing of nomination petitions, statement of facts have made that the signatures attached to the foregoing nomination paper are in the proper handwriting of the qualified electors named therein. Direct-primary elections are of two types open or closed.

In Wisconsin these have printed on separate sheets but have fastened together at the top and folded. Or they may become printed on the same sheet, with perforated lines between the tickets of the various meetings. Retiring to his booth, the voter privately separates the ticket of the party he wishes to vote from the others, marks and folds it, and upon emerging deposits it in the open.

This corruptions neve will occur in my Fusion Electoral System because nominations are out the hand of corrupts politicians and Boss, even though the candidates may form their particular followers' groups to support his or he candidature, but cannot nominated them.

Reference: Report on the Jury Wheel Crime of 1912, published by the People's Rights Association of Delaware County, 1915. Solutions to this problem: The New Electoral Fusion System, Nonpartisan Elections.

PARTIES AND ELECTORAL CORRUPTIONS
American Political Parties History

Voters Rate Political Corruption as America's Biggest Crisis. Recognition of political corruption as the nation's biggest crisis should not be much of a surprise, considering the ongoing political debates. On one side, many voters believe that President Donald Trump have elected to clean up the swamp. On the other side, many believe the president is more corrupt than other politicians. But the feeling of political corruption as a crisis goes deeper than attitudes about the president: Most voters (54) percent believe it is likely that their own representative in Congress trades votes for cash. Just (23) percent believe their own representative is the best person for the job. Two-thirds of voters (67) percent believe that big businesses and government regulators often work together to create rules that are harmful and unfair to consumers. An overwhelming majority of voters (82) percent believe that the top leaders of federal regulatory agencies often use their position to pursue their own personal program and impose their standards on the rest of the nation. At the federal level, just (21) percent believe that government contracts are issued to the best company for the job. Seventy-nine percent believe contracts have awarded to the firms with the best contacts in government.

Put it all together and you have a situation where voters find little hope and much pessimism in the political process. Only (26) percent of voters think it is even likely that Congress will successfully address significant issues facing the nation before the next election. Just (17) percent now trust the federal government to do the right thing most or all the time. That hardly sounds like a system where the government enjoys the consent of the governed. In fact, the system has so broken that (27) percent of voters do not think anything would be all that different if Hillary Clinton had won the presidential election in2016, that's why we must change this corrupt system by the Fusion System. Those running for president should focus more on fixing our broken political system and less on making the nation follow a corrupt political system. Tests of party affiliation: Advantages of the open primary regular ballot box, at the same time placing the unmarked tickets in a ballot box reserved for blanks. Under the closed type of direct-primary election, on the other hand, the voter who wishes to take part must send to a test of party affiliation, either sometime prior to, or at the primary itself. These tests differ considerably in kind and in the character of the authorities administering them, as will become explained later, but all of them have one feature in common, namely, that the voter must publicly affiliate himself with one of the political parties engaged in the primaries. Thereupon, he is handed the ballot of that party only.

Voters who have all the qualifications requisite for participation in general elections, but who do not follow the prescribed tests of the closed primary, have not allowed to vote the ballot of any party in the primary election. They may, however, vote nonpartisan primary ballots, if such ballots have become used at the same direct-primary election.

The open primary has the advantage of preserving the secrecy of the voter's party affiliation. This is a matter of considerable importance to many persons who for business, social, or other reasons prefer to keep their party inclinations to themselves. It is easy to condemn such fearful personalities. On the other hand, one should remember that in connection with general elections enormous stress has become placed upon the right of the voter to a secret ballot, and all sorts of complicated devices have been employed to guarantee this right. After a generation of this kind of instruction it is no wonder that has large number of voters resent the tests employed in closed primaries and that a considerable minority of them refuse to comply with such tests, thus, of course, disfranchising themselves as far as primaries are concerned.

Primaries of the open type do not rouse this resentment, nor exclude voters who because of fearfulness or an excess of independence refuse to show their party affiliation.

On the other hand, open primaries suffer from the serious defect that they interpose no barrier to raids made by members of one party upon the primary ballot of another. For example, if a Republican member of Congress who has been a tower of strength to his party comes up for denomination, the Democrats of his district may throw enough votes to his opponent, a weaker and less well-known man, to nominate the last. And, of course, Republicans may interfere with Democratic nominations with equal ease. The temptation to indulge in this sort of guerrilla warfare is particularly strong where, as is often the case, one party, because of lack of candidates, has no important contests on in the primary. while the other party has.

Reference: Voters Rate Political Corruption as America's Biggest Crisis by Scott Rasmussen April 25, 2019, Andrew Harnik, File.

NOMINATIONS AND CORRUPTIONS

American Political Parties History

Politics April 24, 2019 Corruption, Gerrymandering

All these different bits and pieces of the election apparatus in North Carolina have been bent in the favor of entrenchment of one party at the expense of everything else. For months, North Carolina's political framework has become plagued by scandal, a serious case of voter fraud that gave an entire election illegitimate; legal battles over gerrymandered maps and voter ID laws; and corruption implicating top Good-Old-Party' officials. But none of that has come unexpected. The state's electoral system has been slowly sliding the rails over the last decade. In 2010, Republicans won control of the House and Senate in North Carolina, and they have been working to change the Democratic infrastructure of the state ever since.

Reynolds calls their efforts a malignancy, at the center of politics in the state. In late 2016, he wrote an open for the Raleigh News and Observer headlined North Carolina no longer a democracy. Reynolds, who studies international relations, applied models he used for other countries' democratic systems to his own state and found it places us alongside authoritarian states and pseudo-democracies like Cuba, Venezuela, Indonesia and Sierra Leone. He argued that a troublesome voter ID law, arranged fraudulently maps, and the now-infamous latrine bill, which blocked trans-gender people from using the toilet of their choice, added up to a deeply faulty, partly free democracy.

But Reynolds could not have guessed how much worse it could get. When you add all the stuff that I spoke about, and then they steal from the election in the North Carolina 9th District, and then, North Carolina GOP chairperson. Robin Hayes gets indicted for corruption. It's like somebody's making this up as two elections quickly approach, a special congressional election in the fall, and the presidential election after that, the state is being forced into an inflection point. North Carolina has become considered a battleground state for national Democrats who hope to nudge it from purple to blue in 2020. As the state's urban and suburban areas continue to grow, thanks to growing business and technology opportunities there, some politicos are beginning to wonder if that will be enough to finally tip the scales in future elections.

According to a New York Times Magazine story that asked if North Carolina is representative of the future of American politics, seven of the state's 100 counties have accounted for 40 percent of its voter registration growth. Here are the biggest challenges facing North Carolina's voting system. Reference: (By Jacob Rosenberg).

In this respect the open type of direct primary election offers far less protection to party integrity than the old popular caucus. Impersonators, from other parties trying to take part in the latter usually needed sanatorium treatment shortly thereafter. Considering the gravity of this defect in the open type of direct primary election, it is not strange that most states have preferred the closed primary. Such changes as have had made of recent years are also in the latter direction. It cannot become asserted, however, that the closed primary has found a definite solution of the problem of determining party affiliation of voters.

A perfectly working system would have sufficient flexibility to allow voters to pass from one party to the other as issues change or as individual opinions change, and at the same time would prevent the unstable of machine controlled or other voters to the primaries of another party without any intention of supporting the party. It is, however, much easier to tell an ideal of this sort than to realize it in legislation and administration. So far as declarations made by voters with regard to party membership are concerned, they may be reduced to Disadvantages of the open primary Closed primaries generally preferred Cf. the excellent table comparing conditions in 1908 and 1920, in M. McClintock's Party Affiliation Tests in Direct Primary Election Laws. Reference: American Political Science Review, vol. xvi, pp. 465-467 (August 1922). Vermont changed from open to Declarations of voters two main groups: those relating to past allegiance; and (2) those relating to present affiliation or intent. Solutions: The New Electoral Fusion System, Nonpartisan Elections.

PARTIES AND ELECTORAL CORRUPTIONS

American Political Parties History

Political corruption is the use of power by government officials for illegitimate private gain. An illegal act by an officeholder is political corruption only if the act is causally related to their official duties, has done under color of law or involves trading in influence. Forms of corruption vary, but include bribery, extortion, favoritism, discrimination, patronage, implantation, and embezzlement.

Corruption may help criminal enterprise such as drug trafficking, money laundering, and human trading, though not restricted to these activities.

Abuse of government power for other purposes, such as despotism of political opponents and general police brutality, has not considered political corruption. Neither are illegal acts by private persons or corporations not directly involved with the government. The activities that constitute illegal corruption differ depending on the country or authority.

For instance, some political funding practices that are legal in one place may be illegal in another. In some cases, government officials have broad or hostile definite powers, which make it difficult to distinguish between legal and illegal actions.

Worldwide, bribery alone have estimated to involve over one trillion US dollars annually. A state of unrestrained political corruption is known as a Kleptocracy or corrupt leaders, exactly meaning ruling by steals. Some forms of corruption, now called institutional corruption are distinguished from bribery and other kinds of obvious personal gain. Campaign contributions are the prime example.

Even when they are legal, and do not constitute a tradeoff, they tend to prejudice the process in favor of special interests and undermine public confidence in the political institution. They dishonest the institution without individual members being dishonest themselves. A similar problem of corruption arises in any institution that depends on financial support from people who have interests that may conflict with the primary purpose of the institution. Reference: From Wikipedia. https:// en.wikipedia.org/wiki/Kleptocracy.

PARTIES AND ELECTORAL CORRUPTIONS

American Political Parties History

Under the first of these, for example, a voter at the time of registration some weeks before the primary might enroll himself as a Republican. At the primary itself a watcher of that party, suspecting the voter's affiliations to be otherwise, might challenge his vote. Whereupon the challenged party would become needed to take oath that at the preceding general election he had cast his ballot for a majority at least of the candidates of the party with which he had declared himself affiliated. However, party watchers are loath to interfere under these circumstances. In most cases they do not know what the motives of the voters are afraid that a challenge at the hands of a watcher of the party he has just embraced may drive him back to the opposition party in the general election.

No doubt the test as to earlier affiliation works satisfactorily in the case of persons of nice moral principles. Unfortunately, not all the voters wishing to take part in closed primaries belong to that category. In any event, deceitful under oath in this connection is safe from legal penalties for the simple reason that at the preceding, as at all general, elections the ballot was secret.

Obviously, a pledge about a voter's present affiliation or future intention is equally valueless for the same reason. It should not become indirect that personal motives are consciously wicked in the case of all those who make a change in their enrollment contrary to the kind of vote cast in the preceding general election. References: McClintock, op. (it., notes the following subdivisions and the number of states* employing each in 1920.

NOMINATIONS AND CORRUPTIONS
American Political Parties History

A point of considerable practical importance takes part in the designation of the authority which formulates the formulating trial of party affiliation. Under earlier direct-primary party tests election laws it was more common to place such powers in the hands of the political party itself. In the Southern states this enabled the dominant party to exclude negroes from its primaries, and hence from any effective political action, since a nomination is virtually equivalent to election in these states.

Between 1908 and 1920, however, seven states out of the fourteen having regulations of this character withdrew the power to formulate tests of affiliation from the political party. At present thirty-one states vest it in the legislature, and six others divide it between the legislature and the party. Less objectionable than the various tests noted above would be to a form of declaration that within a prescribed kind of interval the voter had not took part in the primary election of another party.

Reinforced by an adequate system of party registration, this would effectually prevent capricious or dishonest changes of party affiliation. But such a solution is open to three important objections: First, it interposes too rigid a barrier to the prompt redistribution of voters among the parties in response to a sudden change in the dominant party issues.

Secondly, it tends to prevent a different party affiliation in federal and in local politics in response to differences in the attitudes of parties toward federal and local issues. Thirdly, it tends to encourage an unnatural concentration of voters of divergent political sympathies in the primary of a dominant party.

The tendency of the establishment by law of an effective test of party affiliation is, therefore, to perpetuate obsolete party divisions, to confuse distinct party issues, to undermine minority party organizations, to divide majority party establishments. References: A. N. Holcombe, Direct Primaries, and the Second Ballot. dm. Pol. Scu Rev., vol. v, pp. 535-55 (Nov. 1911). Solutions: To this corruption is The New Electoral Fusion System, Nonpartisan Elections.

Tendency of recent primary legislation to give to a minority of voters, namely, the dominant faction within the dominant party, a disproportionate influence upon the result of elections. Confronted by this political contradiction, the general tendency of recent legislation is toward the more strictly closed primary, and the introduction of increased difficulties in the way of a voter who wishes to change his party affiliation. In practice, however, no direct primary has absolutely closed. All that can become said is that change of party affiliation is much more difficult in some cases than in others.

Apart from the South the states fall into two groups on this point. First, those which are more populous and urban, Eastern, which keep stringent party tests by law or tradition. Secondly, those less populous and inner-city, primarily Western, North-central, or mountainous states, where party ties sit more loosely and whereby law or by practice primaries tend to become open. In states of the last named group a marked disintegration of parties is taking place and groups such as the Nonpartisan League political organization founded in 1915, and today Fusion no partisan System is not related to that organization due that present Fusion have no affiliation to any party and is not a party, is just an Electoral system.

That no partisan group are able at times to play a dominant role. all the states having the direct primary election system provide that nomination for certain kinds of offices shall be made by a Fusion Electoral System primary. This has held at the same time as the party primary. It differs from the latter, however, in that the ballots used have no party designation whatever. The candidates whose names appear on nonpartisan primary ballots nominated by petition as in the case of candidates on the party primary ballot Nonpartisan primaries A. N. Holcombe, op. cit. The undermining of minority party organizations is particularly clear in a state like Pennsylvania. Thus, in the writer's district with a Republican enrollment of (831) and a Democratic enrollment of (113), the average vote for Democratic candidates in a recent election was (234). This would show that slightly more than half of the Democratic party's strength locally enrolled and takes part in the primaries of the majority party. For a thorough survey on this and other points.

References: R. S. Boots, The Trend of the Direct Primary, Am. Pol. Sci. Rev., vol. xvi, pp. 412-431 (Aug. 1922). Ray, Recent Primary and Election Laws, ibid. vol. xiii, pp. 264-274 (May 1919). Solutions: To this corruption is The New Electoral Fusion System, Nonpartisan Elections system.

NOMINATIONS AND ELECTORAL NO PARTISAN SYSTEM.

American Political Parties History

Also, at the primary election itself qualified voters may receive and vote nonpartisan ballots regardless of whether they have met the tests prescribed for participation in a party primary. The purpose of the nonpartisan primary is, of course, to reduce this narrow-mindedness to a minimum in the making of nominations to certain offices which because of their nature it has felt should become kept free from this influence.

In municipalities the tendency has been strongly in favor of this form of nomination. Judicial and school offices have also commonly placed on a nonpartisan primary ballot. In Minnesota it has even used in connection with members of the legislature.

The names of the two candidates receiving the highest votes in such primaries have placed on a nonpartisan ballot, also, as its name implies, without party designation of any kind, for the general election. The success of this device depends upon the degree of independence and intelligence of the communities in which it is employed. Unquestionably the nonpartisan ballot, whether used in primaries, makes a stronger demand upon the intelligence of voters than the partisan ballot.

In fact, groups form behind the so-called nonpartisan candidates both in the primary and general elections, which are parties in all but name. In those states or cities where the organization is strongly entrenched, it is usually able to pass the word to a sufficient number of its ruler henchmen prepaid to engage in crime or dishonesty to secure the nomination and election of those candidates who have been placed upon the nonpartisan ballot at its request. To make it clear Fusion has no political machinery, for ended is not a party and do not recommends any candidates, they are nominated by an application in the Fusion Electoral Tribunal.

One of the arguments urged most strongly in favor of the direct primary election system was that under its aspirants for nomination would be more many than under the convention system. Also, often under the latter it was machineries of the nonpartisan primary. On the actual workings of the direct primary in various states, Reference: C. Kettteborough on Indiana, Nat. Mutt. Rev., vol. x, p. 166 (1921); F. E.,

PARTIES AND ELECTORAL NOPARTISAN SYSTEM

American Political Parties History

Greater number of candidates under direct primary perfectly well known that only those persons who had secured in advance the approval of the Boss had any chance to get a place on the ticket. overall, this argument in favor of the direct primary has justified itself in practice. At times there is an excess of candidates.

Thus in 1921 a Philadelphia primary ballot had the names of (218) competitors for eleven nominations to the office of magistrate. In general, there is seldom any shortage of candidates for desirable offices on the primary ballots of parties which have a fair chance of success in the general election.

At the Illinois primary of 1916 there were from one to eighteen candidates for each office on the Democratic ticket, and from two to seventeen on the Republican ticket. Ordinarily, however, the average number of candidates for each nomination does not exceed two or three.

On the tickets of minority parties there will often no contests, only one name presented for each nomination. This condition manages the tendency noted above, on the part of members of minority parties to enroll and take part in the primaries of the dominant party.

Frequently the primary ballots of the Prohibition, Communist, and other smaller minority parties left blank as far as names of candidates are concerned, except for a few prominent statewide offices.

In such cases enrolled voters of these parties may write in the names of candidates under the titles of the various offices.

With more than two aspirants in a primary it must frequent devices frequently happen under the generally accepted plurality rule, prevent that the nomination is carried off by a candidate who has behind him less than a majority of the votes of his party, presentations to remedy this condition various devices have been employed if only one name written in under such circumstances, it goes on the ballot for the general election as the official candidate of the party for that office. Of course, under these circumstances 'candidates belonging to the majority parties often try to capture the nomination of a minority party in addition to that of their own. Thus, it may happen that a notoriously wet Democrat secures a place on the prohibit blanks in minority party ballots Horack, Primary Election} in Iowa; Millspaugh, Party.

In the New Fusion Electoral System, this ballot is irrelevant, there are only: (7) seven Presidential candidates (3) three candidates per states for officer's administration's position, peoples elect states and cites officials and the officials will be representing the voters, to elect the President in the presidential election, there will be no political parties involved in the election.

References: Organization and Machinery in Michigan; N. H. Debel, Direct Primary in Nebraska; R. S. Boots, New Jersey, Direct Primaries; and nominations.

NOMINATIONS AND CORRUPTIONS PROBLEMS
American Political Parties History

Nomination ticket or a notoriously capitalistic Republican on the Socialist ticket. With more than two aspirants in a primary it must frequent devices frequently happen under the generally accepted plurality rule, prevent that the nomination is carried off by a candidate who has behind him less than a majority of the votes of his party, presentations to remedy this condition various devices have been employed. circumstances' candidates belonging to the majority parties often try to capture the nomination of a minority party in addition to that of In a few states the preferential system of voting is employed by that office. Of-course, under these circumstances' candidates belonging to the majority parties frequently try to capture the nomination of a minority party in addition to that of nomination ticket or a notoriously capitalistic Republican on the Socialist ticket decision inconclusive, and nominations made by the state convention. A few other states once had similar percentage plans but have abandoned them for an ordinary plurality requirement.

Experience shows that where there is a sharp division upon a question of principle the number of candidates will be small and the contest is likely to resolve itself into a struggle between two of them. But if the battle is a personal contest between individuals with no principles at issue, there is no great harm done by allowing the one receiving the highest vote to take the nomination. However, the most widely accepted device of this kind is the double primary which has been adopted either by party rule or by law in Florida, Georgia, Louisiana, Maryland, Mississippi, North Carolina, Tennessee, and Texas.4 In these states there is a first or free-for-all primary, open, that is, to all aspirants who have secured the required number of signatures to their petitions. For legal texts. Reference: Ala., L. 1915, No. 78; Idaho, L. 1909, p. 196. 8 See pp. 443-44; American Yearbook, 1915, p. 86, and of the Wisconsin law, ibid., 1912, p. 69. 8 C. E. Merriam, The American Party System, p. 268.

PARTIES AND ELECTORAL CORRUPTIONS

American Political Parties History

This is decisive in the case of nominations to offices if any aspirant receives a clear majority vote. In the case of other offices there is a second, or run off, primary to decide between the two candidates who received the highest votes in the disorganized fight ballot. Of course, this plan involves a great deal of extra trouble and expense, but it does place a majority vote behind the party nominees. In the states where it is employed this is a matter of more than usual importance because nomination by the Democratic party is virtually equivalent to election.

Taking advantage of provisions for the formation of new parties or for running as independents, candidates who have become defeated in the primary of their own party sometimes secure a place on the ballot for the ensuing general election. Naturally, they have censured as brawl fight by their successful rivals and former party associates.

In a few states the direct primary election laws have recently become amended to prohibit such candidacies. Thus, Kentucky makes any candidate defeated in the primary ineligible for the same office during the same year; Maryland, Oregon, and California forbid a candidate of this kind to become the candidate of any party or to run as an independent; and Indiana has provided that the name of an independent candidate may not be printed on the general election ballot unless he shall have filed his declaration thirty days before the primary.

Another argument often urged in favor of direct, primary elections is that they bring out a better class of candidates and so a higher type of public officials. That they have increased the number of aspirants there can be no doubt, but among these are always some who are without organized support and hence are not really in the running. 198.

However, this seldom happened unless the machine expects type of candidates under direct primary a sound drubbing at the hands of the voters because of its recent misdeeds. It argued that men of this type, particularly those whose eminence has expanded in other fields than politics, will not thrust themselves? Under the old convention system men of high type had sometimes appointed by the machine without the necessity of any effort on their part. forward and make the fight necessary to gain a nomination at a primary election. Can someone explain me why this brain wiling none sense; Cal. L. 1921, chap. 710; Ind. L. 1921, chap. Reference: S. Boots, op. cit., K.y. L. 1920, chap. 156; Md. L. 1922, chap. 399; Ore. L. 1921, chap. 4

THE OLD CONVENTION

CHAPTER 24

NOMINATIONS AND CORRUPTIONS PROBLEMS.

American Political Parties History

Opinions differ about this point. Secretary Charles E. Hughes takes it very seriously, but Professor Merriam regards it as a pleasant fiction without much basis in the facts of political life. In the absence of accepted standards of measurement to Occasional determine political ability and virtue it is, of course, in primary possible to prove that the direct primary election system.

Over' the has produced candidates of superior type. Certainly, its machine debars no politician capable of cutting a figure in the old-time caucus or convention. And it gives great advantage to the smooth man who is willing to spend money in making himself known, or to the aspirant who keeps himself much in the public eye, regardless of the way in which he gets himself there.

It must, though, be conceded that, given a popular revolt against the machine of sufficient magnitude, it is possible to break the bill of the last in the primary election even when it is so completely in control of the party machinery that under the old convention system it could dictate every nomination on the ticket. Such events happen only occasionally, as in the 1922 primaries of Indiana when Beveridge was nominated for the Senate, and of Pennsylvania in the same year, when Pinchot was nominated for Governor.

However, the possibility of such unfortunate events induces to a certain restraint on the part of political bosses that is doubtless salutary. overall, this is the greatest distinct advantage that can claimed for direct primary elections after twenty years 'experience with them. Of course, if the electorate is quiescent, party organizations find it easily post Cf. pamphlet on.

Reference: The Direct Primary, published by the National Municipal League, 1921, pp. 5, 14. W. B. Munro, Government of American Cities, p. 134.

PARTIES AND ELECTORAL CORRUPTIONS PROBLEMS

American Political Parties History

The Boss and the direct political-primary Bible to secure the nomination of their schedules under the direct primary election system. In one party bosses have said to find a certain satisfaction in direct primary elections. Under the old convention system, prospective candidates knew that their chance of success depended entirely upon the word of the boss. If that word were not forthcoming, they made as much trouble for him as they could. Under the direct primary election system many candidates still eagerly seek the approval of the Boss.

He may tell those to whom he is in reality opposed that he has nothing to do with nominations, that everything is in the hands of the people under the direct primary election system, and that, of course, if they wish to try it, they have the same right to do so as anybody else. Nevertheless, he may use his influence quietly and often successfully for his friends in the primary. If afterward there is any accusation from disgruntled aspirants the boss tells them not to blame him, but the people who manage their defeat.

Direct primary elections are sufficiently simple and open in their methods to encourage active participation by the ordinary people of party members. Undoubtedly, they bring out a vote heavier by far than have ever registered under the old popular caucus system. Even in dull primaries from (25) to (55) per cent of the party vote has polled. In hot fights the participation runs from (55) to (85) per cent. Of course, objection have made to direct primary elections on the ground that only a minority may nominate even under the most favorable circumstances.

Thus with (85) per cent participation and only two aspirants, the successful one needs only (43) per cent of the party enrollment to win. However, few, if any, nominations have made under the old convention system that could claim to have become supported by anything approaching this percentage of party strength.

Further it should become remembered that a considerable element in all parties is indifferent. Voters of this kind pre-Vote in direct primaries fear to let others make nominations, reserving to themselves the right to reject any or all candidates of the party in the general election. It must be remembered also that under the direct primary system every vote counts directly for every office on the ballot from governor to tax assessor, whereas in the old popular caucus it counted directly only for a handful of local offices and indirectly through the hierarchy of delegate conventions for offices of greater importance.

Reference: P. O. Ray, op. clt., p. 148; C. E. Metriam, op. tit., p., American Political Parties History

NOMINATIONS AND CORRUPTIONS PROBLEMS
American Political Parties History

The direct primary election system applies the same method to all nominations made under it, and in this respect, it is simpler than the convention system. Finally, under the old convention system an unsubstantiated candidate might become presented soundlessly in such a way as to carry off the nomination at the last-minute. Under the direct primary this time damaged fake of political jockey-ism is impossible. On the other hand, the direct primary election system defects of suffers from certain obvious defects. Where it is so commonly, the direct gather that all conventions have abolished, no party authority still is which is capable of drafting platforms.

If conventions have supported, it may happen that they have dominated by a faction hostile to-the candidates nominated in the direct primary elections. Of course, in such cases the candidates may formulate and at times have formulated and proclaimed their own platforms, but the situation is an awkward one, nevertheless. Also, under the direct primary election system it may happen that majority of the party offices have secured by members of a faction hostile to candidates.

As a result, the last must either accept support of party officials whom they distrust or improvise a campaign organization of their own. It has become suggested that this difficulty might become removed by allowing candidates to appoint Balanced tickets their own campaign managers. an attempt was made to formulate paramount issues in national, state, and county affairs, summarizing each of them in eight words upon the ballot used in primary elections, but this portion of the law was re-pealed in 1921.

References: The Richards law in South Dakota (L. 1917, Ch. 234) (L. 1921, Chaps. 329, 331), American Political Parties History.

PARTIES AND ELECTORAL CORRUPTIONS

American Political Parties History

Balanced tickets, created on July13, 2019 in Brooklyn, NY., their own campaign managers doubtless this would work as well as it does in national elections, if the candidates agreed among themselves, but under the direct primary election system easily possible that the candidates may represent bitterly opposed factions.

Of course, similar cases of internal conflict occurred under the old convention system, but they were less likely because the party which dominated the convention not only nominated the candidates, but also wrote the platform and chose the party officials who were to manage the campaign. Party conventions also resulted in the nomination of a well-balanced ticket, that is, one with candidates representing the various geographical sections of the district and even more important industrial, racial, and religious elements of the party.

Unworthy bargains may have become accomplished in connection with such arrangements, but on the other hand, considerations of ability, party service, and party welfare must have become considered. The point is that the direct primary election system supplies no facilities for producing a balanced ticket. It may result in the success of a single narrow party and the nomination of a ticket leaving large sections of the district and essential elements in the electorate out of consideration. Of course, since all parties run under the same primary election law, each of them is equally exposed to this danger.

Opponents of direct primaries originally made a great deal of the argument that they would unduly favor the mass vote of cities as against the widely scattered rural vote, but as a rule this has not been the case. In many ways the old convention system worked for lures of the party integration and harmony. It supported periodical meetings between leaders and active party workers from all parts of the county, district, state, or nation.

No hesitation leaders and delegates alike at such meetings were more interested in projects for the division of the political multiplication of loaves-and-fishes, referred to the patronage-winning papers of his party, presumably than in the higher issues of statecraft, but at least they met one another face to face and formed per social cold convocational relationships of esteem and cooperation. Even today it is impossible to talk to a politician of the old school without noting the vivid and pleasant, one might al-most say sentimental, memories he retains of his convention experiences.

As predictable, some conventions were thundery activities, making it necessary for the members of the dominant faction to throw out, in the literal sense of the word, their opponents. In general, surprisingly little permanent resentment resulted from these struggles. A year later former antagonists might be working shoulder to shoulder, or the dominant faction of the earlier fight, now in a minority, might find itself thrown out in its turn. And no matter which side won there was a clear-cut decision. The argument which has used with the greatest force and effectiveness against the direct primary election system is the heavy burden which it imposes upon both the public imposed by purse and the private purses of candidates.

The state forced to pay for extra registration in advance of the primary, for the printing of primary ballots, the rent of polling places, and the salaries of election officials. And the successful candidate has obliged to fight two campaigns, one for nomination, the other for election. In the first of these he stands not as the representative of the party, but as a personal aspirant.

If he wins at the primary, he may expect some support out of the party funds for his final campaign. But it is manifestly improper to use party funds to advance the interests of any candidate in the primary, and in some states, it has specifically forbidden by law. Of course, a candidate may form a personal campaign committee and receive financial help from it. In general, primary to however, the tendency is to look to the candidate for a candidate large part of the money needed for his primary campaign.

The laws of several states, mostly in the South where direct primary elections are conducted under party control, empower the party authorities to collect fees from candidates sufficient in amount to pay some portion at least of the cost of the primary. Thus, in Alabama party authorities may make assessments upon candidates not to exceed (4) per cent of the first year's salary of the office sought, nor more than ($35) in the case of payment of offices.

Reference: Cf. N. Y. L. 1911, chap. 891; 1913, chap. 820.

PARTIES AND ELECTORAL CORRUPTIONS

American Political Parties History

In Nevada fees varying from ($12.50) for candidates for the legislature to ($100) for United States Senator may be collected. This relieves the state treasury, of course, but it does so by transferring the weight to the candidates. However, the trend of primary legislation is toward the payment of all common costs out of public funds. Advantages small towns and districts the financial problem imposed to candidates upon candidates under the direct primary election system, large campaign is not great enough to determine from entering the primary campaign funds marry.

If allowed under the law the first of these alternatives. But in larger cities or states one may expect to make little headway unless he is able either to contribute large sums from his private funds, or can count upon contributions considerable has the aggregated from persons or interests friendly to his candidacy is objectionable because it means that millionaires with political ambition enjoy an enormous advantage under the direct primary election system. Some of the most offensive political scandals of recent date are cases in point.

The second alternative is objectionable because it may mean, that the poor man obtains his success in the primary only by silently pledging his future official conduct to the interests which have financed his campaign. Of course, candidates under the old convention system have often compelled to contribute or raise considerable sums to secure nomination, although the absence of publicity laws at the time leaves us without definite figures as to amounts thus exacted.

No doubt the money has sometimes used to bribe delegates. One of the arguments in favor of the direct primary election system was that while you could buy a nomination from a convention you could not buy it from the whole electorate of the state. However, largescale corruption has been employed to obtain nominations within the gift of the people. Further, the direct primary election system indisputably opens the way to the disbursement of much larger sums than have needed under the delegate convention system for per-primary campaigns of education, or rather of advertisement, and for other purposes not in themselves corrupt.

NOMINATIONS AND CORRUPTIONS PROBLEMS

American Political Parties History

In conclusion, it needs a much larger amount of effort on the part of political workers and leaders, and to that extent makes such services even more essential than they were before. The massive amount and detail of corrupt practices acts applying to direct primary elections give testimony eloquent as to the difficulty of this problem.

Throughout the last few years' outbreaks have become made upon direct primary elections in many states. Enemies of the party system ascribe this hostile movement to the deficiencies which it has shown in practice. Its friends assert that the movement is a conspiracy of discontented machine politicians looking to recover the power they had under the old convention system. Some encouragement has given to the outbreaks upon direct primaries by the administration at Washington, and the movement occurred in so many sections of the country and on an enough scale to become described as nationwide. Nor has it been without results, for conventions have been restored to a large degree in New York and Idaho.

However, the direct primary has windswept the tempest. Between 1919 and 1922 bills to repeal the direct primary law were introduced on one or more occasions in eight states, but all failed with the exceptions noted above. Bills designed to restore the convention specifically Preprimary campaigns of advertisement Recent attacks upon the direct primary.

Reference: New York L. 1921, chap. 479; L. 1919, chap. 107. In New York, write« R. S. Boots, op. eit.,1 R. S. Boots, The Direct Primary Weathers the Storm, Nat, Mun. Rev., vol. x, pp. 328-324. (June 1921).

Direct primary weathers the storm 263.

PARTIES AND ELECTORAL CORRUPTIONS

American Political Parties History

Elections primary laws unlikely for minor state offices were also introduced in ten states, and none was successful. In Montana an act of 1919 to restore conventions for the nomination of certain officers was referred to popular vote by the legislature and defeated by 77,549 to 60,483.1 The primary conditions the tempest and annul of draws referred to popular vote by the legislature and defeated by 77,549 to 60,483.1 And in Nebraska an act of the same general character was beaten by a referendum vote of 133,115 to 49,410 On the whole, there is little immediate likelihood of the sweeping repeal of direct primary election laws. Despite the heavy burdens and manifest defects of this method of making nominations, it keeps the support of a large part of the people as a functional means of beating the machine at least occasionally.

Presidential preference primaries, which will become discussed later, have shown themselves so ineffective, however, that abandonment may occur in that field. But there is not the slightest prospect of a return to the old and thoroughly discredited system of unregulated popular caucuses and conventions. Even if other states should follow the lead of New York and Idaho in restoring conventions for more important offices, they will, as these two states did, surround the processes of conventions with many legal safeguards designed to insure fairness and openness, and further, they will provide for the election of delegates to such conventions in direct-primary elections also regulated by law so as to prevent the abuses of the old popular committee.

If the direct primary system is to remain for the present, as seems likely, what means may be taken to improve its operation? Since in so many primary elections resemble general elections, it is obvious that reforms which would work well in connection with the latter should prove applicable also to the former. Outstanding among such reforms is the short ballot,

NOMINATIONS AND CORRUPTIONS PROBLEMS.

American Political Parties History

Reforms in other political fields, as, for example, the merit system, should have a beneficent reaction upon both general and primary elections. Also, it is evident that many states, especially those which enacted direct primary laws several years ago might do well to revise them in the light of the experience gained by more progressive states. We are, however, sadly in need of an adequate scholarly survey of that experience. Such a survey would be a task of colossal size which could be performed successfully only by cooperative effort.

One proposal for reform has been brought forward repeatedly by theorists, practical politicians, and officials, that of a preprimary recommending resolution. This would permit party commission person regularly chosen at the preceding election to make designations from the list of those who had filed nominating positions, in other words, to put a regular ticket in the field prior to the date of the primary election. If the party ordinary people accepted this ticket, no election need become held, thus saving a great deal of expense and trouble.

If opposition developed, independent designations could become made, and a decision reached in the ordinary way at the primary election. It is unlikely that such contests would be many. As a result, the primary ballot could become shortened, a consummation devoutly to become wished. On the other hand, independent candidates who forced a decision at the primary would no doubt become denounced by the regulars as party rebels.

According to a recent writer, the pre-primary conference plan seems to possess other advantages, as follows: It would permit effective party conference; it would secure the choice of committee members by, and their responsibility to, the full party vote.

Reference: C. E. Merriam, Recent Tendencies in Primary Election Systems, Nat. Mun. Rev., vol. x, pp. 87-94 (Feb.,1921).2 Recommended by Charles E. Hughes when governor of New York, P. O. Ray, op cit., p. 144. The Fate of the Direct Primary, Nat. Mun. Rev., vol. x, pp.3-31 (Jan., 1g).

Pre-primary recommending conventions.

PARTIES AND ELECTORAL CORRUPTIONS

American Political Parties History

On New York and Colorado plans Nominations by petition irresponsible organization in many states, and permit an enrolling of candidates in the states where now everything is left to the self-advertisers; it would not lessen the opportunity which the primary now affords, of combating objectionable candidacies and reducing the organization to submission. While much can be said in favor of the above plan, the New York law of 1911, since revoked, went too far in its provisions for preprimary meetings and designations. It gave candidates selected by regular party committees a preferential place on the primary ballot and authorized them to use the party emblem, thus favoring unduly the organization and opening the way to straight-ticket voting.

A more promising plan have introduced in Colorado, where representative party assemblies Have held and all aspirants receiving (10) per cent of the vote thereof become official party candidates in the primary.

Unquestionably, however, there is a growing conviction among authorities on the subject that tries to reform the direct primary election system will result primarily in adding to its problems and complexity.

Various suggestions have become made looking to the substitution for it of something simpler, less costly, and more effective. Among these suggestions, nomination by petition has become widely discussed.

This plan takes two forms, according to the number of signatures required for a place on the ballot used in the general election. The first aims to prevent a multitude of candidates by the requirement of many signers. Thus, in Boston any voter may appear upon the municipal ballot as a candidate for mayor by filing nomination papers with (5,000) signatures, and as candidate for the city council or the school committees by filing nomination papers with (2,500) signatures.

This plan does not restrict the race to the two strongest candidates. It gives a chance to every large group in the city to make its nominations. But it has not put an end to the preliminary caucus and it suffers from all the abuses and waste of effort apparently inherent in the collection of large numbers of signatures, the Fusion System, purpose consist in select Officers to represent the voters in a Presidential Election. Reference: R. S. Boots, op. cit., p. 431.

This is the fusion idea of Democracy-Republic System

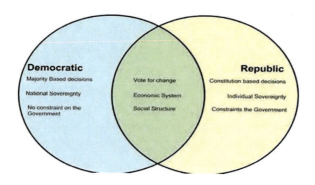

NOMINATIONS AND CORRUPT ELECTORAL SYSTEM.

American Political Parties History

The second form of nomination by petition, sometimes referred to as the free nomination system, proposes to nomination throw open the ballot for use in the general election to all system persons whose names are proposed by a very small number of electors. This system has produced excellent results in England and in several of her self-governing colonies. For parliamentary candidacy all that had now required is a nomination petition in writing signed by a proposer, seconder, and eight others, all registered voters. Moreover, if only one candidate has proposed for a seat, he has forthwith declared elected. In general, parliamentary elections from one fourth to one third of the candidates and in a community and district council elections even larger proportions have thus returned unopposed.

There are many reasons for the shortage of candidates in England. Parliamentary candidates have obliged the system to deposit in advance a sum of money which may amount in England to from five hundred to a thousand pounds, to pay the expenses of the election. If in the later poll a candidate receives one eighth of the votes, his money have returned to him; if not, he loses it forever. Elective office holders have paid exceptionally low salaries or none. There is no patronage to distribute. There is no hierarchy of offices, local, county, state, and national, as in the United States, to encourage candidate is eager for future advancement. Other traditional and social reasons peculiar to England discourage political ambition in large classes of the people. In the United States most of these limitations do no poll existed.

Reference: A. L. Lowell, Government of England, vol. ii, pp. 46-56. Democratic way.

PARTIES ELECTORAL SYSTEM AND CORRUPTIONS

American Political Parties History

In the United States the ambition to hold public office is widespread. Overall, it is well. For an admirable discussion of this topic. In the Fusion Electoral System is less complex and operative, because, first in the Fusion

Electoral System is less complex and operative, because, first there are no political party in this system, second the selected Officers will represent the voters to chosen the new President. Other workable solutions that this is the case, although at times thoroughly unfit men manage to get themselves nominated and chose. Also, Americans seem to be more willing to stand up and take a political beating, although, of course, there are many more ways of deriving advantage even from defeat in this country than in England. Apart from the motives influencing candidacies in the two countries, however, it is undeniable that the comparatively large number of signatures required under our existing primary-election laws does not prevent an excess of candidates in many instances.

If we were to reduce our requirement to the English standard of ten names only, and, further, if we were to eliminate the necessity of fighting for a decision in a primary election, it seems probable that we would be overwhelmed with candidates, at least for all desirable offices. Our ballots, already too long for discriminating voting, would become uncontrollable. Nomination by petition, whether with a large or a small number of signatures, so, offers no perfect solution to the problem proposed by direct primary elections. There stays, however, one further possibility.

With few or comparatively few nominations, the primary election might become eliminated and decision made in a final election held under the privileged voting system, or, better still, under the single transferable vote system of proportional representation. These voting systems will become explained later. Suffice it to say here that both of them provide methods whereby if no candidate receives a majority of the voters' first choices, which, of course, would elect him in any event, the second or third choices of voters are canvassed until a decision is reached presumably representing the major choice of the electorate. The single transferable vote system of proportional representation arranges for the ascertainment of the will of the voters with a precision which seems to cover every shade of preference which could be brought out in two elections, one primary, the other now being made along this line in a number of cities should prove successful, we may be able to substitute for the direct-primary election system not something just by means of good, but something better, simpler, and cheaper. general. By doing so it saves an enormous amount of trouble and expense, in the New Electoral System have all requirements you are looking for. Amusing me how we still are politically attached to the colonial Monarchy Elections System, when basically what we have to do is abolishing the election trough political party system, when my Fusion Electoral System will be basically simple, and effective free of corruptions, and political struggles.

NATIONAL CONVENTIONS AND NOMINATIONS CORRUPTION

American Political Parties History

If the experiments Meanwhile it is well to remember that if once in a dozen years the direct-primary prevents the capture of a city or a state by the machine, the resultant money saving alone, leaving moral values wholly out of the calculation, may amount to much more than the cost of primaries during the whole period.

As originally adopted, the Constitution of the United Constitution States devoted less than one hundred words to the method of choosing a President. It was the sincere hope of the president Fathers Founders that parties would play no part in the process thus briefly formulated, but rather that men of high standing and wide vision would be appointed presidential electors and left free to select from among the country's greatest statesmen the one best fitted to be chief magistrate.

Even with the addition of the amendment the Constitution tells us comparatively little of the actual process of President making. It does support three steps: (I) the choice of electors; (2) the voting by electors; and (3) the counting of the votes. Of these, however, the second and third have become mere formalities, while the first has preceded and determined by an enormous amount of party effort culminating in the national conventions and continued at white heat throughout the subsequent campaign. And until quite recently the structures and forces engaged in this work were outside the purview of the constitution and the laws, having been developed solely under party rules and traditions.

The first formal steps preliminary to the national congress Democratic-Conventions of the two great parties are taken at meetings preliminary to their respective national committees in January of a conventions presidential year or in December of the preceding year. Usually the sessions of these committees are held in Washington to meet the convenience of members holding congressional or other federal offices. The principal matters of business coming before the meetings are (I) fixing the date This first farewell address, from our only really independent president in American History, he distinguishes guidelines back to an age when distrust of political divisions was perhaps higher than it is now, and suggestions of a solution to what troubles us today. As President Washington, Fusion is of the same conclusion, we are demanding for the exclusion of all political parties in United States and come back when there was no a political party in the two terms of the Commander in Chief George Washington.

PARTIES AND ELECTORAL CORRUPTIONS

American Political Parties History

For the last thirty years the Republicans have fixed dates falling between June 7th and 21st of the presidential year for the opening of their convention, the Democrats following with dates from one to three weeks later. In 1888 the Democratic convention have held two weeks earlier than the Republican.

With this exception the Republican convention has preceded the Democratic in every campaign year from 1864 to 1920, inclusive. The course pursued by the former is bolder and gives them the dubious advantage of a longer campaign period. By their more cautious policy the Democrats stand to profit from any errors or omissions occurring in the convention of their adversaries. Before deciding upon the place for holding the convention the National Committee gives a hearing to delegations of prominent politicians and businesspeople coming from all the cities which want that honor.

Spokespeople chosen by each of these delegations recite in glowing terms the advantages of their respective cities. Immunity from the heat common to other American cities in June and July had promised by one orator for the very good reason, as he averred, that we do not keep that kind of weather. Members of the committee are, of course, not moved by such elocutionary effervescence.

They are intent upon the solid advantages offered by large cities located as near the center of population as possible, and possessing adequate hotel accommodations, excellent railway connections with all sections of the country, and an auditorium colossal enough to seat delegates, alternates, and the vast crowds which flock to the sessions of the convention. It is desirable also that the city should have several daily papers of metropolitan circulation, some of which should be favorably inclined to the party holding the convention. Political influence upon a doubtful section or pivotal state may become considered.

NOT ONE NOR THE OTHER

NATIONAL CONVENTIONS AND ELECTORAL CORRUPTIONS
American Political Parties History

Finally, but by no means least in importance, is the size of the financial guaranty toward the expenses of the convention or the party funds offered by each of the competing cities. Money talks, and B-S walk, it said, and a sum more than $100,000 have become pledged for such purposes, mainly from business men who expect to reap a profit from convention hordes.

Prior to the Civil War Baltimore was the favorite privileged of the national convention city. But with the western movement of population Chicago has distanced all competitors. From 1864 to 1920, inclusive, thirteen conventions, nine Republican and four Democratic, have become held in that city.

St. Louis ranks second with one Republican and four Democratic conventions, and Baltimore third with one Republican and two Democratic conventions during the same period. Other convention cities since 1864 are as follows: Philadelphia, two Republican conventions; Cincinnati, one Republican, one Democratic; New York and Minneapolis, one Republican each; Kansas City, Denver, and San Francisco, one Democratic each. The most surprising choice of recent years was that of San Francisco by the Democrats in 1920. Included in the call for the convention issued by the Ca]1 f h Democratic National Committee is a statement of the number of delegates to which each state and territory had authorized.

The Republican call, goes into some-what greater detail, prescribing in general terms the process by which and the period within which delegates are to become chosen, the forwarding of their credentials to the secretary of the National Committee, and outlining the procedure in the case of contesting delegations. For an actual discussion of these points by the Democratic National Committee, Jan. 8, 1920, resulting in the choice of San Francisco. Reference: Official Report of the Democratic National Convention, 1920, appendix, pp. 548-566.

PARTIES AND ELECTORAL CORRUPTIONS
American Political Parties History

Apportionment of delegates reservation of the South in Republican conventions in state and minor conventions, as has already had noted, delegates were apportioned among the districts according to the strength of the party vote in each. Until a quite recent date, on the other hand, apportionment of delegates to national conventions has been based upon the size of the total representation of each state in Congress.

Prior to 1852 the number of delegates to national conventions from each state was usually equal to the number of its Senators and Representatives. From 1852 to the present time in the case of the Democratic party, and from 1860 to 1916 in that of the Republican, the number of delegates of the total congressional representation of each state.

From 1852 to 1872 each delegate in Democratic conventions had one half vote. Since 1872 in Democratic conventions and since 1860 in Republican conventions each delegate has had one vote. As an occasional exception half votes had still recorded in the national conventions of the two great parties. Usually this is because contesting delegations coming from a few states are both seated, each member of such delegations become given one-half vote. In addition to the delegates from the states there were in the Democratic national convention of 1920, delegates from the Canal Zone and six delegates from each of the following: Alaska, District of Columbia, Hawaii, and Puerto Rico.

The present rule of the Republican party its regard to delegates from the District of Columbia outlying possessions will become found below. Party strength had distributed equally throughout the country this rule would have worked satisfactorily. But such was far from being the case, particularly with the Republican party.

For example, in the 1912 convention of that party, Georgia, which had cast only 41,692 Republican votes in the preceding presidential election, had entitled to twenty-eight delegates, whereas Iowa with 275,210 Republican votes in 1908, had entitled to only twenty-six dele-gates.

Similarly, four others Southern states, Alabama, Louisiana, Mississippi, and South Carolina, with a total Republican vote of 42,592, had eighty-two delegates, while Pennsylvania with a Republican vote of 745,779 had only seventy-six.

NATIONAL CONVENTIONS ELECTORAL CORRUPTIONS.
American Political Parties History

This monstrous disproportion was made even more Reform glaring by the fact that the states favored under it were proposals almost never found in the Republican column when the electoral vote was counted.

And the practical danger of the situation had enhanced because of the notorious subservience of Southern Republican delegates to Republican administration influence in Washington or to corruptions acting in the interests of certain candidates.

As early as 1883, the matter came up for discussion before the Republican National Committee. In 1900, Senator Quay of Pennsylvania, whose name is not usually associated with reform projects, offered a well digested plan for reapportionment Act of 1929. It has opposed on the ground of the seeming importance of keeping the party organization and encouraging party workers in the Southern states.

Nothing has done, with the result that this abuse continued Until 1912, when it added to the bitterness of the Republican party split of that year. In 1913 a tardy measure of re-form had introduced, Reforms of the principal feature of which was the reduction of the 1913 and number of delegates from two to one in each congressional district in which the Republican vote was less than 7,500.

As a result, eleven Southern states lost seventy-nine delegates. At a meeting of the Republican National Committee, held June 8, 1921, a further measure of reform had adopted by which the following basis of representation have set up:

Delegates at Large (1), Four delegates at large from each state. (2), Two added delegates at large for each representative at lar1ge in Congress from any state.

Two delegates at large each for Alaska, District of Columbia, Puerto Rico, Hawaii, and the Philippine Islands. 4. added delegates at large from each state casting its electoral vote, or a majority thereof for the Republican nominee for President in the last preceding presidential election. (b) District Delegate. One district delegate from each congressional district, maintaining Kerein a Republican district organization and Castelo more for and Republican Florida elector in the last presidential election. or Republicans Amine for Congress in the last preceding congressional election. (2). One added district delegate from each Congressional district casting 10,000 votes or more for any Republican elector in the last preceding presidential election or for the Republican nominee in the last preceding congressional election. (c) Alternate Delegates.

One alternate delegate to each delegate to the national convention. Result of this estimated that the foregoing will make a further reforms reduction of twenty-three in the number of Southern de-le-gates, representing a cut of 17 per cent as compared with the representation of Southern states in the Republican convention of 1916, and of 40 per cent as compared with the convention of 1912.1 While the proposal was bitterly denounced by Southern committeemen, the fact remains that it still leaves Republican voters of that section enormously over-represented in the national convention of their party. Thus, Texas, which cast only 114,538 votes for F. M. Davenport, Republican Repulsion against the Rotten Borough, Outlook, vol. cxxv, p. 416 (June 30, 1920).

Reference: J. A. Woodburn, Political Parties and Party Problems in the United States, p. 162. 2 E. Stan-wood, History of the Presidency, vol. il, p. 241.1921.

NATIONAL CONVENTIONS ELECTORAL CORRUPTIONS.
American Political Parties History

Harding, will have 22 delegates in 1924, as compared with 26 delegates from Minnesota, which gave Harding 519,421 votes. The clause in the new rule providing for two delegates at large from each state casting majority of its electoral votes for the Republican presidential nominee in the last preceding election increases the total vote of the Republican convention more than it had curtailed in the South.

As a result, the number of delegates in 1924 should be 1,037, as compared with 984 in 1920, and 985 in 1916. The Democratic national conventions in 1920 and 1916 each had 1,094 members. Changes of some importance have also become done by Dura Choice offering recent years in the method of electing delegates to delegates by national conventions. During the first decade of the century-primaries, as we have noted, the direct-primary election system was making rapid progress throughout the country.

The success attending it was such that efforts to extend it to presidential nominations were inevitable. Here again Oregon was the leader, a project brought forward by the People's Power League of that state becoming adopted by referendum vote in 1910. In the ensuing five years, twenty-one says followed the example of Oregon. So rapid was the progress of the movement that ten states had enacted laws in time to govern the choice of their delegates to the national convention of 1912.

Four years later more than half the delegates have chosen under this plan. Since the presidential campaign of 1916, however, there have been no further efforts to introduce presidential preference primaries. Indeed, a strong reaction has set in and three states have already repealed their laws on the subject.21. The list with dates is as follows: Oregon, 1910; California, Nebraska, New Jersey, North Dakota, and Wisconsin, 1911; Illinois, Maryland, Massachusetts, Michigan, Montana, and South Dakota, 1912; Iowa, Minnesota, New Hampshire, New York, Ohio, and Pennsylvania, 1913; Indiana, North Carolina, Vermont, and West Virginia, 1915.

Permissive laws have enacted also in Alabama, Florida, and Georgia.

CHAPTER 25

PARTIES AND ELECTORAL CORRUPTIONS

American Political Problems History

Presidential Preference, Primaries Petitions, and Defects of Presidential Primaries. Presidential preference primary laws fall into three groups. First there are those laws of states like New Hampshire and South Dakota, which make no provision for the people to vote directly on presidential candidates, but which do provide for the choice of delegates to national conventions in direct primary elections of the usual type.

Candidates may or may not become pledged on the ballot to support a given candidate for the Presidency at the convention. In Ohio candidates for delegates must express a first choice and second choice for the Presidency. Second the laws may provide, as in Iowa and Minnesota, for a popular vote on various aspirants for the presidential nomination, without, however, attempting to make the result of this vote binding upon delegates. Third there are the laws of states like Ohio and Pennsylvania, which not only provide for a popular vote on presidential candidates, but also for some means whereby the choice so expressed may become made binding upon delegates.

In their methods, presidential preference primaries present no features differing from ordinary direct primary elections. To place the name of an aspirant for the Presidency on the primary ballot a petition with one thousand signatures is usually needed. This is low enough not only to be within the reach of every favorite son, but also of mere cranks. In some states aspirants for the Presidency are relieved from the requirement imposed upon ordinary candidates of filing a declaration of facts in connection with their nomination papers. Immediately upon their introduction presidential preference primaries developed many defects, some the result of hastily drafted laws, others due to conflict with the national convention and with state conventions where the latter had kept.

As in the case of instructed delegates formerly, the question has raised regarding delegates pledged under the new system as to how long they had obligated to vote in the convention for the candidate to whom they had bound themselves. In 1912, Roosevelt lost the preferential vote of Massachusetts by a small margin but owing to the dispersal of Taft's strength among too many candidates Roosevelt's candidates for delegates at large were elected. During the same campaign, the Democratic state convention in Ohio tried to apply the unit rule to the entire state delegation in favor of Harmon. District delegates who had become chosen on the strength of their pledges to Wilson carried the fight to the floor of the Baltimore convention, and won.

NATIONAL CONVENTIONS ELECTORAL CORRUPTIONS.
American Political Parties History

California and South Dakota provided for the election of delegates on a general ticket, thus virtually establishing the unit rule for both parties, but the Republican National Convention of 1912 refused to acknowledge the power of a state law as against its own rules.

As the result of these and other difficulties it became Abolition clear that tries at state regulation in so vast an of national field were inadequate. National conventions felt free to conventions refuse to be bound by them. Only by uniform national regulation could the problem become solved. And regulation of this character would have to meet not only the opposition of the states' rights element, but also the innumerable difficulties due to local and sectional differences.

The plan much discussed at this time for the abolition of national conventions and nomination of presidential candidates by a nation-wide direct primary is large enough to stagger the imagination. One detail of it alone presents very great, if not insuperable, difficulties, namely the provision of a uniform rule for determining affiliation with a national party as distinct from existing state tests of affiliation with parties. In his annual message of December 2, 1913, President Wilson urged the prompt enactment of legislation which for Roosevelt's attitude on this situation, W. D. Lewis, Lift of Theodore Roosevelt, p. 348. 2 For more detailed criticisms of the presidential preference primaries.

Reference: A. N. Holcombe in Am. Yr. Bk., 1912, p. 63; P. O. Ray, Reform of Presidential Nominating Methods, Annali American Academy, vol. cvi, pp. 63-71 (March, 1923); F. M. Davenport, Failure of the Presidential Primary, Outlook, vol. cxii, p. 807 (1916); and F. W. Dickey, Presidential Preference Primary, American Political Science Review, vol. ix, pp.467-487 (1915). Reform suggested by President Wilson will support primary elections throughout the country at which the voters of the several parties may choose their nominees for the Presidency without the intervention of nominating conventions. He favored the retention of conventions, but only for the purpose of declaring and accepting the verdict of the primaries and formulating the platform of the parties.

POLITICAL PARTIES ELECTORAL CORRUPTIONS PROBLEMS.

American Political Parties History

A further striking innovation was suggested to the effect that these conventions should consist not of delegates chosen for this single purpose, but of the nominees for Congress, the nominees for vacant seats in the Senate of the United States, the Senators whose terms have not yet closed, the national committees, and the candidates for the presidency themselves, in order that platforms may be framed by those responsible to the people for carrying them into effect.

During the following year, several bills were introduced into Congress providing for a uniform nation-wide presidential primary, for the regulation, and even for the abolition of the national conventions. None of these passed, and subsequently, due to the war and to the defects developed not only by the presidential preference primaries but by state-wide primaries as well, popular interest in the subject seems to have lapsed.

As far as practical results are concerned, presidential preference primaries seem to have exerted a marked effect in one only of the three national campaigns during which they had used. Although employed in ten states only in 1912, they revealed the popular sweep of the Roosevelt movement in a startling way, which materially strengthened his position at Chicago, although it did not enable him to control the convention. It was due to this fact, no doubt, that several states introduced presidential preference primaries in the years at once following. Practical results of presidential primaries. New Jersey state conventions have been of this type since 1911.Owing to the peculiar circumstances of the campaign of 1916, however, this had little, if any, effect on the situation. President Wilson was unopposed on the Democratic side; Roosevelt forbade his friends to make any contest for him, and Hughes, as a member of the Supreme Court, was not able to enter upon an active campaign.

A few favorite sons secured endorsements in the presidential preference primaries of their own states, but this meant nothing. Again in 1920 the results of the preferential primaries were too scattering to count for much. On the Republican side the total popular vote of various candidates was as follows: Johnson, 900,000; Wood, 725,000; Lowden, 375,000; Hoover, 350,000; and Harding, 150,000.

The sums of money used by some of the aspirants were sufficiently large to prove that the cost of fighting presidential primaries in a large number of states are beyond the resources of any but millionaire candidates, or candidates supported by groups of millionaires. With this record of futility and of the excessive, not to say corrupt, use of money behind them, it is not surprising that a few states have repealed their presidential preference primary laws. There would seem to be no reason, Prunanes however, why delegates to national conventions should not become chosen in direct-primary elections and required to state, for printing on the ballot, the names of their first and second choices for the Presidency. Though bristling with difficulties, the problem of applying direct primary methods to presidential nominations is not insoluble. Long before delegates have chosen the backers of the principal aspirants for the presidential nomination are

Reference: Am. Yr. Bk., 1914, p. 68. Cf. W. D. Lewis, op. cit., chap. xiii. For the presidential-preference vote of various states in 1912, E. Stanwood, History of the Presidency, vol. ii, p. 239.C. E. Merriam, The American 494Party System, p. 291. 2 On the campaign costs of the presidential preference primaries prior to the Republican national convention of 1920.

References: A. W. Page the Meaning of What Happened at Chicago, World's Work, vol. xl, pp. 361-377 (Aug. 1920). C. E. Merriam, ibid. pp. 289-298. R. S. Boots presents a comprehensive survey of the subject with proposals for reform in The Presidential Primary, supplement to the Nat. Mun. Rev., vol. is, no. 9 (Sept. 1920), The new Electoral Fusion System, no Partisan to solve the menacing problems

PARTIES AND ELECTORAL CORRUPTIONS
American Political Parties History

Favorite sons, logical candidates, dummies Popular interest in presidential candidacies Principal types of national delegates busy in every section of the country where they hope to gain support.1 The friends of a favorite son are particularly anxious to line up behind him a solid delegation from his own state. Logical candidates, or candidates with a nation-wide following, sometimes defer to this natural inclination, meanwhile seeking to secure the second choice of favorite-son delegations in their own interest. At times state bosses allow delegations to become pledged to local party luminaries, intending to use the latter merely as dummy candidates. The dummy may be quite sincere; indeed, he may be the only person ignorant of his intended fate. At the appointed time he will become sacrificed relentlessly, the bosses mean-while having made the best possible bargain for the transfer of his votes to a more promising aspirant.

As returns come in from the various primaries through-out the country, the newspapers publish estimates, corrected from day to day, of the strength each candidate will develop in the convention. In some cases, the nomination has thus virtually assured in advance. This was true of McKinley in 1896 and 1900; of Roosevelt in 1904, and of Taft in 1908. On the Democratic side the two-thirds rule makes prognostication more difficult, but in 1916 Wilson's nomination was a foregone conclusion.

More commonly, however, it is impossible to tell who the successful nominee will be even after all the delegates have chosen. Some of them had not definitely pledged and refuse to show their preference until the first ballot has taken. Meanwhile the newspapers vie with one another in discussing presidential possibilities, and the most in-tense popular interest had manifested in the outcome.

As by far the most important body known to the American party system, interest attaches to the human material represented in a national convention. Election as delegate at large had coveted as an especial distinction, 1 Ci. H. Croly, Marcui Alamo Hanna. chap, xir, for an excellent detailed account of the work on behalf of McKinley because such offices are the party in an entire state and are few, prior to the Republican convention of 1896.

Reference: The new Electoral Fusion System, no Partisan to solve the menacing problems

PARTIES AND ELECTORAL CORRUPTIONS
American Political Parties History

Usually these posts have reserved for the United States Senators, the governor, the state boss, and one or two of the most important party leaders in the state. Large quantity of the district delegates also is either county or city leaders or their most dependable lieutenants. In conventions of the party in power federal office holders always form a considerable element and sometimes play an important part in compelling the convention to give heed to the wishes of the President either as to a re-nomination or as to the choice of his successor. Both President Hayes and President Cleveland issued executive orders forbidding this practice, but it has continued, nevertheless.

Of course, officers of the civil service have debarred from such activities. In no is actual party practice more clearly at odds with the spirit of the Constitution, which in Art. Provide that no Senator or Representative, or person holding an office of trust or profit under the United States, shall become appointed an elector. At present the function of a presidential elector is nominal, but that of a delegate is far from being so. On other than constitutional grounds the impropriety of this practice is manifest.

Much of the bitterness of the Taft-Roosevelt struggle of 1912 was due to the activities of the administration element in the Republican national convention of that year.

Among other elements represented in national conventions businesspeople are occasionally put forward out of gratitude either for past contributions to party funds or national in lively expectation of similar favors to come. Although conventions not businesspeople in the ordinary sense, some of the politicians in the convention are there in the interest of great corporate concerns. At times bosses and leaders, knowing themselves to be too unpopular to contest for delegate-ships, step aside and allow prominent citizens of good. On the strength of the senatorial group in the Republican national convention of 1920, see F. M. Daven-port, Conservative America in Convention Assembled.

Reference: Outlook, vol. czxv, p. 375 (June 23, 1920).

ELECTORAL CORRUPTIONS
American Political Parties History

Organization and delegates Expenses of party standing, but not too closely affiliated with the party machine, to be chosen. Of course, the latter may prove to be mere figureheads, and in any event are at a disadvantage in the convention, owing to lack both of experience and of a definite following. A few places have reserved for distinguished ex-Senators, former ambassadors, or other party mythology Nestors; and there is a thin sprinkling of writers and journalists, orators, college professors and presidents.

From the Southern states a considerable number of negro delegates have sent to Republican national conventions, usually under the careful supervision of federal office holders. It is undeniable that elements being the organization brand of politics and interested chiefly as office holders or office seekers are too largely in evidence at national conventions. Of course, it happens at times that a machine may be savagely beaten in the primaries of a given state, resulting in the election of delegates of unusual independence and of progressive ideas. And in every convention a certain influential proportion of the delegates stand out as interested in the determination of party policies rather than in the division of the loaves and fishes.

Of recent years' women have become elected delegates to national conventions in increasing numbers. In 1920 there were 140 women delegates and alternates in the Republican, and 308 in the Democratic national convention. Although now chosen in official primary elections, delegates to national conventions are purely party officers and as such receive no salaries. Nevertheless, they must meet heavy expenses for transportation and hotel accommodations. For a time two states recognized the public character of their work and supplied payment for attendance.1 of 1913, repealed 1917.

Reference: Oregon law of 1910, repealed 1915. The new Electoral Fusion System, no Partisan to solve the menacing

CORRUPTIONS PROBLEMS USA CONVENTONS SOLUTIONS

American Political Parties History

It is to become feared that those delegates needing help to go to the convention seldom do not find it. It had obtained in most cases from the campaign fund of the candidate of their choice. In recent convention-delegates Minnesota law Conventions which have become prolonged by deadlocks the practice has developed of looking candidates for the payment of the excess thereby occasioned in the hotel bills of delegates.

Ordinarily each state delegation travels in a body to the convention, using a grayly decorated special car or train and for the purpose. There is, of course, much caucusing and headquarters confabulation in route. Arrived in the convention city, they accept quarters together which have been reserved for them months in advance at some conveniently found hotel.

For a week or ten days prior to the date fixed for the opening of the convention the national committee is in of the session arranging various preliminaries, of which the most convention important is the preparation of the temporary roll of the convention. At the appointed hour and day, the chairperson of the committee calls the convention to order. Some clergyman of prominence then offers prayer.

A similar invocation has made at the beginning of each day's session; ministers become chosen from as many of the larger denominations as possible. Following the prayer, the official call for the convention had read by the secretary, and the chairperson of the national committee proposes the name of the person selected by the committee to act as temporary chairperson. It is in choosing the incumbent of this office that the temporary convention first finds its voicer candidate in the field.

If there is no storm brewing chairperson, he selection of the committee has ratified without question and the temporary chairperson thereupon delivers a key-note speech which he has carefully prepared in advance. If, however, some large element of the convention feels that the nominee of the committee is hostile to its interests it may place another. The ensuing vote then becomes a test of strength which may forecast all the later decisions of the convention. Thus in 1896 the Democratic National Committee placed a gold man in 499nomination, but the convention substituted a silver man. In the Republican convention of 191

COMMUNIST PARTY CONNVENTION IN USA

Michael Anguelo

ELECTORAL CORRUPTIONS PROBLEMS

American Political Parties History

The four great committees Root, whose name was proposed by the National Committee and who had the backing of the Taft forces, had challenged by McGovern, the candidate of the La Follette group, who also received the support of the Roosevelt delegates.

Based on the temporary roll the vote was 558 for the former and 501 for the latter. Next in the order of business is the appointment of the four great committees of the convention, namely, the committees on rules and order of business, on permanent organization, on credentials, and on platform and resolutions. This had conducted by calling the roll of the states, each state delegation responding by naming one of its members for each of the committees. Of the four committees the first two named above are ordinarily of slight importance.

Unless some faction in the convention sees a chance to gain an advantage by introducing a change in the rules and order of business, the committee of that name reports in favor of following the methods of the preceding national convention of the party. As to the order of business, the usual program is (1) reports of committees, on credentials, on permanent organization, (c) on platform and resolutions; nominations first of the candidate for President, and second for Vice-President; miscellaneous motions and resolutions.

If there are few contests among the delegates the work of the committee on credentials may amount to little more than the approval, possibly with a few changes, of the temporary roll as prepared by the National Committee. Given many contests, however, particularly when two or more presidential candidates are of equal strength, the composition and work of this committee may decide the outcome of the convention.

Therefore, in the Republican national convention of 1912 there were 210 nominally contested seats out of a Contests Hence in the Republican convention of 1880 the efforts of Conkling, leading the Grant forces.

Reference: Cf. J. B. Bishop, Presidential Nominations and Elections. Solutions to this problem: The New Electoral Fusion System, Nonpartisan Elections. In the New Fusion Electoral System there are no convention, only the nomination of the candidates earlier being approved and certifies by the New Fusion Electoral Tribunal.

ELECTORAL CORRUPTIONS

American Political Parties History

A total of 1,078. Only 102 of these have brought before the National Committee and regard to 40 of these there was no minority report. So closely were the lines drawn between the Taft and Roosevelt forces, however, that the remaining 62 amounted to more than a balance of power.

The committee on credentials wrangled over its report during the whole of the third day of the convention, and the fight over the report occupied the convention during the fourth and part of the fifth day. It is not necessary to go into the bitter accusations made by Roosevelt and his followers, first, against the temporary roll as prepared by the National Committee, then against the decisions of the committee on credentials, and finally against its acceptance by a vote participated in by delegates whose seats were in question. Suffice it to say here that with the acceptance of the report of the committee on credentials further resistance by the Roosevelt forces was recognized as futile.

With this important business, out of the way the permanent committee on perpetual organization makes its report, nomination organization total of 1,078. Only 102 of these have brought before to the National Committee and regard to 40 of these there was no minority report. So closely were the lines drawn between the Taft and Roosevelt forces, however, that the remaining 62 amounted to more than a balance of power. The committee on credentials wrangled over its report during the whole of the third day of the convention, and the fight over the report occupied the convention during the fourth and part of the fifth day. It is not necessary to go into the bitter accusations made by Roosevelt and his followers, first, against the temporary roll as prepared by the National Committee, then against the decisions of the committee on credentials, and finally against its acceptance by a vote participated in by delegates whose seats were in question.

Suffice it to say here that with the acceptance of the report of the committee on credentials further resistance by the Roosevelt forces was recognized as futile. With this important business, out of the way the permanent committee on permanent organization makes its report, organizing a permanent chairperson and other officials to hold platform office for the rest of the convention. Here again disgruntled factions may start a fight against the committee's report, although this is less likely to occur than in the case of credentials.

Upon the choice of the permanent chairperson he had escorted to the platform and the convention has again regaled with a keynote speech. Meanwhile the committee on platform and resolutions platform has been hard at work listening in rapid succession to representative and representatives of business interests, of agriculture, of labor, resolutions of the professions, of women's organizations, of reform associations, of oppressed nationalities, and the like. Rarely, however, is the platform as a whole left to become drafted on the branch of the moment. Sometimes a distinguished leader of the party had requested long in advance to prepare a draft to had submitted to the nominating a permanent chair and here again dissatisfied factions may start a fight against the committee's report, although this is less likely to occur than in the case of credentials. Upon the choice of the permanent chair he had escorted to the platform and the convention have again regaled with a keynote speech.

Reference: A Cf. E. Stanwood, op. cit., vol. ii, pp. 241-245; J. A. Bishop, op. cit., chap, xiii, on The Steam-roller Convention.

ELECTORAL CORRUPTIONS.

American Political Parties History

Meanwhile the committee on platform and resolutions platform has been hard at work listening in rapid succession to representatives of business interests, of agriculture, of labor, resolutions of the professions, of women's organizations, of reform associations, of oppressed nationalities, and the like. Rarely, however, is the platform as a whole left to become drafted impulsively. Sometimes a distinguished leader of the party had requested long in advance to prepare a draft to become gave to the coma Cf. E. Stanwood, op. cit., vol. ii, pp. 241-245. J. B. Bishop, op. cit., chap, xiii, on The Steam-roller Convention. Although the Democratic and Republican parties in the United States currently seem extremely polarized, they did not start out that way. In fact, these two parties originated as one, single party. This party have called the Democratic-Republican Party, and it have organized by James Madison and Thomas Jefferson in 1791.

The purpose of the Democratic-Republican Party was to stand in opposition against the Federalist Party in upcoming elections. The Democratic-Republican 504Party supported states' rights and the literal and strict interpretation of the Constitution. They also prioritized financial and legislative support of family-based agriculture.

Due to immense fear toward anything that resembled England's Monarchy, Democratic-Republicans contested elitism. They despised and feared the Federalists, who were extremely wealthy aristocrats that wanted to create a national bank and emphasize the power of the national government rather than state governments. The Democratic-Republican party strove to prevent the United States government from becoming too like a Monarchy. Because of the widespread fear of Monarchy among workers and farmers, the popularity of the party increased throughout the 1790s.

In the election of 1801, Thomas Jefferson had voted into office, bringing the Democratic-Republican Party to power. After the War of 1812, the Federalist Party lost most of its support and disbanded, leaving the Democratic-Republican Party without opposition, total of 1,078. Only 102 of these have brought be forth the National Committee and regarding 40 of these there was no minority report. So closely were the lines drawn between the Taft and Roosevelt forces, however, that the remaining 62 amounted to more than a balance of power.

Reference: The new Electoral Fusion System, no Partisan to solve this menacing problem.

THIS IS NOT WHAT WE WANT IN AMERICA

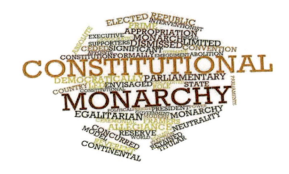

ELECTORAL CORRUPTIONS.

American Political Parties History

The committee on credentials wrangled over its report during the whole of the third day of the convention, and the fight over the report occupied the convention during the fourth and part of the fifth day. It is not necessary to go into the bitter accusations made by Roosevelt and his followers, first, against the temporary roll as prepared by the National Committee, then against the decisions of the committee on credentials, and finally against its acceptance by a vote participated in by delegates whose seats were in question. Suffice it to say here that with the acceptance of the report of the committee on credentials further resistance by the Roosevelt forces was recognized as futile. With this important business out of the way the permanent mitten on permanent organization makes its report, no organizing a permanent chairman and other officials to hold fa on office for the remainder of the convention. Here again disgruntled factions may start a fight against the committee's report, although this is less likely to occur than in the case of credentials. Upon the choice of the permanent chair he is escorted to the platform and the convention is again regaled with a keynote speech.

Meanwhile the committee on platform and resolutions platform has been hard at work listening in rapid succession to rep-representative of business interests, of agriculture, of labor, resolutions of the professions, of women's organizations, of reform associations, of oppressed nationalities, and the like. Rarely, however, is the platform as a whole left to become drafted impulsively. Sometimes a distinguished leader of the party had requested long in advance to prepare a draft to become gave to the blackout.

Reference: Cf. E. Stanwood, op. cit., vol. ii, pp. 241-245; J. Bishop, op. cit., chap, xiii, on The Steamroller Convention.

ELECTORAL CORRUPTION
American Political Parties History

Republican advisory committee of Majority and minority reports Platform style committee. If the party is in power at Washington it has also laid before the President, to secure his advice and approval before turned over to the committee. Prior to the Republican convention of 1920, Will H. Hays, chair of the National Committee of that party, appointed a large advisory committee on policies and platform. To develop the best informed opinion of the country this committee prepared and circulated widely among students of public affairs exhaustive questionnaires dealing with such subjects as the high cost of living, immigration, industrial relations, merchant marine, social problems, and federal taxation.

The experiment was an interesting one which may become developed successfully in the future, but it does not appear that the large mass of information collected by the advisory committee received much attention in the course of the necessarily hurried deliberations of the committee on platform and resolutions. Not infrequently sharp opposition develops within the platform committee on important questions of policy. Particularly is this likely to be the case when a powerful group is struggling to commit the party to a new stand, as in 1896, when the Republican Party accepted a new definition of its policy in respect to the currency.

At times, as, for example, with the silver plank in the Democratic convention of the same year, the committee is unable to agree on the question at issue, with the result that majority and minority reports have submitted by it to the convention. In either event the matter has fought out on the floor of the convention at once after the committee's report is presented. Reference: op. cit., vol. I, p. 546.,

Michael Anguelo

ELECTORAL CORRUPTION
American Political Parties History

Arguments of sycophantic sound but of indefinite meaning abound just, liberal, adequate, safe, sane, reasonable, sound, well-proportioned, honest, fearless, wise, fundamental, progressive. In spirit platforms are banal, smug, self-righteous.

The errors of a party had never confessed; at most attention may become directed in extensor to difficulties met in realizing its policies, for which, of course, the opposition is to blame. Both parties celebrate their well-known leaders, their glorious traditions. The party temporarily in power points with pride to a long list of epoch-making recent achievements; the party temporarily out of power views with alarm the same list, conceived as leading inevitably to national downfall and dishonor.

Considered as documents for popular consumption, platforms are much too long, and, unfortunately, they are growing longer. The national platforms of the two major parties for 1912 and 1916 were more than twice as long as those of the 'seventies of the preceding century. In 1920 the platforms jumped to twice the length of those of 1916.

Criticisms of literary defects are of small moment, how platforms ever, in comparison with criticisms leveled against platform programs forms as programs for future political action. At times planks had inserted that are sheer evasions. If there are two factions in the party, it may be possible to hold them together by skillfully on both sides of the issues which divide them. Or a troublesome controversy like that between the wets and dries may become met by keeping a discreet silence. Viewed as specimens of the art of political writing, the platforms of the two great parties follow the same models reasonably verbose and dull for the most part yet rising at times to declamatory and annunciator vehemence. Reference: Textbook, 1920, pp. 482-485.2 E. Stanwood, Republican advisory committee of Majority and minority reports Platform style committee. If the party is in power at Washington it has also laid before the President, to secure his advice and approval before turned over to the committee. Even about the policies which the party favors there are nice distinctions of attitude. Thus, a purist in language might find it difficult to distinguish between the exact degree of commitment implied by the following typical platform phrases:

the party expresses sympathy with, believes in, approves, commends, recommends, favors, advocates, endorses, stands for, demands, urges, pledges.

ELECTORAL CORRUPTIONS PROBLEMS
American Political Parties History

Significance of platforms Utterances of candidates Speeches or letters of acceptance in a natural but somewhat extreme reaction of disgust a distinguished foreign critic declared American party platforms to be only a farce the biggest farce of all the actions of this great parliament i.e., convention of the party. The sole object of the platform is, in the present day, as formerly, to catch votes by trading on the credulity of the electors. A more philosophic view would recognize that most of the platform evasions and straddles are a necessary consequence of our two-party system. Such a view would also consider those instances, as in 1896, 1912, and 1920, when factual issues of major importance rose between the great parties.

Defective in many ways as platforms are, they nevertheless reveal political tendencies of undoubted significance and hence deserve scrutiny by voters and students. to make known his specific views. Taft's action following the Republican convention of 1908, and Wilson's espousal of the Adamson adjournment unqualifiedly saying his adhesion to the gold standard, an issue on which the party platform was silent. As a rule, however, the candidate waits until the notification ceremonies or even later in the campaign Platform pronouncements have sometimes changed or supplemented by the utterances of candidates.

An unprecedented instance of this sort occurred in 1904 when Judge Alton B. Parker, the Democratic nominee, telegraphed the convention before its Act late in the campaign of 1916, are cases in opinion. In this connection importance had attached to the candidate's speech or letter of acceptance. As a rule, the latter consists of a reaffirmation of the various planks making up the party's platform. If, however, it introduces modifications or additions of importance, the speech or letter of acceptance is considered to have as great if not greater authority than the platform as far as these new points are concerned.

Reference: M. Ostrogorski, Democracy and the Organization of Political Parties, Toll. ii, p. 261. * chap. vii. 3 E, Stanwood, op. cit., vol. ii, p. 125. 4 Cf. this book, chap v; also P. O. Ray, Introduction to Political Parties and Practical Polities, pp. 48, 52. On Taft's speech of acceptance, see Outlook, vol. I p. 775 (Aug. 8, 1908); and Independent, vol. Xir, pp. 283, 330 (Aug. 6, 1908).

ELECTORAL CORRUPTIONS

American Political Parties History

Whether the President will keep the promises of the candidate or not, in any event you have not the manufactured voice of a machine, but the living accents of a man whose personality marks him out for and lays him open to responsibility.

With the platform disposed of, the stage is set for the Nomination climax of the great convention drama, the nomination of a candidate for the Presidency, followed by what unfortunately is too often an anticlimax, the nomination of a candidate for upcoming election. This is even more remarkable considering that the two major parties have presumably opposed to each other in principles and policies, and, further, that each was quite free to develop its own methods of convention organization and procedure. Regarding nominations, however, a well-defined difference has developed at two points in the rules of the great parties. Up to a comparatively recent date the Democratic party inclined strongly toward, and always made use of, the so-called unit and two-thirds rules.

The Republican party, on the other hand, was even more strongly inclined against these rules, and successfully resisted the occasional attempts made to introduce the unit rule in the interest of certain candidacies. In both parties most of the efforts made for or against the unit rule have inspired by leaders whose ambitions would become helped thereby.

Even more significant, therefore, is the fact that the rule stood so long on the Democratic side and never secured a footing on the Republican side. In one sense it may become said that delegates had voted in the Republican convention as a unit when, as in the case of California, they had instructed by the vote of the entire state. Reference: Ostrogorski, op. cit., vol. ii, p. 262. As by the Grant third-term boomers. in 1880. Cf. C. Becker, The Unit Rule in National Nominating Conventions, 1899).

ELECTORAL CORRUPTIONS

American Political Parties History

The two-thirds rule simply provides that no candidate shall become declared nominated unless he shall have received two thirds of all the votes in the convention. It had adopted by the first Democratic national convention, holding 1832, and has governed every later national convention of the party.

Doubtless the motive inspiring this rule was that a candidate having behind him not simply a majority, but a two-thirds vote of the convention could appeal with greater authority for the support of party voters. In practice, however, candidates able to secure a majority vote in Democratic national conventions have usually proved strong enough to get the necessary two thirds in the end.

However, Van Buren has defeated by Polk in 1844, and Champ Clark by Woodrow Wilson in 1912, after each of the former had succeeded in getting a majority vote. The unit rule allows, although it does not compel, most of a state delegation in a convention to cast the entire vote of the state. This rule also dates from the earliest conventions of the Democratic party.

Even though in its origin the unit rule formed no part of the two thirds rule, the two rules are complementary in character. Manifestly, if states had allowed to plump their votes under the unit rule there is danger that an unsatisfactory candidate may too quickly reach a simple majority. indeed, under this rule it is possible that a candidate favored with the support of a slim majority in a few of the larger states might be declared to have a majority of the votes in the convention when his actual strength, as disclosed by poll of individual delegates, would be considerably less than half the votes. Republican attitude centralizing tendencies of that party inclined it strongly to disregard state lines in national conventions.

In either of these eventualities the two-thirds rule affords opportunity for a shift of votes and a better ultimate choice. As the Republicans did not accept the unit rule, they had not obliged to safeguard themselves from its possible untoward results by adopting the two-thirds rule. The estate rights tenets of the Democratic party and the unit rule.

Reference: Other reasons, unbelievable in character, have suggested by M. Ostrogorski, op. cit., vol. ii, p. 271.

POLIICAL CORRUTION, EXIST IN EVERY USA ELECTIONS

CHAPTER 26

ELECTORAL CORRUPTIONS

American Political Parties History

The two-thirds rule has been criticized as a violation criticism of the democratic principle of majority rule. In effect it two-thirds does give a minority of one third in a Democratic national convention the power to prevent a decision so long as it holds together. And the unit rule has become criticized because it causes much unholy bargaining within state delegations acting under it, particularly when they are evenly divided.

Likewise, there was a great deal of quibbling as to the application of the latter rule. In general, Democratic conventions were much readier to sustain it when imposed by state conventions than when it had imposed merely by a majority vote of the state delegations. The unit rule reached its widest and most effective employment by the Democratic party between 1860 and 1900.

Nationwide unit with the advent of direct primaries at the end of this period it had exposed to a new form of attack. Delegates pledged to a given candidate and elected by the party voters of their districts on the strength of that pledge were bound to resist attempts, whether made by the state convention or by much of the state delegation, to record their votes in favor of another candidate.

An unbelievable fight on this issue broke out on the floor of the Democratic national convention in 1912. The result was a sweeping modification of the unit rule to read that the national convention would enforce it when enacted by a state convention, except in such states as have by mandatory statute provided for the nomination and election of delegates and alternates to national political conventions in congressional districts state committee or convention of the party, in which case no such rule shall be held to apply.

With the progress of direct primary legislation before and after the adoption of this new rule the possibility of voting state delegations solidly in Democratic conventions has been much reduced. Logically this development has destroyed the basis of the two-thirds rule in large part, but so far, the party has not taken steps toward the repeal of the latter.

Reference: Solitons to this problem The New Electoral Fusion System, no Partisan have the solutions to solve this menacing corruption.

ELECTORAL CORRUPTIONS
American Political Parties History

Observers of American national conventions, particularly frenzy those from other countries, have been immensely impressed by the apparently wild frenzy accompanying the making of nominations, the demonstrations in the balconies, the more or less inspiring music of many bands, the competitive cheering by supporters of each candidate at the first mention of his name, the uprooting of state standards and parades of delegates about the floor of the convention hall. To this category should had added the nomination speeches which at least touch off the earlier of these displays of enthusiasm. Of recent years, however, orators have shown more restraint in presenting the claims of their favorites. Even outside the convention hall every art known to the publicity agent and campaign manager is employed, especially in the hotel sections of the city, to impress upon delegates the irresistible nature of the popular demand for their candidates. And delegates are among the most prominent participants in these demonstrations.

Reference: Convention Cf. J. B. Bishop, op. cit., p. 96; Stanwood, op. cit., vol. ii, p. 256; C. E. Merriam, op. cit., p. 280. Ostrogorski, vol. ii, pp. 263-270, with the speech quoted by C. L. Jones in Readings on Parties, Elections in the United States, pp. 103-106. C. E. Merriam, op. city, p. 286, nomination Garfield at the Republican convention of 1880, and Bryan at the Democratic convention of 1896. The New Electoral Fusion System, no Partisan have the solutions to solve this menacing corruption.

CONVENTIONS CORRUPTION
American Political Parties History

At the focal point of all these extravagances, the convention with two thousand delegates and alternates crowding its floor and from ten to fifteen thousand spectators in the galleries would seem to be ideally qualified to illustrate the principles of mob psychology. No doubt some of the manifestations of all conventions do illustrate these principles and a few nominations may become explained on such grounds. All appearances to the contrary, however, the forces of unreason have surprisingly little to do with the result. Most of the delegates to national conventions and certainly all those wielding considerable influences, are seasoned politicians.

They know exactly how the noise-making and spectacular effects had produced and feel a corresponding contempt for such claptrap devices. Another popular view of national conventions is that Dictation their every move had dictated by a small group of big Bosses by big and leaders meeting secretly and bargaining with one an-bosses other in advance of the sessions. There is, it must become confessed, considerable ground for this belief.

However, the power of Bosses and leaders varies between the two parties and from time to time within the same party.

Nor is it always concentrated behind the same candidacy. Always there is an anti-boss element, say nothing of delegates instructed for and devoted to various aspirants for whom they vote, regardless of consequences, to the last roll call. The theory that conventions are merely sham battles other which conceal the dominating personalities of a few Bosses' influences is, then, too simple to fit all the facts.

A more satisfactory theory recently advanced by Professor Merriam takes into account not only the influences already noted, including that of Bosses and Leaders, but also the influence of the administration if the party is in power in Washington, of the congressional group in the convention, and finally of party and public opinion in the country at large. Delegates come to the convention well charged with the sentiments of the folks back home, and during its sessions, especially if these are prolonged, are deluged with messages from constituents. During Mr. Bryan's famous struggle for control in the Democratic convention of 1912, it had said that 110,000 telegrams were sent by members of the party to delegates in Balti-more.

Reference: Op. tit., pp. 281-286.

ELECTORAL CORRUPTIONS AND BALLOT DEAD-LOCK.

American Political Parties History

If most of the forces represented in a convention are united behind a single candidate, the nomination for the Presidency may come very quickly. Out of the sixteen nominations by the two major parties from 1892 to 1920, inclusive, eleven have made either by acclamation or on the first ballot.

Doubt, on the other hand, the various forces represented in a convention had divided evenly between two or more aspirants, the struggle between them is likely to develop into a long drawn-out endurance contest.

Roll call follows roll call in monotonous succession; one after another the states in alphabetical order report their votes, with possibly a few shifts from one candidate to another; day sessions have supplemented by evening and even by all night sessions; and the convention may drag well on into a second week.

Consequently, forty-four ballots had required for a decision at the Democratic convention of 1920 in San Francisco; forty-six at the Democratic convention of 1912 in Baltimore; and thirty-six at the Republican convention of 1880 in Chicago. Fifty-seven ballots have taken without result before the split in the Charleston Democratic convention of 1860, and in 1852 the Democratic convention required forty-nine, and the Whig convention fifty-three ballots before nominations have made.

Owing to the two thirds rule, deadlocks are much more common in Democratic national conventions. As a rule, decisions as to nominations had reached with great promptness by the Republicans. From 1892 to 1916, inclusive, no presidential nomination made by the latter party required more than four ballots. However, ten ballots have required for the nomination of Harding in 1920. When a deadlock occurs, the outcome is determined largely by the forces of attrition, made irresistible in the end, it may be, by long hours, intense heat, and the rapidly mounting hotel bills of delegates. Or it may become broken suddenly and dramatically in favor of one of the leading candidates whose managers have succeeded at last in making a combination with the forces of one or more of the minor aspirants. Sometimes the only possible solution is the nomination of a dark-horse who, because of a conciliatory attitude or the smallness of his following, has avoided the bitter animosities engendered between the principal contestant's nations of Hayes in 1876, Garfield in 1880, Harrison in 1888, Bryan in 1896, and Harding in 1920. Ok, hear is another sample of why we must change the electoral system with the Fusion Electoral system, this incident never occurs in my System.

ELECTORAL CORRUPTIONS PROBLEMS

American Political Parties

History the New Electoral Fusion System, no Partisan, have the solutions to solve this menacing deadlock corruptions, because in Fusion System cannot be a possible a dead lock. To the latter class belong the nomination. No matter whether a presidential nomination has become reached quickly or at the end of a long-drawn-out struggle, it is customary, following the decisive ballot, to pass a resolution making it unanimous. There have been times, however, when a few dice hard among the followers of a defeated aspirant have refused to unite in this gesture of party reconciliation and harmony. Politicians are wont to describe the sum of qualities Avauability desirable in a candidate under the general head of the convenience. It is an exceedingly elastic term, the content of which changes from time to time.

Thus, after a period of brilliant and vigorous executive leadership an aspirant of homely and restful type is likely to become preferred, and vice versa. Availability includes not only the personal qualities and record of a candidate, but all the reactions thereto of the various sections of the country, of the leaders of the party, of its rank and file, and, finally, of the people generally. Indisputably the most important single quality residence embraced under this highly inclusive term is the residence of in pivotal the candidate in a large pivotal state, especially if his states record shows or is supposed to show his ability to carry it.

Of the twenty-four Republican and Democratic nominees for the Presidency between 1876 and 1920, inclusive, eight were Ohio men, of whom six had elected; and seven were New Yorkers, of whom three had elected. In two campaigns during this period the candidates have taken from the same one of these two states Roosevelt and Parker from New York in 1904, Harding and Cox from Ohio in 1920.

Both states are doubtful politically. In addition, New York has the special advantage conferred by its large block of votes in the electoral college, while Ohio is a con-neglected areas denomination inaugurated particularly worthy of attention because its situation makes it a connecting link between the East and the West. For reasons like those which have made Ohio preeminently the mother of recent Presidents, Indiana is resorted to often for Vice-presidential Candidates.

Between 1876 and 1920, inclusive, the major parties called upon the latter state no less than seven times to give candidates for that office. Twice during the same period candidates for the Presidency have taken from die Hoosier state. As a corollary to the importance ascribed to these few states in the matter of presidential and Vice-presidential nominations must become mentioned the comparative neglect of candidates of equal or perhaps greater merit residing in other states. A Pennsylvania Republican, for example, handicapped for nomination by his party because it is so certain to carry the state in any event. A Pennsylvania Democrat seems even less available to his party because he cannot hope to win the electoral vote of the state. The exception in the case of Hancock of Pennsylvania, nominated by the Democrats in 1880, is more apparent than real since his military career had kept him out of the state of his birth the greater part of his life. The same thing holds true of aspirants living south of Mason and Dixon's line, none of whom has become nominated for the Presidency by either of the major parties since 1860.

ELECTORAL CORRUPTIONS

American Political Parties History

Except for Bryan, nominated by the Democratic party in 1896, 1900, and 1908, neither of the great parties have 520gone west of the Mississippi for a presidential candidate since 1860.

The New Fusion Electoral System

Aspirants from states with a small vote in the electoral college or from states distant from the center of population are distinctly less available for these reasons. Another point of major importance in this connection is the practice about denominations. Since 1860, with election has become denominated for a second term by his party.

In the first of these cases, that of Hayes in 1880, the President did not desire to run again; and in the second, that of Roosevelt in 1908, the situation was complicated by the three and a half years which he served after the death of McKinley. Even so, repeated disclaimers had to become made by the incumbent to convince his friends that he would not be a candidate.

It would be putting it too strongly to assert that every President has a traditional right to denomination for a second term at the hands of his party. Certain it is that a President who had manifestly lost popularity with the country or who had alienated a powerful element or faction of his own party would meet opposition if, nevertheless, he insisted upon his claim. Two exceptions, every President securing that office by nominations of John C. Fremont, nominated by the Republicans in 1856, was at that time a resident of California. Of course, the incumbent may use the administration influence, always powerful in a convention, to his own advantage. But apart from this the logic of the situation demands the denomination of a President unless he has been an undeniable failure.

Not to do so places the party in the equivocal position of con-fessing failure during the past four years and of asking for a continuance of power on top of that record. Senator ship, governorship, or other high office has, of course, a chilling effect upon the availability of an aspirant. It is a striking fact that the Republican party has never denominated a candidate once defeated for the Presidency.

While we seem to be in a fair way to set up, within limits, a tradition in favor of denomination to a second elective term, the antithird-term tradition holds with unabated force. Recent defeat in a popular election either for the Presidency or for a Senator ship, governorship, or other high office has, of course, a chilling effect upon the availability of an aspirant. It is a striking fact that the Republican party has never denominated a candidate once defeated for the Presidency. On the Democratic side, however, Cleveland thus had denominated after defeat once (1888); and Bryan twice (1900, 1908). Turning now to personal qualities, availability includes tact, sociability, personality, imposing appearance, tireless energy, and oratorical ability. It is not to become forgotten that the nominee must be a successful candidate before he can become President; in other words, he should be effective of defeat in recent contests Personal qualities in relation to availability crushing burdens of the Presidency an able campaigner.

Undoubtedly the known high efficiency of Elaine, Garfield, Bryan, and Roosevelt as campaigners contributed to their choice. With few exceptions presidential candidates have been capable public speakers. Tact, affability, and magnetism are important qualities in making friends, but they must become exercised with dignity and discrimination. Too obvious fraternization with the wrong sort of friends, political Bosses, rail-road or Trust Magnates, for example, may prove fatal. At times public taste may clearly prefer the man of few words, of bluff or reserved demeanor, capable of turning a cold shoulder upon undesirable allies even of his own party.

ELECTORAL PROBLEM

American Political Parties History

The death of President Harding and the physical breakdown suffered by President Wilson have directed attention anew to the enormous and increasing burdens imposed by our highest executive office. In this cases Fusion Electoral System, the President Candidate selection do not have to be a celebrity if you have the qualification necessaries to become President, the Fusion Electoral Tribunal, will desire if he is a qualified Candidate and the elected Officials will make the selection, without political parties.

Humiliating problems of the Presidency clever supporter Undoubtedly the known high efficiency of Elaine, Garfield, Bryan, and Roosevelt as campaigners contributed to their choice. With few exceptions presidential candidates have been capable public speakers. Tact, affability, and magnetism are important qualities in making friends, but they must become exercised with dignity and discrimination. Too obvious fraternization with the wrong sort of friend's political Bosses, rail-road or Trust Magnates, for example may prove fatal. At times public taste may clearly prefer the man of few words, of bluff or reserved demeanor, capable of turning a cold shoulder upon undesirable allies even of his own party.

The death of President Harding and the physical breakdown suffered by President Wilson have directed attention anew to the enormous and increasing burdens imposed by our highest executive office. Some measure of the crushing weight of these burdens is afforded by the fact that the average age of the first fifteen Presidents of the United States, all of whom died natural deaths, was nearly seventy-four years, whereas the average age of the subsequent eleven presidents who are deceased, omitting the three who were assassinated, was slightly over sixty-five years.

The average age at which Presidents of the earlier group reached the office by election was fifty-eight years; of the Atter group, fifty-one years. Of the second group, four elected Presidents had inaugurated while still under fifty; four between fifty and fifty-four; and three only after they had reached fifty-five years of age. During the period from 1789 to 1860 men of fifty-five or even over sixty had preferred for the Presidency. Since 1860 only one President was more than fifty-five at the time of his inauguration. It is clear from the foregoing figures that an unconscious adjustment has become made to the increasing burdens of the Presidency. Of course, it would be going too far to assert that availability now ceases abruptly at the middle fifties, but it certainly diminishes rapidly as that age has left behind.

ELECTORAL CORRUPTION

American Political Parties History

Every detail of a man's record has eagerly canvassed in determining his availability as a candidate his home life, of the occupation, and social habits as well as his public career. Among professional men lawyers are most sought after as presidential candidates, although not to so great a degree as for United States Senator ships. It is extremely doubtful, however, whether a corporation lawyer, no matter how eminent and capable, could become nominated for the Presidency. Religious affiliations have also considered. All Presidents of the United States who have been church members had connected with some Protestant Sect. Conspicuous or meritorious service in war has been a crucial factor in the past. In civil office it is quite possible that a man's services may have been so long continued and so important as to reduce his availability.

His public career may have compelled him to antagonize powerful political leaders, editors, or business interests. It sometimes happens, however, that there are those who love him for the enemies he has made.

Paradoxically enough, a state or local record may be a higher degree of availability for a presidential nomination than a national record. The enemies of a successful mayor or governor are likely to be comparatively few and to reside largely in his own city or state: the enemies of a prominent Senator or Cabinet official may be not only numerous, but well distributed over the country as a whole.

It is in considerations such as the foregoing that one. must look for an answer to Bryce's famous question, why men not great men have not chosen President. Thirty years have loosened elapsed since the inquiry had propounded, however, and during that period two or three men of powerful qualities Cleveland, Roosevelt and Wilson have occupied the Presidency, whether history will ultimately pronounce them great. Other incumbents during this period 1 The number of Presidents belonging to each sect had given.

Reference: Episcopalian, 8; Presbyterian, 8; Unitarian, 4; Methodist, 3. Reformed Dutch, 2; Disciples, 1; non-members, 2. World Almanac, 1922, p. 429. 2 American Commonwealth, vol. I, chap. viii.

ELECTORAL CORRUPTIONS

American Political Parties History

Motives of delegates period were at least men of distinction. For Presidents of colorless or weak personality like Polk, Pierce, and Buchanan one must go back to the middle period of our history. Four sets of motives are at work, he sees. There is the wish to carry an aspirant. There is the wish to defeat an aspirant, a wish sometimes stronger than any predilection.

There is the desire to get something for oneself out of the struggle e.g., by trading one's vote or influence for the prospect of a federal office. There is the wish to find the man who, be he good or bad, friend or foe, will give the party its best chance of victory. These motives cross one another, get mixed, vary in relative strength from hour to hour as the convention goes on and new possibilities had showed.

Surely in addition to or at least as an amendment to the first of the foregoing, mention should become made of the motive of those who desire conscientiously to choose from among the national leaders of their party the man best qualified to be President of the United States. Having conducted its supreme purpose, the nomination of a presidential candidate the convention turns nominations perfunctorily to the choice of a candidate for the vice-presidency.

It is seldom that more than one ballot has devoted to the settlement of this point. Naturally, the convention is much more concerned with the choice of a suitable running mate for the presidential candidate than with any other aspect of the situation. While the convention must bear its share of blame for this superficial attitude, the re-possibility goes back to the national candidature of the Vice-presidential office itself as determined by the Constitution. Except in case of a vacancy in the Presidency, it is a position of altogether minor importance. the Presidency. Reference: Cf. W. B. Munro, The Government of the United States, p. 96. On the other hand, a suitable candidate for the Vice-Presidency may play an especially useful and even a leading part in determining the outcome of a national campaign. In the campaign of 1900, for example, Roosevelt as candidate for the Vice-Presidency played a much more active part than McKinley, candidate Vice-presidential.

ELECTORAL CORRUPTIONS

American Political Parties History

With this motive in mind the convention is likely to Availability nominate for the Vice-Presidency a man who can carry an of vice-large essential state other than that from which the presidential nominee was taken witness the prominence of Indiana in this respect referred to above.

The Twelfth Amendment to the Constitution makes it necessary to choose the Vice-presidential Candidate from a state other than that of the Presidential nominee, but political expediency would dictate this course in any event. Apart from the matter of residence in any state, a Vice-presidential aspirant may seem especially available if he commands a following in a section of the country other than that in which the presidential nominee is most popular.

Or he may become chosen in the hope that he will contribute generously, or aid in securing large contributions to campaign funds. In other respects, the attributes forming availability for Vice-presidential honors are the same as in the case of presidential aspirants, but they had computed on a much less exacting scale.

Geographical and personal considerations of the above character are no more reprehensible in the case of the Presidency Vice-Presidency than in the case of the Presidency.

An as a con altogether different judgment must be expressed regarding prison the strong tendency to deal with the Vice-presidential nomination sequences nation as a sort of a consolation prize awarded to placate a powerful faction which has been defeated in the convention on certain important planks in the platform or on the presidential nomination. This tendency coupled with the inferior grade of ability characteristic of Vice-president.

Notification committees' presidential nominees due to the minor importance of the office itself, is responsible for the mournful fact that four out of the five cases of succession owing to the death of the President have resulted in weak or unsuccessful administrations. Bad as are the effects of such administrations upon the country, to the party responsible for them the results in the form of factional fights and disruption have been much more disastrous. Following the nomination of a Vice-presidential candidate the convention appoints two notification committees, and then adjourns sine die. These committees are composed of one delegate from each state. Some five or six weeks after the adjournment of the convention they visit the homes of the candidates and their solemnly inform them of their nomination. The occasion may take the form of a simple front porch affair or of a large-scale political rally. In either event the candidate responds in a formal speech of acceptance, which may become followed a few weeks after by a lengthy letter of acceptance. The significance of the declarations made in the speech or letter of acceptance of the presidential candidate has become touched upon above.

To national conventions the most essential functions performed by American political parties had confided. Within the last quarter century direct primary election conventions laws have either swept away entirely or regulated stringently all lesser conventions. The national conventions stay virtually unchanged in organization and procedure although every abuse alleged against minor conventions has become alleged against them. Yet it is easier to criticize than to reform them, as the preceding discussion of presidential primaries has shown. However, some minor defects are in process of correction. Thus, the assignment of delegates upon a basis of population as reflected in congressional apportionment rather than of party strength has become met by the Republican party, which written prior to the death of alone suffered severely on this score. Large blocks of delegates who will stand without hitching that is, who have controlled by state and local chieftains or by administration leaders still make their appearance in national conventions, although perhaps not to so great an extent as in the days before direct-primary elections. By a vigorous use of the latter device on the part of electorates this evil could become reduced. President Harding and the succession of Coolidge. Reference: The New Electoral Fusion System, no Partisan have the solutions to solve this menacing corruption.

ELECTORAL CORRUPTIONS

American Political Parties History

More serious is the criticism that national conventions are at entirely times irresponsible and sometimes arbitrary in powers managing their great powers. They may, for example, admit or reject delegations a will, regardless of the primary election laws of any state. However, these laws have now become sufficiently set up to make nullification at the hands of a convention exceedingly dangerous business. Abuse of power to make up the temporary roll by the holdover National Committee and by the committee on credentials, as in the Republican convention of 1912, is more likely to occur. Of course, it may lead to party schism and defeat of the national ticket; but most of the delegates who manage the abuse have not directly touched by these penalties. They are not themselves candidates or, if so, expect to win in their petty local contests. In their factional frenzy such delegates are not unwilling to risk party defeat, supplied only they can keep their grip on the organization. Of course, no amount of prevision can prevent or should try to prevent a party split when it is due and needed.

But deliberate party wrecking to keep control of the machine is another matter. In this connection President Wilson's suggestion previously quoted might prove helpful. A convention composed of delegates who were themselves' candidates for conspicuous offices could become punished promptly and severely for its misdeeds. Finally, national conventions are grossly incompetent as organs for the formulation of party policies which, in case for the of success at the polls, may become the nation's policies. As we have already noted, they are unsuited in personnel and they are far too large, too hurried, and too irresponsible for the proper performance of this weighty function. Moreover, they are too much engrossed with the choice of a presidential candidate to give enough attention to party policies.

If these two functions are in trusted to the same body the latter had doomed to suffer partial neglect at least. It is a curious fact of American politics that since presidential candidates had needed only once every four years, the party's content themselves with definitions of their national policies in platforms spaced by that interval of time. In several countries of continental Europe parties are accustomed to hold diets or congresses which define and change their policies from year to year or as critical issues arise. Moreover, these diets make no nominations and are thus free to devote their time exclusively to questions of policy and tactics. The practice has its disadvantages, but it does tend to keep the parties alert and up to date on issues. If we in the United States are to develop interest in political policies and principles as opposed to interest merely in nominations and patronage, it will be necessary for us to devise party institutions capable of real deliberation and frank expression on national affairs.

Reference: Chapter I C. E. Merriara, The American Party System, pp. 274-307 (1922). R. Michel's, Political Parties, pt. ii, chap, iv; E. McC. Saint, Government and Politics of France, chap, x; and the author's Government and Politics of Switzerland, chap. xiii. The New Electoral Fusion System, no Partisan have the solutions to solve this menacing corruption.

ELECTORAL CORRUPTION

American Political Parties History

Estimate and criticism of national from 1815 to 1832, the organization of the Democratic Republican Party hesitated. Without the pressure of competition, they no longer needed a united front. States began nominating local electors, who had their own personal interests in mind.

This split up the party several diverse ways. Particularly the split led to, in 1828, the modern Democratic Party, along with another political party known as the Whig Party. The Democratic Party, led by Andrew Jackson and Martin Van Buren, had made up of farmers, urban laborers, and Irish Catholics.

Although the Democratic Party was not exactly popular in newest England states, it gained immense popularity in New York, Pennsylvania, Virginia, and western states. supported the Democrats at this time strongly opposed aristocracy, a national bank, and programs which pushed to modernize American industry instead of family-based agriculture. Additionally, they Mexican-American War and the expansion of farmland into the western territories. They also opposed anti-immigration legislation and monopolies. Although the Democratic Party was much more popular in comparison with the Whig Party, the Whigs had access to more wealth, and thus more funding and influence.

In 1848, the Democratic National Committee have created at the elector nomination convention. General Lewis Cass had nominated for candidacy, but he lost the election to a Whig named General Zachary Taylor. The Free-Soil Party of New York influenced the outcome of the election. The Free-Soil Party had set up for one reason, to oppose the expansion of slavery into the new western states. The Free-Soil Party have made up of members from both the Whig Party and the Democratic Party who felt that free men on free soil should remain free.

They also fought for the rights of free men in many Midwest and northern states. Because of the party division over this issue, many Democrats voted for General Taylor instead of General Cass, which contributed to the loss of the Democratic Party in the election of 1848. In 1850, Democratic members of Congress passed what is known as the Compromise of 1850, which was a set of bills that tried to prevent civil war over slavery. The Compromise essentially outlawed slavery in the Western states; however, it also included a bill called the Fugitive Slave Act of 1850, which demanded that slaves who ran away to northern states had returned to their masters in the South. After the Compromise of 1850, Democrats gained small increments of popularity, while the Whig Party began to lose its unity. The Whig Party became increasingly divided over the issues of slavery and anti-immigration. In 1852, the Whig Party disbanded, leaving weak opposition against the Democrats for that year's election. Democrat Franklin Pierce had elected, followed by James Buchanan in 1856. Democrats who opposed slavery eventually left the party and joined those who were left over from the Whig Party in the North to form the Republican Party in 1854.

ELECTORAL CORRUPTION
American Political Parties History

From 1840 through 1850, certain Democrats began supporting the reform and modernization of industry. They argued that modernization would pave an effortless way for farmers to market and sell their goods. Although this stance may seem drastically different from the original Democratic vision, these Democrats argued that it still supported the same goals because industrialization would indirectly lead to prosperity among farmers and laborers. By the election of 1860, the anti-slavery Republican Party gained widespread popularity. Throughout the election, the Republican Party focused on the issue of slavery. They felt that the slaveholders and slavery supporters had taken over the government, and that these pro-slavery Democrats were voting against the progress of liberty. This incredibly powerful message led to the election of Republican Abraham Lincoln in 1860, who was as you may have deduced, the first Republican President.

After the onset of the Civil War, the Northern Democrats had divided into two factions based upon support for Lincoln's military policies: The War Democrats, who supported them, and the Copperheads, who opposed them. To prevent conflict that would injure wartime unity, no party politics have allowed in the Confederacy during the Civil War.

Confederates viewed political parties as bad for governance, so they avoided political division as much as possible. In general, Northern Democrats supported Lincoln throughout the war; however, Democratic support began to drop off after two key events. Around the year 1862, an anti-war push for peace gained strength among the Democrats. The Copperheads especially wanted to focus on ending the war as soon as possible. The Democrats went on to lose the election of 1864 after running their candidate, George McClellan, on a peace platform, despite most of the War Democrats supporting Lincoln.

In the congressional elections of 1866, the Radical Republicans won enough seats to have a two-thirds majority in both houses of Congress. The Republicans controlled all reconstruction policies since the Democrats had so few votes. In response to this political helplessness, the Democratic Party tried a New Departure. The aim of the New Departure was to downplay the war. The Democrats tried to distance themselves from the pro-slavery stance.

Although the Democrats wanted to disassociate themselves from the pro-slavery stance, they did gain voter support from white Southerners who felt hostile toward the Republican Party because of the war. In 1873, the country experienced an economic depression. This allowed the democrats to win back the House in 1874; however, they would not win another presidential election until Grover Cleveland had elected in 1884.

President Cleveland was the leader of a Democratic faction known as the Bourbon Democrats. The Bourbon Democrats opposed the annexation of Hawaii as well as Bimetallism, corruption of city bosses, imperialism, and US overseas expansion. They fought for and supported banking, railroad building, the Civil Service Reform, and non-interventionist capitalism.

ELECTORAL CORRUPTION

American Political Parties History

In 1893, an economic depression known as the Panic of 1893 hit due to the collapse of railroad over-building and under-financing. Because the Bourbon Democrats pushed railroad building, they had blamed. In 1894, the Republicans took full control of the House.

Another factor that contributed to the evolution of the Democratic Party was religious affiliation. The Republicans of the North were mostly Presbyterian, Methodist, and Congregationalist, while most Democrats Were Catholic, Episcopalian, and German Lutheran. Because of this sharp division, issues like prohibition became difficult to settle.

Like the current political atmosphere, the Republicans felt that the government should interfere with morality issues, like drinking alcohol, for example, to protect citizens from sin, while Democrats felt that the government should not become allowed to make religious or moral legislation.

Over the next century, the Democratic and Republican parties began to materialize into the polarized, two-party system that we have today. Although some qualities, such as general moral stance and socioeconomic status, can become traced back to the origin of each party, other traits like economic view and stance on government power, have led to prosperity among farmers and laborers.

By the election of 1860, the anti-slavery Republican Party gained widespread popularity. Throughout the election, the Republican Par-ty focused on the issue of slavery. They felt that the slaveholders and slavery supporters had taken over the government, and that these pro-slavery Democrats were voting against the progress of liberty.

This incredibly powerful message led to the election of Republican Abraham Lincoln in 1860, who was as you may have deduced, the first Republican President. After the onset of the Civil War, the Northern Democrats had divided into two factions based upon support for Lincoln's military policies: The War Democrats, who supported them, and the Copperheads, who opposed them.

The New Fusion Electoral System

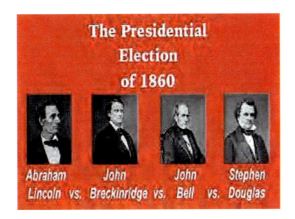

CHAPTER 27

ELECTORAL CORRUPTION PROBLEMS.

American Political Parties History

To prevent conflict that would injure wartime unity, no party politics were allowed in the Confederacy during the Civil War. Confederates viewed political parties as bad for governance, so they avoided political division as much as possible.

Over-all, Northern Democrats supported Lincoln throughout the war; however, Democratic support began to drop off after two key events. Around the year 1862, an anti-war push for peace gained strength among the Democrats. The Copperheads especially wanted to focus on ending the war as soon as possible. The Democrats went on to lose the election of 1864 after running their candidate, George McClellan, on a peace platform, despite most of the War Democrats supporting Lincoln.

In the congressional elections of 1866, the Radical Republicans won enough seats to have a two-thirds majority in both houses of Congress. The Republicans controlled all reconstruction policies since the Democrats had so few votes. In response to this political helplessness, the Democratic Party exasperated a new Exodus. The aim of the New Departure was to downplay the war. The Democrats tried to distance themselves from the pro-slavery stance.

Although the Democrats wanted to disassociate themselves from the pro-slavery stance, they did gain voter support from white Southerners who felt hostile toward the Republican Party because of the war. In 1873, the country experienced an economic depression. This allowed the Democrats to win back the House in 1874; however, they would not win another Presidential Election until Grover Cleveland had elected in1884.

President Cleveland was the leader of a Democratic faction known as the Bourbon Democrats. The Bourbon Democrats opposed the annexation of Hawaii as well as Bimetallism, corruption of city Bosses, imperialism, and US overseas expansion. They fought for and supported banking, railroad building, the Civil Service Reform, and non-interventionist capitalism. In 1893, an economic depression known as the Panic of 1893 hit due to the collapse of railroad over-building and under financing.

Because the Bourbon Democrats pushed railroad building, they have blamed. In 1894, the Republicans took full control of the House. Reference: The New Electoral Fusion System, no Partisan have the solutions to solve this menacing corruption.

CAMPAIGN FUNDDS AND CORRUPTION ACTS

American Political Parties History

The Federalist Party was the first American political party. It existed from the early 1790s to 1816, the era of the First Party System; its remnants lasted into the 1820s. The Federalists called for a strong national government that promoted economic growth and fostered friendly relationships with Great Britain, as well as opposition to revolutionary France.

The party controlled the federal government until 1801, when its exclusiveness had overwhelmed by the democratic spirit of the Republican opposition led by Thomas Jefferson. It came into being between 1792 and 1794 as a national coalition of bankers and businesspeople in support of Alexander Hamilton's fiscal policies.

These supporters developed into the organized Federalist Party, which was committed to a fiscally sound and nationalistic government. The only Federalist president was John Adams; although George Washington was broadly sympathetic to the Federalist program, he remained officially nonpartisan during his entire presidency. The Democratic-Republican Party was the American political party in the 1790s of Thomas Jefferson and James Madison formed in opposition to the centralizing politic.

In conclusion political partisan are a Mafia that corrupt the Democracy and the Republic Systems is an unnecessary their existence, I have studied the system through researches and experiences that in a rational mind the political parties are a business of corrupts politician and their helper lawyer.

The prohibitive cost of campaigning has more than outrun the High cost prohibitive cost of living in the United States. In the Buchanan-Fremont campaign of 1856 the total amount at the command of the Democratic National Committee was less than $25,000. Four years later the Republican National Committee spent a little over $100,000 on behalf of Lincoln. This sums in today's money is a vast amount.

Estimates are lacking as to the sums spent during the period of reconstruction, but no doubt they were extremely modest as compared with more recent developments. Most of the money collected at that time came as personal contributions in lesser amounts from office holders, candidates, job hunters, and enthusiastic partisans.

With the emergence of the tariff issue in national politics it became possible for Republican campaign collectors boiling to secure large contributions from protected manufacturers a process known as a vulgarly expression as Fat-Frying. At the same time the Democrats had accused of bleeding the large importing interests of the country, which were naturally interested in lower duties. Of these two sources, however, the former was much more productive. The consequent growth of campaign funds in the eighties led to the figures quoted for 1856 and i860 are given by Perry Belmont. Reference: The New Electoral Fusion System, no Partisan have the solutions to solve this menacing corruption.

CAMPAIGN FUNDDS AND CORRUPTION ACTS

American Political Parties History

Abolition of the Secrecy of Party Funds, U. S. Senate Doc. No. 405, 62d Cong., 2d Washing-ton, 1912. In contrast with these very modest figures, however, it should be noted that Seward's candidacy in the Republican national convention of 1860 was seriously damaged by the charge that his backers had procured a campaign fund of from four to

$600,000, by the corrupt granting of franchises for street railways in New York City.

The Electorate Suffrage and sovereignty Who shall vote in an autocracy the ruler has only to make up his own mind to determine the will of the state. In narrow aristocracies or oligarchies, it is also a comparatively simple matter to find the will of the small group of rulers. But with the extension of political power to masses of people in a democracy there can be, as Montesquieu French politician and philosopher arguments available in his book The Spirit of Law political theory, no exercise of sovereignty but by their suffrages, which are their own will. Now the sovereign's will be the sovereign himself.

The laws, therefore, which set up the right of suffrage are fundamental to this government. And indeed, it is as important to regulate in a republic, in what manner, by whom, to whom, and concerning what suffrages are to be given, as it is in a Monarchy to know who is the Prince, and after what manner he ought to govern.

Historically four principal answers have been given to the most fundamental of these questions: by whom are suffrages to be given, which, of course, involves the further question, who shall be debarred from suffrage? Among Greeks and Romans, the right to vote had considered to belong to all citizens as a necessary accompaniment to their membership in the state. It must become remembered, however, that citizenship itself has narrowly restricted even in the most democratic of ancient states. During the Middle Ages men voted because of the lands or titles they seized. It must become remembered, however, that citizenship itself has narrowly restricted even in the most democratic of ancient state. Reference: The French Revolution T. Nugent, bk. ii, chap. ii. C. Seymour and D. P. Frary, How the World Votes, chap. L.

THE RECALL PROBLEM

American Political Parties History

The recall has been well denned as neither more nor defined than a special election to determine whether an official shall become superseded before the ordinary end of his term. As such its field of operation is completely different from that of direct legislation.

On the other hand, their recall uses petitions in much the same way as they had used in initiative and referendum procedure. Also, it had advocated in the same way as a means of increasing popular control over government, and has found acceptance largely in states which have been most active in the use of the initiative and referendum. For these reasons it may not become judged amiss to discuss the recall in connection with direct legislation, although it might have taken up more logically under elections.

Unlike the statutory initiative and referendum, the recall seems to have become invented a new in the United States. Tension in although in fact a similar institution still survives in the constitutions of various Swiss cantons. It has first introduced in the Los Angeles charter of 1903,3 and has obtained its widest distribution subsequently in municipal charters, chiefly of the home rule, During the Middle Ages men voted because of the lands or titles they seized.

In the other seven it applies to judicial on the same terms as to other officials. Colorado alone supports the recall of judicial decisions. In Kansas, the recall may become invoked against appointive as well as elective officials. The North Dakota amendment of 1920 attempts to make it apply to representatives in Congress.

All recall laws guarantee a certain period of grace to official's subject to their provisions Usually this is six months, dating from the beginning of their terms, but in some states, it is a short as three months and in others has long as a year. In the case of members of the legislature the term has usually fixed as five days after the beginning of the first session following their election to that body. After this period has elapsed petitions may become circulated which must give the reasons briefly upon which the demand for recall is based.

To be effective they must become signed by a certain percentage of the voters of the state or district represented by the official who is under fire. Usually this has fixed at 25 per cent, a stiff requirement, higher, it will become noted, than the percentages commonly set up in the case of the initiative and referendum. In some states and cities, however, the percent-age required for recall petitions is as low as 10, in ethers as high as 35, per cent. The Illinois requirement of 55 per cent applying to officials of commission, and commission manager types. In 1908 Oregon, which had already been the innovator in other political fields, made the recall applicable by constitutional amendment to elective state officers, as well as to elective officials in districts such as counties, cities, and the like governed cities are, of course, so high as to be prohibitive. No doubt it had inserted with this intent, for it is a favorite device of opponents of direct legislation and recall bills when their rejection in toot cannot become brought about, to amend them by fixing impossible percentages. In view of the relatively greater ease of securing signatures locally it is interesting to note that the Kansas constitution requires 10 per cent for the recall of state officials, 15 per cent for the recall of officials of districts smaller that the state but greater than the county, and 25 per cent for the recall of officials of counties and smaller districts.2 Similarly the California recall amendment of 1911 requires 12 per cent in the case of state officials elected at large and 20 per cent in the case of state officials elected in political subdivisions of the state.

California also endeavors to secure a degree of geographical distribution by the requirement that petitions for the recall of officials elected by the state as a whole must be circulated in at least five counties and must secure the signatures of at least 1 per cent of the voters in each. Signatures for recall petitions had gotten in much the same way as signatures for direct-primary and direct legislation petitions. In all three the same abuses occur, and the same legal safeguards are necessary.

One state only, Kansas, makes the requirement that petitions must certify that the signers voted for the officer to become recalled, or, if his position is appointive, that they voted for the elective official appointing him. With the secret ballot, however, it is obvious that this requirement can be effective only as a moral obligation. In some cases, a single petition may become circulated against more than one official, and a single election used to conduct the recall of several officials.

References: J. D. Barnett, The Operation of the Initiative, Referendum, and Recall in Oregon, 1915. An Am. Pol. Sci. Rev., vol. vi, pp. 41-53 (Feb., 1912), A. H. Eaton, The Oregon System, pp. 99-104, T. Bourne, Jr., and G. W. Guthrie in Ann. Am. Acad. Pol. Sci., vol. xliii (Sept., 1912). For Government and Politics of Switzer-land, p. 321. The first resort to it in the history of the country occurred in Los Angeles, Sept. 16, 1904. E. Pomeroy, The First Discharge of a Public Servant, Independent, vol. lviii, p. 69 (Jan. 12, 1905). Commission, and commission-manager types. In 1908 Oregon, California followed this example, 1911; Arizona, 191112; Nevada, Colorado, Idaho, and Washington, 1912; Michigan, 1913; Kansas and Louisiana, 1914; and North Dakota, 1920. Of the eleven states, four expressly exempt judicial officials from recall, viz., Idaho, Washing-I ton, Michigan, and Louisiana. H. S. Gilbertson, Public Control under the Recall, Annals American Academy, vol. xxxviii, pp. 833-838 (Nov., 1911; and The Recall, list Provisions and Significance, same magazine, vol. xl, p. 216 (Sept., 1912) The Illinois law had passed March 10, 1910. Constitution, art. iv, § 193. 3 Constitution, art. xxiii. S. G. Lowrie, Am. Pol. Set. Rev., vol. v, p. 248 (May 1911.

THE RECALL PROBLEM

American Political Parties History

Upon their completion recall petitions go for verification resignation to avoid recall to the city clerk, county clerk, or secretary of state for resignations to examination and verification. Usually the officer whose avoid recall has sought may resign within five days from the filing of his petition. If he does not, and if the petitions had found enough, a special election must become ordered to take place within from twenty to ninety days. In Arizona, for example, the period is twenty to thirty days; in Colorado, thirty to sixty days, if a general election is not to occur within ninety days; in Louisiana, three to five months. Some states provide that if a regular election is to occur at a not too distant date, say within ninety days, the recall election may become postponed for that length of time.

Candidates who wish to run against the incumbent are Recall ballots thereupon nominated by petition or in such other manner as the primary laws may provide. Of course, those who are backing the recall have a strong motive to center the strength upon a single opposition candidate if this can become done. Originally most recall elections consisted simply of a choice between the incumbent and those nominated against him, the candidate who received the largest vote holding the office to the end of the term. This has been modified until at present in nearly all cases the ballots used in recall elections present first the question, shall be recalled from the office of with space in Arizona, for example, the period is twenty to thirty days; in Colorado, thirty to sixty days, if a general election is not to occur within ninety days; in Louisiana, three to five months. Some states provide that if a regular election is to occur at a not too distant date, say within ninety days, the recall election may become postponed for that length of time.

Candidates who wish to run against the incumbent are Recall ballots thereupon nominated by petition or in such other manner as the primary laws may provide. Of course, those who are backing the recall have a strong motive to center the strength upon a single opposition candidate if this can become done. Originally most recall elections consisted simply of a choice between the incumbent and those nominated against him, the candidate who received the largest vote holding the office to the end of the term. This has been modified until at present in nearly all cases the ballots used in recall elections present first the question, shall be recalled from the office of with spaces for a cross mark or stamp opposite the answers, is yes and no. Underneath this question names of candidates are printed with the usual spaces for voting.

In some cases, also the top of the recall ballot had occupied by a printed statement giving the reasons for the recall as advanced by those who circulated the petitions, followed by a justification from the official under attack, each not to exceed 200 or 300 words in length. Under the more modern arrangement answers to the of first question had first counted. If many answers ballots Recalls had recorded, in the no, the recall has failed, and the incumbent still is in office. If a majority vote in the yes, on the question of recall, the votes of candidates are next counted and the candidate who has received the largest number of votes is entitled to hold the office to the end of the term, for forms of petitions and ballots used in Oregon.

References" J. D. Barnett op. cit., appendix.

THE RECALL CORRUPTION PROBLEMS

American Political Parties History

Usually the law provides that only those ballots may be counted on candidates which are also marked in answer to the recall question. Two methods prevail regarding the number of times Name and the name of the incumbent may appear on the recall ballot, incumbent assuming that he does not resign within the time allowed ballot for this purpose, his name goes on the ballot automatically at least so far as the question of recall is considered.

In some states it does not appear again as a candidate against the. field. Under this arrangement, of course, the official whose recall have sought must get most of all voting on the first question to keep his position. If he does not do so his successor may win by a bare plurality. In other states the incumbent's name appears first in the question referred to above, and again in the list of candidates.

It was a valid criticism against the 546 original form of recall elections in which the incumbent simply stood for reelection against candidates pitted against him, that the result did not Under this arrangement it is possible for the recall to defeat itself that is, for the question as to the recall to become answered affirmatively by a majority, while, nevertheless, the incumbent retains his seat by winning over the other candidates with a bare plurality. If, on the other hand, it was the practice to vote first on the question of the recall only, leaving the vacancy created in case the recall succeeded to be filled either by form of the appointment or in the same way as any vacancy caused recall by death or resignation, this criticism would be avoided.

THE KANSAS RECALL CORRUPTION PROBLEMS
American Political Parties History

At times, of course, the latter method would involve the added trouble and expense of a second special election, which is no doubt one of the reasons it has not become adopted. So far Kansas alone has taken the latter horn of the dilemma, its constitution providing simply that if the popular vote is in favor of recall a vacancy in the office shall exist to be filled as authorized by law.

It should become remembered in this connection that Kansas makes the recall applicable to appointive as well as to elective officials. In Louisiana and North Dakota, the recall may not be call elections resorted to a second time against the same official during the same term. Colorado pays the election expenses of an official against whom the recall had invoked unsuccessfully and makes the practically impossible requirement of a 50 percent petition for a second recall election against him during the same term.

California also repays election expenses of state officials against whom the recall has failed and provides that a second recall shall not become undertaken within six months. In other states it is usually if those who wish to launch a second recall against the same man during the same term must first pay into the public treasury the costs of the first recall election.

Kansas is the only state which expressly provides that methods of the existence of the recall shall not exclude the use of other removal means of securing the removal from office of unsatisfactory officials. In all other cases this had assumed. Prior to the introduction of the recall, American states and municipalities had supplied many methods to secure the dismissal of officials. These methods included, to mention a few types only, impeachment; dismissal of appointive officers by their executive superiors either acting alone or with the consent of the upper legislative house; removal of judges by joint resolution of both branches of the legislature; and removal by higher court judges of prosecuting attorneys, minor judicial officials, and minor county and town officers.

Opponents of the recall have always urged that these arguments methods were sufficiently numerous, that they were more based on deliberate and impartial than removal by popular vote, methods and that they met the needs of the situation fully, or at least might be made to do so by certain modifications of procedure. Advocates of the recall, on the other hand, held that these earlier methods were too cumbersome, that they offered too much scope for the use of political influence and the introduction of legal technicalities, that in spite of them, many officials were subservient to bosses and machines and unmindful of the loyalty they owed to the interests of the people. Acute political observers have often noted the unsatisfactory nature of the reasons publicly advanced for the re-advanced call of officials.

These do not have to be misdemeanors or legal offenses enough to justify dismissal by other t methods. Corrupt or illegal conduct, misrepresentation of constituents, incompetence or any other grounds that may seem enough, may become alleged as reasons for recall. As a matter of fact, the reasons stated may amount to nothing more than alleged errors of judgment spending too much money for one purpose rather than another, in one section of a state or county rather than another, or upholding appointive officials whose conduct or opinion has given offense. There is a general tendency to state reasons broadly, or to state part of the reasons only, leaving the real motives of the recall movement undisclosed. Fear of libel suits accounts partly for this reticence. Sometimes the real motives are not very creditable, involving, as they may, many petty, personal, local and property interests. For example, wet and dry animosities become invoked freely in such campaigns, if not in petitions. These conditions often give a sordid air to recall movements. It must become remembered, however, that the lower motives play a very influential. A recall election, also called a recall referendum or representative recall, is a procedure by which, in certain polities, voters can remove an elected official from office through a direct vote before that official's term has ended. References: Constitution, art. iv, sec. 192.

ELECTIONS AND CORRUPTION PROBLEMS

American Political Parties History

Recall elections differ from other elections only in the necessity of formulating reasons, which tends to bring these lower motives to the surface. Of course, they are unpleasant to contemplate, but it is more sanitary to bring them out into the sunlight and air of publicity than to ignore their existence.

Supporters of the initiative, referendum, and recall frequently urged the adoption of all three of these tools of direct popular power not because they had needed for frequent use, but because of their cautionary effect upon public officials.

THE RECALL CORRUPTION PROBLEMS

American Political Parties History

There has been but one instance On the Los Angeles recall of 1909, of the use of the recall against an official elected by vote n homely phrase they were to resemble the farmer's shotgun behind the door, to become taken out only in case of emergency.

Contrary to this expectation, as we have seen, the initiative and referendum developed a frequency of use that constitutes one of the chiefs

The New Fusion Electoral System

of current objections to these institutions. The recall alone has become used so sparingly as to justify the earlier prediction of its friends. Oregon, which has had the longest statewide experience resort to the with the recall, saw only seventeen instances of recall its use in seven years following its introduction. Thirty-five office holders were involved, only nine of whom succeeded in keeping their offices. No incumbents of state offices had attacked in Oregon.

Until 1921 the most prominent officials against whom the recall had invoked in other states were the mayor of Los Angeles in 1909, and the mayor of Seattle in 1911.1 In both cases the incumbents were removed.

References F. T. Stillson, National Conference on City Government, 1909, pp. 326-333; Independent, vol. lxvi, pp.431, 861 (Feb. 25, March 26, 1909). The Seattle recall of 1911 has dissing-cussed fully by F. W. Catlett, The Working of the Recall in Seattle, Ann. Am. Acad. Pol. Sci., vol. xliii, pp. 227-236 (Sept. 1912). Cf., McClures, vol. xxxvii, pp. 647-663 (Oct., 1911); Outlook, vol. xxxvii, p. 295 (Feb., 1911 In 1915, however, the mayor who have recalled in 1913 have again elected mayor of that city on a platform pledging reform. See W. M. Baine, Seattle Changed Its Mind. H. Gill, Am. Mag., vol. lxxx, p. 51 (Sept. 1915).

There has been but one instance On the Los Angeles recall of 1909, of the use of the recall against an official elected by vote of the state as per a complete. In 1920 North Dakota adopted the recall through the influence of the Nonpartisan League.

A year later it was employed with success to remove from office the governor of the state who had become elected, also with Nonpartisan League support, at the same time the recall had introduced. The figures in this case is particularly interesting because of the slight margins in the two votes. In 1920, Lynn J. Frazier have elected governor with Republican and Nonpartisan League support by a vote of 117,188 to 112,488 for his opponent, J. F. T. O'Connor, who had Democratic and Independent support. In the recall election a year later Frazier have beaten by a vote of 107,333 to I14,432 for this opponent, R. A. Nestos.

At the same election, the state commissioner of agriculture and attorney general had recalled. Nevertheless, little animus seems to have survived against Frazier for he has elected to the Unite State Senate in 1922. In general, therefore, the recall has shown itself to be an instrument serviceable primarily against local officials whose acts touch constituents closely and hence often rouse their resentment.

Considering the very large of such officials through the country now subject to recall number would seem to indicate that little animus against him survived from the recall has shown election which cost him the governorship. In general, therefore, the recall has shown itself to be Recall Prim aria instrument serviceable primarily against local officials primarily for whose acts touch constituents closely, and hence often 1186 rouse their resentment. Considering the exceptionally substantial number of such officials throughout the country now subject to recall, its use must become described as sporadic only.

Under the circumstance's critics doubt whether its cautionary effect upon officials is much greater than the moral and religious effect upon individuals due to the knowledge of the latter that lightning may strike them. There is one possibility in this connection which is evil. Enemies of a given office holder may circulate recall petitions against him until they have secured signatures to a number slightly less than the required quota. There is secured signatures to a number slightly less than the required quota. Then as the phrase has it, they may hold the petition in un-emotional storing, threatening him with its completion unless he conforms to their wishes. This practice, which is alleged to have occurred been used as evidence of popular instability alleged to be caused by the recall, but it seems to prove nothing on that score which might not be alleged against ordinary popular elections, in certain instances, might be broken up by fixing a definite period of time within which the required number of signatures would have to be obtained, failing which petitions would be void.

POLITICALPARTIES

American Political Parties History

On the rare occasions when they do occur, recall elections usually attract an intense popular interest. The issues presented touch citizens closely and often they are quite sensational in character. An element of sharp personal antagonism, like that of the duel, is present. The ballots used are short enough to satisfy the most thoroughgoing short-ballot advocates. However, extreme interest has not always manifested.

In the same state there have been other recall elections characterized by general apathy and in which less than a third of at times recall elections develop a good deal of noise and some violence may occur or become threatened, but unwelcome incidents of this kind are no more directly attributable to the recall than to ordinary elections, which also occasionally marred by them. In a few Oregon recall elections, the vote cast was more than the registered vote had polled. Careful observers find it difficult to appraise the effectiveness of the recall. Experience is not sufficiently in those states and cities which have had it longest for final judgment. It is not difficult to imagine circumstances under which the recall might become galvanized into a much more frequent use than has hitherto become recorded.

It has prevented some of the more conspicuous political sins of commission, such as bad franchise grants and the establishment of segregated vice districts. Also, it has fostered some political sins of omission. Tax officials subject to recall had said to be afraid to make assessments at full value as required by law. Theoretically, the recall may become used as readily by the machine against faithful servants of the people as by the people against servants of the machine, but experience shows that the first contingency is little to be feared.

References: A. M. Kales, Unpopular Government in the United States, pp. 112-127. 1

POLITICAL PARTIES AND THE RECALL CORRUPTIONS

American Political Parties History

Critics of the recall were wont to argue that it would make voters careless. Since they could get rid of an official at any time, they would be inclined to elect officials without careful consideration of their fitness. This argument overlooked the very considerable amount of effort and even of expense necessary to successfully conduct a recall movement.

And there is no evidence to show that voters are more indifferent to the character of candidates with the recall than they were before its introduction. Another argument was that if the menace of the recall had added to other disadvantages attached to many elective positions such as low salaries, hard work, constant criticism, and short terms there would be a dearth of candidates. Nevertheless, candidates, good, bad, and indifferent, present themselves quite as freely after the recall has become adopted as before. And although the recall has not made statewide advances in recent years so rapidly as during the period 1911-14, in general those states and cities which have already adopted it seem well enough satisfied.

At least movements for its abolition occasionally heard of, although there is some discussion of methods by which it may be perfected. Perhaps the greatest single gain which may become credited to the recall is that indirectly it has aided materially in bringing about a much-needed lengthening of the terms for of certain elective officers. In fact, the recall is of little use as against short term office holders.

For example, if petitions must be halted for the first six months of a two-year term, and if elections may take place not earlier than sixty to ninety days after petitions have been completed and approved, it is evident that the time during which such an office holder may be attacked is limited. Moreover, the loss inflicted upon a short-term office holder by a successful recall, and consequently the cautionary effect of the institution, are likely to be much less than in the case of a long-term office holder.

POLITICAL PARTIES AND THE RECALL CORRUPTION

American Political Parties History

To be sure, these are negative results, but on the positive side the same considerations incline the electorate to look with more favor upon an increase of official tenure and powers, provided the incumbents are at the same time made subject to the recall. As far as legislative officials are concerned, the initiative and referendum tend to have the same effect, although not to so great a degree as the recall.

In all probability the short ballot, and the commission and commission-manager forms of municipal government, all of which involve longer terms and greater concentration of powers, would have made much less rapid progress throughout the country had it not been possible to offer the electorate at the same time the sop of the recall. Great readjustments of a similar character are impending in state administration, and these may also find the recall a useful adjunct.

Even more than the initiative and referendum, the recall judicial had denounced originally as unconstitutional and revolutionary in that it substituted a dangerous form of direct democratic rule for representative republican institutions. But the bitterest condemnation had reserved for those who proposed to make it applicable to judicial officials. As typical of the more extreme of these expressions one eminent writer who conceded that the introduction of the referendum as a check upon the legislature might become considered progress nevertheless insisted that if it is progress it is also revolution.

The initiative he held to be the most preposterous and the most vicious" of all the proposals brought forward in the name of direct democracy.

References: A. B. Hall, Popular Government, pp. 203-241; S. Further the recall of executive and legislative officials, while meddlesome and disturbing to leadership, was not a violation of the principles of representative government as are the initiative and referendum. Applied to the judiciary, however, the recall is much more than a piece of imprudent foolishness. It is an outrage of the first size. McCall, Representative as against Direct Government," Atlantic, vol. cviii, pp. 454-466 (Oct., 1911); H. J. Ford, Direct Legislation and the Recall, Ann. Am. Acad. Pol. Sci., vol. xliii, p. 75 (Sept., 1912). Also, articles by R. G. Brown, J. A. Metcalf, and A. H. Snow in the same issue of the Annals. The New Electoral Fusion System, no Partisan have the solutions to solve this menacing recall corruptions.

THE RECALL AND THE POLITICAL PARTIES

American Political Parties History

Criticism directed specifically against the latter point was not without its effect since, as we have already noted, four of the eleven recall states expressly exempt judicial officials of all grades from recall.

The action of Arizona on this point attracted much attention in 1911 and 1912. The first constitution with which it sought admission to the union provided for the recall without excluding judges. Congress passed an enabling Act stipulating, however, that an amendment become gave to the people of the state at the first ensuing election by which judicial officers should become exempted.

Even with this condition President Taft vetoed the enabling Act in a message which presented fully and forcibly the arguments against the recall of judges. Thereupon Congress amended the enabling Act by inserting the words, except members of the judiciary, as applied to the proposed recall provisions in the state constitution. A year following its admission; however, Arizona restored the judicial recall to its constitution.

Opponents of the recall of judges laid great stress on necessity of leaving the courts free from every gust on recall of popular passion in their work of interpreting constitutions and laws.

With a sword of Damocles forever suspended over their heads in the form of the recall, judges would lose their independence and constitutional guaranties would become swept away.

Advocates of this use of the recall argued that judges sometimes fall under the sinister influence of political bosses and machines, or of great corporations, and that they, as well as other officials, needed to become re-minded occasionally that they were servants of the people. As elective officials in most of the states they must give their claims to the people from time to time in any event.

References: N. M. Butler, Why Should We Change Our Form of Government? pp. 25, 32. 2 The message may become found in House Doc. 106, 6iA Cong., Beard and Schultz, Documents on the State-Wide Initiative, Referendum and Recall, pp. 246-256. 3 Am. Yr. Bk., ton, p. 262; 1912, p. 47.

THE RECAL AND THE SWRD OF DAMOCLE

In the aftermath of the War of Recapture, however, dissent was growing among the one-time allies; your ancestors didn't want to give lands to the Clradians on their home continent, while at the same time they owned significant properties back in Calradia. Your grandparents did their best to avoid a new conflict, but after their deaths, there was nothing to stop a new war from emerging.

This chaotic period became known as the War for Equality. In the end, your majestic parents, may their names be blessed for eternity, ended the war with a peace treaty: they gave up their Calradian lands, and afterwards neither they nor the Calradians would try to take each other's' properties. Trade between the two continents flourished, and more importantly, to signify the unity between them, the people of the two continents organized a great expedition fleet in search of new lands. The expedition was successful, for they found a third continent...

This mass of land was called Ponasova by its native inhabitants-primitive tribes of humans fighting among themselves. They were savage warrior cultures, garbing themselves in skins of wild beasts and bearing strange, exotic weapons. That is, until the expeditionary troops wiped them out completely. Some of the native tribes yet endure, but most of the new continent now belongs to the invaders - us, and our Calradian allies.

However, we live in a time when sailing between continents takes over a month and homing pigeons are the fastest way of delivering messages on short distances. Under such conditions, holding the new colonies in check is difficult if not nigh impossible. As such, the representatives of the various nations are likely to start infighting eventually, especially since the peace treaty signed at the end of the War for Equality is about to expire. More worrying yet, your royal parents recently died under mysterious circumstances. The investigation found no evidence of illness, poisoning nor assassination so far, but both your father and mother dying so suddenly and at the same time is quite strange. In any case, this is where YOU come into the picture...circulating petitions against them.

During the first seven years of the statewide recall in Oregon, it had invoked on two or three occasions against local judges, but they had attacked because of the alleged miss performance of certain duties imposed upon them in an administrative capacity, not because of their conduct on the bench.

In general, the conclusion seems well founded that the people not only have a high respect for the courts, but are little interested in purely legal decisions, and therefore are not likely to resort to the use of the recall against judges on such grounds.

An off shoot of the controversy over the recall of judges judicial which provoked an enormous amount of superheated discussion during the campaign of 1912, was the proposed recall of judicial decisions. In the platform of the Progressive party of that year, the plank on this subject was as follows: When an act passed under the police power.

References:1 A. N. Holcombe, op. cit., p. 375.2 For details see the Independent, vol. lxxiv, p. 1014 (May 8, 1913); Literary Digest, vol. xlvi, p. 1048 (May 10, 1913). 3 P. Eliel, Corrupt Judges Recalled in San Francisco, Nat. Mun. Rev. vol. x, p. 316 (June 1921). 4 J. D. Barnett, op. cit., p. 206. The New Electoral Fusion System, no Partisan have the solutions to solve this menacing recall corruptions.

CHAPTER 28

THE RECALL AND THE POLITICAL PARTIES

American Political Parties History

The recall proposed merely to hold them to account in cases and at time when gross abuses were suspected against them. In the light of our experience to date the controversy seems barren. No judge has yet been recalled because of popular dissatisfaction with a decision involving constitutional interpretation. The recall has not yet become invoked against a member of any superior or supreme court.

The most sensational case on record involving a judge has directed and carried to a successful conclusion against a San Francisco police magistrate in 1913. In this case the accusation was that of collusion in the escape of prisoners charged with serious crimes against young girls. Two other San Francisco police judges have recalled in 1921, an interesting feature of the case being the fact that the Bar Association aided in

THE RECALL AND POLITICALS PARTIES

American Political Parties History

Recall of the state is held unconstitutional under the state constitution by the courts, the people, after an ample interval for deliberation, shall have an opportunity to vote on the question whether they desire the Act to become a law, notwithstanding such decision. Colorado adopted this proposal in the form of a fraud accepted by constitutional amendment in 1913, but no other state has followed its example. According to this amendment no court lower than the supreme court may declare laws unconstitutional.

If the supreme court takes this action about an Act passed by the legislature, its decision is not binding for a period of sixty days. During this period petitions may become circulated demanding a referendum vote on the law. If these petitions have signed by 5 per cent of the voters an election must become held within ninety days, and if a majority vote favors the law it has upheld regardless of the decision of the supreme court.

The same provisions hold have had about judicial decisions averse to city charters except that in such cases petitions have circulated and the election has held only in the city affected thereby. Even though, this amendment has been in force ten years, no decision of the Supreme Court has become attacked under it.

At this distance of time it is difficult to see anything Futile revolutionary or dangerous in the recall of judicial decisions rather than as proposed in 1912. It had the advantage of being much less invidious than the recall of judges themselves, which was doubtless one of the reasons it has taken up. On the other hand, it amounted simply to a new method of constitutional amendment by popular vote, and, as such, was narrower and less effective than the constitutional initiative. In short, the proposal was unsuccessful rather than essential, and has ceased altogether to figure in politics.

References: O. Ray, op. cit., pp. 499-503. W. L. Ransom, Majority Rule the Judiciary, 1912; and by W. D. Lewis, A New Method of Constitutional Amendment by Popular Vote, Ann. Am. Acad. Pol. Sci., vol. xliii, pp. 311-325 Sept., 1912. W. F. Dodd, Social Legislation and the Courts, Pol. Sci. Quar., vol. xxviii, pp. 1-17 March 1913; and A. B. Hall,

The New Fusion Electoral System

THE RECALL AND POLITICALS PARTIES

American Political Parties History

Excepting only its application to the initiative and referendum, all the manifold forms of the voting process discussed in preceding chapters are employed in the choice of elective public officials. The fundamental importance of this process under any form of representative government fully justifies the large share of popular attention given to it. He is through the officers thus chosen that the will of the people had expressed in even more important affairs of government. What is not so clearly versioned in the public mind is the fact that elective officials form an extremely small proportion of the great army of public officials taken as a whole, all of whom are engaged in some major or minor part of the work of government.

In the federal system, for example, there are only 533 Large number elective public officials the President, the Vice-President, 96 Senators, and 435 Representatives. From a body of less than three hundred officials at its organization the national government has expanded until in 1922 it had 560,863 appointive civilian employees of the executive civil service, making it the largest employer of labor in the world. In state governments also the appointive is more than the elective personnel. New York In 1919, at the peak of the demand caused by the war, the number was 917,760.

References: Cf. Thirty-ninth Annual Report of the United States Civil Service Commission for the Fiscal Year Ended June 30, 1922, p. vii. The New Electoral Fusion System, no Partisan have the solutions to solve this menacing spoil corruptions.

Michael Anguelo

SPOIL ELECTORAL SYSTEM

American Political Parties History

These figures do not include the comparatively small number of places within the appointive power of the legislative and judicial branches, nor, of course, the armed forces of the army and navy. State has 18,00c,1 Illinois something like 10,000 employees.

Metropolitan cities have even larger labor in rural counties and local governments, the disparity between the numbers of elective and appointive offices are not so great, but as a rule the latter are much more numerous. federal government and all the states, counties, towns, cities, and villages there are three million persons. According to a recent estimate in the entire public service of the one in every thirty-five per-sons man, woman and child attractions pay from the government. And we pay them in a year, all told, something more than three billion dollars.

Every head of a family puts his hand into his pocket each year and takes out on the average more than one hundred dollars to contribute to the pay of his public servants. The foregoing estimate includes both elective strength of and appointive officials.

The latter, as we have just noted, holders are in a great majority, and since most of them are adults they constitute a considerable proportion of the voting population, perhaps one in twenty or twenty-five. In large cities this proportion runs much higher.

Professor Munro estimates that in New York city the number of municipal employees is 8 per cent of the registered voting population. In Boston it is about 12 percent.

SPOILS ELECTORAL SYSTEM

American Political Parties History

Outside the metropolitan centers of population, the mere voting strength of public employees is not great enough to make them an important political factor. Moreover, taking the country, it is in all probability evenly divided between the parties.

On the other hand, the possibility of the misuse of so large several places to build up a political machine is so omnipresent and threatening that it constitutes one of the major problems of American Politics. Even during the administrations of Washington and origin Adams partisan considerations were by no means disregarded in making federal appointments.

With the defeat of the Federalist party the demand for patronage was materially increased. Finding himself faced by the quandary, how has vacancies to become obtained? Jefferson remarked, plaintively, those by death are few, by resignation none.

At that time public opinion would have been outraged using the presidential power of removal on any considerable scale to secure offices for distribution. The old English view that once in private hands a public office takes on something of the nature of a vested property right, still survived.

Meanwhile, however, this traditional barrier was breaking down in the larger cities and states of the North. With the disappearance of property qualifications for suffrage there had added to the electorate in this part of the country many new voters who had no sympathy with the political ideas of the dominant local aristocracy.

A race of politicians grew up who were not the men to entertain scruples about disturbing gentlemen in their comfortable moorings.

The longer the office holders had been in the more reason they should get out to make room for others and give everyone a chance at the public housing.

References: Tammany Hall to organize the new mass of poorer voters, Aaron Burr succeeded in wresting the control of New York city from Hamilton in 1800. Thus inaugurated, the Government of American Cities, p. 266. 2 H.J. Ford, The Rise and Growth of American Politics, p. 148

Michael Anguelo

SPOILS ELECTORAL SYSTEM

American Political Parties History

Using Tammany Hall to organize the new mass of poorer voters, Aaron Burr succeeded in wresting the control of New York city from Hamilton in 1800. Thus inaugurated, use of patronage as a political weapon spread apace through other Northern cities and states.

It was another New York state leader, Senator Marcy, who some years later evolved the phrase destined to become the catchword of the new political conception: To the victor belong the spoils of the enemy. In 1820 the first breach has made in the federal bulwark by the passage of an act limiting to four years the tenure of district attorneys, collectors, surveyors of customs, navy agents, paymasters, and some other officials.

Primarily the purpose of this Act was to enable Secretary Crawford to build up a machine that would help him to reach the Presidency. By automatically ejecting dwelling holders at the end of four years the Act of 1820 was, of course, much more productive of vacancies than the tardy processes of death and resignation.

Then came the popular disturbance which made Andrew Jackson President. Although held responsible for the introduction of the spoils system into the federal government, Jackson made no clean sweep. According to Benton, he left most offices in the hands of members of the opposing party even in the executive departments at Washington.

However, the number of removals made by Jackson during the first year of his administration, variously estimated at from 690 to 734, was so large and startling as compared with the record of his predecessors that it may become taken as the mark of a new era in politics. In 1836, the last year of Jackson's second term, another law had placed upon the statute books which materially eased the operation of the spoils system.

It provided that all mail carriers whose compensation was one thousand dollars a year or more should become appointed by the President with the confirmation of the Senate and that their term of office should be four years. Further, they have made removable at the discretion of the President.

References: Used in a debate in the United States Senate, 1832; Register of Debates in Congress, viii, pt. I, 1325.

Following Jackson's administration, the spoils system made rapid progress not only rapid progress not only in the federal government, but also in state and city governments except in the South, where for a long time its introduction locally was successfully resisted. After each defeat at the polls deserving members of the victorious party raised the cry, Turn the mischief-makers out, and clean sweeps became the order of the day. leaders in Congress and out constantly brought pressure to bear upon heads of departments to dismiss employees in order that their own followers might become rewarded. At its extreme development the spoils system was capable of producing results similar to those summed up in the first annual report of the Civil Service Commission as follows: When Draper, a Republican, was collector of the port at New York, he removed a subordinate as often as every third day for a whole year.

When Smyth, another Republican, succeeded Draper as collector in 1866, he removed 830 of his 903 Republican subordinates at the average rate of three every four days. When Grinnell, another Republican, succeeded Smyth as collector in1869, he removed 510 out of his 892 Republican subordinates in sixteen months. When Murphy, another Republican, succeeded Grinnell as collector in 1870, he removed Republicans at the rate of three every five days until 338 had become cast out.

Thus, during a period of five years in succession, collectors, all belonging to one party, for the purpose of patronage, made removals at a single office of members of their own party more frequently than at the rate of one every day. In 1,565 secular days 1,678 such removals have made. Of course, such speedy results were exceptional. Exceptions The principle of rotation in office have seldom applied universally either in the federal or in state and local government. A new party taking power had virtually forced to keep certain experienced or especially capable employees in technical positions.

Reference: The New Electoral Fusion System, no Partisan have the solutions to solve this menacing spoil corruptions.

Michael Anguelo

SPOIL ELECTORL SYSTEM

American Political Parties History

Nor were all other appointees without training, for some men succeeded in obtaining a long intermittent term of office, coming in and going out repeatedly with the ups and downs of their party or faction. At times of stress when it became advisable to pander a little to the moral element in the com-munity, a few conspicuously good appointments might become made. In Pennsylvania, this process is known as sprinkling political perfumery. Professor Merriam relates a story of the head of a great spoils system who once decided to make an eye of the school trustees. He had found late one night in his favorite saloon and had asked to make one of the customary types of appointments; but to the surprise of the solicitor he answered. We stay appointing no stiffs here. Give us a guy of some class. In favor of the principle of rotation in office explain some respectable authorities and precedent may have quoted.

Jefferson thought that it would prevent the creation of an autocracy. Jackson himself was convinced that long tenure of office lead to laxness and corruption Defense of respectable authorities and precedents may be mad. Jefferson thought that it would prevent the creation of a bureaucracy. Jackson himself was convinced that long tenure of office leads to laxness and corruption. Provisions had included in many state constitutions and city charters making certain prominent office holders ineligible to succeed themselves.

In the case of financial posts limitations of this kind had held to be particularly valuable because they compel the settlement of accounts at regular intervals. There is little in common, however, between changes of the above sort and the indiscriminate rotation of innumerable offices, most of them petty in character, which lies at the basis of the spoils system.

Nevertheless, rotation in its extreme form has not lacked apologists, most of them, to be sure, spoils politicians themselves. Few of these apologists go the length of Plunkitt, who held that while the civil service law lasts there cannot be no real patriotism. References: The American Party System, p.353.W. L. Riordon, Plunkitt of Tammany Hall, p. 19.5,

SPOIL ELECTORAL SYSTEM AND PARTIES.

American Political Parties History

All of them assert that without patronage parties cannot exist. Since parties have conceded to be necessary and beneficent, every advantage spoils system by this argument. Unfortunately for it, however, our party life is most intelligent, vigorous, and successful in the field of national government where civil service reform has made the largest inroads into the volume of patronage.

Despite powerful local machines, undoubtedly built up in large part by spoils, party life is distinctly less intelligent and efficient, even less honest, in state, city, and county governments where the most abundant supply of spoils, relatively speaking, is to become found. Parties functioned efficiently in the United States during the pre-Jacksonian era, when spoils were virtually unknown.

The experience of many European countries, notably of England since the reform of her civil service, shows that a vigorous party life is possible without the use of patronage. One of the earliest arguments in favor of the spoils Rotation System was that it fostered an ambition to serve the country alleged to be on the part of a great many poorer citizens, formerly democratic excluded by a caste of stiff and arrogant aristocrats.

Hence it was democratic and by the natural equality of men. If you do not believe that "one man is as good as another," at least you may accept the dictum of George III, himself an adept in the use of spoils, that every man is good enough for any place he can get.

At the time the anti-aristocratic argument has advanced in favor of rotation it did not lack a certain justification. Applied as it often is to-day in favor of turning out a trained and selected force for the benefit of incompetents, it takes on quite an assorted color.

Descending from argument to epithet, spoils men glorified their practice as the American system, deriding snivel service reform as the Chinese system. A favorite assertion, according to Roosevelt, was to call the reform Chinese, because the Chinese had constructed an inefficient governmental system based in part on the theory of written competitive examinations.

References: P. O. Ray, Introduction to Political Parties and Practical Politics, p.373. The New Electoral Fusion System, no Partisan have the solutions to solve this menacing spoil corruptions.

SPOILELECTORAL SYSTEM AND POLITICAL PARTY.

American Political Parties History

The argument might have become applied still further. For instance, the Chinese had invented gunpowder and uses it for centuries; gunpowder used in Springfield rifles; so, Springfield rifles were Chinese in part. One argument is quite as logical as the other.

Arguments against the spoils system are based upon its effects in the fields of party organization and method, spoils system of a ministration and legislation, and of political life and morals in general. As far as the misuse of patronage is responsible for the machine and notoriously it is one of the foundation stones of such structures the numerous malpractices characteristic of machine rule may become charged to spoils.

The methods and consequences of machine domination have become discussed at length in an earlier chapter and need not become repeated here. Suffice it to say that the anti-Aristocratic arguments and democratic pretenses of spoils politicians cannot become reconciled with that actual practice of a highly centralized party organization. The latter is a narrow oligarchy, if indeed it does not become a virtual Autocracy under Boss rule.

It does not open wide the avenues to public employment on a democratic basis; on the contrary, it places the power of appointment in the hands of one or a few men who in most cases are not responsible to any governmental authority for their exercise of that power. Also, machine rule restricts the number of those eligible in fact to appointive office.

Disgracefully, the principle of selection which it employs is not that of fitness for the duties to become performed, but that of service to the machine, sometimes service of a demoralizing or even criminal character. With occasional exceptions citizens who are unwilling to perform such partisan service have as effectually excluded from office as they would be under any other kind of Oligarchy. In the fields of legislation and administration the con effects on sequences of the spoils system are many and sinister, these consequences. References: Autobiography, p. 151.

SPOIL SYSTEM AND ELECTIONS

American Political Parties History

Under the spoils system members of Congress, state legislatures, and city councils must spend a large part of their time blockading executive officers and administrative departments in a constant search for the jobs demanded by their constituents.

As a result, the legislative work in trusted to them must suffer, while at the same time administrative officers are worried and distracted beyond human endurance. A governor or legislator who attempts to perform the proper functions of his office, neglecting demands made upon m for patronage, soon finds his position made untenable by deserving Democrats or deserving Republicans back home.

Of one such governor, a party manager, quoted by Professor Merriam, remarked, I simply do not understand Governor. He takes no interest in these appointments. He spends all his time thinking about bills in the legislature, or about his speeches. He does not seem to care a dam up about politics.

Until a President, governor, or other executive officer end or has disposed of the patronage under his control he may, which former executive officer ends of course, use it to induce legislators to do his bidding. Its manager at. was in this fashion that Lincoln procured the passage by used Congress of certain needed war measures and that Cleveland obtained the support of silver Congress people in 1893 for the repeal of the silver purchase clause of the Sherman Act.

While executive patronage has been employed at times for praiseworthy ends, it may become turned to the up building of a personal machine, to secure action from a legislature contrary to the will of the electors, or to other sinister purposes. On the other hand, once the patronage has become disposed of, disgruntled legislators and others who feel that they have become defrauded of their fair share, do not hesitate to turn against the executive and his policies. It is for this reason in large part that a governor or mayor is so much more influential at the beginning than at the end of his term.

Reference: Of. cit. 104. The New Electoral Fusion System, no Partisan have the solutions to solve this menacing spoil corruptions.

Michael Anguelo

POLIITICAL SYSTEM AND CIVIL SERVICE REFORM
American Political Parties History

When the supply of sponsorship is not enough and it and padded never is the legislative body is under strong temptation payrolls to create useless jobs.

Pressure has also brought to bear upon administrative departments to pad their payrolls. From the spoils seeker's point of view such sinecures are eminently desirable, not only because they entail few if any public duties, but also because they leave him free for the performance of the partisan tasks imposed upon him by the machine. If free play has given to the pressure for jobs regardless of the need for them, supernumeraries swarm in the public service.

A striking instance of this sort occurred in the Bureau of Printing and Engraving at Washington in 1877.

Having become exempted even from the weak rules in effect at the time it became a dumping ground for the favorites of members of Congress. An official report made to the Secretary of the Treasury said that over 500 employees, or 56 per cent of those in the Bureau, were unnecessary.

Some of these supernumeraries were so much in the way of the regular workers that shelves had to become provided on which they spent part of their time in sleep. The unnecessary cost involved amounted to a total of $390,000 a year. Under the spoils system, incompetents as well as supernumeraries' multiply in the public service.

The few men of ability who receive appointments soon grow disgusted with their slipshod environment and turn to private employment. On the other hand, inefficient employees are extremely hard to remove, for the same political influence which got them their places always has ready to protect them if possible.

Constant intervention by legislators and political leaders in disciplinary and other matters breaks down the morale of the administrative departments. Men who try to serve two experts soon learn which of the two must become obeyed. Under the spoils system it is not the official master, but the political master, who has the means to enforce obedience. A newly appointed bureau chief may have the most praiseworthy determination to improve the work of his force, but he soon discovers that efforts to get rid of incompetents are likely to prove futile if the latter have a political jerk.

Reference: Discipline vs. pull. p-195. The New Electoral Fusion System, no Partisan have the solutions to solve this menacing spoil corruptions.

SPOILS SYSTEM AND CIVIL SERVICE REFORM
American Political Parties History

If, nonetheless, he persists until he succeeds, a berth is soon found for the discharged sufferer for a cause in some other bureau where standards are not so high. It is in the field of political life and morals 1ncrease that the reactions of the spoils system are most deplorable, increased cost, poor services.

The increased cost of government due to inefficient public servants, the substantial number of superfluous employees, and the heavy labor turnover, is, of course, reflected in heavier tax burdens. Even greater loss had inflicted upon the people by the inferior quality of administrative service supplied them under the spoils system, because of which they suffer in convenience, business, and health.

Statistics quoted by E. C. Marsh, show that for the seven years preceding the classification under civil service rules of the Railway Mail Service, employees handled an average of 1,230,731 pieces of mail annually with an average of 335 errors.

The average number of errors fell from an average of 183 per employee for the first decade of this period to 131 for the second decade. Better conditions of work and better administrative methods contributed to the improvement, but the competitive examination system must become given its share of credit, particularly for the decrease of errors.

The illustration had cited because of the large possibilities of delay and loss in business due to errors in handling mail matter. In the broader view parties themselves had harmed by pcs the injection of patronage. It may become admitted freely harmed by that the use of spoils contributed materially to the up and about benefaction building of great party organizations in the United States.

Benefactors does not really help a party. It helps the Bosses to get control of the machinery of the party. But this growth of organizations dominated by the spoils motive had not conducted without some loss to party life on the side of principles and policies. Instead of becoming directed to the settlement of critical issues political contests were lowered in tone and envenomed in spirit by constant malicious disputes over jobs.

References: Roosevelt, Autobiography, p. 147.

ELECTORALPROBLEMS.

American Political Parties History

Under these circumstances males of higher type turned in disgust from candidacy for elective offices. To seek appointive office on any other basis than service to the organization was, as we have already noted, unsuccessful in most cases. Large numbers of citizens who would have responded eagerly to campaigns involving factual issues relapsed into apathy because of the perpetual repugnant struggles for benefaction. Lowered standards in politics had reflected in contemporary morals. As early as 1835, Calhoun, with rare prescience, wrote of the spoils system. Were a premium offered for the best means of extending to the greatest the power of benefaction, to destroy the love of country, and to substitute a spirit of subservience and man worship, to encourage vice and discourage virtue, no scheme more perfect could be devised. Evils of such size led naturally to demands for Beginnings of civil reform.

It is a curious fact that during the same period Term when the United States was sinking deeper and deeper into the spoils system, England, aroused by conditions in her administrative service both in India and at home, was gradually working out the means of extricating herself from ancient abuses of benefaction.

Reformers m the United States were thus enabled to draw upon English experience in the solution of our own problem. However, the struggle was to prove much longer and harder on this side of the Atlantic, nor are the results reached at present so complete and so generally accepted as in England.

THE SPOIL SYSTEM

American Political History

In the United States, the spoils system is the culture of firing and hiring federal employees when the presidential administration changes. The phrase was introduced in 1929, when Andrew Jackson replaced an unprecedented number of federal workers with people, he promised office during his presidential campaign. Many people thought this method was corrupt, and the phrase "spoils system" was coined by U.S. senator William L. Marcy as an offensive term. Andrew Jackson and the former president John Adams were political opponents, and most of the people in government had opposed his presidential bid. They blocked his core initiatives in what he interpreted as sabotage. He found a solution by firing people from key federal posts and replacing them with loyalists. Earlier presidents, including George Washington, hired loyalists to influential positions, but under the new president, this kind of purging reached its peak. His supporters justified the move by claiming that some people had served in government since the administration of George Washington.

DENOUNCE OF CORRUPTION

American Political History

Jackson's political opponents denounced the spoils system, though they were powerless against the president. Future president and Jackson's ally Martin Van Buren are credited with proposing the policy. Unofficial reports suggested that more than 700 federal works were fired within the first year, a move that degraded the economy of Washington D.C. Though this was exaggerated, it was indeed a controversial policy. In 1832, Jackson's political opponent Henry Clay Assailed Senator William Marcy of New York accusing the pro-government loyalist of importing corruption vices from New York to Washington.

Michael Anguelo

REFORMING THE SPOILS SYSTEM

American Political History

Every successive president after Jackson appointed political supporters to key posts in federal government. Though it appeared as an effective method of curbing political sabotage and ensured the president's initiatives were supported, it was criticized for denying people jobs based on their political beliefs. During the Civil War, President Abraham Lincoln became annoyed by people camping in the White House, pleading for employment. The proposal to change the system was finally considered after a deranged and disappointed office seeker shot President James Garfield. The Pendleton Civil Service Reform Act was enacted to help protect federal employees and civil servants from the spoils system.

Marcy appeared a hero after the War of 1812. He briefly served in the Senate before he became the governor of New York for twelve years. President James Polk appointed him the Secretary of War before President Franklin Pierce appointed him the Secretary of State. Regardless of his long political career and achievements, he is well known for the phrase "spoils system."

References: Kiprop, Victor. "What Is a Spoils System?" World Atlas, Dec. 13, 2019, worldatlas.com/articles/what-is-a-spoils-system.html.

CHAPTER 29

SPOILS SYSTEM AND CIVIL SERVICE REFORM.

American Political Parties History

It was assumed that in the interest of the department he would devise tests the passing of which would guarantee fitness to perform the duties involved.

Unfortunately, however, the administrative official usually feared the influence of the Congressperson or other politician who was backing the applicant. Consequently, the standards set in such examinations were often ridiculous. At the best they excluded only impossible blockhead. According to Prof. A. B. Hart questions such as the following had asked: Where would you go to draw your salary? How many are four times four? What have you had for breakfast? Who recommended your employment? Of course, spoils politicians found little to complain of in the pass examination system, and the weak laws of 1853 and 1855 gradually fell into neglect.

In 1864 an Act had passed providing for the appointment of consular clerks by examinations in the State Department, but it applied to only thirteen places. The era following the Civil War was marked by an Attitude of large increase in the number of appointive offices which had promptly converted to spoils uses, and by administrative scandals so gross and far reaching that they threatened to smirch the integrity of the Presidency itself.

Sluggishly public opinion began to develop against the abuses of benefaction.

The Democratic platform of 1868 demanded reform of abuses in the administration, the expulsion of dishonest men from office, the abrogation of useless offices. Four years later both parties declared civil service reform to be necessary, and after planks on the subject have become inserted in their national platforms with two or three exceptions. The civil service of the government has become a mere instrument of partisan tyranny and personal ambition, and an object of selfish greed.

It is a scandal and reproach upon free institutions and breeds a demoralization dangerous to the perpetuity of Republican Government. We therefore regard a thorough reform of the civil service as one of the most pressing necessities of the hour; that honesty, capacity, and fidelity constitute the only valid claim to public The Republican plank of the same year position of the government are considered rewards for mere party fanaticism is fatally demoralizing, and we therefore favor a reform of the system by laws which shall abolish the that. employment: that the office of government ceases to be matter of arbitrary favoritism and patronage, and that public station become again a port of honor.

References: Actual Government, p. 289. 2The Democratic plank of 1872 was as follows. The New Electoral Fusion System, no Partisan have the solutions to solve this menacing spoil corruptions.

Reference: The New Electoral Fusion System, no Partisan have the solutions to solve this menacing spoil corruptions and patronage worries.

THE TWO PARTIES TRAGEDY

The Two-party Perpetuating System

- Winner-Take-All Rules
- One Winner (loser gets nothing)
- Strategic voting, Wasted vote theory
- Voters don't support parties not in contention
- Formation of Minor Parties discouraged- (due to lack of voter support)
- Fewer parties Flourish
- Existing parties perpetuate system that brought them to power

POLITICAL PARTIES AND ELECTORAL PROBLEMS
American Political Parties History

Nevertheless, the declarations of the parties were to become taken with a grain of salt, and civil service reformers continued to receive the unmitigated abuse of unfaltering practical politicians of both camps.

How little platform planks on the subject really meant have shown by the fate of the promising reform measure enacted in 1871, following the agitation started by Congressman Thomas A. Jenckes, of Rhode Island. This law authorized the President to make regulations to find the fitness of candidates in respect to age, health, character, knowledge, and ability.

Grant showed his good faith in the matter by appointing a leading reformer, George William Curtis, chairperson of the commission to enforce the law, but embarrassments had heaped upon it, and after 1873, Congress refused even the manager appropriation necessary to carry on its work. Not till the assassination of Garfield by a disappointed office seeker in 1881 did civil service reformers find themselves backed by a public demand that was irresistible.

While Garfield lay dying at Elberon the National Civil Service Reform League had organized. Ever since it has done valiant service both in agitating for legislation on the subject and in watching over its later administration. A year later Senator George H. Pendleton, of Ohio, Pendleton introduced a civil service bill which passed both houses of Congress and became law with the approval of President Arthur on January 16, 1883.

The Pendleton Act was one of the most skillfully devised statutes ever passed by a legislative body, and after forty years of experience it stays the basis on which the federal civil service breaks. Claim to public employment; that the offices of the government cease to be a matter of arbitrary favoritism and patronage, and that public station become again a post of honor.

Michael Anguelo

ELECTORAL SPOILS SYSTEM AND CIVIL SERVICE REFORM
American Political Parties History

An important feature of the Act was the placing of large discretionary powers in the hands of the President. The extent to which these powers have become exercised have shown by the following statement giving the number of offices, exclusive of the growth of the service, which have become transferred to the classified list by each successive administration.

Arthur, 15,573; Cleveland, first term, 11,757; Harrison, 10,535; Cleveland, second term, 38,961; McKinley, 3,261; Roosevelt, 34,766; Taft, 56,868; Wilson, to June 30, 1917, about 40,000. Curiously enough, a motive akin to that of spoils men aided in the extension of the reform. By executive orders bringing offices which had had filled on bigoted grounds under the classified service, the incumbents had protected to some extent against the assaults of the opposition party when it succeeded to power.

At least it could not dislodge them without seeming to take a step backward in a reform movement which had come to command wide popular support. Turning from the federal service to that of states, Civil service counties, and cities, the picture is much less encouraging, reform in New York was the first state to adopt a civil service Act in May, 1883. Massachusetts followed the example of movement New York a year later.

From that date until 1905 the movement lagged, but, beginning with the latter year, ten other states have enacted civil service laws. One of the ten, Connecticut, after passed a repealed, the only case of backsliding so far recorded. Although differing widely in scope and effectiveness, the state laws on the subject follow the main outlines of the Pendleton Act. Some of the state laws apply to the state service only. In four states, New York, Massachusetts, New Jersey, and Ohio, permissive or mandatory clauses applying to cities had included. Considering he bitter opposition of Illinois and Wisconsin, 1905; Colorado and Indiana, 1907; New Jersey, 1908; Ohio, 1912; California, 1913; Connecticut also in 1913 but re-pealed the law in 1921; Kansas, 1916; Maryland, 1920. New York, Ohio, California, and Colorado have constitutional provisions relating to this matter.

Reference: The New Electoral Fusion System, no Partisan have the solutions to solve this menacing spoil corruptions and Electoral problem.

ELECTORAL AND CIVIL SERVICES PROBLEMS
American Political Parties History

Classified and unclassified positions United States civil service commission the politicians to every extension of civil service reform, it is a matter for distinct congratulation that more than 350 cities are now under some form of the merit system. The list includes all the twenty largest cities in the country and seventy-two out of the one hundred largest according to the census of 1920.

County government, however, stays a stronghold of the spoils system. Out of the 3,065 counties in the United States only a score has adopted any form of civil service tests. Under the rules drawn up during the first year of the Pendleton Act 14,000 offices have classified, i.e., made subject to examination, leaving about 96,000 federal positions outside the merit system.

On June 30, 1922, there were in the executive civil service of the United States approximately 420,688 classified and 140,175 unclassified employees.1 In other words, while the percentage of federal offices filled by competitive examination rose from 12.7 in 1883 to 75 in 1922, the growth of the service as a whole was so tremendous that at the end of the period the number of places still not under the merit system showed an increase of 44,000.

The same expansion has gone on, although probably to a less degree, in the service of state and local governments, which as we have just noted have lagged considerably behind the federal government in the application of the merit system. Despite the progress made since 1883, therefore, the volume of political patronage in the country is undoubtedly greater than ever before. Under the Pendleton Act the President is authorized to appoint, by and with the advice and consent of the Senate, a Civil Service Commission composed of three members, not more than two of whom shall be of the same party.

Reference: The New Electoral Fusion System, no Partisan have the solutions to solve this menacing spoil corruptions and civil services exploitations.

Michael Anguelo

SPOILS ELECTORAL SYSTEM

American Political Parties History

Each commissioner receives a salary of $5,000 annually and necessary traveling expenses. It is important to note. According to an estimate kindly supplied by Mr. John T. Doyle, secretary of the United States Civil Service Commission, possibly 50,000 of the unclassified employees were laborers, of whom some 20,000 are subject to tests of physical fitness, that the Civil Service Commission is not attached in any way to any of the executive departments, nor subject to the direction of any of the heads of those departments.

On the contrary, it is an independent agency of government free from all control except that of the President himself. The duty of the Commission is to aid the President, as he may ask, in preparing suitable rules to carry the Civil Service Act into effect. When such rules have become issued it becomes the duty of all officers of the United States in the departments affected by them to aid in their enforcement.

Moreover, the Commission has given power to make investigations into and reports upon all matters concerned with the administration of the Act and its own rules and regulations. To this extent, therefore, the Commission may even sit in judgment upon the executive departments subject to the civil service law.

Among other things the rules of the Commission shall provide for open, competitive examinations for evaluating the fitness of applicants for the public service now classified or to become classified hereunder. Such examinations must be practical in their character, relating as far as may be to matters which will fairly test the relative capacity and fitness of the persons examined to discharge the duties of the service into which they seek appointment.

Selections shall fill all classified offices according to grade from among those graded highest as the result of competitive examinations. The Commission is authorized to appoint a chief examiner and such other employees as are necessary to hold examinations in Washington and in one or more places in each state, and in general, to carry out the provisions of the law and its own rules. The meat of the great reform of 1883 to become found in the foregoing provisions of the Pendleton Act. To certain positions appointments may become made without examination or upon noncompetitive examinations.

References: Schedule A, p. 84, Thirty-ninth Annual Report, 1922. Also, by an amendment of July 25,1914. The New Electoral Fusion System, no Partisan have the solutions to solve this menacing spoil corruptions. The New Electoral Fusion System, no Partisan have the solutions to solve this menacing spoil corruptions and Civil Services exploitations.

ELECTORAL PROBLEMS

American Political Parties History

Safeguards against political influence Particularly important 582is the clause supporting open, competitive examinations for evaluating the fitness of applicants. In other words, merit, not favoritism, was henceforth to decide appointments.

So clearly is this its purpose that Civil Service reform itself is often and more aptly called the merit system. Next to the disregard of fitness the fundamental malevolent of the spoils system was that under its appointments were anything but open. Under the merit system they had opened wide to all citizens of the United States possessing the necessary qualifications as set forth in the rules and in the announcements for each examination prepared by the Commission.

The spoils system made appointments depend upon the favor of Senators or Congressmen, but the Pendleton Act specifically enjoins them from furnishing recommendations to examiners and appointing officers except as to the character and residence of the applicant. Another safeguard against the use of influence had provided by a rule prohibiting questions concerning the political or religious opinions of any applicant.

Recommendations which make such disclosures had not considered or filed and the persons sending them are so informed. Although commonly used in the narrower sense, Civil Service reform might become taken to include any change designed to improve the Civil Service, as, e.g., a better ordering of departmental work or organization.

The term merit system, on the other hand, is perfectly definite in meaning. While the two terms are interchangeable in ordinary usage there have been instances of politicians who asserted that although unalterably opposed to Civil Service reform, they were thoroughly in favor of the merit system.

By an amendment of July 25, 1914, the Commission may, if there is a lack of eligible a who are citizens, examine persons who are not citizens, but the latter shall not have certified for appointment so long as citizens are eligible. Under state and municipal Civil Service rules, also, examinations restricted to citizens, a fact which places a considerable premium on naturalization.

References: W. B. Munro, The Government of American Cities, p. 11o. The New Electoral Fusion System, no Partisan have the solutions to solve this menacing spoil corruptions and Civil Services exploitations.

ELECTORAL SPOILS SYSTEM

American Political Parties History

One of the commonest objections to the value system among the uninformed is that examinations are too theoretical or too legendary in character, thus excessively favoring college students or other persons who have book is the merit system academic knowledge only.

In this connection spoils men of the resolute variety frequently indulged in stories of a type like that of the applicant for a position as letter carrier who had alleged to have become asked in a Civil Service examination, how many miles is the sun distant from the earth? According to the tale the applicant said in reply that he did not remember the exact number of miles, the distance from Earth to the Sun in miles is 92,955,887.6 miles. but was certain that the sun was so far distant that it would never interfere with him in the performance of his duties as a Mailman.

It need hardly be said that such stories were pure inventions, designed solely to cast ridicule on the merit system. One may well contrast with them the action taken by Roosevelt following the issuance of his order that Texas rangers be placed under the rules of the Civil Service Commission.

Congressperson and others joined in a lively outcry over this order, declaring that men fit for so strenuous a job could never become chosen by examination. The President asked the objectors, what qualities had needed and had told, men who can ride a horse, shoot a gun, and speak Spanish is qualify. Immediately Roosevelt issued an order to the Civil Service Commission directing them to examine applicants for Texas Rangers as to their ability to ride a horse, shoot a gun, and speak Spanish. Every effort has made, as the Civil Service practical examination of the law itself directs, to employ tests in all examinations of a tests practical character, designed to discover special fitness for the kind of employment concerned. For many minors' mechanical jobs, the only hypothetical or fictional performance required of competitors is the mere filling in and signing of an application blank. In examinations for the various trades so called real, operational, or presentation tests had used. References: Autobiography, p. 153, W. D. Lewis, The Life of Theodore Roosevelt, p. 92 The New Electoral Fusion System, no Partisan have the solutions to solve this menacing spoil corruptions and Civil Services exploitations.

POLITIC PARTIES PROBLEM

American Political Parties History

Thus, applicants for employment as truck drivers, chauffeurs, or motorcycle operators are required to take out their respective machines and demonstrate ability to handle them in the midst for the way in which one such story was run down by Roosevelt while a member of the U. S. Civil Service Commission of ordinary traffic. Applicants for paving jobs in the department of streets and highways had supplied with the tools and materials of their trade and tested as to the amount and quality of the paving laid in a given time.

Applicants for positions as stenographers and typists had required to take dictation of fair material and transcribe it at standard rates of speed or do actual typing.

In many examinations for technical jobs a larger or smaller part of a man's final rating depends upon the amount of experience he has had in his line of work. For this reason, high school, and college students, instead of being at an advantage, are really at a disadvantage since few of them have had time to gain practical experience.

Far from being too academic, American Civil Cervices tests are often criticized as being too narrowly practical for the best results in permanent appointments. English examinations for higher grade offices lay much more stress on university training, the object being not so much to discover the immediate fitness of candidates for the work they are to take up first as to ascertain what their ability to do the work will be after they have learned it by experience in service.

Selecting Tests of the sort commonly employed by larger cities police officers for the police force give a clever idea of the range and flexibility of Civil Service methods. Applicants must have the requisite certificates of good character and must qualify as to height and physical stamina before becoming admitted to the mental examination. The latter may include a few simple tests in the common branches and it will certainly include questions regarding the location of police stations, fire stations, and hospitals in the neighborhood where the applicant lives. In addition, after being told to be observant, the applicant is taken for a brief period into a room containing a variety of furniture and other articles, and upon coming out is asked to give a description of what he saw therein, a fair test, one would think, of his ability to observe and to give evidence in court. Or a notice describing a certain fugitive from justice had read to the assembled applicants which they must reproduce as closely as possible from memory. Reference: The New Electoral Fusion System, no Partisan have the solutions to solve this menacing spoil corruptions and Civil Services exploitations.

PARTIES SPOILS SYSTEM.

American Political Parties History

All Civil Service examinations to fill positions where the employee must become in contact with the public, or where he must use unusual discretion and judgment in performing his duties, lay great stress upon the oral interview, carefully handled by qualified examiners.

Having passed all the foregoing tests, the applicant for a job on the force must then present himself for an oral interview, conducted by men of considerable experience in choosing police officers. Questions had asked with the purpose of ascertaining the probable bearing of the applicant in dealing with citizens in various emergencies, his real reasons for desiring to get on the force, and the like. Incidentally, applicants who admit, as some do, that their motive is to wear a uniform, twirl a club, or play in the police band, do not create the most favorable impression.

Finally, before recommendations for appointment had decided upon, a painstaking inquiry has made into the past life of all who succeed in passing the various tests. Loafers, men who have engaged in shady pursuits or who have a bad record in any way, had excluded. An objection frequently made to the merit system is that while it may become applied successfully to minor clerical no ensemble test and technical jobs, it is quite unsuited to positions of a professional character.

Admittedly the problem presented by the latter is a difficult and delicate one. A crowd of doctors cannot become brought into a room and their examined like so many schoolchildren to discover the one best fitted for the post of health officer. The best men would refuse to give to such an examination and only incompetents would present themselves. The difficulty has met in part at least by the no assembled test. This means simply that candidates had not required to meet in given room and take the examination simultaneously. Instead, a suitable task is set, as, for example, the writing of a thesis in the case of candidates for appointment as engineer, statistician, or economist; the work on this assignment is done individually and when all the papers have been sent in, they are passed upon by eminent specialists. Reference: The New Electoral Fusion System, no Partisan have the solutions to solve this menacing spoil corruptions and Civil Services exploitations.

ELECTORAL PROBLEMS

American Political Parties History

In addition, a searching investigation has made of the candidates' education, training, achievements, and personal qualifications, each of which may give a certain predetermined weight and counted in making up the final averages.

By no assembled tests the United States Civil Service Commission has filled successfully hundreds of highly technical positions requiring executive and organizing ability in the Bureau of Mines, the Interstate Commerce Commission, the Public Health Service, and many other bureaus and departments. Cities and states are also employing this method for positions ranging in salary from $3,000 to $8,000 a year.

There is a possibility which is now engaging the serious study of Civil Service administrators that examinations may be somewhat shortened and their results improved by the use in connection with some of the tests already given of intelligence tests like those employed in the army during the World War I.

In the federal civil-service examination papers had rated on a scale of 100, the subjects there become given such relative weights as the Commission may prescribe. All competitors rated at 70 or more are eligible for appointment. Following the marking of the papers a list of eligible has made out, rating them in the order of their grades from highest to lowest. From the head of this list the commission certifies to the appointing officer three names for each vacancy to become filled.

References: Intelligence Tests in the Public Service, by C.N. Amsden of the Los Angeles County Civil Service Commission, an address yet unpublished given before the June, 1923, meeting of the Assembly of Civil Service Commissions in New York City., H. J. Filer and L. J. O'Rourke of the United States Civil Service Commission, in the Journal of Personnel Research, vol. I, no. 2 (March, 1923). The New Electoral Fusion System, no Partisan have the solutions to solve this menacing spoil corruptions and Civil Services exploitations. Also, wives of injured soldiers, sailors, and marines.

SPOILS ELECTORAL SYSTEM

American Political Parties History

Certification has made without regard to sex except in cases where the appointing officer has otherwise specified eligibility and appointments officer has otherwise specified. Unless the latter objects to any of the persons certified and had sustained by the commission in his objection, he must make selection for the first vacancy with sole reference to merit and fitness from among the highest three names on the list.

Selections for second and later vacancies has made in the same manner. Certification of the highest three is a peculiarity of the American practice. In England, the appointing office does not have the right of choice, candidates become appointed in the exact order of the standing they have earned. Within limits the American method enables the appointing official to give preference, if he so wishes, to desirable personal qualities in the applicants which have not registered in their examination averages.

Also, if inclined to disregard the plain injunction of the law to consider merit and fitness only, he may consult somewhat his own racial, religious, or political prejudices, assuming him to have pro-cured information regarding candidates on these points through channels not connected with the Civil Service Commission.

During the first six months or the first year, if so, fixed by regulation, the civil Service appointee is on probation. If after full and fair trial his conduct or ability is not satisfactory to the appointing officer, the probationer had notified in writing with a full statement of reasons and his employment ends. Retention in the service during the probationary period confirms his absolute appointment.

In the United States service the proportion of failures on probation is exceedingly small, being about one half of 1 per cent. One of the greatest technical difficulties in the administration of the Federal Civil Service Act is due to the clause requiring that appointments to the public service in Washington shall had apportioned among the several states and territories and the District of Columbia upon the basis of population at the last preceding census. Distant states and those which are retrograde in educational facilities do not give enough supplies of qualified food.

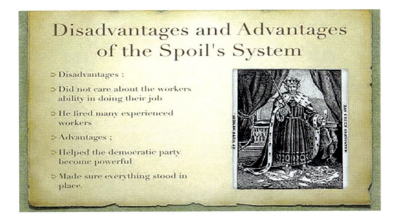

CHAPTER 30

POLITICAL PARTIES AND ELECTORAL PROBLEMS

American Political Parties History

The District of Columbia and states near at hand, because of the willing Probation Apportionments of their applicants to accept low salaries, have always had a much larger share of appointments than that to which they had allowed.

By an amendment of March 7, 1918, several offices in the Bureau of Engraving and Printing, Government Printing Office, and elsewhere, which were particularly hard to fill under the apportionment rule, had exempted from its provisions. Honorably discharged soldiers and sailors enjoyed certain preference preferences in the service of the United States prior to the passage of the Pendleton Act.

These had continued by the Act and have become extended by more recent enactments. At present preference is given to honorably discharged soldiers, sailors, and marines, and their widows, and to the wives of injured soldiers, sailors, and marines who themselves nonexistence qualifications, but whose wives are qualified, as follows: (I release from all age limitations, and for many positions also from height and weight requirements; (2 requirements of an average of 65 per cent only instead of 70 for eligibility; (3 appointment without regard to apportionment by states; and (4 the placing of their names in the order of their ratings above those of all competitors who did not have military service.

Veteran preference has not limited to veterans of the war with Germany. It applies to all former soldiers, sailors, and marines, including commissioned officers, army field clerks, the S. A. C., enlisted or commissioned army and navy nurses, persons who enlisted in officers' training camps during the war with Germany, persons who served in the S. Coast Guard, and members of the National Guard who were mustered into the federal service. Also, the commission may exempt from the physical requirements for any position a disabled and honorably discharged veteran upon certification of the Federal Board of Vocational Education that he has been specially trained for and has passed a test demonstrating his physical ability for the class of positions in which employment sought.

POLITICAL SPOILS SYSTEM

American Political Parties History

When reductions had made in the force of any executive department ex-service men who are equally qualified must become kept in preference to others. There has been a great deal of intense argument, pro arguments, and fraud, and not a little political agitation, over veteran on veteran preference.

It may become conceded that service in the army preference or navy develops certain qualities useful in various branches of civil administration, notably municipal and state police forces, where such experience is often heavily weighted. Loyalty to the government as shown by a willingness to defend it in time of war should be a valuable element in the morale of any departmental force. On the other hand, the mere fact of honorable discharge is no certain index to the spirit and quality of a man's Military Service. moral, mental, and physical development under army instructions and training.

If accepted uncritically it may lead to the anomaly of rewarding with public offices thousands of men who were inducted into the army in spite of their efforts to escape their military obligations, who did not engage the enemy, and whose entire time was spent in enforced furtherance of their own. As far as disabled soldiers and sailors and their wives' effects of are concerned, gratitude is a national duty and privilege of Veteran the first rank. It should become met not by making public of effects of Veteran preference a gratuity, but by a generous compensation policy. Consideration of the various preferences granted former soldiers and sailors shows that all of them lower the standards required for effective service.

The harmful consequences are not great at present, but they are certain to become so when the average age of veterans of the World War passes the expectation of efficiency. Despite assertions often made on this subject it may become doubted whether the demand for soldier preference has anything like a popular majority behind it. Out of more than half a million appointments made between 1883 and 1921, 27 per cent fell to them. Such discrimination in favor of men as still exists is due to the legal right of appointing officers to specify whether people may want. Regardless of this right, women have now admitted to all examinations. During the earlier period of the merit system they made up only one seventh of the classified service, occupying clerical, or sub-clerical positions. With the advent of typewriters, stenography, card indexes, and telephones, the number of women employees increased rapidly.

In scientific work also appointing officials found that for the lower salaried positions they could secure much better prepared helpers by calling for women. During the World War the proportion of women appointed rose to 70 per cent of the total. Subsequently the preference gave men who had been in military service has caused a decrease in the number of women appointed. In 1920, Ms. Helen H. Gardener have appointed one of the members of the United States Civil Service Commission, the first woman to hold that office. The Pendleton Act supplies various privileges and safeguards for persons in the classified service. It states specifically that they are under no obligation to contribute to political funds or to render any political service, and that they will be protected against removal or being otherwise prejudiced for refusing to do so. Corresponding to this privilege, civil servants are obligated not to use their official authority or influence to coerce the political actions of protection of civil servants are not to use their official authority or influence to coerce the political actions of others. References: Cf. Thirty-ninth Annual Report, State Civil Service Commission. New York, 1921, p. 12. The New Electoral Fusion System have the solutions to solve this menacing spoil corruptions and Civil Services exploitations.

ELECTORAL SPOILS SYSTEM

American Political Parties History

Under an Act of Congress approved August 24, 1912 (37 Stat., L. 555), which has been called the Magna Charta of government employees, no person in the classified civil service of the United States may be removed therefrom except for such cause as will promote the efficiency of the service and for reasons given in writing.

The person whose removal has sought shall have notice of the same and of any charges preferred against him, and become furnished with a copy thereof, and become allowed a reasonable time for personally answering the same in writing and affidavits in support thereof. No examination of witnesses nor any trial or hearing had required except in the discretion of the officer making the removal.

The Act of 1912 also provides that membership in any Organization of Postal Employees designed to improve working conditions, including hours of labor and wages, employees shall not become ground for dismissal nor for reduction in rank or compensation. However, such organization of postal employees must not be affiliated with any outside organization imposing an obligation or duty upon them to strike or proposing to assist them in any strike against the United States.

Further, civil servants individually and collectively have the right to petition Congress or any member thereof, and to give information to either House of Congress or to any committee or member thereof. By an Act passed in 1892 (27 Stat, 340), laborers and mechanics employed by the federal government or by con-tractors on public work had restricted to an eight-hour workday. Under the provisions of the Act of August 24, 1912, more than two hundred and seventy-five units of the Federal Employees Union have become formed and twenty-five others now become organized.2 These units had located in forty-six states, the District of Columbia. In certain European countries organization of civil servants has gone much further than in the United States.

Bureaucracy is necessarily hierarchical, first because of the Iron Law of Oligarchy, and secondly because bureaucracy grows by adding more subordinate layers. Since, lacking a market, there is no genuine test of merit in government's service to consumers, in a rule bound bureaucracy seniority is often blithely adopted as a proxy for merit. Increasing seniority, then, leads to promotion to higher ranks, while expanding budgets take the form of multiplying the levels of ranks under you, and expanding your income and power. Bureaucratic growth occurs, then, by multiplying levels of bureaucracy.

References: Cf. E. M. Sait, Government and Politics of France, p. 119, Government of Switzerland, pp. 218, 247. 2 E. J. Newmyer.

PARTICIPATION IN SPOIL POLITIC SYSTEM

American Political Parties History

Voting is not merely a right. In a much truer sense, what intelligent voting requires as we have already had occasion to note, it is a duty. Nor is it a duty easy to perform properly. Registration is a prerequisite; both primaries and elections are of frequent occurrence; ballots are long, involving many kinds of offices and extended lists of candidates; initiative, referendum, and recall votes are increasing in number.

Moreover, to vote intelligently requires some knowledge of our government, national, state, and local; some familiarity with its history, particularly in recent times; some acquaintance with our public men; some insight into the economic, sectional, racial, and other groups that are struggling for mastery; and finally, some conception of the issues which this struggle has brought forth for contemporary solution. Even these requirements, imposing as they may seem, no longer suffice. Since 1914, the voter in our national elections has had called upon to consider supreme questions involving a knowledge not simply of domestic but of world politics. Active citizenship begins, but it does not end, with the mere poking of a ballot into a box at the polls. Voting, services in with all the details thereby involved, is the bare minimum addition to of what a democracy must ask of many of those upon whom it has conferred the franchise. If popular government is to succeed, it must secure, particularly from its more capable citizens, a variety of added services. Fortunately for us, this higher obligation has recognized and privileged by men of light and leading from the earliest days of the republic.

Every year, however, more than two million of our young men and women reach the age of twenty-one, the vast majority of whom thereupon buy the legal right to vote. Political consciousness may have come much earlier, but political interest and a desire for public service are often not manifested until after an economic foothold has secured and a family has become founded.

Owing to the short time that has elapsed since the adoption of the Nineteenth Amendment the number of American women of all ages who are sincerely eager to be of public service is extraordinarily large. For the more promising citizens of these and other classes some discussion of the various avenues of approach to political activity may be helpful. To the vast majority, of course, political service can be and should be a part-time occupation only. For this reason, the advice given by President Hadley of Yale is of peculiar value. Starting with the assumption that every American citizen ought to assume political responsibilities, he holds that there are at least four diverse ways in which this can become done. One may want to go into politics as a most important part of the business of his life. Another may strive to influence the conduct of our public affairs indirectly, by his activity on behalf of civil-service reform and other measures calculated to promote better government.

References: As to the dawn of political consciousness, C. E. Merriam, American Party System, p. 28, The New Electoral Fusion System, no Partisan have the solutions to solve this menacing spoil corruptions and Civil Services exploitations.

ACTIVE PARTICIPATION IN SPOIL POLITICS

American Political Parties History

A third party may reserve his political activity for special emergencies, when some crisis, national or local, justifies him in an exceptional expenditure of time and strength. A fourth may content himself with that general influence on the conduct of public affairs which is exercised by every citizen who forms his moral judgment independently and expresses it fearlessly.

Leaving the professional attitude for detailed discussion and strength Reform or later, some suggestions may become made for that much larger reform organizations and extremely useful class of persons who must play on the scrub team of politics. President Hadley cites civil service reform as an example of the measures calculated to promote better government.

In preceding chapters, several other worthy political causes have become noted, among them direct primary elections, Corrupt Practices Acts, the short ballot, proportional representation, the initiative, referendum, and recall. Special organizations national in extent exist to promote some of these measures. Citizens who intend to dedicate themselves to one of these specialized forms of political activity will find membership in such organization's indispensable. There are other organizations, also national in extent but more general in their purpose, which publish periodicals, supply literature, maintain speakers' bureaus, and send experts to communities which are engaged in the solution of certain political problems.

Both types of organizations welcome all citizens interested in their work who are eligible under their rules. A small annual fee had charged for membership. Citizens interested in city government will find that field well cultivated.

References: e.g., the Municipal Government Association of New York state, the Ohio Municipal Association, and the Massachusetts Civic, Standards of Public Morallty, p. 133.The National Civil Service Reform League, 8 W. Fortieth St., New York city; the Short Ballot League, 261 Broadway, New York city; the Proportional Representation League, 1417 Locust St., Philadelphia., The National Municipal League and the National League of Women Voters., Fusion Electoral System Nonpartisan Elections The New Electoral Fusion System, no Partisan have the solutions to solve this menacing spoil and Civil Services exploitations. Corruptions

POLITICAL PARTIES AND SPOIL ELECTORAL SYSTEM
American Political Parties History

There is a national organization, general well-known in scope the National Municipal League; various state organizations, also general in scope League; a national organization of limited aims the City Planning Conference; national associations composed of municipal corporations or city officials, e.g., the League of American Municipalities, associations of city engineers, health officials, police chiefs, fire chiefs, park superintendents, and the like.

In each of the larger cities of the country there are a great variety of local organizations directly concerned with municipal affairs e.g., voters' leagues, taxpayers' associations, improvement societies, the city club, the bureau of municipal research. Other organizations, although primarily commercial, industrial, or professional in purpose, devote some share of their time to the welfare of the city.

Among these may had mentioned chambers of commerce, boards of trade, merchants' associations, labor unions, architects' associations, and medical associations. Political bosses of twenty-five years ago were wont to sneer at all this activity, but they have since learned to take good government movements more seriously.

Among the many notable achievements of the latter the rapid extension of the home rule and optional charter systems and the numerous adoptions of commission and City Manager types of Municipal Government may become mentioned as contributions of the first importance to the political development of our time.

Reform organizations are so many in American County Government Cities that part or their work overlaps. County Government, on the other hand, has become appropriately called The Dark Continent of American Politics.

CHAPTER 31

ACTIVE PARTICIPATION IN POLITICS

American Political Parties History

A recent systematic investigation of county government reveals the encouraging fact that such organizations as the National Short Ballot Organization, the National Municipal League, the various political science as associations and clubs and civic bodies everywhere, are turning their attention to this problem.

State government has received much more attention than county government. As earlier chapters have made clear, em1nent most of the reforms dealing with nominations, elections, and party methods have conducted by state legislation. Many stays to become done, however, particularly in the line of administrative reorganization. The experience gained under the more progressive forms of city government will be helpful and such organizations as the National Short Ballot Organization, the National Municipal League, and the National Institute of Public Administration are giving a large share of their attention to this field.

At Washington there are so many investigating and reform organizations that Congress and the departments Federal government grow restive at times under their constant prodding and Argus-eyed glare.2 We are not concerned here with the innumerable lobbying agencies representing various corporate and selfish interests at the national capital. Powerful profession-al and trade associations interest themselves persistently in federal legislation and administration.

References: e.g., the National Association of Manufacturers, the Chamber of Commerce of the United States, the Grange, the American Federation of Labor, the Rail1K. H. Porter, County and Township Government in the United States, p. 290. 2, National Voters League. Lynn Haines, 737 Woodward Building, Washington, D. C. The Spotlight, Senator Robert La Follette, The Progressives: What They Stand Federal for and Want, Saturday Evening Post, vol. cxcv, no. 37, p. 27 (March 1, 1923. parties' exploitations.

POLITICAL PARTIES AND SPOIL ELECTORAL SYSTEM

American Political Parties History

Other forms of political activity road Brotherhoods, the National Education Association. Besides these there are many purely reform organizations which devote themselves to the public welfare, as they conceive it, among them the Anti-Saloon League, the recently formed International Reform Bureau of the World Temperance Foundation, the American Peace Society, the Navy League, the National Security League, the National League of Women Voters, the National Consumers' League, and the American Association for Labor Legislation.

As the foregoing paragraphs show, President Hadley's second method of assuming political responsibilities requires for effectiveness some measure of specialized study of the reform or reforms chosen as calculated to promote better government. In consequence this method is more likely to become followed by people of scholarly training or habit. However, the other three suggested methods of assuming political responsibilities may become undertaken with success by people of all walks in life.

Regardless of the tenure of College Degrees or High School Diplomas citizens may come to the front in times of crisis, or they may always exert an influence upon the conduct of public affairs by independent judgment and fearless expression of their opinions. Those who go into politics with the purpose of obtaining office may even find a college degree somewhat of an embarrassment at an early stage of their career.

Certain it is that the effort to be politically effective in any one of these three ways, and particularly in a professional manner, will involve active membership in political clubs and on political committees. There is no single method of contravention into the organization, as Roosevelt phrased it.

Much depends upon, the intelligence, training, character, and purposes of the person who is making the start. It is obvious also that methods admirably adapted to one kind of community might prove unsuccessful elsewhere. On the other hand, the door to political opportunity always stands wide open and to all classes and conditions of men infringement into the organization.

References: Cf. C. E. Merriam, The American Party System. p.224. 2 Autobiography. 63. The New Electoral Fusion System, no Partisan have the solutions to solve this menacing spoil corruptions and the Electoral system.

ACTIVE PARTICIPATION IN SPOIL POLITICS

American Political Parties History

Political parties require a vast variety of services involving every grade of talent from the highest to the lowest. For part only of this are they able to pay, hence willing workers are always welcome. Moreover, political parties can win only by collecting majorities and therefore are much more catholic in welcoming adherents than churches, clubs, corporations, or any other form of association.

So true is this that a study of the careers of many prominent American statesmen and of nearly all politicians and office holders of lesser degree will show that they did not choose politics deliberately as a profession; rather they drifted into it partly by chance, partly because so many political doors stood invitingly open to them.

As a recent writer puts it in the vernacular, the typical member of a political club joins in his youth, because he finds that, after a fellow has spent one evening a week at each of such diversions as taking in a vaudeville show, seeing a movie, calling on a girlfriend, going to a dance, etc., there still remain one or two evenings a week when a fellow can think of nothing better than to go up to the club and play Pinochle or Shoot Pool.

Of course, most of such tyros are content merely to pay dues and to take advantage of the social opportunities offered by the club.

As far as its political activities are concerned, they simply go end to end. Nevertheless, the control of a large mass of mere dues payers and voters is a political asset of extreme value. On the other hand, a few of the new members of such clubs discover within themselves a real political interest in, and certain aptitudes for, political work.

References: B. Deutsch, College Students and Politics, School and Society, vol. xvi, pp. 673-680 (Dec. 16, 1922). W. G. Shepherd, How Men Get into Politics, American Boy, vol. xxiv, p. 12 (Dec. 1922) The jersey by H. Curran on John Citizen's Job in the Saturday Evening Pott, April 7, 21, May 26, June 30, and September 30, 1923.

ACTIVE PARTICIPATION IN SPOIL POLITICS
American Political Parties History

In consequence they had found useful, soon become active party agents and the abler become leaders of greater or less power. What advice may become offered to persons who wish to assume active political responsibilities? On this point the writer has consulted personally and by correspondence many political leaders and politicians of various party affiliations, whose combined experience covers a wide range of activities, national, state, and local, in both public and party offices. To a surprising extent these authorities agree in the advice they offer, on no point are they more unanimous than that the beginner must make a start in his own precinct, ward, or division. As Senator Hitchcock phrased it: Like charity, politics should begin at home, to succeed a man must begin with local questions in the precinct, the ward, the city, or the county.

They are the natural steppingstones up to the questions in the larger fields of state and nation, and most men who have come into public life have come by that route. It may not interest a young man to go to meetings where the subjects of discussion are paving or grading or local taxation, but those are the questions that most men must naturally begin with.

And the best avenue of entrance, according to former Secretary Newton D. Baker, is by association with a ward or other local organization of the political party or group most to his liking. He can there find a group sufficiently small to be within the range of his possible intimate personal acquaintance, and a forum in which whatever talents for political helpfulness and organization he as can become developed.

Reference: F. Dunne, James R. Mann, Illinois; John D. Katherine Bement Davis, New York; Maude Bassett Gorham, Massachusetts; Mary H. Ingham, Pennsylvania, Works, California; Miles Poindexter, Washington.

ACTIVE PARTICIPATION IN SPOIL POLITICS

American Political Parties History

Thu Mrs. Antoinette Funk wrote; The first observation of the workings of politics should become made in the home, that connects the electors directly with matters largely municipal, such as the Schools, the Fire Departments, the Roads, the Pavements, the Sewers, Garbage Disposal, the Police Department, the Health Department, etc.

Intermit personal acquaintance, and a forum in which whatever talents for political effectiveness and organization he has can become developed. Every letter received emphasized the necessity of making a local beginning. It is a near step then to the study of questions gave about these matters.

Every people can frame a sound opinion whether new jails had needed, new bridges or public improvements of a general character. To begin locally, then, means to get into touch with the getting in local committee member or with certain local leaders. A word of caution had needed hear.

A citizen may have chosen his national party with due deliberation and yet man be completely ignorant of the character and purposes of its unquestionably make the acquaintance of the election district and county organizations.

Not of necessity that these organizations should become supported by the man in question, but that he should know about them firsthand, and not through his reputation created by opponents.

As we have already learned, leadership in any district usually reflects the quality of the citizenship of that district. If the beginner finds the character and aims of the party's local leaders such that he can support them overall, he may offer them his cooperation. If, on the other hand, it will become observed that this is the point of view of the community civics now so largely taught in the schools of the country.

Since his association with the latter is bound to be close, it is essential to study them carefully. This is not to become done in any pharisaic spirit, nor should too much credence be given to local conversation.

Thus, William Barnes of New York writes: First I should

Reference: K. C. Levis, Community civic now (1923). The New Electoral Fusion System, no Partisan have the solutions to solve this menacing spoil corruptions and Electoral System

PARTIES AND ELECTORAL SYSTEM

American Political Parties History

Formation of independent clubs if necessary, beginners he finds them worthless of support he will do well to look up the leaders of the opposing faction. Certainly, one must accept Roosevelt's pronouncement that no man who is worth his brackish has any right to abandon the effort to better our politics merely because he does not find it pleasant, merely because it involves associations which to him happen to be displeasing.

In certain districts it is possible that the citizen may find the local situation hopeless in that the leaders of both factions are pursuing aims which he feels bound to oppose. Let him then get out among his friends and organize a club of his own, aided by which he may become an independent political factor and, in time, perhaps, win the leadership himself. In any event, if he can succeed in rallying any considerable number of adherents to his banner, he will find the older leaders inclined to treat with him for his support.

On this point the late Franklin K. Lane, Secretary of the Interior under President Wilson, wrote: I suggest that you tell your young friend to join the political club in his neighborhood. If there is no political club that fits his fancy, see if there are enough of his chums to form an organization. A political organization is just like a fraternal organization, men will rise in it who do the work for it and who show wisdom and tact.

The best kind of political organization for a young man to join is one made up of all grades of people; the Poorest Kind of political organization is one made up of what the boys call intellectuals. I have never been a practical politician, but I think that if I were going into practical politics, I would try to organize the Workingmen, the Streetcar Drivers, Brakemen, Firefighters, Clerks and use them as a club to induce well-thought-of Electoral System as The New Fusion Electoral System. It may happen that the services of beginners, especially if they seem too ambitious in their aims, will not had welcomed by the local leader or Boss. The latter may fear that, once having gained experience and skill in party methods, the newcomers may turn out to be rivals or at least usually welcomed must be booked.

American Political Parties History

Professor Merriam tells a story of one local boss who was asked why he had dropped the meetings of the ward club in his district. Because, he said, it is only a nursery for upstarts, and I have too many political leaders on my hands now. In general, however, this attitude toward beginners is unusual. If a faction or party is in thorough control of a given territory, if, moreover, it already oversupplied with active workers and with plentiful campaign funds, such an attitude may indeed become manifested.

Thus T. Henry Walnut, at that time (1914) member of the state legislature from the seventeenth Philadelphia district, wrote: It is much more difficult to break into a Republican organization as an active factor than it is into our independent organization. We are continually hunting for men who will take an interest, and any man who will work will find plenty to do, plenty of chances for the assumption of political responsibility.

If on the other hand, the strength of the two parties had evenly divided or if there is any threat of factional warfare, it might prove suicidal to refuse the proffered aid of newcomers. Also, as we have already noted, there is an unlimited amount of party work to become done.

Finally, most established political leaders or Bosses have a robust, an even overweening, confidence in their ability to deal with newcomers. Once having made connection with his local organization, all the political authorities consulted agree that the newcomer in politics should with due modesty begin by the side of the lowest and exhibit a readiness to undertake any kind of work for which he is fitted and which the interests of the party at the time may require.

Charles Edward Merriam. Charles Edward Merriam, Jr., November 15, 1874 – January 8, 1953, was a professor of political science at the University of Chicago, founder of the interactive approach to political science, a trainer of many graduate students, a prominent intellectual in the Progressive Movement, and an advisor to several U.S. Presidents. Reference: The American Party System, p. 106.

SPOIL ELECTORAL SYSTEM

American political parties History

Political work suitable for beginners to membership in whatever may be the simplest form of political organization or association in the locality and will find himself provided with plenty of work to do. It may be extremely far from the advocacy of principles and influence upon the policies and direction of government in which he would like to engage.

He cannot begin by leadership or by dictating party policies, and he probably cannot assume in the beginning any such position of superiority as he may think his education and intelligence entitle him to have. The work in which he will be engaged at first may be simply the details of local organizations, which will perhaps seem of little consequence; or engaging in struggles between candidates for small offices, in which he does not take very much interest; or canvassing from house to house to ascertain the political affiliations or preference of the residents. There are many forms of political work suitable for beginners in addition to those mentioned by former Secretary Root. They range from addressing and stamping campaign literature, filing and card indexing, to bell ringing, collecting campaign contributions, and making stump speeches in the little red schoolhouse or on street corners.

The beginner may gain experience to his advantage in any of these lines of work, but naturally he will prove most effective by testing out his aptitudes and devoting himself as soon as possible to the work for which he had best fitted. He may discover that he has ability for independent leadership, readily attracting a following willing to accept his direction. Or without such ability, he may have the loyalty and industry needed in dependable assistants and trusted lieutenants. Those who are looking forward to candidacy for office will naturally try to secure such forms of party work as will bring them most often and favorably to the notice of voters. Some details about the work of a beginner in Politics Learning to may prove helpful. He should give much study to the set out the election laws, a knowledge of which is essential.

The question of getting out the full vote on registration days, at the primary election, and at the general election, becomes one of absorbing interest. He should be resourceful in knowledge of the right to challenge a vote when illegal, and, if he can, he ought to serve on the election board, or as watcher at the polls, to be present when the vote has counted.

The opportunity offers, writes Robert D. Drips of Canvassing; Philadelphia, the experience gained by a personal can canvasser from house to house in the interest of the party and other of his choice is of deep value. It tests out a man's theories, sometimes in a rather trying way; it provides him with new political connections; if his work is well done it commends him tremendously to the political leaders of the district; it gives him a basis for conversation on political subjects of a very practical sort, and in general is of the first standing. The beginner should also secure an introduction as soon as possible to the council members, representatives, state senators, and other office holders of the general character showed, being the section in which he lives.

If he is willing to engage in stump speaking, he should make the fact known, both to the ward leaders and to the office holders. Very often fundamentally speaking can be better undertaken through assignment by a city or state committee to some locality other than that in which a man lives, for then if he makes a fool of himself in his early efforts, he is not so suitable to leave disagreeable reminiscences behind in the district where he lives. Whether or not he engages in counterfoil speaking, he should make it his business to attend political meetings and listen to the speeches there made, captivating them to learn.

Reference: D. Lloyd Claycomb, formerly member of the Pennsylvania legislature

POLITICAL PARTIES AND ELECTORAL PROBLEMS
American Political Parties History

Ideals and principles Advice of radical leaders' particular pains to note the effect which they seem to have on the audience and taking notes, either then or later, of the points which seem especially impressive. Such a man should be urged to keep in touch with several newspapers rather than with one only, and he should read at least one paper representing the best thought of the leading party in opposition to his own. But what of devotion to ideals, loyalty to principles and policies, formal knowledge of the science of government as necessary to the equipment of the beginner in politics? It must become admitted that considerable difference of opinion exists among active political workers as to this question. On the one hand are those, primarily of independent and progressive tendencies, who glorify ideals and principles.

On the other hand, those who have had long experience with the regular organizations are inclined to question the value of these factors, or to preach caution in their use, at least in the earlier stages of a political career. So important is this point that it may be well to estimate at some length from the two types of advice offered. As illustrative of the first type Virgil Hinshaw, a well-known Prohibitionist leader, wrote: First one should have at heart some great cause, the success of some issue vital to the nation's welfare. Whittier said: Young man, associate ward self in district youth with some virtuous, disliked cause and live and work to make that cause popular

One would have to spend at least a year's assiduous study if he wants to master the Communist philosophy. Our attitude is to examine carefully into social conditions and ascertain what ought to be-come done, regardless of the ignorance of the people and regardless of whether they want it or not. We believe that if they understood they would want at once what we think has needed. This attitude forces us to take a stand far in advance, a stand which is necessarily unpopular, but which in time will become popular, if it is right and in line with progress.

Contrasting with the foregoing the following from an advice of Pennsylvania Republican of independent affiliations: It had pled party naturally of supreme importance that a man should be thoroughly acquainted with the current literature not only of his own party, but of those with which it is in conflict. It seems to me that his efforts to obtain information as to the problems before the electorate would become better directed if he attempted to question the voters of his own partition and the local political leaders and office holders of the same political faith as himself. In a similar mood leader, particularly the references in the former to campaigning. It would be possible to give from letters received many similar pieces of advice. Thus, former Governor William C. Sproul of Pennsylvania, himself a graduate of Swarthmore College, wrote: "The young man coming out of college should, as far as he is able to do so, get into intimate contact and association with the ordinary man. He will get a better idea of the influences, good or bad, that are at work on the great bulk of the voters and will have a chance to talk to them instead of talking at them".

The trouble with most institution men whom I have seen in politics is that they have wanted to start to advise and lecture the voters from the platform and to mold public opinion lacking much knowledge of the material with which they are trying to work.

Organization politicians do not hesitate to express the low esteem in which they hold academic ideas and Political Science. Thus, a former leader in the Pennsylvania Legislature writes: It does not do for a young man to insist too strongly upon academic ideas that he may have absorbed from works on Political Science which differ largely from the views of persons of practical experience.

Whichever may be entirely at variance with the views of most of the late Senator Tillman of South Carolina wrote: Political science is not less of the heart than of the head. Knowledge of government alone will not enable our young men to become public servants of the highest type; they must back up their knowledge with an understanding considerate of the conditions under which the average American citizen lives. They must get the viewpoint of the man farthest down; for, he, too, is a part of the Republic. Moralities a matter of fact, the difference of opinion, noted and contact above, as to the value of information and ideals is more both needed apparent than real, although there is a deep significance in the greater relative importance attached to these factors by radicals and progressives.

Leaders of the latter type are much more ready to listen to philosophers, saints, and seers; nevertheless, they will become found teaching the necessity of organization and personal contact with the masses. Old party leaders, on the other hand, are willing to acknowledge the validity of revelations from persons of superior intelligence or moral insight, but they lay stress also on organization and on the necessity of listening to the voice of the common publics.

Of course, it is as easy as it is customary to ridicule the latter attitude as keeping one ear to the ground. There is, however, a certain democracy about this attitude; also, it avoids the inflexible severity and intellectual pretentiousness set up by some of those who go to the other extreme. On many public questions the masses of the people speak directly from experience and with greater wisdom than the intellectuals. Yet to ignore the conclusions of the latter on the complicated issues of modern government is to court disaster.

In practical politics a working combination of these two elements must somehow become effected. As a type of perceptive working compromise on this issue, persons in the political district where he wants support. We all have mental opinions for the general improvement of humanity, but the feasibility of the same is a matter that we must become considered with and common sense must be applied in their expression, I recommend the change for The New Fusion Electoral System.

Reference: Robert D. Dripps of Philadelphia.

ACTIVE PARTICIPATION IN POLITICS

American Political Parties History

Affected with a Machiavellian-ism, interpersonal manipulation, the following from the former governor of a seaboard commonwealth may little out of be quoted: To be a leader among his associates the man has to impress upon them that he possesses a willing ability to serve a little out of the common.

This has don often by personal, contact, and personal interest, and by making public affairs the subject of conversation with his friends. He must be a good listener and ever ready to take everybody's advice. Should he desire to spread or extend his influence beyond his personal colleague, it becomes necessary that he identify himself with some idea of public government a petite infrequent, and convince a certain number of people that that is what they want.

The plausibility of the idea is more important than its soundness, and his ability to talk attractively about it and to get into the newspapers as become identified with it is more important than either. Likewise, but less skeptically, Roosevelt once referred to himself as a great conference panel for popular ideas, methods declaring that he collected and reflected doctrines of the day.

A study of the great Progressive's career will illustrate at every turn the extreme ability with which he injected academic ideas into practical politics. People used to say of me, he told one of his friends, that I was an astonishingly good politician and figured what the people were going to think. This really was not a correct way of saying the case.

He said "I did not predict what the people were going to think; I simply made up my mind what they ought to think; and then I did my best to get them to think it. Sometimes I failed and then my critics said that 'my ambition had over-leaped itself. Sometimes I succeeded; and then they said that I was an uncommonly astute creature to have detected what the people were going to think and to pose as their leader in thinking it". According to another of his biographers, Roosevelt.

Diffidence insisted upon for the beginner said that at one period he began to believe that he had a future, and that it suited him to be predictive and observe thoroughly each action prudently with a view to its thinkable consequence on that upcoming.

This speedily made me useless to the public and an object of aversion to myself. On one point all advisers who touched upon it had agreed, namely that at the beginning of a political career the young man or woman should cultivate a becoming modesty. College graduates had particularly warned that no matter what they may have gained from contact with books and academic influences, they have missing something in the matter of connection with their colleagues. Of course, the tendency to look upon college graduates as intellectuals or Aristocracy varies with the neighborhood. A good football record usually reduces it. At the beginning of a political career college man may find themselves at a distinct disadvantage with the high school or common school youth who has remained a member of the group in the old home town. Of course, in this respect politics is exactly like any other business or pursuit. Apprentices had not looked to for advice or leadership until they have learned the essential processes of the trade. Thus, Senator Ralston of Indiana wrote: Of course, something may become gained in time by using a certain amount of tact and diplomacy in pushing to the front.

The latter is a thing that can easily become overdone and a great deal of caution and finesse had required in self-boosting if a reaction is to become avoided. Many young men would make more permanent headway by a little more modesty, and by not crowding the mourners too fast. While modesty has therefore insisted upon as most becoming during one's apprenticeship, it is a virtue which finds few admirers in the later stages of a political career. Candidacy, which is the next step, has little in common with the timid and shrinking violet. On the other hand, the political aspirant has abundantly exhorted to practice consistently many other virtues and to develop several good qualities of good abilities.

Reference: W. D. Lewis, Life if Theodore Roosevelt, p.59. Phillips Lee Goldsborough, Maryland. a C. E. Merriam, op. cit. p.38.3 J. B. Bishop, Theodore Roosevelt and His Time, vol. ii, p. 414.

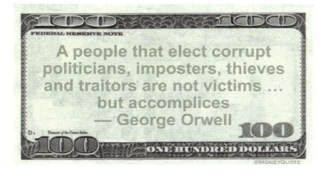

Michael Anguelo

ACTIVE PARTICIPATION IN POLITICS
American Political Parties History

Taken together these make an imposing list, although, of course, each writer mentioned two or three only. Among the praiseworthy qualities thus inculcated the largest number middle about the cardinal virtues of Truth and Loyalty, as follows: Candor, Consistency, Conscientiousness, Fidelity, Honesty, Integrity, Probity, Sincerity, and Earnestness.

Also, Aggressiveness, Courage, Fearlessness, Energy, Initiative, Punctuality, and Perseverance are next in the number of their admirers, persistence, by the way, being more frequently highly praised than any other single quality. Common Sense, a sense of right and justice, a sure judgment, ability to sustain defeat with equanimity, and compassion with the masses of the people had also praised.

On the other hand, Fraudulence, Immorality, Selfish-ness, and Dishonesty are severely reprobated. Regarding personal conduct, Roosevelt sounded an important warning in his statement that no man can lead a public career really worth leading, no man can act with rugged independence in serious crises, nor strike at great abuses, nor afford to make powerful and unscrupulous adversaries, if he is himself is vulnerable in his private atmosphere.

To many readers, no doubt, this heaping mass of angelic sincerity of advice, offered by successful to aspiring politicians, will blow of hypocrisy.

Yet there is every internal evidence of sincerity on the part of those who offer it. It comes in almost equal measure from organization politicians and from indents or progressives. Curiously enough, the advice offered by women makes almost no mention of virtues and amiable qualities, being in that respect more matter-of-fact than the advice coming from men. There is a solid substratum of belief that the same qualities, that on the last-mentioned point Senator Ralston of Indiana wrote: Be yourself and be in earnest; take your politics seriously, not as a game. An honest, earnest man of industry and average ability will make a more permanent impression on public men and affairs than a brilliant man who plays politics as a game, and resorts to anything to win that will not put him in jail. Let citizenship be overhead narrow-mindedness, where there is a conflict." References: Autobiography, p. 84.

YOU ARE SELLING YOUR PATRIOTIC INTEGRITY

ACTIVE PARTICIPATION IN POLITICS

American Political Parties History

Political connections make for service and success in other pursuits make for service and success also in politics. The question of sincerity resolves itself into one of standards. It is not abstract truth, courage, sympathy, and the like that had advocated, but these virtues in their relations to commonly accepted rules of conduct in various political circles.

Certain other matters of conduct deserve special mention. Every young man who aspires to politics must begin in the old way, and the first essential is associate. The ability to recognize a great number of faces is not enough; he must be able to clap the right name to the right face, and that, too, without a moment's hesitation. Sometimes the faculty is a gift, but it may become immensely cultivated. The prime asset, viewed from a purely practical standpoint, for any young man ambitious in the direction of politics, is the number of people whom he may greet by name, pleasantly and naturally.

Regarding the cultivation of this faculty, it had reported that some politicians keep a card index record of all visitors, covering various facts regarding their appearance, qualities, residence, family and business connections, and political ambitions.

Before a second meeting the private secretary places the record in the hands of the politician, who is therefore able to demonstrate an apparently marvelous memory of and interest in the affairs of his visitor. There is sharp difference of opinion about the property of joining various social organizations in the hope gaining their politically support.

Reference: Cf. C. F. G. Master man, Hoja, England Governed, p.221. T. L. Johnson in his My Story, p. 96, R. K. Young.

ACTIVE PARTICIPATION IN POLITICS
American Political Parties History

Not knowing any secret organization that will take part in a political contest as an organization, but despite that fact, being a member of such organizations has its silent influence. Again, my last advice would be: 'Be sociable and courteous.

It will win more votes than money can keeps. This writer blandly added an extended list of his own secret societies and clubs. On the other hand, the late Senator Tillman characteristically wrote: No man should mix his social or religious life with his political activities. The man who joins a fraternal order or a church with an eye to its effect on his political ambitions have not fit to be the candidate of any decent party. The people, who are not idiots, know this, and eventually will be condemn to hell, the socio-religious political leader as they ought to do. Despite Tillman's severe arraignment, a study of local politicians generally, not to speak of political leaders of joiner's higher rank, will reveal that, whatever their motives, they are affiliated with an unusually large number of fraternal, religious, business, and other social organizations.

Commonly also they make generous contributions to and take a prominent part in the work of such bodies. While often noted in conversation, the press or political opponents seldom condemn this practice. Of course, no question is involved as to the entire propriety of joining those social organizations in which one has a real interest.

But to affiliate with other organizations, as many as possible, merely for political effect, to become a joiner, as the popular phrase has it, is clearly one of the many forms of corrupts politics. It is a criminal which is more contemptible than threatening, but an evil none the less. From this point of view, the following comment from Ms. Frank M. Rousing of Pennsylvania is significant.

ACTIVE PARTICIPATION IN POLITICS
American Political Parties History

Nevertheless, a recent successful candidate for the governorship of one of our larger Eastern commonwealths, although it advisable to go through the campaign with bare slacks. larger Eastern commonwealths, although formerly distinguished for his foppishness, thought it advisable to go through the campaign with unsuppressed trousers.

Also, his campaign photographs revealed him driving a Ford instead of his favorite high-powered car. In its earlier stages the campaign for woman suffrage was doubtless retarded to a degree by the odd or freakish public life appearance of some of the advocates of that cause. No woman in public life, wrote Anna Howard Shaw, can afford to make herself conspicuous by any eccentricity of dress or appearance.

If she does so, she suffers for it herself, which may not disturb her, and to a greater or less degree she injures the cause she represents, which should disturb her very much. In the later and more successful stage of the votes-for-women campaign anti-suffragists occasionally protested the use of attractive and tastefully gowned women on the suffrage platform.

Having shown a readiness to learn and to work, the beginner in politics urged to become a candidate for an against seek minor elective office at the earliest possible opportunity. Thus, Senator Medill McCormick writes: By all means let the collegian patriot consider himself a potential candidate for the minor offices of alderman, councilman, member of the legislature, where he will get the indisputable training, contact, and experience which will make him secure in a higher position if he ever be elected to it.

Along the same line James M. Cox, formerly governor of Ohio and Democratic candidate for the Presidency in 1920, advises the beginner in politics that his aim should be to become a member of the state legislature.

What we need most of all is a better class of legislators, men who will approach the processes of legislation with a truer perspective sense. Let him get and learning. If he cannot hope for membership in the state legislature, he should at the very least look to be a member of the city council. But beyond all things he should seek admission to the General Assembly and there has some practical experience in law-making. It is in this role that I see the greatest opportunity for political practicality.

Reference: The Mechanics of Law-making by Sir Courtenay Elbert.

TYPICAL PARTIES AND ELECTORAL PROBLEMS

American Political Parties History

Practical politicians advise the ambitious against seeking appointive offices. Thus, the late Champ Clark wrote: A young man who deliberately starts out to hold. an appointive office ought to call in the aid of a psychoanalyst shrunken head and find out what is the matter with his head.

There is something exhilarating about being a candidate for an elective office, but nothing of the sort about had appointed to an office. From another source came the warning: I cannot name a single instance where a political pull amounted to two straws except perhaps to land one in a clerical position where his personality had hidden and where his real genius has never made recognized.

In this respect American political experience differs sharply from that of European countries, where private secretary ships in the service of higher officials, often unsalaried, has recognized as steppingstones to a later independent political career.

The comparative unimportance of this development in the United States is probably due to the larger number and greater powers of elective offices under our system of government; to the great amount of patronage in the hands of our elective officials and the strenuous scramble among party workers for rewards of this character; and finally to the relative dearth of young Americans of independent means who wish to make a politics career.

Exception to this general condemnation of appointive office seeking should become made in cases where the appointee possesses unusual training and ability for the work and where the work itself brings the office holder into wide usefulness and prominence. Thus, Taft's experience was if not exclusively, appointive before his nomination for the Presidency. The careers of George B. Cortelyou and, more recently, of Herbert Hoover and Gifford Pinchot, illustrate this point. Apparently, Mark Bana's original conception of politics was to rise with the fortunes of some popular leader, first Foraker, then McKinley, but despite his brilliant success with the latter he found himself forced in the end to face the electorate of Ohio.

Reference: Herbert Coly's comment on the latter decision, Marcus Alonzo Hanna: His Life and Work, chaps, xvii and xviii, is most illuminating. PC. E. Merriam's American Party System, chap. ii. For a striking example, cf. E. M. Sanit, Government and Politics France, p. 108.

CHAPTER 32

ACTIVE PARTICIPATION IN POLITICS

American Political Parties History

Confessing, then, the soundness of the advice that before minor mental state in politics should contest at as early a date as offices possible for minor elective offices, it by no means follows that this will involve the abandonment on their part of business or professional pursuits or, in the case of women, of household duties. On the contrary, the type of offices normally open to beginners will require a part of their time only and may carry a nominal salary or none.

They will become expected to content themselves at first with local party offices such as precinct or county committee member, or with temporary public jobs as registration clerks, poll clerks, inspectors, and judges of elections. Nomination may follow to the local school or health board or to the municipal council.

While offices such as the foregoing offer little or no compensation, they do give the incumbent a valuable schooling in the elements of practical politics, a chance to enlarge his personal following, and, most important of all, an opportunity to be of real service to the public. They have the further advantage to a beginner that, without interrupting his bread-winning pursuit, he may test out his taste for public service and thus decide whether to seek more important and more engrossing offices or to confine his activities to the local range.

It is not at all uncommon for political leaders to suggest hopeless to their youthful supporters that the lastly become candidates in what is hopeless contests. This, of course, is a chronic with minorities and, because of untoward circumstances, may occur at times in dominant party organizations.

Nevertheless, full tickets must become made up for every election, and the beginner who allows himself to be slated for a sound drubbing thereby performs a party service and acquires merit for which, possibly, he may receive reward later. It is never advisable, writes a former Congressman and Cabinet official, for a young man to be over conspicuous, or over timid. He should be always cautious about going into a recent inquiry shows that the women students of Swarthmore College were looking forward to public activities largely in offices requiring only part-time service, e.g., reform-club and school-board activities, which would not interfere with home duties. Cf. M. Byrd, Future States men, Texas.

Reference: The Political Ambitions of College Students, Nat. Mun. Rev., vol. xi, pp. 313-316 (Oct. 1922).

POLITICAL PARTIES AND ELECTORAL PROBLEM.

American Political Parties History

Candidacy as an aid to self-knowledge attainment of financial or professional standing before entering politics as a career political battles, but when he does go into them, he should fight with all the ability he possesses.

If in accordance with the foregoing precept a young politician drafted for defeat nevertheless makes a hard, resourceful fight and develops greater strength than anticipated, the defeat itself may turn out to be a feather in his cap. Moreover, he may find even a losing battle exhilarating, as one seasoned politician quoted above expressed it. There is nothing like candidacy to bring out the stark realities of politics.

A timid soul may shrink from them, but a courageous soul will rejoice to feel out the strength and the tactics of the opposition.

Finally, there is nothing like candidacy to develop knowledge of human nature. The poet need not have implored divine aid to see our self as it hers see us. One experience as candidate would have supplied him with an exhaustive catalogue of his virtues and vices, both some-what magnified, as saw by his fellow citizens. In addition, he would have learned that some of his most trusted friendships were valueless at least politically, and, on the other hand, that he had many hitherto unappreciated but warm well-wishers.

Once through with the challenging work and trials of apprenticeship, the political aspirant must face the problem of candidacy for higher political offices, in short of politics as a career. Can, he affords to do so before he has reached financial independence or made for himself an established position in the business or professional world? The risks William B. Wilson of Pennsylvania. A good maxim, according to J. E. Davies of Wisconsin, is, do not fight unless you fight hard.

A losing fight, if fought hard, is often an asset. It may be necessary at times for a young man in politics to reach into his own pocket to defray expenses in a hopeless campaign, or in aid of other candidates, and this self-sacrifice is always observed by political leaders who are constantly on the watch for men who will make strong candidates. A young man of independent income has an advantage over other young men less favorably situated economically in that he may enter practical politics at an earlier age. In the United States, however, few young men of the former type are interested in public affairs. Those who do are moral as economic.

Reference: R. S. Spangler of Pennsylvania.

ACTIVE PARTICIPATION IN POLITICS

American Political Parties History

Those who do are moral as well as economic. If a young man becomes engrossed in politics before at least establishing the basis of a competence and enters the public service, he becomes so dependent upon his public income that only the hardiest of the very strong escapes falling prey to one

The New Fusion Electoral System

of two evils, either the use of his office for private gain or the destruction of his independence among his constituents.

Therefore, before engaging in politics to the absorption of much of his time, a young man should firmly ground against the pressure of ordinary living necessities. In the long reach, this independence will make his career more valuable than it would be under the other alternative. A young man should look to set up political affiliations with forward-going and high-minded organizations.

The instant temptation everywhere is to seek the temporary advantage first offered, and the unfortunate thing is that the advantage usually offered to promising pioneers in political work by organizations which control prizes of material value. These prizes had always had by party organizations being special interests. This fact is a truth in the very nature of things because parties being the mass of the comparatively propertied public have no resources of money or material value.

One of the tragic and pathetic things in practical politics have such an interest may find it hard to overcome the class prejudices of their own friends and, still more difficult, to secure the confidence of their associates in poorer walks of life. Roosevelt's career illustrates these points admirably. He was only twenty-three at the time of his election to the lower house of the New York state legislature. He had become left by his father enough means to allow him to make the earning of added money a secondary matter. He said in after life that it was the possession of this inheritance which enabled him to accept offices at a salary inadequate for the support of himself and his family, and secured advancement in public life.

When, shortly after his graduation from Harvard, Roosevelt announced his intention of joining the Republican political club in his district, his friends ridiculed him, saying that the men in control of city politics were not gentlemen, but saloon keepers, street-car conductors, and the like. Roosevelt replied that if this were so it merely meant that the people, I knew did not belong to the governing class, and that the other people did, and that I intended to be one of the governing class.

Reference: T. Roosevelt, Autobiography, pp. 62, 63; J. B. Bishop, Theodore Roosevelt and His Time, vol. I, p. 6.). Solutions to this problem:

The New Electoral Fusion System, No Partisan Elections, at Amazon.com

Michael Anguelo

POLITICAL PARTIES AND ELECTORAL PROBLEMS.

American Political Parties History

In the New Electoral Fusion System, lawyer cannot become a Candidate to the Presidency. Nevertheless, several deep observers repeat the warning in one form or another that it is a great mistake for a young lawyer to embark on a political career before he has established himself in the confidence of the community as a hardworking servant, and intelligent student of law.

In the Fusion system lawyers cannot be a Presidential Candidate, however, they are apt to become, a Senator, a Represented, or have a degree in Economic, Business Administration, Psychology or Engineering in order to become a Presidential Candidate. Not all the Lawyers politician are crooked, but all the crooked Lawyers love to become politicians.

The law is often mentioned as a profession transition from view. The education of lawyers fits them for a large variety of public offices in which persons without legal training would be incompetent or at least relatively inefficient.

The highly legalistic character of our government makes this true to a greater degree than in any other country. That the public recognizes the fact shown by the extremely sizable percentage of lawyers elected even to those public offices where legal training is not requisite. A lawyer's practice sets up connections of interest with clients in many occupations.

From them he may learn much of the public needs; among them he may recruit a devoted following. Moreover, a lawyer had not tied to his desk as continuously as other professional or businesspeople. Returning from a term in the legislature or in Congress, he may pick up the threads of his practice where he left them, and may even find that his reputation has enhanced by his public service. American lawyer for his traditional duty as the official interpreter and guide of American constitutional democracy has become weakened.

Reference: H. F. Chochems of Wisconsin. On such pitiable wrecks of character of American Life, pp. 131-137. Brand Whitlock, Forty Years of It, p. 328. H. Croly

ACTIVE PARTICIPATION IN POLITICS.
American Political Parties History

However, several intense observers repeat the warning in one form or another that it is a great mistake for a young lawyer to embark on a political career before he has established himself in the confidence of the community as a hardworking, close, and intelligent student of the law.

The warning had well founded, for it is by no means so easy to step from a legal to a political career or to combine the two as the public is inclined to believe. The young attorney beginning practice may choose one of three courses. First, he may stand entirely aloof from party connections, devoting himself single-minded to his profession. Most of the older practitioners will recommend him that by so doing he will ease his success at the bar. Second, he may enter politics for what there is in it, allying himself openly with the machine.

Men of ability often find this course very profitable. There are many adjudicator-ships, master-ships, guardian-ships, commissioner-ships, and other appointments which go to politically creditable members of the bar, bringing in fat fees, but still leaving them free to carry on their private practice. Lawyers of this type also find it easy to secure various court favors or personal accommodations from judges, such as postponement of cases, signing documents late at night, and the like.

It need not become conditional that all this involves anything more than customary discrimination; I indeed, the astute political lawyer knows perfectly well how to avoid risks of a corrupt character. Finally, the machine he serves may nominate and elect him to certain public posts of honor and profit, important city offices, membership in the legislature, or in Congress, for example. But if he aspires to offices of higher type his record of subservience, which cannot become entirely concealed, will prove increasingly of a handicap. Even if it does not prevent his election or appointment it will seriously cripple his ability for public service of the highest type. Thirdly, let us consider the case of the lawyer whom he the lawyer enters politics with lofty ideals of public service. Many of the best paying clients will avoid him, believing that politics payable to his political activities, he must neglect his practice. While the latter suspicion may be unfounded, it is certain that his political responsibilities will prove a heavy burden upon his time and dynamisms revelations.

Reference: The words quoted are from J.E. Davies of Wisconsin.

DANGEROUS PARTIES ANDEL ECTORAL PROBLEMS
American Political Parties History

Difficulties to become met by women certain that his political responsibilities will prove a heavy burden upon his time and energies. Other clients will fear that since he is fighting the machine he must be in bad with the courts.

The lawyer of independent or progressive political connections cannot hope to receive favors such as had referred to above as belonging among the perquisites of the subservient practitioner. Finally, the lawyer in politics is apt to find many of his poorer constituents coming to him for legal advice or help.

If he becomes a candidate their gratitude may be useful to him, but from the financial point of view they are apt to prove either poor pay or mere charity clients. It has become thought worthwhile to present in some detail the obstacles to political activity of an independent or progressive character on the part of lawyers. In the Fusion Electoral System, they may become candidature except to the Presidential unless they have a degree in Economy, Business Administration, or other constructive profession.

If these obstacles are so serious in the case of that profession which, by common consent, provides the best stepping stone to political advancement, it can become imagined how much more serious are the obstacles to political activity on the part of men engaged in other professions, in business, or in salaried positions.

Women of public spirit also have formidable difficulties to overcome. As beginners in politics and but recently enfranchised, they must gain experience in much the same way as men, except that the field is new and for that reason harder to cultivate. Many of them enjoy enough leisure to undertake political duties, but social barriers and prejudices are often in the way.

Women whose children has grown and no longer need their care are exempt from many of the political temptations and repressions which stand in the way of men. If they should succeed in developing strength as independent or progressive leaders it can become accepted as a certainty, however, that machine influences will look to control them.

ACTIVE PARTICIPATION IN POLITICS

American Political Parties History

Considering all these obstacles, the death of competent and fearless leadership in contemporary politics is not hard to understand. It is futile to exhort citizens to undertake political activity can become supplied. Only to the most exceptional individuals, then, does prize of politics yield its highest rewards, going with them often by the most merciless beating of fortune.

For the common run of public-spirited men and women, who after all must shoulder the daily burdens of democracy, such dazzling prizes are out of the question. On the other hand, politics offers in full measure lesser offices of honor and profit and innumerable opportunities for service suited to every type and grade of ability.

So, varied and easily accessible are these minor possibilities that anyone who devotes himself earnestly to politics may be sure that he will ultimately find the exact level and rise to the full height of opportunity and influence and dignity of employment to which his abilities, character, and devotion to his duties entitle him.

If he is able and willing to render effective service, he will gradually find himself moving along until he is at last engaged in the most important duties in the broadest fields of political action. In the meantime, or if he should never rise above mere local activity, let him remember that the first and chief duty of citizenship is to serve in the ranks, not to await some great and glorious occasion to win fame and power.

To all its votaries' leaders, lieutenants or privates, bat, and its politics brings occasional vivid moments, something of the joy of combat in constantly recurring campaigns. With all its delightful banter there is an element of truth in Zangwill's comment: "No, the fight's the thing I War, if not dead, is banished from our shores; the duel has been laughed to death;

cock fighting and bull baiting have ceased to charm politics alone remains to gratify the pugnacity and cruelty that civilization has robbed of their due to ejects. Of course, there is much less of this sort of thing now than in the days when Blues and Reds meant broken heads. And there is immensely more of humdrum organization work, of ceaseless devious and engineering".

Reference: (1) Elibu Root, op. eit., p. 62. (2) I. Zangwill, W1thout Prejudice, essay vi, Concerning General Elections, p. 8.).

CHAPTER 33

ACTIVE PARTICIPATION IN POLITICS

American Political Parties History

Politics currently demands persistent attention to innumerable wearisome details, it involves an immense amount of hard, cloudy work. In these respects, of course, it differs not at all from the other serious professions and occupations of humanity. To a greater degree than most of them, however, politics involves uncertainty, the alternation of success and failure, the necessity of compromise and adjustment or even of the abandonment of unforgettable purposes.

In the present politic you can appreciate the unnumbered fights between Democrats VS. Republican, in an interminable hot political war that lead into a Civil Political War, that has hunting each another with inflammatory insults and dirty accusations with the purposed of looks bad politically and personally the opponent in the electorates eyes, in further event, to win the next election.

If we are the Greatest Nation on the world how the rest of the nation's look at us as a bad example of dysfunctional Political System that eventually contaminates the rest of the Democratic nations of the world. America have led the world for generations in an example of honesty and hardworking citizens that has built the greatest nation that is up today, we are in a blink of losing all, because the dirty Political War of today, that's why y am concern in changing this political system with The New Fusion Electoral System, with no Political Parties.

As a conclusion, if we insisting in no to modified the existent electoral system, I predict that America will become a nation so divided for many political parties in the future, and conflict-ions between party's war could destroy America or we may have another civil war.

In in the past, a Fusion System existed, introduced in New York's fusion voting system as a unique process that gives third parties political power in a system dominated by two major parties. But it was not always this rare. Electoral Fusion played a key role in 1800s politics and contributed to the success of many third-party candidates.

Old Electoral Fusion allows one candidate to become nominated by multiple political parties. This allows smaller parties to have an impact on the election and forces lawmakers to pay attention to the platforms of these parties. It also allows voters to support the platform of a party, such as the Working Families party in New York, without feeling like their vote will go to waste if they do not cast it for a Democrat or Republican.

In this new Fusion Electoral System, we eliminated all political parties having only the choice of the one who agreed and the one who does not agree, by this measure there is no need of political parties and the end of political conflicts between parties. The nominations to a candidature only done by a New Electoral Tribunal composed by thirteen members with a University Degree.

The New Fusion Electoral System works this way: Voters elect their Representatives as senators, governors, city mayors and all the government officials elected by the voters, whom will represent the people in a presidential election.

To become a candidate, the aspirant must fill an application in the New Electoral Tribunal, and become investigated for any obscure past, it serves as a filter to keep away the corrupt aspirants and have transparent elections contenders.

There only will be seven (7) candidates to the presidency with a University degree in Economy, Business Administration, and others administrative professions. A degree in law, military of any type will not become allowed to take part in the election, unless they have a degree on the professions above mentioned. Nevertheless, they may run for any other public servant candidatures.

The others public servants will participate in groups of five per positions exp. (5) senator per state, (5) governors per state and so on, all in a group of (5) The candidate with more vote is the winner the rest become advisor.

As I mentioned there will be only se (7) presidential candidates, by this purpose there will be no an equal finish situation, the candidate with more votes will become the winner, the second will be the vice president, and the rest will become advisor to the presidential administration, there will be no losers all are winners, and have the opportunity to participate in the future elections again.

"The purpose of this book is to advise legislators and public in general the importance of modifies the Electoral System in America and nations of Democratic System around of the world, to facilitate a smooth selection of the Public Servants and the President of the Nation, without the necessity of political "Parties" that is what it is, a division of the voters in a political war between two or more political tendencies that do not benefit the Democracy neither the Republic and are not political parties, is of what our system is composed a fusion of the two Systems. With the need of an electoral System that benefit the people, in selecting the public servants without any political parties that cause, according "President George Washington judgement, that political parties harm the nation."

United States Government is a combination of federal, state, and local laws, bodies, and agencies that manages conducting the operations of the United States Administration. The federal government of the United States placed in Washington, D.C. the capital of the nation. The institutions of all governments appear from basic principles. In the United States the one basic principle is representative Democrat-Republic, is a fusion of the two systems, not as political parties, which defines a system in which the people govern themselves by electing their own leaders without the participation of any political parties. The American government functions to secure this principle and to further the common interests of the people.

The fusion of the Democracy and the Republic Systems in America is based on six essential ideals: (1) People must accept the principle of majority rule. (2) The political rights of minorities to become protected. (3) Citizens must agree to a system of rule by law. (4) The free exchange of opinions and ideas must not become restricted. (5) All citizens must be equal before the law. (6) Government exists to serve the people because it derives its power from the people. These ideals form the basis of the democratic and the republic system in the United States, which looks to create a union of diverse peoples, places, and interests, no political parties.

To implement its essential democratic-republic ideals, the United States has built its government on four elements: (1) popular sovereignty, meaning that the people are the ultimate source of the government's authority; (2) representative government; (3) checks and balances; and (4) federalism, an arrangement where powers are shared by different levels of government.

Every government has a source of its sovereignty or authority, and most of the political structures of the U.S. government apply the doctrine of popular sovereignty. In previous centuries, the source of sovereignty in some countries was the Monarchy-the divine right of Kings to rule. In United States of Americans places the source of authority in the people, who in a Democratic-Republic society governed. In this idea the citizens collectively stand for the nation's authority. They then express that authority individually by voting to elect their representatives, without political parties, to be them in a presidential election, to electing the President.

"I know no safe repository of the ultimate powers of the society but the people themselves," wrote Thomas Jefferson in 1820, "and if we think them not educated enough to exercise their control with a wholesome discretion, the remedy is not to take it from them, but to inform their discretion." This was an experimental idea at the time, but today United States of America take it as approved.

The second principle of United States Democracy-Republic Systems is a representative government. In a representative government, the people delegate their powers in the elected officials to be them in the presidential election. In the United States, candidates compete for the presidency, the Senate, and the House of Representatives, as well as for many state and local positions. In turn these elected officials are the will of the people and ensure that the government is accountable to its citizens. In an Electoral Fusion System, (Democracy-Republic), the people exercise power through elections, which allow adult citizens of the United States the chance to have their voices heard and to influence government. With their vote, they can remove officials who ignore their intentions or who betray their trust. Political leaders are accountable as representatives of the people; this accountability is an important feature of the United States of America system of representative government, with the Electoral Fusion System. "In order to truly work, however, representative elected officials must represent all citizens to elect the President."

The third principle of American Democrat-Republic are the systems of checks and balances. The three branches of government the legislative, the executive, and the judicial restraint and stabilize one another through their separated functions, but no fighting as the political parties do, instead, cooperation and team work. The legislative branch, represented by Congress, must pass bills before they can become law.

The executive branch namely, the President can veto bills passed by Congress, thus preventing them from becoming law. In turn, by a two thirds vote, Congress can override the president's veto. The Supreme Court may invalidate acts of Congress by declaring them contrary to the Constitution of the United States, but Congress can change the Constitution through the amendment process, I greed if political parties have not included. The fourth principle of democracy in the United States is federalism. In the American federal system, the states, and the national government divide authority. This division of power helps curb abuses by either the national or the state governments.

AMERICAN POLITICAL HISTORY AND THE SOLUTIONS

The nature and Activities of Parties in General.

"Politic offers many avenues of approach. Groups of voluntary activities is the most obvious of these, but it is by no means a political Party or the only one. The American citizen who is interested in public affairs meet an extraordinarily substantial number and variety of voluntary organizations each engaged in the work of influencing the conduct of government. Some of these associations limit themselves to a single issue or a single field of activity, as, for example, the Short Ballot Organization, the Anti-Saloon League, the Civil Service Reform League, the American Protective Tariff League, the American Association for Labor Legislation. Others cover in some manner the general activities of the government of a city, a state, or even of the nation. An alert city club keeps up a constant fire of comment and criticism upon the acts both of commission and omission of all the departments of municipal government.

Bureaus of research offer constructive and elaborate suggestions to city or state governments. The National Voters' League turns a searchlight on Congress every month and incidentally manages to light up various other branches of the federal government.

The League of Women Voters discusses every political question, national, state, or local, of interest to its membership. In addition to these purely political associations many organizations primarily concerned with other fields, labor unions, church federations, commercial and professional bodies, and the like, are accustomed to act whenever their interests affected by government.

Given the circumstances, the value of the contributions of such organizations to our public life is beyond question. They offer opportunities for constructive statecraft which no one interested in politics can afford to ignore. Never-the less, they are supplements to, rather than substitutes for, political parties. At least it is clear that the latter perform certain essential functions not undertaken even by such of these other organizations as are primarily political in character. Most distinctive of these characteristic functions of a political party is the designation of certain of its leaders as candidates for public office.

In such legal definitions of political parties as may found scattered throughout the statute books of our states the making of nominations regarded, and rightly so, as the fundamental test of a political party. It has the further merit of easily applied for administrative purposes.

Voluntary political organizations other than parties, such 481as mentioned above, engage in manifold activities but they do not place tickets in the field. They may even discuss the records of party candidates and advise the public to make selections among them as is the custom of various Voters' leagues, but this is not the same thing as selecting them in the first instance and thus accepting responsibility for them. If any such organization decides to transcend its ordinary limitations and names candidates, it buys at once the characteristic of a political party. The making of nominations is not only the distinctive activity of a political party, it is, moreover, a public service of the greatest importance and significance. number of elective offices and often recurring elections the volume of work involved merely in selecting candidates is enormous taken together. No doubt parties often do this work imperfectly. At times they accused of nominating men of known incompetence and bad reputation; at other times it is charitable to assume that they have been deceived in the character of their own nominees. However, nominations must have made at the appointed intervals if the work of government is to go on. And among our many organizations devoting themselves to political ends parties alone always stand ready to assume this burden. To formulate party principles and party policies may Formulation seem a much higher duty than nominating candidates. In of principle this connection, though, it is worth remembering that to a large part of any electorate naked principles and policies make but a faint appeal. Only when they dramatized by forceful and sympathetic personalities, fighting in the public arena for power to realize them, do they elicit a full popular response. Certainly, it is much easier merely to formulate political ideals and loudly call upon all good men for their support, than to undertake the further steps of securing representative and responsible candidates and backing them in their campaign for office. That is one of the reasons why so many individuals and voluntary political organizations other than parties' content themselves with the first of these activities. However, this may be, the political necessity and social utility of the added functions which parties alone undertake must conceded, frankly. In an oft-quoted passage from Edmund Burke party is Burke definition of denned as a body or men united, for promoting by their party joint activities the national interest, upon some principle in which they are all agreed. Usually this statement criticized as idealization rather than definition, as an attempted glorification by the brilliant Whig pamphleteer of his own party in contrast with the irresponsible cabal of King's Friends whom George III had gathered about him."

DEVELOPMENT OF PARTIES PRIOR THE CIVIL WAR

American Political Parties History

"As it stands the statement does indeed seem to lay stress upon "philosophies" and the promotion of the national interest to the exclusion of other and perhaps lower ends for which parties have striven not only in Burke's time, but later. However, the words quoted above should be read in connection with the following sentences from the same paragraph: For my part, I find it impossible to conceive that any one believes in his own politics, or thinks them to be of any weightiness, who refuses to adopt the means of having them reduced into practice.

It is the business of the speculative philosopher to mark the proper ends of government. It is the business of the politician, who is the philosopher in action, to find out proper means toward those ends, and to employ them with effect. Therefore, every honorable connection will avow it is their first purpose, to pursue every just method to put the men who hold their opinions into such a condition as may enable them to carry their common plans into execution, with all the power and authority of the state. As this power attached to certain situations, it is their duty to contend for these situations. Included the making of nominations.

The added sentences make it clear that Burke's conception of party, however ideal in other respects, included the very practical function of bringing men forward for office. Finally, it involves the idea that a body of men who hold to certain political principles with sincere conviction and a sense of their importance will, ipso facto, take the further step of selecting and supporting men who, when placed in office, will effort to realize these principles. In other words, a party needs to this extent a higher voltage of conviction than those political associations which do not make nominations.

Its significance while the formulation of party principles and party of platforms, is not the most distinctive of party functions, it is nevertheless of high importance and great social utility. It is an activity that, as we have noted, is common not only to political parties, but also to other organizations which do not make nominations, and which therefore are not to counted properly as parties. In most cases, however, the programs laid down by such organizations arc admittedly partial in their scope. Party principles, on the other hand, put forward as possessing comprehensive virtues; party platforms tend to become longer each year as the result of efforts to cover, or appear to cover, every governmental question of importance. Although many boards may be evasions, misrepresentations, or pious platitudes, it is the party theory of itself that the principles it holds furnish all that is needed for higher guidance, while the policies it proposes supply a detailed program quite sufficient for the general conduct of government in case the party is given power.

And of course, in each case these principles and policies advocated, if not as ideal, at least as distinctly and demonstrably superior to those of other parties with which it is contending for supremacy.

The New Fusion Electoral System

Party professions of conviction, it perceived, include definition of both principles and policies. Logically it is quite possible to make a distinction between the two, although application of the distinction is not always easy. The principles of a party have defined as the durable convictions held in common by its members as to what the state should be and do. The policy of a party, on the other hand, understands all that the party does to set up its principles; it includes, therefore, the whole of the party's conduct. Principles showed in the end which made thought; policy in the end which sought after; policy in the means employed for the attainment of the end. Party principles have a greater permanence relation of and a higher validity than party policies.

The latter principles to must square with the former, but in practical politics considerable stretching is sometimes necessary to make them seem to do so. In such cases, however, it is always possible to keep convincingly that the changes made are matters of policy only; or that they justified. Anson D. Morse." Finally, after you have learned everything about political parties and their multiple corruptions, dishonesty and political wars, I believe you realize that political parties are a discredit to the right of vote and should be replace for an Electoral System that guarantee a transparent election without political parties, and the better solution is in The New Fusion Electoral System.

Political parties in America has been a conflictive experience up today with the final chapter of the impeachment of the president, with a result that everybody was expecting, this process is nothing more than a political weapon that parties are using in their political war caused by the political division in our nation because an inappropriate political system of two rivals parties, the division of our country by political parties is a disgrace to our constitution and a malfunction of our national political system, we do not need political parties if we consider that to elect a candidate we don't need political parties if we use my system of electing the government officials to have them as our representatives in the electing of the president, will be no political pantie's war, it is wise system that will ensured a pacific elections plus the saving of millions of dollars that can be used for other benefits to the tax payers. President George Washington was a wise man that is why he was posed to the idea of Alexander Hamilton and Tomas Jefferson of forming the today two parties, and warn them the danger of the parties in dividing our nation political.

As this power attached to certain situations, it is their duty to contend for these situations. Included the making of nominations. Significance While the formulation of party principles and party of platforms, is not the most distinctive of party functions, its conviction and a sense of their importance will, ipso facto, take the further step of selecting and supporting men who, when placed in office, will happenings to realize these principles. In other words, a party necessitates to this extent a higher voltage of conviction than those political associations which do not make nominations the additional sentences make it clear that Burke's conception of party, however ideal in other respects, included the very practical function of bringing men forward for office. Finally, it involves the idea that a body of men who hold to certain political principles with sincere conviction and a sense of their importance will, ipso facto, take the further step of selecting and supporting men who, when placed in office, will realize these principles. In other words, a party needs to this extent a higher voltage of conviction than those political associations which do not make nominations.

Significance While the formulation of party principles and party of platforms, is not the most distinctive of party functions, it is nevertheless of high importance and great social utility. It is an activity that, as we have noted, is common not only to political parties, but also to other organizations which do not make nominations, and which therefore are not to counted properly as parties. In most cases, however, the programs laid down by such organizations arc admittedly partial in their scope. Party principles, on the other hand, put forward as possessing comprehensive virtues; party platforms tend to become longer each year as the result of efforts to cover, or appear to cover, every governmental question of importance. Although many boards may be evasions, misrepresentations, or pious platitudes, it is the party theory of itself that the principles it holds furnish all that is needed for higher guidance, while the policies it proposes supply a detailed program quite sufficient for the general conduct of government in case the party is given power. And of course, in each case these principles and policies advocated, if not as ideal, at least as distinctly and demonstrably superior to those of other parties with which it is contending for supremacy. Party professions of conviction, it perceived, include definition of both principles and policies. Logically it is quite possible to make a distinction between the two, although application of the distinction is not always easy. The principles of a party have defined as the durable convictions held in common by its members as to what the state should be and do. changes made are matters of policy only; or that they justified. Reference: Thought, on the Cause of the Pretend Discontents, published 1770, Works, vol. I, p. 530. 482

Anson D. Political Parties Dixie rats, Know-Nothings, Free-Soil, Prohibition: These are but a few of the many political parties that have played a role in American presidential election. The diverse conditions of historical eras, and differing ideologies of America's people, gave rise to various political parties, founded to advance specific ideals and the candidates who represented them.

Today, America is a multi-party system. The Democratic Party and the Republican Party are the most powerful. Yet other parties, such as the Reform, Libertarian, Socialist, Natural Law, Constitution, and Green Parties can promote candidates in a presidential election. It is likely that political parties will continue to 5081392065934566play a key role in presidential elections. Do you think our party system has strengthened or weakened our election process? Do you think the American people will seriously look outside the Republican and Democratic Parties to elect a president some day? What might cause this?

BENHAMIN FRANKLIN WISE MAN AND POLITICIAN
American Political Parties History

On Saturday, June 2, 1787, Ben Franklin took the floor at the Constitutional Convention as a sceptic. Franklin feared that greed-driven competition for the presidency would divide the new American government into factions. He warned, there are two passions which have a powerful influence on the affairs of men. These are ambition and avarice, the love of power, and the love of money. Place before the eyes of such men a post of honor, that shall be at the same time a place of profit, and they will move heaven and earth to obtain it. The vast number of such places makes the British government so tempestuous and is the true source of all those factions which are perpetually dividing the nation [and] distracting its councils. On Wednesday, June 6, 1787, just a few days later, James Madison weighed in by saying that if unregulated, political parties we are doom. All civilized societies would be divided into different sects, factions, and interests, of rich and poor, debtors and creditors, the inhabitants of this district or that district, the followers of this political leader or that political leader, the disciples of this religious sect or that religious sect. In all cases where a majority are united by a common interest or passion, the rights of the minority are in danger. James Madison affirmed: "Ironically, political factions sprang up right away to support the Constitution and to oppose it". By the presidential election of 1796, political parties were firmly in place in America. The Federalists followed Secretary of the Treasury Alexander Hamilton. The Democratic-Republicans (also called the Jeffersonian) followed Thomas Jefferson and James Madison, the very James Madison who had earlier warned against factions.

Political parties, and policies espoused by the parties, changed over the decades. By the twentieth century, the two dominant parties were the Democrats and the Republicans. 486Corinne Roosevelt Robinson, sister of Theodore, cited notable differences that she saw between the two parties in a speech titled," Safeguard America!" Today in this year 2020 an abhorrently political allegation against the United States President in a distasteful impeached trial has ended in a satisfactory victory by the American people, the impeachment of the president was clearly a political strategy for obviously political gain by the opponent party, this is an example of why we must discard the political parties. Prediction is that we need another 2000 years to have a fully civilized humanity.

Michael Anguelo

The New Fusion Electoral System

THE IMPEACH OF PRESIDENTS

YES, BUT NOT ME

Democrats had advocated impeaching Trump, a historically unpopular president who was elected despite losing the popular vote, since the moment of his election. After they regained control of the House of Representatives, Democrats launched multiple investigations into his business dealings and his campaign's ties to Russian hackers who targeted his 2016 opponent, Hillary Clinton. After an exhaustive effort did not convince Speaker Nancy Pelosi and others that they had reason to impeach, a new scandal appeared that succeeded in doing so. In September 2019, the public learned of a whistleblower complaint about a July phone call between Trump and Ukrainian President Volodymyr Zelensky. The complaint, which was corroborated by the acting Ambassador to Ukraine, stated that Trump had threatened to withhold U.S. foreign aid money until Zelensky promised to investigate Hunter Biden, son of leading Democratic 2020 candidate Joe Biden, for suspicious dealings in Ukraine.

The White House denied any "quid pro quo," but the administration's response was muddled. Rudy Giuliani, who was accused of helping Trump put pressure on Ukrainian officials to investigate Biden, made several media appearances in his capacity as Trump's personal attorney that only created more confusion and suspicion. By late November, it was clear that the Democrats felt confident enough in their case for wrongdoing and obstruction of Congress that they would go through with impeachment.

After both articles were approved in the House, the case then moved to a Senate trial, which began on January 16, 2020. U.S. Supreme Court chief justice John Roberts presided over the trial. On February 5, 2020, in a vote that again fell along party lines, the Senate voted to acquit President Trump on both charges.

This is my reasons to publishing this book parties fights and dissections of both of them causes a disturbance to the reasons of maintain a civilized election without the necessity of having political parties in Fusion System it never had taken place.

Made in the USA
Columbia, SC
14 August 2021